THE ETHNIC
PHENOMENON

THE ETHNIC PHENOMENON

Pierre L. van den Berghe

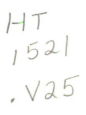

ELSEVIER
New York • Oxford

Exclusive Distribution
throughout the World by
Greenwood Press, Westport,
Ct. U.S.A.

Elsevier North Holland, Inc.
52 Vanderbilt Avenue, New York, New York 10017

Sole Distributors outside the USA and Canada:

Elsevier Science Publishers B.V.
P.O. Box 211, 1000AE Amsterdam, The Netherlands

© 1981 by Elsevier North Holland, Inc.

Library of Congress Cataloging in Publication Data

Van den Berghe, Pierre L.
    The ethnic phenomenon.

Bibliography: p.
    Includes index.
        1. Racism. 2. Ethnicity. 3. Sociobiology.
        4. Social ethics. I. Title.
HT1521.V25   305.8   80-21092
ISBN 0-444-01550-7

Desk Editor   Louise Calabro Schreiber
Design   Edmée Froment
Mechanicals/Opening pages   José Garcia
Art Editor   Glen Burris
Art rendered by   Vantage Art, Inc.
Production Manager   Joanne Jay
Compositor   Crestwood Press
Printer   Haddon Craftsmen

Manufactured in the United States of America

History itself is a *real* part of *natural history*—of nature developing into man. Natural science will in time incorporate into itself the science of man, just as the science of man will incorporate into itself natural science: there will be *one* science.

Karl Marx
The Paris Manuscripts, 1844

It follows from the information thus acquired [from a questionnaire constructed by Darwin in 1867] that the same state of mind is expressed throughout the world with remarkable uniformity; and this fact is, in itself, interesting as evidence of the close similarity in . . . mental disposition of all the races of mankind.

Charles Darwin
The Expression of the Emotions in Man and Animals, 1872

CONTENTS

PREFACE

No book in social science is produced in a vacuum; this one is no exception. As I will show presently, the field of "race and ethnic relations" has been buffeted by ideological currents and countercurrents. Waves of revisionism have succeeded one another and supposedly "objective" scholars have been embroiled in heated controversy. The publication of Gunnar Myrdal's *An American Dilemma* (1944) established the salutory precedent of explicity stating the author's ideological biases in an attempt to relate them to the substance of the work, or at least to give the reader some clues and caveats about the possible intrusion of the writer's beliefs on his perception of reality.

This is an example I have always tried to emulate. Instead of seeking to hide my opinions and to avoid value judgements, as many of my colleagues told me I should do as a scientist, I have always striven to bring them out as openly and as self-consciously as I could. Previous statements of my position regarding issues of intergroup relations can be found in many of my previous writings [see inter alia, van den Berghe (1965, 1967, 1970, 1975b, 1978d)].

I have come to my position through a growing conviction that phenomena are fully comprehensible only in the broadest possible framework of comparison. This was the position I took in my earlier books on the subject of race and ethnic relations (van den Berghe, 1967, 1970). There I criticized the provincialism of much of the literature, especially the American literature that was so overwhelmingly based on the very special American experience. Happily, my 1967 strictures against my colleagues in the field are less valid than they were, because comparative studies have multiplied in the last decade and a number of important analytical works, reflecting a wide range of viewpoints, have appeared since that date (Fredrik Barth, 1969; Francis, 1976; Leo Kuper, 1974; Leo Kuper and M. G. Smith, 1969; Le Vine and

Campbell, 1972; Mason, 1971; Rex, 1970; Schermerhorn, 1970; W. J. Wilson, 1973).

Here, I am merely extending that comparative approach one crucial step further by comparing our species with other species. The arguments in favor of this strategy will be presented later, but the ideological significance of that step must be addressed now. The mere mention of biology in connection with human behavior often elicits passionate rejection, not least among those who share with me a liberal outlook. Much of that unthinking revulsion is based on ignorance of modern biology and evolutionary theory. Many erroneously assume that any attempt to integrate the social sciences into the mainstream of biological evolutionary theory heralds a return to Social Darwinism, racism, eugenics or any of the ideological aberrations of the last century that claimed a linkage, however tenuous and wrong-headed, to biology.

To be sure, any scientific theory has a potential for political misuse. Sociobiology—the application of Darwinian evolutionary theory to the social behavior of animals, including *Homo sapiens*—is no exception. It is just as easy, however, to draw liberal conclusions from sociobiology as conservative ones. For instance, human sociobiology stresses how similar the basic repertoire of human behavior is across cultures, and it can thus be read as a ringing reaffirmation of the unity of mankind and of the biological trivialness of "racial" differences. Indeed, evolutionary biology and sociobiology are fully compatible with much contemporary "radical" thinking—and certainly with Marxism with which it shares a materialist conception of the world and a view of human behavior as motivated by the pursuit of self-interest. Classical and neoclassical economics, Marxism and Darwinian evolutionary theory all have their intellectual roots in the thinking of Malthus, Ricardo and Adam Smith.

In an attack on sociobiology, Marshall Sahlins (1976) treats it as a status quo ideology grown out of late capitalist society. Sociobiology, he claims, only bears a seeming relationship to external reality because our Western capitalist culture has developed the particular brand of biology from which sociobiology evolved. The idea of kin selection, for instance, appeals to Westerners because we have this strange notion that family, kinship and marriage have to do with biological relatedness and reproduction. All that, according to Sahlins, is purely coincidental. Other people, he claims, think otherwise. Sociobiology is merely the folk biology of late 20th century capitalism.

For the historian of science, the social context out of which scientific theory develops is a fascinating subject in its own right. So are the political uses and the ideological twists to which scientific paradigms are put. There is an evident relationship between science and ideology, which becomes all the more relevant when the subject matter of the scientific theory includes human behavior itself. The protest against sociobiology is only raised when sociobiology is applied to *human* behavior. Had E. O. Wilson (1975, 1978) confined himself to ants, nobody would have raised a whisper of dissent, except perhaps for a few entomologists. Hamilton (1964) and Maynard

Smith (1964), who more than anyone else are primarily responsible for the early theoretical development of sociobiology but who generally refrained from applying it to humans, are hardly mentioned in the attacks.

The issue is not whether science and politics, or theory and ideology are related. They obviously are. Science always develops in a social and temporal context. It is often used to serve political interests. Scientists are no less corruptible than other mortals, nor any less prone to let their wishes and opinions color their perception of reality.

The proof of a scientific theory is not in the moral fiber or the ideological orthodoxy of the scientist, but in its congruence with a reality external to it. In the last analysis, a scientific paradigm is a way of looking at the world. It is not true or false in an absolute sense. It is merely a more or a less useful, parsimonious and elegant way of reducing the enormous complexity of the world to a manageable number of normative and predictive statements. The more that is accounted for with the fewest number of principles, the better the theory. In biology, the Darwinian theory of evolution by natural selection has been without serious rivals for over a century. It is now found to be equally applicable to the evolution of animal behavior and morphology. Indeed, behavior may be seen as a special kind of morphology. To exclude our species from the purview of sociobiology is becoming as untenable as to invoke an act of special creation for the origin of the human animal itself.

In one fundamental respect, the view of ethnicity and "race" that I am about to present, and which is derived from sociobiological theory, does clash with the two dominant ideologies of industrial societies—liberalism and socialism. Ethnicity and "race," I will argue, are extensions of kinship, and, therefore, the feelings of ethnocentrism and racism associated with group membership are extensions of nepotism between kinsmen. The central theoretical importance of nepotism as a genetically based mechanism of animal sociality will become clear later. If my argument is correct, then it follows that ethnocentrism and racism, too, are deeply rooted in our biology and can be expected to persist even in industrial societies, whether capitalist or socialist.

This perspective and this prognosis conflict with both the liberal and the socialist views of ethnocentrism and racism as purely cultural products peculiar to certain types of society. In liberal ideology, ethnocentrism and racism are archaic, irrational residues of preindustrial societies, which can be expected to yield to universalism under conditions of "modernization." In the socialist tradition, these phenomena are seen as the product of the capitalist mode of production and as misguided forms of "false consciousness" destined to wither away after the advent of socialism. Both ideological traditions have been equally at a loss to explain the persistence, indeed the resurgence, of ethnic and racial sentiments in both the advanced capitalist and socialist societies. These sentiments will not obligingly go away, as both ideologies predict.

A scientific theory is an attempt to understand the world; an ideology (or ethic, or religion) is an attempt to live with it—or to make others accept it. Unfortunately, most ideologues (and religionists) do their best to obscure the distinction, claiming that their beliefs are grounded in natural law. For my part, however, I see no reason why our values should not be antithetical to natural law. To say that nepotism and ethnocentrism are biologically evolved mechanisms serving the pursuit of individual self-interest, as I will argue in this book, is not to be in favor of these things. It is merely a statement that the behavior of most people most of the time is consistent with that paradigm, whether one likes it or not. Conversely, the common (and correct) assertion that ideology is often self-serving says nothing of its validity or falsehood.

Both the attempt to dismiss a scientific paradigm by linking it with an ideology or an interest, and the endeavor to discredit an ideology, ethic or religion by pointing to its disparity with the natural order are equally misguided. Theory and ideology are complexly linked—often inextricably as I will try to show presently—but they nevertheless serve different ends, and therefore need not be congruent in their conclusions.

Unlike some who, like E. O. Wilson (1978), see in sociobiology a scientific basis for a new ethic, I see the value of sociobiology as providing us with a model of what we are confronting ethically. Sociobiology is a utilitarian model of behavior that sees organisms as blindly selected to maximize their reproductive success. Humans have been so spectacularly successful in this evolutionary game that they are now becoming the victims of their success: they are destroying, through overreproduction and overconsumption, the habitat that supports them. The fundamental ethical problem of the industrial age is to find a solution to the tragedy of the commons. Unless we stop behaving naturally—that is, being our selfish, nepotistic, ethnocentric selves—we court collective extinction.

To develop this new ethic, that we must have if we are to survive the unnatural conditions of the industrial age, we need a workable model of what kind of an animal we are. It is as an anti-ethic that sociobiology holds its greatest promise. We must know the nature of the beast within us to vanquish it. Unless we achieve both—and quickly—we are doomed as a species.

Ethnicity is not lightly shed. There must be powerful material incentives to make one change one's ethnic group. Furthermore, once shed, an ethnic affiliation is almost invariably replaced by a new one, although there are a few genuine cosmopolites who feel equally at home (or equally alienated) in all cultures.

This book is obviously an intensely personal statement. In a sense, this book is in part an attempt to exorcize ethnicity by trying to understand it. I abhor its narrowness, its bigotry, its intolerance, its violence and its outbursts of irrationality. I am not sure whether I succeeded, but I hope to convince the reader that the task is not easy and that it must be done if we are to survive as a species and as a civilization.

ACKNOWLEDGMENTS

This work represents my first book-length statement on race and ethnicity since the publication in 1967 of my *Race and Racism*. My thinking has evolved considerably since then, and the two books are thus quite different. While my comparative methodology has remained much the same, this work is more explicitly evolutionary; it is also twice as long, much wider in scope, and more conceptually ambitious (or pretentious, depending on how the reader assesses the results of my efforts). It continues to bear the mark of my earlier associations with distinguished scholars like Georges Balandier, Hilda and Leo Kuper, John Rex, Richard Schermerhorn, and Michael G. Smith; but it also shows the imprint of more recent influences of the 1970s.

Among them, I should like to mention two groups of people. First, I associated closely with a group of colleagues at the University of Washington called the Committee on the Comparative Study of Ethnicity and Nationalism. Among them I owe a special debt to Paul Brass, Daniel Chirot, Michael Hechter, Charles Keyes and Simon Ottenberg, partners in innumerable discussions on ethnicity. Second, I became exposed to sociobiology and its implications for human behavior by reading and conversing with Richard Alexander, David Barash, Napoleon Chagnon, Richard Dawkins, Irvin DeVore, William Hamilton, Joseph Shepher, Robert Trivers and Edward Wilson. Among my students, my association with Malka Applebaum-Maizel, Penelope Greene, Gary Hamilton, Karen Hansen, Cullen Hayashida, Gene Mesher and George Primov has been especially fruitful. All of them have read and commented on some of my recent writings, including portions of this book. Sammy Smooha introduced me to the complexity of Israeli ethnic relations. Herbert Adam and Leo Kuper gave this manuscript a critical reading, as well as discussed South Africa at length with me. Jorge Flores Ochoa, Fernando Fuenzalida, José Matos Mar and Benjamin Orlove greatly contributed to my understanding of Andean society.

The Spivak award granted me by the American Sociological Association gave me both material support and moral encouragement in the writing of this book. For cheerful secretarial work in converting my unsightly scribblings into a useable typescript, I am indebted to Lilly Karas, Sylvia Moul, Evalinda Skiby, Kim Seymour and Pat Vonasch. Finally (in chronological order), my friend and editor, William Gum, undertook the thankless task of copy-editing this book, the sixth one of mine he had the good sense of publishing. This makes him, I am sure, one of the most persistent readers, and the most consistent improver of my prose. To all these people I am deeply grateful. Any residual wrong-headedness is, of course, altogether my own. God knows they all tried to make me mend my ways.

Pierre L. van den Berghe

Seattle, February 1981

THE ETHNIC
PHENOMENON

INTRODUCTION:
THEORIES AND IDEOLOGIES
OF ETHNIC RELATIONS

It is probably fair to say that the academic specialty usually called "race and ethnic relations" is rich in literature but poor in theory. The same might be said of the social sciences as a whole, with the partial exception of economics and linguistics. In my view, the two main reasons for this state of affairs are that the social sciences are riddled with ideology, and that they have so long divorced themselves from the life sciences. They have treated the study of human social behavior as a phenomenon almost entirely *sui generis*—disembodied from the evolution of the human organism. The two reasons are interrelated and their effects are especially evident in the field of race and ethnic relations, which has long been in the maelstrom of political controversy.

IDEOLOGICAL AND INTELLECTUAL CURRENTS

Concern for "racial" and cultural differences between human groups, and for the consequences thereof in terms of behavior and interaction, antedates the birth of the social sciences as self-conscious disciplines in the second half of the 19th century. The *philosophes* of the 18th century were preoccupied with questions of racial and cultural differences and tended to be Lamarckians and climatic determinists. Peoples differed in customs, temperament and appearance because they lived in different climes and passed on to their descendants the different characteristics acquired in their different geographical settings. Sages of the Enlightenment, like Thomas Jefferson (especially in his *Notes on Virginia*), wavered back and forth between what today we might call genetic and environmental explanations of human differences, but they tended to lean on the environmental side of the fence.

By the middle, and increasingly in the second half, of the 19th century, the European and American social science traditions entered into a phase of genetic determinism, giving rise to racism and social Darwinism (Hofstadter, 1959; Gossett, 1963; Banton, 1977). Human differences in behavior, abilities, character and culture were now attributed principally to in-born differences in biological make-up. A theory of genetic determinism and evolution was being developed 50 years or so before Gregor Mendel's discovery of the genes themselves was rediscovered in 1900. Through the influence of scholars like Herbert Spencer in England and William Graham Sumner in the United States, the social sciences entered a phase of racism and social Darwinism that was to dominate the social sciences during the last quarter of the 19th and the first quarter of the 20th century.

Then, the intellectual pendulum began to swing once more in the environmentalist direction. By the 1920s and 1930s, the United States had become the centerstage of the social sciences, and the students of Franz Boas in anthropology and Robert Park in sociology began to spread the gospel of extreme cultural relativism and determinism that held sway through the 1960s. The political and ideological context of this triumphant cultural determinism was as clear and as evident as that of the social Darwinism of the previous epoch. Much as social Darwinism first became the ideology of laissez-faire capitalism and finally found its political expression in Fascism and Nazism, environmentalism and cultural determinism served the political ends of the Communist–liberal alliance of the Second World War.

Many landmark studies of, and statements about, race and ethnic relations in the quarter-century following the outbreak of World War II bear an unmistakable ideological imprint. German anti-Fascist refugees like Theodore Adorno et al. (1950) influenced a whole generation of studies of the "authoritarian personality." A Swedish Social Democrat, Gunnar Myrdal (1944), was commissioned to study the "Negro problem" in America and predictably pronounced it a white problem. A leading French-Belgian intellectual, Claude Lévi-Strauss (1952), published under UNESCO auspices, the official United Nations line on "race." The American anthropologist, Charles Wagley (1952), was sponsored by UNESCO to study race relations in the supposedly tolerant Brazil. The great American liberals of the period—W. Lloyd Warner (1941), Gordon Allport (1954), E. Franklin Frazier (1957), Otto Klineberg (1944), John Dollard (1939) and many others—all presented a monolithic ideological front—a genuine party line on race and ethnicity. Indeed, that tradition still largely holds sway today in America and Europe.

The liberal tradition in race and ethnic relations held these truths to be, if not self-evident, at least established beyond reasonable doubt:

1. All humans are members of a single species, and there are no biologically meaningful subspecies within it. "Races" are social constructs corresponding to no biological reality.

2. Differences *between* human populations are smaller than *within* them, and such differences as exist (e.g. in I.Q. test performance) are largely if not entirely the product of the social environment.

3. Racism and ethnocentrism are irrational, dysfunctional attitudes, if not downright aberrations, to which certain rigid, authoritarian types of per-

sonality are especially prone. Such attitudes must be combatted through a social therapy promoting equal status contact between groups.

These tenets were part of a general social science world view that nearly all human behavior could be explained in terms of learning, conditioning, socialization, acculturation—in short, the cultural environment. Suggestions that one should *also* look at the genetic evolution of man, as one species of organism interacting with many others in a physical and biotic milieu *as well as* in a cultural environment of his own making, were clearly unfashionable and drew considerable ideological fire.

Along with that environmentalist creed went, in many cases, an assimilationist ideology. The notion of the "melting pot" and the experience of European immigrants groups in the industrial cities of North America in the late 19th and early 20th centuries had given rise to Park's "Chicago school," which saw assimilation as the final phase of the "race relation cycle" (Park, 1950). For a wide variety of reasons, assimilationism seemed a convenient and ostensibly liberal way of solving "minority problems" for the ruling classes of centralized, bureaucratic states, whether capitalist or socialist. To be sure, some anthropologists, fearing the disappearance of "natives" to be studied, continued to plead the cause of cultural diversity, but the main thrust of social science thinking during that era was that ethnic and social sentiments were, on the whole, bad. The value judgment was generally hidden under pretentious jargon such as "particularism," "traditionalism" and "tribalism," but the general view was that race and ethnicity were dysfunctional in industrial societies, represented traditional residues of previous eras and would therefore be eroded by the forces of urbanization, industrialization, modernization and all those impressive-sounding processes so dear to the functionalists.

A very similar ideology developed in the Marxist tradition and was translated into "nationality policy" in the communist countries. The Marxist tradition, with the exception of Lenin, was notoriously unsuccessful in addressing problems of ethnicity, attempting to reduce them to class problems and treating them as residuals of capitalism to be supplanted by proletarian internationalism.

As for the "new nations" of Asia and Africa, and the highly centralized Napoleonic states of Latin America, they also found environmentalism and assimilationism a convenient doctrine to squash separatist movements and to foster "national" unity. A neat semantic trick of semantic mislabeling took place here with the nearly universal cooperation of Western social scientists. All states were now declared to be nation-states. The real nations within these artificial multinational creations of European colonialism were proclaimed to be mere "tribes," and any genuine nationalism that might develop within them was stigmatized as "tribalism." As for the amorphous, anticolonial ideology of the new ruling classes of the Third World, it was dignified with the label of "nationalism." Ethnic groups could now be suppressed, short of physical extermination, with the blessings of the United Nations.

In the late 1960s, and increasingly in the 1970s, the ideological climate changed once more, and social science followed, once again, like a weather vane. The United States and, to a lesser extent, other industrial societies like Canada and Britain went on an ethnic binge. The very word "ethnicity" was coined during that period. It became fashionable to discover, cultivate and cuddle "ethnic identities" and "roots." "Nationalist" movements (e.g. "black nationalism" in the United States) sprang up, and governments, universities and intellectuals followed suit with alacrity with quota systems, affirmative action, ethnic studies programs, offices of minority affairs and the like. All of a sudden, social scientists began to proclaim that the melting pot had failed and had been a sham to start with, that ethnic identities were precious, that assimilationism was a sinister policy of "ethnocide," and that the state should give full recognition to ethnic and racial sentiments and should base its policies of resource distribution on criteria of race and ethnicity. In the 1950s, for example, any social scientist who suggested that American blacks were anything but darkly pigmented, poor and oppressed Anglo-Saxons was called a romantic at best—a fascist at worst. By the late 1960s, social scientists were busy discovering black soul, black culture, black English and so on. Some, like Arthur Jensen (1969), went as far as to discover a special kind of black intelligence.

All these ideological twists and convolutions would be merely amusing if they were not fraught with practical consequences. Although it is probably true that social scientists have followed, rather than preceded, public opinion, political pressures and government policies, they have certainly provided an impressive array of pseudoscientific findings to support whatever was fashionable. The common charge of radicals that social science has always been a handmaiden of power and mainstay of the status quo is not *always* correct. For instance, in South Africa, social scientists have generally been far to the left of the government. But there is no doubt about social scientists' susceptibility to intellectual fashions, uncritical acceptance of views that support their ideology, and blind resistance to evidence that seems to challenge established beliefs.

The events of the seventies threw the overwhelmingly liberal academic establishment in the United States into a quandary. The great liberal coalition of blacks, Jews, students and intellectuals forged during the integrationist phase of the civil rights movements was effectively shattered in the late 1960s by the rise of black "nationalism." Many intellectuals were alienated by civil rights issues. A few timidly reasserted the old liberal ideology of meritocracy, universalism and complete equality of individual rights, but they were clearly out of fashion. Those traditional liberals who wanted to remain in favor had to do an ideological somersault: they now had to support racial classification, ethnic quotas, reverse discrimination and policies based on treating people not according to individual merit or need, but according to group membership. The revival of feminism gave rise to a politically unrealistic coalition of "women and minorities," half-heartedly and ineptly bolstered by federal bureaucrats, but the new coalition fell apart almost as rapidly as it formed. By the time the inevitable white and traditional backlash got organized against blacks and other minorities (e.g. the "white ethnic" movement and the antibusing movement) and against feminism (e.g. the anti-ERA and the "Right to Life" movements), ideological and political disarray, anomie and cynicism reigned in the academic establishment that once espoused the civil rights movement and provided a well-integrated rationale for it. Such has been the background that led me to a search for a more satisfying approach to race and ethnicity.

THE NEED FOR A BROADER PARADIGM: GENES, ENVIRONMENT AND CULTURE

Increasingly over the last decade, it became clear to me that it was not enough to compare human societies with each other—and most assuredly not from the culturally determinist perspective that still dominates the social sciences. An understanding of many fundamental features of human behavior will continue to elude us unless we compare our behavior with that of other species. Indeed, how else are we to determine the nature of human nature, except by establishing similarities and differences with other species? Most social scientists either flatly deny that there is such a thing as human nature or, while granting its existence, proceed to ignore it and to take it for granted. Most social scientists are still content to declare our species sufficiently unique as to limit drastically the value of cross-specific comparisons and as to justify the continued isolation of the social sciences from biology. Most social scientists continue to subscribe to an almost infinitely plastic model of human behavior, shaped overwhelmingly by the cultural environment created by man himself. In my view, these basic premises of so many social scientists are quite untenable and are rapidly rendered obsolete by recent developments in sociobiology (Barash, 1977; Daly and Wilson, 1978; Dawkins, 1976; Shepher, 1980; van den Berghe, 1979a; Edward O. Wilson, 1975, 1978).

In several other places, I have suggested a broader framework for the study of human behavior (van den Berghe, 1978a, 1978b, 1978c, 1979a). Here I shall give a mere sketch of it. Human behavior must be analyzed at three distinct but interrelated levels: (1) genetic, (2) ecological and (3) cultural.

First, like all other organisms, we have evolved biologically through natural selection. The fundamental mechanism for natural selection is the differential reproduction of alternative alleles of given genes. This is obvious enough when we consider our anatomy and physiology. Many social scientists even readily concede that human capabilities (for deductive reasoning, symbolic language, culture and so on) have evolved biologically. The overwhelming majority, however, vigorously deny that our behavior continues to be under genetic control. Instead, they argue, despite evidence to the contrary, that, once the capability for symbolic language and culture developed, culture almost entirely took over as a mechanism of evolution, and that human behavior, by some magic, became infinitely plastic and totally freed of genetic constraints. There is no denying the importance of culture, but culture is a superstructure that builds on a biological substratum. Culture grows out of biological evolution; it does not wipe the biological slate clean and start from scratch.

Second, like all other organisms, we evolved in adaptive response to a multitude of environmental conditions. The phenotype (appearance) of an organism is the product of the interaction of genotype (genetic make-up) and environment. Darwinian evolutionary theory, far from disregarding ecological conditions, is inconceivable without systematic attention to environmental factors. Only naive social scientists oppose heredity and environment; biologists see them as the two complementary sides of the same evolutionary coin. Ecological factors are complex and multiple; they include physical conditions of climate, altitude, space, light, water, salinity and so on, and the biotic environment made up of other animal and plant species, which may be parasites, prey or symbionts. The environment is internal to the organism as well as external, for it includes endoparasites. Indeed, even the genes have a complex interaction effect on each other and can thus be said to constitute part of each others' environment.

For humans, however, the story does not stop there. There is a third crucial element necessary to an understanding of human behavior and human evolution. Our species has developed an impressive bag of tricks, called culture, to control, modify, indeed, create an important part of our environment. Culture is part of our environment, but it differs from the rest of it in being created and transmitted by our own species according to mechanisms fundamentally different from genetic natural selection. Cultural evolution is much faster than biological evolution, and its transmission is Lamarckian rather than Darwinian. Acquired cultural characteristics, unlike in genetic evolution, can be transmitted, modified, transformed or eliminated through social learning. Cultural artifacts can be passed on and utilized from individual to individual through nongenetic inheritance.

Culture is important but not *all*-important. It cannot be divorced from either ecology or genetics. All three levels are intertwined. Genes are selected through environmental pressures, and they impose limits on culture. Culture grows out of biological evolution and responds to multiple environmental forces, but it also shapes the ecology and therefore the biological evolution of our entire planet. Nothing is gained by trying to maintain a categorical distinction between nature and nurture.

The most fundamental question posed by the social sciences is the question of human sociality itself, or what has often been called the "problem of order." Why and under what conditions do humans cooperate? Why is not human existence a war of all against all, at least not all the time? Cooperation and conflict have long been regarded in the social sciences as two sides of a single reality, but it is now becoming apparent that human sociality is a special case of animal sociality in general. Humans, in short, compete and cooperate for much the same reasons as other animals. Organisms compete with each other for scarce resources that are convertible into the ultimate currency of biological evolution: fitness—defined as *reproductive success*. Natural selection operates through a process of differential reproduction, for it is through differential reproduction that different alleles of the same genes change their relative proportions in successive generations of an animal population.

KIN SELECTION AND INCLUSIVE FITNESS

As Dawkins (1976) so elegantly argued, the ultimate unit of biological selection—that is, the smallest unit of genetic material that replicates itself—is the gene. But genes are not free-floating. They are bunched together in chromosomes, which are themselves carried in these little bags of protoplasm we call cells, which are in turn clumped together in more or less complex organisms, i.e. individual plants and animals. When we study behavior, the most convenient unit of analysis is that enormously complex and differentiated assemblage of genes and cells that makes up the individual organism. From the point of view of evolution by natural selection, however, change takes place at the genic level, and organisms are but ephemeral "survival machines" (in Dawkins' phrase) for potentially eternal genes. An organism is but a gene's way of replicating itself—through the organism's reproduction.

Genes cannot be directly observed to behave, however. Rather, genes have an effect on the behavior of organisms (often complex, indirect and flexibly modified by environmental conditions). We can only infer the effect of genes from the phenotypic behavior of individual animals or plants. Since organisms are survival machines for genes, by definition those genes that program organisms for successful reproduction will spread. To maximize their reproduction, genes program organisms to do two things: successfully compete against, and thereby hinder reproduction of, organisms that carry alternative alleles of the genes in question, and successfully cooperate with (and thereby contribute to the reproduction of) organisms that share the same alleles of the genes. In simpler terms, the degree of cooperation between organisms can be expected to be a direct function of the *proportion of the genes they share*; conversely, the degree of conflict between them is an inverse function of the proportion of shared genes.

This formulation at the genic level can be made more intuitively understandable by expressing it from the perspective of the organism. Whenever cooperation increases individual fitness, organisms are genetically selected to be nepotistic, in the sense of favoring kin over nonkin, and close kin over distant kin. The more closely related organisms are, the higher the proportion of the genes they share. Therefore, genes that favor nepotistic behavior in organisms will enhance their own replication more effectively than genes favoring random cooperation. The more closely the beneficiary of a nepotistic act is related to the nepotist, the higher the probability that a given gene is present in both of them. By increasing the fitness of relatives through nepotism, the nepotist indirectly enhances the reproduction of his genes via his kin.

We shall return to this genetically selected propensity for nepotism, also called *kin selection*, in the next chapter, for it seems to underlie much animal sociality (including human) and is of central interest to our subject matter. There is now overwhelming evidence, ranging from social insects to vertebrates, that animal societies are held together in good part by nepotism (E. O. Wilson, 1975). Related animals enhance each others' fitness by cooperating. Animals are social to the extent that they increase their fitness by staying together (e.g. to nurture their young, defend against predators, or forage and hunt more effectively). If, in addition to cooperating, they favor their kin, they further enhance their fitness by fostering not only their own direct reproduction, but also the reproduction of relatives who share a proportion of their genes. Kin selection, though a partially conscious process in humans, need not, of course, be conscious, and in fact is probably not conscious in most animals. Nepotism is blindly selected for because nepotistic individuals in social species have higher fitness than nonnepotistic ones. This is equally true whether the nepotism is conscious (as in humans) or unconscious.

RECIPROCITY

Nepotism is not the whole story of animal sociality. Unrelated animals also cooperate, even across different species, as when they establish a symbiotic relationship. Some fish for instance let smaller fish enter their mouths with impunity to allow them to eat their parasites. Sexual reproduction itself is a basic form of cooperation between frequently unrelated animals. Typically, mating and reproduction take complex and protracted cooperation between male and female, involving at least some of the following: courtship, copulation, nest building, provisioning the young and defending territory. At a minimum, the female has to stay in place long enough for the copulation to take place, but generally the cooperation is much more extensive than that; females, for example, often actively seek and/or signal their readiness to mate to males.

In short, even unrelated animals cooperate when it is mutually beneficial for them to do so, that is, when cooperation increases fitness. The basis for that cooperation may be termed *reciprocity*. Humans, being the intelligent animals they are, have developed systems of reciprocity well beyond the level of complexity found in other species. Humans are highly self-conscious animals, capable of self-consciously pursuing their interests. Therefore, their systems of reciprocity typically involve some kind of mental "book-keeping" of favors given and returned—a balance sheet of gifts extended and received. Such book-keeping presupposes, of course, two cerebral capabilities (which we probably share with many other higher vertebrates): long-term memory and recognition of individuals. Although, in industrial societies, that ability of individual recognition is often taxed beyond our biological potential, any human of normal intelligence has no difficulty recognizing several hundred individuals with whom he interacts regularly. Until a few thousand years ago, the size limits of recognition were roughly coterminous with the size of human societies.

Reciprocity can, of course, operate between kin, but unlike kin selection, it is not *limited* to kin. It thus greatly extends the limits of human sociality. There is, however, a catch to reciprocity, especially to self-conscious reciprocity of the human type: it is open to cheating or free-loading. The temptation not to return a favor received is irresistible. Therefore, systems of self-conscious reciprocity have to detect and control cheating, excluding cheaters from subsequent interactions. This, in turn, selects for more and more complex and subtle forms of cheating, hence, for increasingly sophisticated detection devices, and so on, ad infinitum. The evolution of complex human systems of reciprocity was probably one of the major selective forces for the growth of human intelligence beyond the simian or australopithecine level.

Many animals have evolved simple and presumably unconscious forms of deceit, such as camouflage and mimicry of a predator or of a dangerous prey. Monkeys and apes are perhaps intelligent enough to evolve rudimentary forms of conscious deception and are certainly not easily fooled by crude forms of human deceit. But humans are deceitful on a scale that dwarfs anything we know in the rest of the animal world.

The ultimate individual form of human deceit is *self*-deceit. Since we have developed very subtle ways of detecting lying and cheating in fellow humans, lying itself is a difficult art. It follows, then, that the most effective way of telling a lie, especially a self-serving one, is to be convinced that you are, in fact, telling the truth. The ultimate forms of collective self-deceit developed by our species are religion and ideology. Religion is the denial of mortality. Ideology is a sophisticated belief system the purpose of which is to facilitate the transmission of credible, self-serving lies. Religion is universal to human culture because the rise of self-consciousness in our species inevitably brought with it intimations of mortality, and therefore, the existential need to deny death. Ideology is more characteristic of state-level societies because the creation of a state necessarily entails the divergence of class interests between the rulers and the ruled. Ideologies and counterideologies serve the defense of class interests. In state societies, religion itself broadens its functions to become an ideology. State religions are no longer simply answers to the existential fear of death, but rationalizations for the status quo and, therefore, a form of ideology. However, even in classless societies rudimentary ideologies can be found in defense of group interests. Ethnocentrism is one such rudimentary ideology, and so are sexism and "ageism." Men use rudimentary ideologies to control women, and adults to control children.

COERCION

The common denominator of much ideology, then, is that it seeks to hide or to justify *asymmetrical relationships*, that is, relationships in which a fitness gain to ego is achieved at some cost to alter. Asymmetrical (or parasitic) relationships can only be maintained through deceit, coercion or a combination of the two. Deceit, as we saw, is endemic in systems of reciprocity. But systems of reciprocity are vulnerable not only to deceit: they are also open to coercion. To the extent that power imbalances exist in a reciprocal interaction, reciprocity can easily be transformed into *coercion*.

Again, coercion is not a human monopoly. Male animals use force or threats to displace or eliminate competition, to gain access to females in oestrus, to secure submission of subordinates and so on. Some intelligent mammals, such as baboons and lions, are even capable of forming small coalitions of two to four males in order to establish and maintain a collective dominance over individual rivals. Some animal societies can thus be said to have rudimentary "ruling classes." Humans do, however, hold pride of place in their ability to use to good effect conscious, collective, organized, premeditated coercion in order to establish, maintain and perpetuate systems of intraspecific parasitism.

In stateless societies, collectively organized violence has a long history. Hominids early became both predator and prey to their own species. Beyond killing and eating each other, early hominids perhaps began to steal each others' women as well. With the development of agriculture and animal husbandry, the stakes were raised. Human male groups, now larger, better organized and better armed, waged endemic warfare over women, livestock and territory. The rise of states marked the extension of the realm of coercion and parasitism *within* societies as well as between them. Indeed, the very essence of the state is the centralization of power in the hands of the few in order to extract surplus production from the many, within the same society. Police, courts, taxation, forced labor and slavery are so many coercive institutions that thrive together with the development of states. The history of the last six or seven millenia is the history of the rise of bigger and bigger states, ever better organized and armed for outside aggression and internal coercion.

To summarize, I suggested that we look at human behavior in broad evolutionary perspective. *Homo sapiens* evolved as one species among many—through a process of natural selection similar to that of other animals. This is as true of human behavior as of human anatomy. Like those of other animals, human genes were selected in adaptive response to a multiplicity of ecological conditions. Out of this process of natural selection grew a set of specifically human capabilities we call culture. Culture is our species' way of evolving and adapting much faster than would be possible by genetic selection alone. But culture is part and parcel of nature and cannot be dissociated from it.

Like other animal societies, human societies are held together by the self-interest of their individual members. This self-interest is best measured in terms of reproductive success, for it is through differential reproduction that biological evolution of all life forms takes place. Individuals, human or nonhuman, interact competitively or cooperatively to maximize their individual fitness. They do so in three basic ways: through kin selection, reciprocity and coercion. The human variations on these three basic mechanisms are much more complex than those observable in other species, but they are not *categorically* different. Self-consciousness—that outstanding characteristic of human behavior—is probably present to some extent in apes and perhaps in other intelligent mammals as well. Certainly, many higher vertebrates (birds and mammals) show a considerable ability to learn through experience, to modify their behavior accordingly and to transmit socially their innovations—all features once thought unique to human culture. Even the capacity to use symbolic language is present in rudimentary form in apes, although apes do not seem to use symbolic language under natural conditions.

THE SOCIOBIOLOGICAL PARADIGM

This sketch of an approach to the study of human behavior attempts to integrate the biological and social sciences into a single evolutionary paradigm. It places our species squarely in the vast planetary ecosystem where it belongs, together with millions of other evolving species. In some respects, we are genuinely unique, but then so is every species, otherwise it would not be a species. In most respects, we are different from other species only in degree.

Since the publication of E. O. Wilson's book (1975), the label "sociobiology" has gained increasing acceptance to describe the approach presented here. The same general neo-Darwinian approach to the study of behavior has also been termed "ethology," "behavioral biology," "behavioral ecology" and "biosociology." Each of these labels has a slightly different connotation because it has been attached to different groups of scientists doing slightly different research with somewhat different emphases. Labels matter little. What matters is that we improve our understanding of our own behavior. This has not only theoretical appeal: it seems to become increasingly a necessary condition to our very biological survival. We are seemingly the victims of our success as the dominant species of our planet. We have created for ourselves an environment drastically different from the one under which our previous evolution took place. In the process we are not only damaging the biosphere upon which our survival depends; we are unleashing ecological changes at a rate that increasingly outpaces our biological capabilities to adjust.

No doubt, in the long run, our species is as doomed as dodos and dinosaurs. It is only a matter of time before *all* life forms become unsustainable on our planet. But in the last couple of centuries we seem bent on accelerating the pace of our extinction. Unless we learn to modify our behavior (including all kinds of behavior, such as aggression and uncontrolled reproduction, which were once adaptive but have now become catastrophic) we will all be in serious trouble much sooner than many of us expect. To modify our behavior we need to understand it; that is, we must understand what kind of an animal we are. This, in turn, we cannot do in the abstract. We can only do so successfully by comparing ourselves across human societies and across other species. Only then we will be able to establish the parameters of the human condition.

SUGGESTED READINGS

Among the standard general overviews of the field of race and ethnic relations from a broad cross-cultural point of view are Banton (1967), Mason (1970, 1971), Rex (1970) and van den Berghe (1978a), at a more introductory level, and Francis (1976), Le Vine and Campbell (1972), and Schermerhorn (1970), in a more analytical vein. For a sweeping critique of American race and ethnic relations studies from a sociology of knowledge perspective, see Bash (1979).

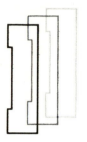

AN
EXPLANATORY
FRAMEWORK

ETHNICITY AS KIN SELECTION:
THE BIOLOGY OF NEPOTISM

The notion that ethnicity has something to do with kinship or "blood" is not new. Indeed, descent seems to be, implicitly and very often explicitly, *the* essential element of the definition of those groups of "significant others" that go under a wide variety of labels: tribe, band, horde, deme, ethnic group, race, nation and nationality. This is clearly the case in the Western tradition where the ideology of nationalism is replete with the rhetoric of kinship: fellow ethnics refer to each other as brothers and sisters; soldiers are said to die for the *mère patrie* or the *Vaterland*, depending on the gender ascribed by language to the collective parent; mystical notions of blood are said to be shared by members of one nation and to differentiate them from other groups.

True, the legacy of two world wars and of virulent racism in Nazi Germany somewhat dampened nationalist fervor in some intellectual circles in Europe and America during the 1950s and early 1960s. No sooner did intellectuals pronounce nationalism dead or dying in the "advanced" industrial countries, however, than it resurfaced within long-established states in the form of multitudinous movements for regional autonomy, ethnic separatism, racial pride, cultural identity and the like.

Nor is the irrepressible nature of ethnic sentiments a uniquely Western perversion. The most common origin myth of "primitive" societies ascribes the birth of the nation to an ancestral couple, divinely created or descended. In the simplest form of the myth, the ancestral couple is thought of as the progenitors of the entire society. In stratified societies, the royal family often attempts to monopolize divine ancestry, but then it quickly makes up for it by claiming paternity over its subjects.

For the followers of the monotheistic religions of Judaism, Christianity and Islam, the Book of Genesis serves as origin myth, and Adam and Eve as the ancestral couple. More specifically, Muslims and Jews see themselves as decendants of Abraham. Those groups have now become so large and so diverse that these putative ancestors are no longer very meaningful to many contemporary followers of these religions, but the Biblical origin myths are in fact quite similar to those of other traditions. For example, the Yoruba of Southwestern Nigeria place their own origin (which in typical ethnocentric manner, they identify with the origin of mankind) in their sacred city of the Ile Ife. The earth was created at Ile Ife by Oduduwa, one of the main divinities of the Yoruba pantheon, on instructions from Olorun the supreme deity. Oduduwa came down to the earth he created, sired sixteen sons who became the founders of the various Yoruba kingdoms and the ancestors of all the Yoruba people (Bascom, 1969).

The Navajo, an indigenous American group inhabiting the southwestern United States, have a complex myth in which Changing Woman, the principal figure among the supernatural Holy People, was magically impregnated by the rays of the Sun and by water from a waterfall and gave birth to twin sons, Hero Twins, who first dwelt with their father, the Sun. Holy People later descended to earth where they created Earth Surface People, the ancestors of the Navajos, and taught them culture, i.e. the Navajo way of life (Kluckhohn and Leighton, 1958).

The Pathan, stateless agriculturalists and pastoralists of Afghanistan and Pakistan, clearly define their ethnicity in terms of descent in patrilineal line from a common ancestor, Qais, who lived some 20 to 25 generations ago, and was a contemporary of Prophet Mohammed from whom he embraced the Muslim faith. A Pathan is thus a descendant of Qais in the male line who is Muslim and conforms to Pathan customs (Fredrik Barth, 1959, 1969).

Even a large centralized state like Japan has a traditional nationalist myth whereby all Japanese are descended from the same common ancestor of whom the Imperial Family represent the line of direct descent, and all the other families of Japan represent collateral branches formed by younger sons of earlier generations. The entire nation is, thus, one single vast lineage (Dore, 1958). In the words of a Hozumi Nobushige, a Japanese writing in 1898, "The Emperor embodies the Spirit of the Original Ancestor of our race. . . . In submitting to the Emperor of a line which has persisted through the ages, we subjects are submitting to the Spirit of the Joint Parent of our Race, the Ancestor of our ancestors." [Quoted by Dore (1958, p. 94).] This "blood ideology," as Hayashida (1976) called it, has been the essential defining element of Japanese nationhood for centuries.

Examples could be multiplied, but these few illustrations from widely scattered parts of the world will suffice. Ethnicity is common descent, either real or putative, but, even when putative, the myth has to be validated by several generations of common historical experience.

When most of the world's "traditional" societies became incorporated in the colonial empires of European or neo-European countries, ideologues and social scientists of both right and left believed that ethnic sentiments would become increasingly vestigial, and that "modernity" (or "socialist internationalism" in the communist societies) would engulf petty particularisms, giving rise to ever wider and more rational bases of solidarity based on market forces, proletarian consciousness, Third World brotherhood or whatever.

Few, if any, of these expectations came to pass. When imperial rule was securely established, it often managed to suppress emergent nationalisms by violence, but no sooner did these imperial systems collapse in the aftermath of war or revolution than did ethnic sentiments burst forth. Ironically, the only large empire to have emerged relatively intact from the postimperial turmoil of the two world wars is that of the Czars. Even the new successor states to the European colonial empires have been rent by ethnic dissidence: Nigeria, Zaïre, India, Pakistan and Malaysia—to name but a few. Nor were the smaller imperial systems spared the threat of ethnic separatism when the traditional system of rule collapsed, as witnessed by the events of the 1970s in Ethiopia and Iran. Even centuries of centralized despotism cannot suppress ethnic sentiment.

The position that ethnicity is a deeply rooted affiliation is often labeled "primordialist" in social science. Articulated by Max Weber (1968, first published in 1922), and later by Geertz (1967a) and Shils (1957), the primordialist position was under severe attack in the 1950s and 1960s when most social scientists treated ethnicity as one affiliation among many—highly changeable and responsive to circumstances. The Marxists viewed ethnicity as an epiphenomenon, a remnant of precapitalist modes of production, a false consciousness masking class interests, a mystification of ruling classes to prevent the growth of class consciousness (Cox, 1948). To functionalists and other non-Marxists, ethniticy was also a premodern phenomenon, a residue of particularism and ascription incompatible with the trend toward achievement, universalism and nationality supposedly exhibited by industrial societies (Deutsch, 1966).

All the bad things said of ethnicity were of course ascribed a fortiori to race. Sentiments of group-belonging, based on physical attributes, were held to be even more wrong-headed and heinous than group membership based upon cultural attributes, such as language, religion and other customs—the usual diacritica of ethnicity (Comas, 1972; Glazer, 1975; Gossett, 1963; Hofstadter, 1959; Leo Kuper, 1975; Lévi-Strauss, 1952; van den Berghe, 1965). Only recently, with the revival of ethnicity, is the "primordialist" position once more being stated (Francis, 1976; Keyes, 1976).

The conventional primordialist position on ethnicity was vulnerable on two scores:

1. It generally stopped at asserting the fundamental nature of ethnic sentiment without suggesting any explanation of why that should be the case. As a theoretical underpinning, the primordialists had nothing better to fall back on than the nebulous, romantic, indeed sometimes racist ideologies of nationalists to which the primordialists pointed as illustrations of their contention. What kind of mysterious and suspicious force was this "voice of the blood" that moved people to tribalism, racism and ethnic intolerance?

2. If ethnicity was primordial, then was it not also ineluctable and immutable? Yet, patently, ethnic sentiments waxed and waned according to
circumstances. Ethnicity could be consciously manipulated for personal
gain. Ethnic boundaries between groups are sometimes quite fluid.
Smaller groups often merge into larger ones and vice-versa. New ethnic
groups constantly arise and disappear, and individuals may choose to
assert ethnic identities or not as their interests or fancies dictate. How
is all this circumstantial fluidity reconcilable with the primordialist position?

In contrast to the primordialist view of ethnicity, there came to be formulated the "instrumentalist" or "circumstantialist" position that held ethnicity to be something manipulable, variable, situationally expressed,
subjectively defined and only one possible type of affiliation among many
(Brass, 1974, 1976). One of the leading exponents of this position is Fredrik
Barth, who in his classical introduction to *Ethnic Groups and Boundaries*
(1969), explicitly defines ethnicity in subjective terms. Ethnicity is whatever
the natives say it is. It is the natives' perceptions of reality that create and
define ethnic boundaries and ethnic relations. It just happens that the Pathans whom Barth studied so extensively define their ethnicity in terms of
descent from a common ancestor; that ethnographic fact does not invalidate
Barth's position. Indeed, nothing can, if the analytical categories used in
social science must always be defined by the natives who, in turn, are, by
definition, always right! The problem for those of us who try to formulate
scientific propositions, is that natives do not always agree with each other,
even *within* cultures, and that therefore a science of human behavior based
exclusively on native opinion tends to be shaky.

As most controversies based on a simple-minded antimony, the primordialist–instrumentalist debate serves little purpose other than to help Ph.D
candidates organize their examination answers. It is one of the main aims
of this book to show that both positions are correct, although not necessarily
in the way the protagonists envisaged, and that the two views complement
each other. In Chapter 3, we shall see that ethnicity is indeed situationally
variable, according to a multiplicity of ecological conditions. And, in Chapter 4, we shall examine the many ways in which ethnicity is manipulated
in power relationships. Before I turn to the ecology and politics of ethnicity,
and thereby vindicate the instrumentalists, however, a theoretical basis for
the primordialist position must be developed. Briefly, I suggest that there
now exists a theoretical paradigm of great scope and explanatory
power—evolutionary biology—that sheds a new light on phenomena of ethnocentrism and racism. In so doing, I am fully cognizant of the protest that
such an endeavor will elicit.

My basic argument is quite simple: ethnic and racial sentiments are extension of kinship sentiments. Ethnocentrism and racism are thus extended
forms of nepotism—the propensity to favor kin over nonkin. There exists
a general behavioral predisposition, in our species as in many others, to

react favorably toward other organisms to the extent that these organisms are biologically related to the actor. The closer the relationship is, the stronger the preferential behavior.

Why should parents sacrifice themselves for their children? Why do uncles employ nephews rather than strangers in their business? Why do inheritance laws provide for passing property on along lines of kinship? Why, in short, do people, and indeed other animals as well, behave nepotistically. To many, these questions appear so intuitively obvious as to require no explanation. We favor kin because they *are* kin. This is no answer of course, but a mere restatement of the problem. Besides, we do not *always* favor kin. Profligate sons are sometimes disinherited, incompetent nephews not hired and so on. Yet, on the whole we are nepotists, and when we are not, it is for some good reason. Nepotism, we intuitively feel is the natural order of things. Where we feel nepotism would interfere with efficiency, equity or some other goals, we institute explicit safeguards against it and, even then, we expect it to creep in again surreptitiously.

But why? A convincing answer was hinted at by the British biologists R. A. Fisher (1958, first published in 1930) and J. B. S. Haldane (1932) but elaborated on only about 15 years ago by W. D. Hamilton (1964) and J. Maynard Smith (1964). The theorem of "altruism", "kin selection" or "inclusive fitness," as biologists often refer to nepotism, was increasingly discovered to be the keystone of animal sociality. Soon, a theoretical synthesis of population genetics, ecosystem theory and ethology gave birth to the new discipline of "sociobiology" as E. O. Wilson labeled it in his magisterial compendium on animal behavior (1975, ably summarized in Barash, 1977).

The problem that posed itself to biologists was the seemingly self-sacrificial behavior of some animals under some conditions, e.g. the emission of alarm calls to warn conspecifics, the mimicking of injuries to distract predators, or seeming restraints on reproduction under adverse ecological conditions. Wynne-Edwards (1962) answered the problem in terms of group selection. Altruists behave in such a way for the good of their social group; groups that produce altruists have a competitive advantage over those that do not. However, there is one big drawback to the group selectionist argument. Altruism, by biological definition, is behavior that enhances the fitness (i.e. the reproductive success) of others at the cost of reducing the fitness of the altruist. If the altruists do indeed reduce their fitness by behaving altruistically, then genes fostering altruism would be selected against. How can an animal population sustain altruistic genes that reduce the reproductive success of their carriers through enhanced predation, induced sterility (as in the worker castes of social insects) or some other cause?

The answer is so disarmingly simple and convincing that even Wynne-Edwards has recently recanted his group selectionist argument. Seeming altruism is, in fact, the ultimate in genetic selfishness. Beneficent behavior is the product of a simple fitness calculus (presumably an unconscious one in most animals, though often a partially conscious one in humans) that takes two factors into account: the cost–benefit ratio of the transaction between altruist and recipient, and the coefficient of relatedness r between altruist and recipient. Simply put, an altruistic transaction can be expected if, and only if, the cost–benefit ratio of the transaction is smaller than the coefficient of relatedness between the two actors.

The coefficient of relatedness between any two organisms is the proportion of genes they share through common descent. It can range from a value of one (for organisms that reproduce asexually, e.g. through cell division) to zero (between unrelated organisms). In sexually reproducing organisms, parents and offspring and full siblings share one-half of their genes; half-siblings, grandparents and grandchildren, uncles–aunts and nephews–nieces share one-fourth; first cousins, one-eighth, and so on.

Reproduction, in the last analysis, is passing on one's genes. This can be done directly through one's own reproduction or indirectly through the reproduction of related organisms. The fitness of an organism is, by definition, its reproductive success. The *inclusive* fitness of an organism is the sum of its own reproductive success plus that of related organisms discounted for their coefficient of relatedness. Thus, it takes two children to reproduce the genetic equivalent of ego; but the same effect can be achieved through four nephews or eight first cousins.

As brilliantly argued by Richard Dawkins (1976), the ultimate unit of replication is the gene, not the organism. Bodies are, in Dawkins' words, mere mortal and expendable "survival machines" for potentially immortal genes. Such genes, therefore, as predispose their carrying organisms to behave nepotistically will be selected for, because, by favoring nepotism, they enhance their own replication. Nepotistic organisms foster the fitness of relatives who have a high probability of carrying the same gene or genes for nepotism. Nepotism genes, therefore, will spread faster than genes that program their carriers to care only for their own direct survival and reproduction—genes, for instance, that would program organisms to eat their siblings when hungry. This phenomenon of fostering inclusive fitness through *kin selection* or nepotism has been conclusively shown (mostly by studies of social insects, but also, increasingly, of vertebrates) to be the basis of much animal sociality (E. O. Wilson, 1975; Daly and Wilson, 1978).

Animal societies, from social insects to higher vertebrates, are held together primarily by cooperating kin who thereby enhance each other's fitness. This seeming "altruism" is thus the ultimate genic selfishness of maximizing one's *inclusive* fitness. An individual will only behave "altruistically" (i.e. in such a way as to reduce its own direct fitness) if, by doing so, the increment of fitness of a relative more than makes up for the loss to ego. For instance, my full sister shares half of her genes with me; she must, therefore, get more than twice as much out of my beneficent act to her than what that act costs me. For a half-sister or a niece, who only shares one-fourth of her genes with me, the benefit–cost ratio of the transaction would have to be better than four to one—and so on, according to the coefficient of relatedness between giver and receiver. The biological golden rule is "give unto others as they are related unto you."

The applicability of the kin selection paradigm to humans has been hotly debated. While anthropologists and other social scientists can hardly deny that all known human societies are organized on the basis of kinship and marriage, forming relatively stable reproductive units called families and exhibiting preferential behavior toward relatives, a number of them continue to argue nevertheless that kinship and marriage for humans are purely *cultural* concepts showing only fortuitous resemblance to anything biological (Sahlins, 1976; Schneider, 1968). Elsewhere, I have attempted to refute that line of argument. While man is in some important respects different from other species, while man has an enormous capacity to adapt through learning and while most of human behavior is indeed patterned (but not single-handedly determined) by a culture transmitted through symbolic language, man nevertheless remains an animal who shares many features of the mating and reproductive system with that of other mammals (van den Berghe, 1979a; van den Berghe and Barash, 1977). Rapidly accumulating evidence shows how applicable the kin selection paradigm is to humans (Chagnon and Irons, 1979; Daly and Wilson, 1978; Greene, 1978; Hartung, 1976; Shepher, 1980).

Relatedness is a relative matter. Kinship might be schematized as a series of concentric circles around ego, each circle representing a degree of relatedness (Schema I). In the smallest circles are small numbers of highly related ($r = \frac{1}{2}$ or $\frac{1}{4}$) individuals. As the circles become larger, so does the number of persons involved, but r becomes smaller ($\frac{1}{8}$, $\frac{1}{16}$, $\frac{1}{32}$ and so on), and therefore the intensity of kin selection rapidly declines.

In theory, we could have a wide-open network of such overlapping ego-centered kinship circles, with no particular clustering. At the limit, all of humanity would consist of one vast undifferentiated surface of overlapping concentric circles with no cluster or boundaries between them. This con-

SCHEMA I. Ego-centered map of kin selection.

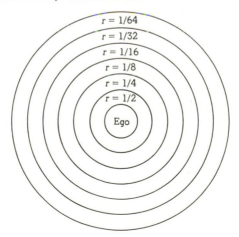

dition would be produced by what population biologists call *panmixia*—that is, random mating. Panmixia never happens in humans, nor in other animals, for a very simple reason: if nothing else, space exerts a passive restraint on who mates with whom. Sheer physical propinquity determines who has sexual access to whom. Geographical barriers, such as mountain ranges, bodies of water, deserts and the like, isolate animal populations from each other, and create breeding boundaries between them, that can and often do lead to speciation or subspeciation.

In humans, however, the story does not stop there. In addition to the purely physical impediments of distance, topography and so on, human groups create cultural prescriptions and proscriptions concerning their mating systems. There is not a single known human group that lacks them and that even approximates panmixia. Rules specify whom one may, may not, should or must marry. These rules and practices are almost invariably of a twofold nature. Certain individuals or members of some kin groups (such as lineages and class) *cannot* intermarry, while a wider group constitutes the people who are normally *expected* to mate and marry.

Indeed, nearly all of the small-scale, stateless, human societies are groups ranging from a couple of hundred to a few thousand people, defined almost entirely by ties of descent and marriage. These breeding populations are internally divided into smaller kin groups that swap daughters and sisters for spouses between the men (Lévi-Strauss, 1969). Elsewhere (van den Berghe, 1979a), I have dealt at length with human kinship and marriage systems and shown how closely they conform to the sociobiological paradigm. The relevance of all this to ethnicity is that the primeval model of the human ethnic group is, in fact, the breeding population of a few hundred individuals, the structure of which we have just sketched. This is what the anthropologists used to call the "tribe"—a group characterized by internal peace, preferential endogamy and common ancestry (real or putative).

At this point, I would like to introduce the neologism *ethny* for "ethnic group." "Ethnic group" is clumsy and "tribe" has many different connotations—several pejorative. The French and Spanish cognates *ethnie* and *etnia* are already in common usage, and it is time to start using such a convenient term in English as well. The ideology usually referred to as "ethnocentrism" might then be more parsimoniously called *ethnism*. An ethny can be represented, as in Schema II, as a cluster of overlapping, ego-centered, concentric kin circles, encompassed within an ethnic boundary. The ethnic boundary is represented by a dotted line, since it is seldom completely closed. More typically, there is some migration, principally of women, among groups.

If the society in question has a rule of unilineal descent, either patrilineal or matrilineal, then the ethny may also be represented, as in Schema III, as internally divided into nonoverlapping unilineal descent groups (clans) that exchange women. In fact, the vast majority of the stateless, tropical horticulturalists and pastoralists, and a considerable number of the preindustrial state societies have unilineal descent and clan exogamy, often combined

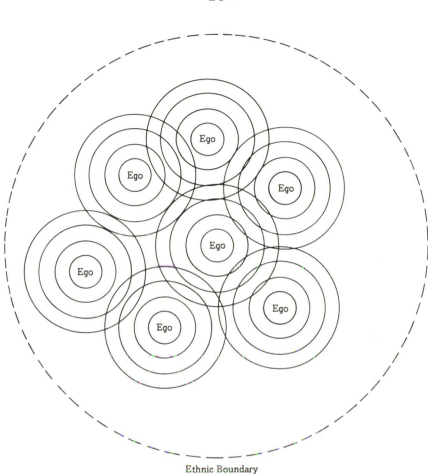

Ethnic Boundary

SCHEMA II. Kinship map of the prototypical ethny.

with preferential cross-cousin marriage. This is not the place to expand on the organizational advantages of this common system, as I have done so elsewhere (van den Berghe, 1979a). Most of the remaining hunting and gathering societies have bilateral descent and a much less structured system of exchanging women but, even in these less structured systems, that were presumably also characteristic of earlier phases of human social evolution, the ethny is also a breeding population of limited size (typically a few hundred), most of whose members are related to each other.

There are, of course, exceptions. Some women are captured from neighboring ethnies. Conquest and peaceful migration periodically mix populations, and newcomers may be fictively related by adoption. It is very difficult and quite exceptional, however, for an ethny to form if the core of the group

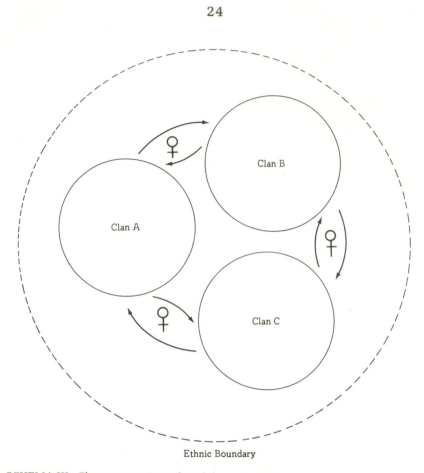

Ethnic Boundary

SCHEMA III. Clan exogamy in unilineal descent ethnies.

is not made up of people who know themselves to be related to each other by a double network of ties of descent and marriage. Ethnicity is thus defined in the last analysis by *common descent*. Descent by itself, however, would leave the ethny unbounded, for, by going back enough, all living things are related to each other. *Ethnic boundaries* are created *socially* by *preferential endogamy* and physically by *territoriality*. Territoriality and endogamy are, of course, mutually reinforcing for without physical propinquity people can hardly meet and mate and, conversely, successful reproduction, with all the lavish parental investment it requires for humans, favors territorialized kin groups. The prototypical ethny is thus a descent group bounded socially by inbreeding and spatially by territory.

Until the last few thousand years, such groups were of limited size as witnessed by many surviving "primitive" societies. The natural ethny in which hominids evolved for several thousand millenia probably did not exceed a couple of hundred individuals at the most. Evidence for this is the great mental and emotional strain on the human brain to "know" more than a few hundred individuals. We can recognize by sight many thousands, but our ability to associate complex personalities with faces and to make reliable enough predictions about people's behavior to render interaction sufficiently unstrained is quite limited. Urban life constantly strains these physiological limits, and when we must constantly interact with a larger and rapidly changing cast of characters the very nature of the interaction changes drastically, as has been repeatedly noted by social scientists and others. There are many fundamental differences between what the German sociologists called *Gemeinschaft* (the small-scale, intimate, face-to-face group of a few hundred people or the prototypical ethny in my terms) and *Gesellschaft* (the large, anomic, impersonal society characteristic of the industrial age).

We have evolved, I am arguing, the kind of brain to deal with small-scale, *Gemeinschaft*-type groups, the prototype of which is the ethny, the "we-group", the "in-group" of intimates who think of each other as an *extended family*. Beyond that kind and size of group, the strain of having to deal with people we do not know well enough, and therefore cannot trust, is of such a nature as to alter radically the very nature of the interaction. In the larger world, we expect ruthless self-interest and cheating to be rampant and to be constrained principally by the coercive power of the state. Furthermore, our brain, which in other respects is a stupefying complex instrument, rebels at "knowing" intimately more than a few hundred people at the limit. If we try to exceed an upper limit of, say, 500, we either have to slough off old acquaintances to allow new ones, or we simply fake familiarity and conviviality beyond our emotional and intellectual capabilities.

The primordial ethny is thus an extended family; indeed, the ethny represents the outer limits of that inbred group of near or distant kinsmen whom one knows as intimates and whom therefore one can trust. One intuitively expects fellow ethnics to behave at least somewhat benevolently toward one because of kin selection, reinforced by reciprocity. The shared genes predispose toward beneficence; the daily interdependence reinforces that kin selection. Fellow ethnics are, in the deepest sense, "our people."

This prototype of the small, endogamous, kin-related ethny is, of course, importantly modified in practice, especially in the larger societies that have arisen since the development of agriculture some 10,000 years ago, of large states some 5000 years ago, and most recently of the industrial revolution 200 years ago. So far, we have merely sketched the evolutionary scenario of the ethny. Now we must fill in the picture by introducing the qualifications.

Ethnic endogamy is seldom strict and prescriptive. Generally, it is merely preferential, and, most importantly, asymmetrical by sex. The double standard of sexual morality that is so apparent in many aspects of our behavior and so readily understandable in terms of the biology of asymmetrical parental investment (Daly and Wilson, 1978; Trivers, 1972) is also glaringly present in the application of ethnic endogamy. Much of the abundant lit-

erature on ethnicity and sex has been psychoanalytically oriented, invoking
elaborate theories of frustration–aggression, sado-masochism, repression of
libidinal urges and attraction of forbidden fruits (Adorno, 1950; Bastide,
1950; Freyre, 1964; Mannoni, 1964; Lillian Smith, 1963; Stember, 1976).
The sociobiological paradigm provides a much simpler explanation. In
nearly all species, the female is the scarce reproductive resource for the
male rather than vice-versa. There are fewer females available for insemi-
nation than males ready to inseminate. Eggs are big, few and therefore costly;
sperms are small, abundant and therefore cheap. Since females invest much
more in the reproductive process than males, they maximize their fitness
by being choosy about their mating partners. They seek to pick the best
possible mates in terms of genetic qualities and resources they have to offer.
The male, on the other hand, maximizes his fitness by being promiscuous
and by outcompeting his rivals in access to reproductive females.

Seen in that light, the ethny is a corporation of related men seeking to
enhance each others' fitness by retaining a monopoly of sexual access to
the women of their own group. This, however, does not preclude men from
further enhancing their reproductive success by making the most of every
opportunity to inseminate women from other groups. In fact, the whole
history of ethnic relations powerfully confirms this interpretation. Men jealously "protect" "their" women from men of other groups, deeply resenting
ethnic exogamy on the part of women, while at the same time seeking access
to women from other groups. In ethnically stratified societies, this double
standard takes the form of polygamy of the dominant-group men, with subordinate-group women becoming secondary wives and concubines. Where
several ethnies live side by side in an unstratified system, the groups constantly raid each other for women.

This sexual asymmetry of endogamy has, of course, one important consequence—namely that no ethny is a completely closed breeding system.
The circulation of women between ethnies continuously brings in fresh
blood. One may then look at ethnic relations from the point of view of the
circulation of women, and arrive at the following formulation. *Within the
ethny*, a group of related men peacebly exchange kinswomen for wives
among themselves. After the system has been in operation for several generations, the wives are also related to their husbands; frequently, they are
preferentially cousins, in fact. This leads to a certain degree of inbreeding
that is all the greater as the ethny is small.

Between ethnies, men use power and violence to secure access to women
from other groups, and this reduces the level of inbreeding. When the ethnies
in presence are equally matched, male competition for foreign women takes
the form of interethnic raids. After an ethnic hierarchy has been established,
subordinate-group men loose all or part of their control of "their" women
and their reproductive success is curtailed, while upper-group men are
polygynous and incorporate subordinate-group women. An ethnic hierarchy, therefore, generally results in a reduced fitness for subordinate-group
males. The classical scenario for conquest is to rape the women and kill,
castrate or enslave the men.

Asymmetry of reproductive strategies for males and females has another important corollary for ethnic relations. In a situation of ethnic hierarchy, ethnic solidarity between men and women is undermined. The men of the subordinate group are always the losers and therefore have a reproductive interest in overthrowing the system. The women of the subordinate group, however, frequently have the option of being reproductively successful with dominant-group males. Indeed, even where forced into relationships with dominant males, they must cooperate in the interest of their children. We shall return to that important point when we examine slavery systems.

Descent, I asserted, is the central feature of ethnicity. Yet, it is clear that, in many cases, the common descent ascribed to an ethny is fictive. In fact, in *most* cases, it is at least *partly* fictive. If such is the case, does not the fictive or putative character of kinship invalidate the sociobiological argument presented here? I think not. Ethnicity, I suggested, is extended kinship. Even in restricted kinship, descent is sometimes a fiction. In most societies, some children are adopted or are not the offspring of their supposed fathers. Nevertheless, these exceptions do not invalidate the general proposition that human kinship systems reflect biological relatedness. Some anthropologists have argued against this proposition (Sahlins, 1976; Schneider, 1968), but they must strain the data beyond credibility to defend their position. A number of anthropologists have argued convincingly against the purely cultural-determinist view of human kinship (Fortes, 1969; Fox, 1967). In a recent book (van den Berghe, 1979a), I have attempted to demonstrate how closely human systems of kinship and marriage fit expectations derived from the sociobiological paradigm.

If kinship in the most restricted circle of the nuclear family is sometimes a biological fiction, it is little wonder that the greatly extended kind of kinship implicit in ethnicity should often be putative. The larger the ethny, the more likely this is. Clearly, for 50 million Frenchmen or 100 million Japanese, any common kinship that they may share is highly diluted, and known to be so. Similarly, when 25 million Afro-Americans call each other "brothers" and "sisters," they know that they are greatly extending the meaning of these terms. The enormous ethnies, running into millions of members, that characterize industrial societies are limiting cases, far removed from the evolutionary prototype of a few hundred people that we have been talking about.

Yet—and this is what begs explanation—the fiction of kinship, even in modern industrial societies, has to be sufficiently credible for ethnic solidarity to be effective. One cannot create an instant ethny by creating a myth. The myth has to be rooted in historical reality to be accepted. Ethnicity can be *manipulated* but *not manufactured*. Unless ethnicity is rooted in generations of shared historical experience, it cannot be created *ex nihilo*. Many attempts to adopt universalistic criteria of ethnicity based on legal citizenship or acquisition of educational qualifications, for instance, failed. Such was French assimilation policy in her colonies. No amount of proclamation of *Algérie française* made it so. Léopold Senghor, that masterful craftsman of the French language, ended up extolling *négritude* (in French!) and becoming the president of independent Sénégal. The Algerian *pieds noirs* were reincorporated into the French ethny despite five or six generations of African experience, while Muslim Algerians with French citizenship find acceptance difficult even after two or more generations of residence in France. Examples could be multiplied of nonacceptance, by industrial as well as Third World societies, of groups perceived as being of different genetic origin, despite their acquisition of dominant group culture and language: Koreans in Japan, Afro-Americans in the United States, Jews in Europe, overseas Chinese and East Indians in Asia, Africa and the Caribbean.

If myths of ethnicity must be credible, what tests of ethnicity are used to decide on their credibility? What criteria do people use to decide whether an individual is a fellow ethnic or not? In the small-scale societies typical of our species until a few thousand years ago, the simple test of acquaintance based on previous association sufficed in most circumstances. We share with other higher vertebrates, such as dogs and monkeys, the ability to recognize individuals and to carry faces in our memories for long periods of time. Occasionally a person kidnapped by another group early in life might face the problem of establishing his filiation with his group of origin, but, in most cases, in societies of a few hundred people the test of membership is straightforward enough: the person belongs if he is known to belong; he does not belong either if he is known not to belong or if he is not known to belong.

Obviously, the larger the society gets, the more difficult the problem of ascertaining membership becomes. Already in "primitive" societies that run into tens of thousands, membership is no longer always established *prima facie*; it must be proven. At that level the test is generally genealogical: the unknown individual claims membership through filiation with known members. Kinship, that is, is explicitly used to establish ethnicity. Australian aborigines are said to have been able to do so across the face of the continent, but this is an extreme case. Usually, tracing filiation only works in groups of moderate size (a few thousand) and spatial dispersal (a few hundred square kilometers).

Where societies run into hundreds of thousands or even millions of members, and cover vast stretches of territory, the situation becomes complicated. Ethnicity can no longer be so easily ascertained and, therefore, it can be faked. If ethnism is a way of maximizing fitness through extended nepotism, then a clever animal like man can be expected to fake common ethnicity for gain. Con games in which individuals gain "undeserved" advantage by exaggerating or counterfeiting a relationship to their victims thrive in large-scale societies that lack the easy controls of recognition and intimacy found in small societies. Ethnicity is one of these manipulable relationships. At the same time, there are occasions where ethnicity has to be established quickly, where one literally shoots first and asks questions later. How, then, can one establish ethnicity quickly and reliably and also keep cheats under control? What features will be chosen as *ethnic markers*?

There are many possibilities, tending to fall into three main categories of traits. The three are not mutually exclusive, and their respective effectiveness varies greatly according to circumstances.

First, one can pick a genetically transmitted phenotype, such as skin pigmentation, stature (as with the Tuzi of Rwanda and Burundi), hair texture, facial features or some such "racial" characteristic. Groups that are socially defined by genetic phenotypes are called "races," and societies that put emphasis on biological traits to differentiate groups within it can be called "racist."

Second, one can rely on a man-made ethnic uniform. Members of one's group are identified by bodily mutilations and/or adornments carried as visible badges of group belonging. These markers range from clothing and headgear to body painting, tatooing, circumcision, tooth filing and sundry mutilations of the lips, nose and earlobes.

Third, the test can be behavioral. Ethnicity is determined by speech, demeanor, manners, esoteric lore or some other proof of competence in a behavioral repertoire characteristic of the group.

A brief review of the three classes of ethnic markers is useful at this point, for each has a different set of properties and of structural consequences. Race would seem the most obvious solution to the problem of ethnic recognition, especially if there is a biological basis for the extended nepotism that we are discussing. Does it not stand to reason that genetically inheritable phenotypes are the most reliable markers of ethnicity, if by ethnicity one means, in the last analysis, genetic relatedness? Would not one, therefore, expect racism to be universal? The answer to the first question, a theoretical one, is "yes," and to the second, an empirical question, "no."

However, before proceeding, I must clarify a common confusion about the term "race." The word has been used in several distinct meanings, *inter alia* as a synonym for nation or ethny, (e.g. "the French race"), as a biological subspecies or inbred population (e.g. "the Chihuahua or Cocker Spaniel race") and as a synonym for species (e.g. "the human race"). None of these meanings is implied here. Where relatively inbred subgroups of the human species are meant, we will speak of "populations" in the genetic sense. What is meant by "race" here is a *social* label attributed to groups of people in particular societies at particular times, on the basis of inherited phenotypical characteristics. If phenotypic criteria are socially used to categorize groups (usually, if not always, invidiously), then races are said to exist in that society, and the ideology supporting that classification and its social consequences is called racism (van den Berghe, 1967).

It is also important to stress that phenotypes chosen for social relevance, while often clearly visible markers of genetic origin, are typically biologically trivial in terms of fitness, abilities, aptitudes and temperament—indeed, anything of social consequence. To suggest that the sociobiological theory presented here is racist in the sense that I have just defined it is nonsensical. Our theory says nothing about racial differences between human groups—much less about any invidious ranking between them. On the contrary, it stresses a common biological propensity, not only of all humans, but also of all social animals, to favor kin over nonkin, a propensity that gets translated into ethnism and sometimes (but only sometimes) into racism.

Having said this, there is no denying that, even though humans share the overwhelmingly greater part of their genetic material with each other (and indeed with other closely related organisms such as the great apes), the relatively small proportion of their gene loci that is multiallelic produces a wide range of individual variation and a smaller, but not negligible, amount of group variation. Human populations are strikingly different from each other in the distribution of some genes, and at least some of these differences have had adaptive significance during some periods of human evolution under certain environmental conditions. For instance, tropical populations of Africa and South India show a much higher incidence of the recessive gene for sickle cell anemia, an allele that, though highly deleterious in homozygous form, confers a measure of immunity to malaria to its heterozygous carriers.

Similarly, there is a close association between the distribution of a gene causing lactose intolerance in adults and the presence or absence of cattle. The lactose-intolerance gene is virtually absent from the gene pool of East African pastoralists but common in other parts of Africa where the tse-tse fly makes the raising of cattle nearly impossible. The several genes that regulate the amount of melanin in the skin are also distributed in a way that shows a close correspondence with climatic conditions. Through skin pigmentation, the amount of absorption of sunlight is regulated: some is needed because of the essential vitamin D, but too much is carcinogenic. Therefore, there is a direct correlation between skin pigmentation and latitude, or at least there was until the mass migrations that accompanied European slave trade and colonialism.

Some human groups are characterized by the significantly higher incidence of some deleterious genes for which no adaptive significance can be found. Examples are the "Tay-Sachs syndrome," a form of genetic idiocy found ten times more often among Askenazic Jews than among Gentiles and Sephardic Jews, and the relatively high frequency of hemophilia (a sex-linked recessive gene on the X chromosome) among the descendants of Queen Victoria, who in the early 20th century populated the royal houses of Europe from Spain to Russia (Stine, 1977). Such phenomena are attributable to what geneticists call the "founder effect" (i.e. the effect of a prolific ancestor) and the resultant "genetic drift" in the gene pool of his or her descendants.

In these cases, however, the incidence of these harmful genes tends to be low, even in the populations where it occurs most frequently. For instance, one Askenazic Jew out of 25 is a carrier of the recessive Tay-Sachs gene, compared to one in 400 among Gentiles. Genetic differences between populations are thus generally a matter of relative frequency of alleles, not of absolute differences.

There is no denying the reality of genetic differences in frequencies of alleles between human groups. None of these differences, however, has yet been shown to bear any functional relationship with the *social* attribution of racial characteristics in any human society nor with the relative positions of dominance and subordination of racial groups in any society. There is nothing, either in the study of human genetics or in sociobiological theory to support any social order or ideology, to vindicate or challenge the position of any group or to buttress or attack any ethical premise or philosophical system. Human genetics and the presence or absence of racial distinctions in human societies are two almost totally discrete orders of phenomena. The only tenuous connection between them is that some human groups, under conditions to be specified presently, sometimes use genetically transmitted phenotypes as badges of membership in social groups. The *socially ascribed* significance of these genetic markers can be enormous, but it bears no intrinsic relationship to their biological, evolutionary significance. Humans use phenotypic characteristics first and foremost as probabilistic markers of common descent.

Now, let us return to the problem of the presence or absence of racism in human societies. With our contemporary knowledge of human genetics, we categorically exclude parenthood on the basis of a single nonmatching allele and, conversely, we can establish kinship beyond reasonable doubt by matching individuals on a multiplicity of alleles of known frequency distribution in certain populations. In practice, however, most people are not geneticists and, indeed, until less than a century ago, people had only the vaguest notions of how characteristics were inherited. The outcome is that while in many, perhaps most, human societies, tests of physical resemblance are used to assess probability of kinship and, by extension, ethnicity, these tests are seldom the only ones or even the main ones that are relied upon, at least as far as establishing ethnic membership is concerned.

The reason for this seeming paradox is apparent enough. At the rudimentary level of folk genetics, racial phenotypes are often very poor indicators of group membership because neighboring populations typically maintain a sufficient rate of migration to create genetic gradients such as that *intragroup* variation on specific loci is much greater than *intergroup* variation. In short, neighboring populations—the very ones that are concerned about maintaining and defending ethnic boundaries—typically look very much like each other. Phenotype is useful to distinguish individuals within groups but not to distinguish between groups. Let us take the example of eye and hair color in Europe. There is a gradient from south to north of increasing frequency of the recessive alleles for blue eyes and blond hair. A Greek army fighting in Finland might make reasonably effective use of these genetic traits as markers of ethnicity—but not in the far more likely circumstance of having to fight Albanians or Turks. Similarly, skin color might be used by a Moroccan army crossing the Sahara, but not between Moroccans and Algerians, or Ghaneans and Togolese. The most crucial ethnic boundaries most of the time are those between groups competing for scarce resources in the same general vicinity. Those are precisely the circumstances under which racial distinctions are most useless.

One can therefore expect racism to appear only where long-distance immigration has suddenly put in presence substantial numbers of people whose physical appearance is different enough as to make genetic phenotype a reliable basis for distinguishing between groups. People must migrate across genetic gradients before their physical appearance can be used as a reliable basis of inferring group membership. Under such unusual conditions, people often develop what Hoetinck (1967), in the Caribbean context, has called a "somatic norm image," i.e. some mental picture of what members of their own and of other groups look like. Even then, however, miscegenation, which typically accompanies conquest and slavery, often blurs racial distinctions within two or three generations. The migration must not only be across large distances, but it must also be rapid and massive enough to make race a useful marker of genetic relatedness between groups. Such conditions have been exceptional in human history, until the colonial expansion of Europe in the past 500 years. If racism is to continue over several generations, it must be buttressed by severe barriers against miscegenation, a rare situation found in only a few countries such as South Africa and the United States (van den Berghe, 1967).

For these reasons, racism, as the primary basis for group distinctions, has been the exception rather than the rule. Racism is not a Western, much less a capitalist, monopoly. For example, when the tall Hamitic Tuzi conquered shorter Bantu speakers to the South, they invented their own brand of racism (more specifically, "heightism") to buttress their domination of the Rwanda and Burundi kingdoms (Maquet, 1961). But there, too, the reason was the same as for the development of Western racism in the wake of European colonial expansion: long-distance migration across a wide genetic gradient—in this case, in body stature. In short, racism can be expected to develop and thrive where genetically inherited phenotypes are the easiest, most visible and most reliable predictors of group membership. When phenotypes lose these properties through intermixture of groups, cultural criteria typically supplant racial criteria of group membership. This happened, for instance, throughout the Spanish American colonies that began as a racial *casta* system (indeed, the word "caste" comes from the Spanish–Portuguese term) and gradually evolved as societies stratified by class and ethnic criteria and only minimally by phenotype (van den Berghe, 1967).

The theory presented here accounts better for the appearance and disappearance of racism in various times and places than competing theories that attribute racism either to ideological factors [e.g. Tannenbaum (1947) on the differences between Protestantism and Catholicism and their respective legal traditions in the Western Hemisphere] or to the capitalist mode of production [e.g. numerous writers of Marxist disposition such as Cox (1948) and Simons and Simons (1969)]. More than anything else, it is long-distance migration over genetic gradients that creates racism; conversely, miscegenation attenuates it. And miscegenation almost invariably occurs because racism as such does little to inhibit it. Dominant-group men, whether racist or not, are seldom reluctant to maximize their fitness with subordinate-group women. It takes extraordinary measures of physical segregation, such as long existed in South Africa and the United States, to preserve a racial caste system. Racism is the exception rather than the rule in intergroup relations, and racially based systems are peculiarly conflictridden and unstable. Attempts at maintaining them often result in cataclysmic bloodshed [e.g. Leo Kuper's (1977) study of revolution in Algeria, Zanzibar, Rwanda and Burundi; the Haitian revolution; and the mounting crisis in Southern Africa]. I shall return to the special case of race later in this book, especially when I deal with racial slavery systems.

Both the second and the third categories of cultural markers are manmade and cultural, but the second is visual and artifactual, while the third is behavioral. The two types of marker are often used conjointly, as multiple tests of ethnicity. If we turn first to what I have called the "ethnic uniform" type of marker, it has the advantage of providing a visible and therefore rapid clue of group membership. This is quite useful in combat or contest situations, for example, as witnessed by the widespread use of uniforms by armies, sport teams and the like. Then the premium is on easy, quick detection at a distance. A drawback of many of these easily visible clues provided by headgear, clothing, plumage, body paint and the like, is that they can be faked. A system of ethnic recognition based solely on these would be widely open to cheating, and indeed cheating does occur as when opposing armies try to infiltrate each other by donning their opponents' uniforms. The sanctions against such cheating, incidentally, are often exceptionally severe, such as immediate execution when, normally, simple capture would be expected.

Ethnic markers based on bodily mutilations, such as facial tatooes, tooth filing, circumcision, nose, lip and ear piercing and the like are not easily reversible, but they are often not so striking and can only be identified at close quarters.

Finally, there are behavioral ethnic markers, which are among the most reliable and hence commonly used. They have the advantage of being difficult to fake, because the performance criteria are often of considerable subtlety and intricacy, but they require skill and time in being applied and hence do not satisfy the criteria of ease and immediacy. Behavioral criteria may include styles of body movement, gesturing, eating or greeting etiquette and the like, but language holds pride of place among them. The way people speak places them more accurately and reliably than almost any other behavioral trait. Language and dialect can be learned, of course, but the ability to learn a foreign tongue without a detectable accent drops sharply around puberty. Therefore speech quality is a reliable (and difficult to fake) test of what group an individual has been raised in. Moreover, acquisition of foreign speech is extremely difficult except through prolonged contact with native speakers, another safety feature of the linguistic test.

Although language is a relatively subtle test, certain easily detectable phonemes give the foreigner away. A classical historical episode concerns the massacre of French troops by Flemings in the city of Brugge (or Bruges as the French say) in 1302. The Flemings wanted to kill the French army of occupation in their beds without raising the alarm, so the problem was how to identify Frenchmen quickly and reliably, in the dark, in order to slaughter them without fuss. The solution was to make them repeat a short Flemish phrase, "schilde en de vriend," ("shield and friend") that contained phonemes unpronounceable to native speakers of French. History books tell us that the stratagem was devastatingly successful. (As the son of a Flemish Belgian father and a French mother, going to a French-medium Belgian school in Brussels, I distinctly remember the disturbing ambivalence that this gruesome bit of Belgian history left me with. It was by no means clear to me on which side I was.)

Besides the difficult-to-fake properties of language that make it a good test of ethnicity, language can also be used to transmit quickly, simple esoteric information, such as passwords that are also easy tests of membership. In addition, language is a powerful vehicle for emotional communication. Not surprisingly, therefore, language is inextricably linked with ethnicity. An ethny frequently defines itself, at least in part, as a speech community; its particular speech is laden with emotional qualities and valued much beyond its efficacy as a means of communication. Second languages, or *linguae francae* adopted later in life for purposes of interethnic communication, can convey complex messages accurately and can become perfectly serviceable media for a wide range of practical purposes such as trade, formal education, technology and so on. However, they are usually bereft of the multiplicity of emotional connotations that are largely restricted to one's "mother-tongue."

The first language learned in infancy is intimately associated with a whole register of emotions first experienced with close kinsmen and, therefore, these affective qualities of kinship become associated with language and rub off onto other members of the speech community. The spontaneous joy of hearing one's mother tongue spoken when surrounded by strangers is probably a universal human experience. It is experienced even after a long exile. One may become quite proficient in a foreign language yet still fail to enjoy and experience it at the gut emotional level. People often report, for instance, that they can only enjoy singing or poetry in their mother-tongue. Language learning is the universal human experience of early childhood through which full human sociality is achieved, and through which one becomes integrated in a kinship network. It is little wonder, therefore, that language is the supreme test of ethnicity. Fellow ethnics are those whose speech is sufficiently like one's own to allow for the unhindered communication of the entire range of human emotions and messages. Other languages are learned for the sake of instrumental convenience; the mother tongue is spoken for the sheer joy of it. It is probably this fundamental difference in the speaking of first versus second languages that, more than any single factor, makes for the profound qualitative difference between intraethnic and interethnic relations. The mother-tongue is the language of kinship. Every other tongue is a mere convenience between strangers.

Let us summarize the argument so far. Humans, like other social animals, are biologically selected to be nepotistic because, by favoring kin, they maximize their inclusive fitness. Until the last few thousand years, hominids interacted in relatively small groups of a few score to a couple of hundred individuals who tended to mate with each other and, therefore, to form rather tightly knit groups of close and distant kinsmen. Physical boundaries of territory and social boundaries of inbreeding separated these small human societies from each other. Within the group, there was a large measure of peace and cooperation between kinsmen and in-laws (frequently both kinds of relationship overlapped). Relations between groups were characterized at best by mistrust and avoidance—but frequently by open conflict over scarce resources. These solidary groups were, in fact, primordial ethnies.

Such was the evolutionary origin of ethnicity: an extended kin group. With the progressive growth in the size of human societies, the boundaries of the ethny became wider; the bonds of kinship were correspondingly diluted, and indeed sometimes became fictive, and ethnicity became increasingly manipulated and perverted to other ends, including domination and exploitation. The urge, however, to continue to define a collectivity larger than the immediate circle of kinsmen on the basis of biological descent continues to be present even in the most industrialized mass societies of today. A wide variety of ethnic markers are used to define such collectivities of descent, but their choice is not capricious. Those markers will be stressed that are, in fact, objectively reliable predictors of common descent, given the environment in which the discriminating group finds itself. Sometimes, but rather rarely, race is the paramount criterion; more commonly, cultural characteristics, especially language, do a much better job of defining ethnic boundaries.

So far, we have suggested the *raison d'être* of ethnicity—the reason for its persistence and for its seeming imperviousness to rationality. Ethnic (and racial) sentiments often seem irrational because they have an underlying driving force of their own, which is ultimately the blunt, purposeless natural selection of genes that are reproductively successful. Genes favoring nepotistic behavior have a selective advantage. It does not matter whether their carrying organisms are aware of being nepotistic or even that they consciously know their relatives. Organisms must only behave *as if they knew*. It happens that, in humans, they often know in a conscious way, though they are sometimes mistaken.

The phenomenon of ethnicity in humans, however, is not in principle different from the phenomenon of boundary maintenance between animal societies. Other animals maintain clear boundaries between themselves and other species, most importantly barriers to matings between closely related species that are the very mechanism making for speciation in the first instance (Mayr, 1963). But humans are not even unique in maintaining societal boundaries *within* the species. Thousands of species of eusocial insects keep different colonies of the same species quite distinct from each other, often using pheromones (smell signals) to recognize each other (E. O. Wilson, 1971). Among mammals, man included, the boundaries between societies are, on the whole much *less* rigid than among the eusocial insects but nevertheless, societal boundaries between groups of conspecifics are clearly marked and defended.

We conventionally restrict the meaning of ethnicity to humans, but we would not be unduly extending the meaning of the term by applying it to troops of macaques, prides of lions or packs of wolves. These other animal societies too are held together by kin selection and must compete with other societies of conspecifics for scarce resources (E. O. Wilson, 1975). In principle, the problems of boundary maintenance are the same for humans and other animals, despite the vastly greater order of complexity of human societies.

Like many other species, man too lives in an environment that includes other societies of his species. Interethnic relations, therefore, must be analyzed not only within the genetic context of kin selection but also, and equally importantly, within an *ecological* context. This is the subject of the next chapter.

SUGGESTED READINGS

The best layman's introductions to sociobiology are to be found in Barash (1977), Daly and Wilson (1978) and Dawkins (1976), after which the reader can then approach E. O. Wilson's (1975) meaty and masterly treatise. For human applications of sociobiology, see Chagnon and Irons (1979), Shepher (1981), and van den Berghe (1979a).

ETHNICITY AND RESOURCE COMPETITION:
THE ECOLOGY OF TERRITORIALITY AND SPECIALIZATION

So far, I have suggested a genetic underpinning for animal sociality in general, human sociality in particular, and most especially, the phenomena of ethnism and racism. Ethnic solidarity is an extension of kin-based solidarity—that is, of nepotism. Merely to give an evolutionary explanation for ethnic solidarity, however, says little about what is generally called ethnic (and race) relations. To say that kin relation is the underlying biological basis of ethnic solidarity allows only the grossest of predictions, because social relationships take place, not in the abstract, but in an environment in which organisms compete with each other for scarce resources. A multiplicity of circumstances dictate the actual content of relationships. The general paradigm is that individual organisms behave, consciously or unconsciously, in such a way as to maximize their inclusive fitness. Degree of biological relatedness is one of the two main terms predicting cooperation or conflict. The other is the cost–benefit ratio of the transactions between actors. Under some circumstances, it pays to cheat or even to kill your brother, e.g. when he stands between you and an amount of resources (inheritance, throne) vast enough to make it worthwhile to forego the benefits of nepotism. Conversely, circumstances can transform unrelated enemies into allies.

The sociobiological model, therefore, does not predict that fellow ethnics will always stick together, or that enmity and conflict will always prevail between ethnies. Behavioral outcomes are always mediated through a vast number of environmental variables. Human ecology is peculiarly complex because, in addition to the physical and biotic (other plants and animals) features of the human habitat that importantly influence human adaptive behavior, humans have developed through culture an impressive capability to modify both the physical and biotic habitat and the very forms of human sociality itself.

Other organisms can also modify their habitat: corals form reefs; beavers build dams; elephant herds can devastate forests or, conversely, carry seeds long distances through their intestines and help regenerate the flora. But man has no rivals in cultural ability to modify (and upset) environment through technology. Other animals also have a limited ability to change their social organization according to environmental fluctuations or phases of their reproductive life cycle. Many birds, for example, form large, non-territorial flocks at certain times, but separate into territorial breeding couples for reproductive purposes (E. O. Wilson, 1975). Male hoary marmots can be either devoted fathers and faithfully monogamous mates or roving philanderers, depending on environmental conditions (Barash, 1977). None, however, have the flexibility with which man can modify behavior and invent new forms of social organization in response to environmental changes. Human culture (including, of course, technology) is thus an increasingly important part of the human environment. Indeed, culture can be described as the man-made part of the human habitat.

HUMAN ECOLOGY AND ETHNIC COMPETITION

This is not the place to attempt a treatise on human ecology. [For recent efforts in that direction, by an anthropologist and an economist respectively, one should turn to Bennett (1976) and Boulding (1978).] The point is simply that an understanding of human behavior must incorporate a synthesis of biological ecosystem theory and of what anthropologists have called "cultural ecology." The implications of that view for ethnic relations is that the latter, as a special category of human behavior, must also be seen in an ecological context that includes two main sets of features: (1) a physical and biotic habitat to which each ethny must adapt and (2) a sociocultural habitat made up of competing ethnies.

Obviously, the distinction between these two sets of variables is analytic, for, in practice, the two are intertwined. Much of the relations between ethnies is shaped by the nature of the natural resources over which they compete, and by the nature of the specific niche within shared habitats to which specific ethnies have adapted. Nonetheless, there is a partly autonomous and man-made component to ethnic relations, especially relations of dominance and subordination, that is not simply reducible to factors in the physical and biotic environment.

Ethnic (and race) relations consist, in the last analysis, of competition over scarce resources, which are ultimately convertible into fitness—that is, reproductive success. Resource competition for humans is more complex than for other species because it includes not only the natural resources of space, food, shelter and so on, but also man-made resources (wealth, prestige and power) that are also convertible into reproduction. The ultimate scarce resource for competing males in the fitness game is, of course, reproductive females. There are always fewer of them around than there are males—ready and willing to inseminate them. Although the males of many species compete individually for females (either by direct dominance contests between males or through attracting discriminating females, or both), human males also organize themselves as *groups* to capture or attract each others' females. Thus, the capture, defense and seduction of women often plays as salient a role in intergroup relations, as it does between the individual members of the same ethny.

THE REGULATION OF COMPETITION

There are basically three mechanisms whereby animals reduce or regulate resource competition: (1) specialization, (2) territoriality and (3) hierarchy. The first operates principally between species. It is well known that two closely related species are seldom sympatric (i.e. share a habitat) unless they adapt to different specialized niches and thus minimize direct competition. Otherwise, one species displaces the other in more or less short order. Thus, several predator species such as lions, leopards and cheetahs can coexist if they specialize on different size preys, or if some are diurnal and others nocturnal. Several primate species share the same habitat if some are terrestrial and others arboreal, or, if all arboreal, if some are fruit-eaters and others leaf-eaters.

The other two mechanisms regulating competition—territoriality and hierarchy—operate mainly within species. Hierarchy or dominance establishes an order of access to resources and typically inequality of access as well. Territoriality divides the habitat into patches monopolistically exploited by individual animals or small breeding groups. Humans make extensive and complex use of both territoriality and hierarchy, in regulating resource competition (van den Berghe, 1974). Indeed, as population density increased and, with it, the range of resources used and the intensity of their exploitation, human territoriality and hierarchy assumed increasingly elaborate and complex forms. Humans are especially striking in the degree to which they establish not only *individual* hierarchies within groups, as do countless other species, but also *group* hierarchies. This ability, as we shall see in Chapter 4, has far-reaching consequences for the development of ethnic relations.

In addition to territoriality and hierarchy, humans have also developed group specialization, so that different sympatric ethnies have adapted to different ecological niches. Many animals have a division of labor by age and sex classes, as do humans as well, and among the eusocial insects different "castes" are almost always sterile (E. O. Wilson, 1971; Oster and Wilson, 1978). In human societies, the division of labor, both within and among societies is carried well beyond anything found in other animals. It is especially unusual in the animal kingdom to have reproductive groups of the same species live sympatrically and symbiotically on the basis of group specialization. Such a situation has developed repeatedly between different ethnies in the last few thousand years (Hechter, 1978). Much of ethnic relations represents niche specialization between ethnies that are thus in much the same ecological relationship to each other as symbionts of different species in the rest of the animal kingdom. Indeed, members of different ethnies often treat each other and regard each other as if they did indeed belong to different species. Treating each other as prey—cannibalism—is but a widespread illustration of this human capacity to draw a sharp line between in-group and out-group, and to create pseudospecific lines between ethnies. Racist ideologies are another example.

STAGES OF ETHNIC RELATIONS

In the remainder of this chapter, I shall examine the ecology of ethnic relations principally from the point of view of territoriality and specialization, reserving hierarchy for the next chapter. If we take these three properties of human groups together, we can see that they fall into a logical and evolutionary progression of types of ethnic relations. One always hesitates to label stages of evolution or types of situations, for categories of any kind are often interpreted too statically and too rigidly. I want to stress, therefore, that the four stages that I am about to introduce shade off into one another. They are merely introduced to suggest gross periods in an evolutionary progression—spans on a continuum of increasing complexity and interdependence. The purpose of these rough stages is to organize the data, and to highlight key ecological features that structure ethnic relations. The general historical trend is from the first to the fourth stage, but different systems and subsystems can simultaneously exist at different stages of evolution. It should also be stressed that I am speaking here of an overwhelmingly *cultural*, not genetic, evolution that has taken place in the last ten thousand years or so since the domestication of plants and animals.

With all these caveats, I would like to suggest the following four stages of ethnic relations: (1) autarchy, (2) trade, (3) symbiosis and (4) parasitism. Schema I gives a capsule summary of what is meant by these terms.* Before proceeding to describe them more extensively and then to illustrate them through ethnographic data, however, these stages must be put in the context of both empirical reality and intellectual approaches thereto.

At one end of the intellectual spectrum are those macrotheorists who look at the world through a telescope, and who deal with large modern states and world market systems. From the perspective of "world system" theorists

---

*The schema bears some resemblance to the three types of ecological interdependence suggested by Fredrik Barth (1969, pp. 19–20); indeed, it elaborates on it, reverses the logical sequence of Barth's first two types and subdivides Barth's third type into our stages three and four by adding the dimension of hierarchy that is curiously underplayed in Barth and indeed in much of the anthropological literature. It is as if anthropologists, having been associated with the colonial enterprise, feel guilty about power relationships and would wish them away. When Barth deals with hierarchical ethnic relations (1969, p. 27), he invokes value consensus rather than coercion as the basis of the stratified multiethnic systems: "[the ethnic groups] share certain general value orientations and scales, on the basis of which they can arrive at judgements of hierarchy." Thus hierarchy, and indeed ethnic affiliation itself, becomes a matter of subjective definition rather than a descriptive outcome of who gets what in a context of ecological competition.

Stage	Characteristics	Type of Relationship
Autarchy	Unspecialized Territorially discrete Unhierarchical	Mutual avoidance or chronic raiding
Trade	Specialized Territorially discrete Unhierarchical	Trade and barter
Symbiosis	Specialized Territorially overlapping Unhierarchical	Niche specialization and ecological interdependence
Parasitism	Specialized Territorially overlapping Hierarchical	Economic exploitation and political domination

SCHEMA I. Stages of ethnic relations.

(Chirot, 1977; Wallerstein, 1974), the modern world looks like a reasonably well-integrated system in which all parts are interdependent, and in which all ethnies are directly or indirectly incorporated in centralized states and are thus in the fourth stage of our schema. From their Olympian perspective, world system theorists are, *grosso modo*, right.

At the opposite end of the intellectual spectrum is what I like to call, with apologies to Raymond Firth (1936), the Tikopia view of the world through a microscope, as a multitude of pristine, insular, isolated ethnies, the "tribes" of traditional anthropology. There have always been a number of laudable exceptions to this antiquarian, ahistorical tradition in anthropology, especially in Southern Africa (Gluckman, 1958; Hilda Kuper, 1947a, 1947b; Monica Wilson, 1936), in the Chicago school of American anthropology (Redfield, 1956; Tax, 1952), in the Mexican school of anthropology (Aguirre Beltrán, 1957, 1967), and among French Africanists (Balandier, 1963). Nevertheless, the main thrust of ethnography until the last two decades has been to treat ethnies as self-contained isolates long after they had ceased to be, to attempt to recapture their pristine condition before Western conquest and to downplay ethnic relations, even between neighboring indigenous groups. From the Tikopia perspective, all ethnies are treated as if they were still in the first of our stages.

The real world is, of course, neither an archipelago of isolated ethnies nor a vast, smoothly integrated system. Different systems and subsystems within larger wholes are differently integrated, and have thus substantially different types of ethnic relations. Neighboring ethnies of the Papua–New Guinea highlands, for instance, whose main form of interaction until recently consisted of killing and eating each other (Berndt, 1962), still have rather different ethnic relations than the Flemings and Walloons of industrial Belgium (du Roy, 1968). There are, to be sure, commonalities and I am not passing any value judgment as to which is better, but Belgian ethnic relations are characterized by a far greater level of complexity and interdependence.

Autarchy: The Yanomanö and the Maori

Now, let us return to our schema. At the first level of autarchy, we have ethnies that are unspecialized, territorially distinct from each other, and not ordered into a hierarchy of dominance and subordination. This was the prototypical situation before the rise of states and the domestication of plants and animals. Self-sufficient groups lived side by side, in contiguous but separate patches of habitat, which they exploited with similar technologies and with similar effect. Each ethny was a close replica of its neighbors; little surplus was produced, and there was little of value to exchange. Therefore, there was little incentive to enter into cooperative relationships between groups, other than for military alliances. Groups directly competed with each; interdependence was minimal and so therefore were ethnic relations. The latter consisted mostly of mutual avoidance, clashes over natural resources, especially the control of territory and what went with it, and raids for woman and livestock.

Except for greater efficiency of hunting and foraging conferred by greater intelligence and the technology that went with it, the ecosystems of pre-agricultural human societies were not fundamentally different from those of nonhuman primate troops or social carnivores, like lions, wolves and African hunting dogs. The hallmarks of ethnic relations were conflict and avoidance between competitors for scarce resources.

Few contemporary human societies still fit the model of primordial autarchy; even the few remaining hunters and gatherers have, by now, virtually all entered second- or third-stage relationships with neighboring pastoralists or agriculturalists. Such is the case, for instance, of the much-studied San Bushmen of the Kalahari and Bambuti Pygmies of the Zaïre rain forest (Lee and De Vore, 1968, 1976; Turnbull, 1961, 1965). However, if one chooses to ignore their incorporation into colonial or postcolonial societies, some of the more isolated ethnies of Melanesia, the Amazon and Africa still had, until one or two generations ago, relations approximating those of stage one.

They lived in contiguous but discrete territories; they were largely self-sufficient; and, therefore, they had little to offer to each other except more of what they already had—principally land, women and livestock.

The Yanomamö. Some remote ethnies of the Amazon and Orinoco basins in South America, for instance, still escape control from the governments of Brazil, Venezuela, Peru, Bolivia and Ecuador, and continue to live in a state of autarchy and to wage war with each other. Such are the Yanomamö of Venezuela and Brazil, swidden horticulturists who live in stateless, classless societies where the village (of size 50 to 200) is the basic peace group (Chagnon, 1974, 1977). Villages are made up of sections of two or more patrilineages that exchange women between them.

Among villages, there is frequent raiding, mostly over—and for—women. Food is relatively abundant and the population has recently been increasing, probably due to the introduction of metal axes which facilitates jungle clearing for horticulture. Women are the scarcest resource, a shortage exacerbated by some female infanticide and by polygyny. Successful older men often have two or more wives. Men therefore fiercely compete with each other for reproductive access to women. This leads to numerous disputes both within and between villages, and these disputes frequently erupt into violence. Violence is carefully graded, from individual stick duels to war raids between villages with several fatalities, but, within villages, violence usually does not escalate beyond a general melee where only nonlethal blows with the blunt ends of weapons are exchanged. Sometimes, however, villages split over these conflicts, forming new villages that can then start raiding each other.

War is the principal relationship between villages. The most valued trade goods, principally metal tools, are obtained from the outside since the Yanomamö have no indigenous metal-working technology. Wives are normally close relatives (cross-cousins) who belong to one of the other patrilineages in the village and such other women as can be captured from neighboring villages during war raids. Each village has its own fields and produces much the same crops: plantains, sweet bananas, manioc, taro, sweet potatoes, palm trees and maize. There is little of value to trade among Yanomamö groups since they are all adapted for the same niche of forest horticulture, supplemented by hunting, fishing and the collecting of wild plants, and since the more desirable trade goods are produced by none of them.

The Maori. The Maori of New Zealand before European contact in 1769 lived largely in an autarchic situation (Buck, 1962; Firth, 1959; Vayda, 1960). They were Polynesian horticulturalists who immigrated in several waves from the North, starting a thousand or more years ago, and settled on the two main islands of New Zealand, in a heavily forested, mountainous, rainy, temperate environment—very different from the tropical setting of Polynesia. They had a stone-age technology, albeit a sophisticated one, and their economy was based mostly on horticulture (mostly tubers), hunting (mostly of rats and birds), fishing along the coast and the collecting of forest products (especially fern roots). The dog was the only domestic animal, though the rat probably came along as a stowaway on the cross-oceanic journeys and became a valuable source of animal protein. The pig, abundant in Polynesia, was not introduced into New Zealand until European times. Thus, there was an absence of large livestock and a chronic shortage of animal protein.

The main tools, stone adzes and axes, imposed severe limitations on the exploitation of a heavily forested environment. Huge trees were killed by fire, but the clearing of land for horticulture was a slow and tedious process, making arable land a scarce commodity. Substantial ecological differences between the warmer Northern Island and the colder Southern Island made horticulture more extensive and successful in the North.

The basic organizing principle of Maori social organization was patrilineal descent, giving rise to what anthropologists call a segmentary lineage system. Other lines of descent were recognized but, for purposes of social organization (such as the transmission of property and authority and the organization of labor and war) the male line of descent and the lineages and clans formed by patrilineal descent, took precedence over other consanguineal ties.

The rule of residence was virilocal, that is, women, at marriage, came in to live with their husband and his kinsmen. Villages, consisting of a few hundred people, were made up of localized segments of patrilineages—one descent group usually forming the core of the village. This segmentary structure of patrilineages gave rise to basically a three-tiered social organization (Vayda, 1960). The *whanau* was an extended virilocal family, a three- or four-generation group of up to a score or so of people, made up of a man, his wife or wives, his married sons and their wives and children, his unmarried daughters, and perhaps his junior brothers and their wives and children. Next, was the *hapu*, a larger patrilineage group made up of several related whanau. The hapu was usually coterminous with the village community, although some villages were made up of several hapus, and, sometimes, a hapu occupied several small villages. At the highest level of social organization was the *iwi*, or clan, made up of any number of related hapu. It is estimated that the 100,000 to 300,000 Maoris who inhabited New Zealand before European contact were split into about 40 iwi. The iwi was thus a group of several thousand people.

The related hapu, which together formed an iwi, occupied contiguous lands, so that the iwi was a territorial as well as a geneological unit. However, social organization at the iwi level was so loose that one hesitates to call it an ethny. It was the hapu—the village community—that best corresponded to the concept of ethny as I have defined it. The hapu was the group of a few hundred people who lived and worked together, owned and used communal property such as land and large war canoes, went to war as a raiding party, and intermarried. Village endogamy was not strict, and there were some marriages between hapu, but marriage within the hapu was considered desirable and was in fact frequent. The hapu, in short, was the peace group (there was never organized hostility within the hapu), the endogamous group, the main territorial unit, the largest effective political group, the prototypical ethny. The iwi, by comparison, was but a loose superethny.

Maori political organization was quite loose and uncentralized. The Maori were, in fact, a stateless society wherein the main principle of authority was seniority in the male line. The so-called "chiefs" were not executive officers with the power to rule over unrelated people. They were merely the respected eldest members of patrilineages, exercising jural authority over kinsmen and their wives. Rank and leadership went by primogeniture, but as members of a hapu considered themselves to be all descendants of a common ancestor, "chiefs" and "commoners" were relatives to each other. Certain senior branches of patrilineages, however, regarded themselves as of chiefly rank and were termed *rangatira*, as distinguished from their commoner kinsmen who were called *tutua* (Buck, 1962).

In addition, there was a third stratum of slaves: war captives became slaves, a degraded, disfranchised status. Slaves were not necessarily ill-treated. Female slaves often bore children for their masters, and their descendants became assimilated into the captor group. However, slaves could also be killed and eaten at the whim of their masters, and they lost all claim to social position, even in their group of origin who regarded them as dead because of the stigma of slavery. Until European conquest, slaves probably accounted for less than 10% of the population, as most war captives were killed and eaten shortly after capture. Thus, the Maori, although they still clearly lacked states, had at least the rudiments of social stratification and what might be termed incipient chieftaincy.

What was the nature of ethnic relations among the Maori? That is, what relations did the hapu have with each other? Apart from occasional inter-marriages and friendly visiting with gift exchanges, hapu ethnic relations were mostly of the aversive type: they waged war with and ate each other in competition over scarce resources, principally land. Although some goods and services were exchanged between hapu, and although there was some limited use of slave labor, members of different hapu regarded each other as actual or potential enemies or, indeed, food, for cannibalism was rampant.

Such limited exchanges of goods as took place did not qualify as trade or barter, for they had a distinctly ceremonial rather than commercial character. People did not consciously trade with each other, exchanging commodities according to agreed upon prices or standards of value. Instead, as Firth (1959, Chapter 12) very clearly states, communities exchanged gifts, especially prized luxury goods such as obsidian, greenstone and bird feathers, and frequently in conjunction with the visits of chiefs. Even when items of direct practical value, such as food, were exchanged, the transaction took the form of gift and countergift rather than barter. According to Firth (1959, pp. 409–410), "Barter implies some agreement as to the rates of exchange, a practice quite foreign to the Maori mode of conducting matters . . . no bargaining or haggling of any kind took place." If a guest expressed admiration for an object, etiquette called for his host giving him the item. Firth cites an example (pp. 411–412) of a man who became abusive in his demands and was killed by his reluctant hosts: "One is almost entitled to conclude from this that in old Maori days true politeness demanded that one should slay a man sooner than hurt his feelings by refusing him a request."

This leaves war as the principal basis of Maori ethnic relations. The Maori have a particularly fierce reputation because they resisted European penetration with considerable vigor, and because the increasing introduction of European firearms starting in the late 18th century led to a frightful escalation in the scope and devastation of interethnic conflicts. Yet, it is clear that the new weaponry merely intensified a well-established pattern. While traditional Maori weaponry was largely limited to wooden and stone spears and clubs of various styles and lengths, wars were nevertheless fought in earnest, with extensive killing of men, women and children, with occasional extermination of entire groups. Hapu waged regular expeditions against each other, involving 100 to 400 warriors on each side; their villages were fortified armed camps that were regularly besieged to the point of starvation (Vayda, 1960). Insults [e.g. quoted by Buck (1962, p. 401): "Who are you? The flesh of your ancestor is still sticking between my teeth."] were often a pretext for war, but war was clearly a real contest to eliminate competitors for scarce resources (game and fish) and to obtain territory, plunder, women, slaves and human meat. Vayda (1960) interprets Maori warfare ecologically in terms of shortage of land in an environment where stone-age technology made land clearing slow, difficult and tedious.

There is evidence of restraint in fighting or, at least, in the slaughter of women and children, between hapu containing close relatives on both sides, and it was common for individuals to change hapu before the battle if the opposing hapu had closer relatives than the one to which he belonged (Vayda, 1960, p. 28). Thus, considerations of inclusive fitness clearly entered warfare. Between insulated hapu, warfare was deadly serious and over tangible stakes; though accompanied by a lot of ritual, it was over spoils and resources. Even cannibalism, often described by anthropologists in religious and ritual terms, was practical. It was largely restricted to fighting men and to what is technically called "exocannibalism" (eating people of outside groups), but it was consciously thought of as the most convenient solution to the logistical problem of feeding the troops in the field. Slain enemies of all ages and both sexes were often eaten on the spot. Surplus meat was carried in baskets by war prisoners, who, as the supply dwindled, were themselves in constant danger of being slaughtered and eaten. Even slaves of long-standing were often killed and eaten (Vayda, 1960, pp. 67–72). In fact, humans were the only large land animals that constituted a regular part of the Maori male diet.

Contacts with Europeans completely disrupted Maori society. Externally, the Maori become increasingly sucked into the larger colonial world dominated by European states, in which they became but one of a multitude of conquered peoples. But even before they were conquered and incorporated into the British colonial empire, trade contact with Europeans brought fire-arms and, with it, a frightful escalation of slaughter. To avoid extermination, you had to secure muskets; muskets had to be traded with Europeans; but the Maoris had little to trade, except for tatooed human trophy heads, which became a sought-after curiousity, and for flax, produced by slave labor. Trophy heads and slaves, in turn, could be gotten through war for which you needed firearms. The infernal cycle was inescapable, and so was the destruction of a whole way of life and the transformation of the Maori from autarchic microsocieties to a conquered minority in a neo-European state.

Trade: Bambuti and Bantu

When two or more ethnies retain their territorial distinctiveness and their political independence, but adapt to different ecological niches, a more complex, cooperative and sustained type of ethnic relations develops, based on an exchange of goods and services through trade, barter or employment. Many systems of ethnic relations, even in complex industrial societies, have features of this second stage of interaction. For example, the "guest workers" who temporarily emigrate from the circum-Mediterranean area to work in the industrial countries of northwestern Europe, who send part of their wages back home and who eventually return home, partake of a system of ethnic relations where the ethnies remain territorially distinct and politi-cally independent, but where a division of labor and specialization creates peripheral contact and economic interdependence. To the extent that the "guest workers" cease to be temporary sojourners, as some of them almost invariably do, their ethnic situation shades off into one of subordinate im-migrant groups in a hierarchical society. Indeed, simpler types of ethnic contact can easily be transformed by disparities of power and wealth into hierarchical relationships. Once more, these stages or types of ethnic contact must not be used in a rigid mechanical way, but merely as convenient analytical constructs.

Another type of ethnic situation of the second stage common throughout the world today, and one which deserves more attention than it has so far received, is tourism. Exoticism becomes a marketable resource; "authentic-ity," or a reasonable facsimile thereof, is the ultimate commodity. In ex-change for putting himself on show, the native receives material considerations: a shilling for a photo, a dollar for a song or a peso for a dive. If necessary, the exoticism is carefully cultured and stage-managed to satisfy tourist de-mand. The situation is clearly a transient one; the tourist is, by definition, a short-timer with a tenuous, peripheral and indeed very special status. He is at once a privileged guest and a ridiculed, unknowledgeable outsider; a pampered recipient of mercenary deference and an impersonally exploited resource. The very type of ethnic contact created by tourism militates against that ultimate goal of the tourist experience: authenticity. But, when the tourist is tired of being given that very special treatment reserved for his breed, he goes home and becomes a native again. Each ethny is a resource for the other, simply by being different. Each specializes in being itself, in cultivating its uniqueness for the amusement of the other.

Naturally, differences in power and in wealth, which so often exist between tourist and "touree," typically make for a strong element of hierarchy in the relationship. Besides tourism is a very special and recent case of trade, made possible on a mass scale only through industrial affluence. (When wealthy and nosy eccentrics like Alexander von Humboldt were few, their travels in search of the exotic were called "explorations," rather than "tourism.")

Let us turn to a less recent and less special example of trade—that of Bambuti–Bantu relations in the Ituri rain forest of northeastern Zaïre (Turnbull, 1961, 1965). The Bambuti are a group of so-called "Pygmies" who live side by side with, but separately from, neighboring Bantu groups of so-called "Negroids." In describing their relations, we shall again ignore the fact that, for the better part of a century, both groups have become incorporated, albeit peripherally, in a centralized state, the former Belgian Congo and now the Republic of Zaïre. Both of these political entities exerted a measure of control, especially on the Bantu whom they forced to pay taxes and cultivate cash crops such as cotton. They also "opened up" the area by building roads and thereby brought in missionaries, traders, administrators and, of course, a variety of trade goods. Again, these external influences were felt much more strongly by the Bantu than by the Bambuti who could easily withdraw into the forest and literally blend into the landscape. Here, however, we shall deal with Bambuti–Bantu relations without reference to the colonial and post-colonial political structure.

Bambuti and Bantu in the Ituri region speak mutually understandable dialects of the same language; that is, the Bambuti have adopted a Bantu language and have none of their own. Other than that, however, they are about as different from each other as any two people on the African continent. Phenotypically, the Bambuti are about 20 centimeters shorter, on the average, than the Bantu. The Bambuti's occupation of Central Africa antedates the Bantu's by many thousand years, and the present "Pygmy" population of Africa, scattered from the Cameroon to Rwanda, constitutes, along with the Xhoisan ("Bushmen" and "Hottentots") peoples of southern Africa, the remnants of a once much more widespread aboriginal population. By comparison, the Bantu are recent interlopers.

The most striking cultural difference between the two groups is that the Bambuti are seminomadic hunters and gatherers living in small temporary camps (they move every few weeks), while the Bantu are tropical horticulturalists settled in much larger and more permanent villages (village sites are changed every few years). The extent of their territorial distinctiveness can be argued since both groups occupy the same general region, keeping largely apart within it. The Bantu villagers concentrate along main roads, rivers and paths, and are much more open to the outside world. Locally, however, they stay close to their settled villages and neighboring fields, cleared from the forest by the "slash-and-burn" technique. They are afraid of the forest and avoid it. By contrast, the primeval rain forest is the Bambuti's world and now their refuge. Bantu and Bambuti meet on the Bantu's ground, that is, in the Bantu villages, but they keep separate most of the time and, hence, cannot be considered to be strictly sympatric.

In terms of social organization the two groups are also strikingly different. Other than age and sex differences that are universal in humans, the Bambuti are a truly egalitarian, classless, stateless society. They have no chiefs, no slaves, no policemen, no courts, no prisons, no taxes and no institutionalized rank differences between adult men, other than individual prestige achieved by age and personal qualities. Such loose authority structure as exists is based almost entirely on kinship, sex, seniority and personal ascendancy. The division of labor is limited to age and sex distinctions, and even these are rather loose; men are dominant over women and more prominent in decision-making, but male dominance is relatively gentle and muted.

Bambuti live in loosely structured bands of shifting composition, made up of a handful to a dozen or so nuclear families (man, wife and their children). They have a bilateral descent, that is, they recognize kinship in all lines and thus have no larger lineages or clans based on unilineal descent. Nuclear family groups commonly shift from one band to another in response to ecological or social conditions, and the band is thus a residential, not a kinship unit. That is, because of the open nature of the bands, a person is likely to have close kinsmen in several bands, and kin ties are thus diffused over large territories. The band is a semitemporary collection of nuclear families who share an encampment and exploit the natural resources of the territory around it.

Marriage rules are also flexible. Marriage may take place within the band or between bands. Within bands, young people simply start cohabiting after the young man has passed the initiation into manhood and brought his prospective father-in-law some meat, and separation is rare after the birth of a child. Marriages between bands are slightly more formal and involve both groups, since the norm is that if a woman leaves a band, her band should receive one in return from the recipient band. There is no bride-wealth, but, between bands, men tend to exchange sisters or other close female relatives. The wife usually joins her husband's band, but not necessarily, nor does the couple necessarily stay in the same band all of their married life. Band composition responds flexibly to ecological pressures. Polygyny is permitted, and some older men have two or occasionally three wives, but most (90% or more) men are monogamously married.

In terms of mode of production, the Bambuti are still pure hunters and gatherers. The women do most of the gathering and contribute the bulk of the caloric intake in the diet. They also build the huts, weave baskets and cook the food. The men do most of the hunting and contribute most of the protein food. In addition, they organize festivals, make bark cloth and collect honey from wild bees. Different Bambuti groups use two different hunting techniques. Some hunt primarily with bows and poisoned arrows, also using spears to kill larger animals. Their hunting is strictly a male activity. Others beat game into long semicircular nets; in those groups, women and children serve as beaters and men kill the animals entangled in the nets.

Being seminomadic, the Bambuti have to travel light and can accumulate few possessions, other than the weapons of men, the few cooking pots and baskets of women and a few items of personal clothing (mostly bark loin-cloths) and adornment. The system of production allows no storage of sur-plus; food collected is consumed within days. Differences of wealth cannot arise, and therefore the very concept of wealth is alien to Bambuti thinking. Resources are exploited and consumed communally at the band level.

The Bambuti are among the few "peaceful" human groups. In recent times, they have not waged war, either between Bambuti bands or with their Bantu neighbors, and they seldom resort to violence in the settlement of disputes either within or between bands. Conflicts and arguments are settled by public discussion, compromise and social pressure—primarily ridicule and witchcraft. Each band has its hunting and foraging territory, and territorial disputes are relatively rare.

Several complementary explanations help to account for this unusually idyllic state of affairs. First, the colonial administration imposed, by superior force, a *Pax belgica* on both Bantu and Bambuti. "Intertribal warfare" was suppressed by the *Force Publique*, the Belgian colonial army. Second, be-tween Bantu and Bambuti, a mutually beneficial relationship exists, as we shall see, that would be destroyed by violence. The two do not directly compete with each other, as each is specialized for completely different niches. Third, the Bambuti, being much less numerous and less cohesively organized than the Bantu, find it prudent not to antagonize them. Fourth, the Bantu would find the Bambuti elusive and hardly worth the effort to attack since they possess little of value that cannot be obtained by peaceful trade. Fifth, while Bambuti bands do compete with each other, forest re-sources are abundant, and therefore the competition is not severe. Sixth, since families frequently change bands and since individuals commonly marry outside their own band, neighboring bands are linked by numerous ties of kinship and marriage, so that the peace group, and indeed the ethny are the Bambuti as a whole, not the individual band.

By contrast to the Bambuti, the Bantu horticulturalists have a much more complex, highly structured social organization. They emphasize patrilineal descent and form virilocal extended families; they recognize lineages and clans, formed by the descendants of common male ancestors. The authority structure, based on male seniority within these patrilineal kin groups, is much more extensive than among the Bambuti, since the kin groups them-selves are much larger. In addition, the Bantu have village chiefs, backed up by police authority—thus the rudiments of a state organization, although they are not clearly stratified into social classes. The lineages and clans are exogamous. Marriage is accompanied by the payment of bridewealth by the kinsmen of the groom to the kin group of the bride and thus involves two extended patrilineal kin groups. Residence is strictly virilocal. Polygyny is desirable, more common than among the Bambuti, and more clearly associated with wealth and power.

The Bantu system of production, based on tropical "slash-and-burn" horticulture, produces an abundance of carbohydrates (bananas, manioc, peanuts, rice, corn and beans). Animal protein is supplied by domesticated livestock, mostly goats and poultry. Food is stored in granaries and livestock is a form of capital accumulation; thus, surplus production is possible, giving rise to differences of wealth which are in turn converted into political power and polygyny.

This more intensive system of production is made possible by a fairly advanced metal technology. Iron working spread among the Bantu of central Africa several centuries before European contact, and the use of iron in both tools and weapons has long been extensive. The combination of iron technology, horticulture and livestock raising makes possible a population density at least 20 times higher than the hunting and gathering of the Bambuti. Bantu villages are cohesive and stable aggregations of hundreds of people—much larger than any of the Bambuti bands.

What *modus vivendi* have these two groups established between them? Depending on whether one looks at it from a Bantu or a Bambuti perspective, the picture is somewhat different. (Turnbull, by the way, distinctly looks at ethnic relations from a Bambuti point of view, perhaps more than the reality of the situation warrants.) The Bantu look at the Bambuti (whom they regard almost as a different and inferior species of doubtful humanity) with a kind of amused condescension, tinged with some fear because of their association with the forest. To the Bantu, the forest and all creatures associated with it, Bambuti included, represent danger, nature and savagery, and are safely avoided. At the same time, the Bantu find the Bambuti entertaining dwarfs and establish with them patron–client relationships.

Indeed, the Bantu refer to particular Bambuti individuals and bands as "theirs," in a proprietary sense. Whole Bantu villages see themselves as collective "owners" of specific Bambuti bands, considering the relationship as hereditary. In addition, individual Bantu patrons are linked to individual Bambuti clients. In the Bantu's mind, there is no question as to who is whose superior.

The Bambuti, for their part, see themselves as free to come and go as they please, and as in no sense dependent on, much less "owned" by, the Bantu. Far from regarding themselves as exploited by the Bantu, the Bambuti think of the relationship as one beneficial to themselves, in which they trick the Bantu into giving them desirable things that are not, strictly speaking, necessary, though they make life much easier and more pleasant. The Bambuti thus see their association with the Bantu as optional, since they can always withdraw into the self-sufficiency of the forest, merely by foregoing the luxuries of the Bantu villages. So, at any rate, Turnbull (1965) tells us, although he may somewhat idealize the Bambuti's situation.

Bambuti bands or individuals periodically drift in and out of the Bantu villages that regard them as "theirs" and enter with their Bantu patrons into multifaceted interactions that include barter, labor, intermarriage, ritual functions and entertainment. In terms of barter, the Bambuti bring two principal forest products much in demand among the Bantu: game and honey from wild bees. In exchange they receive mostly starchy foods, such as bananas and manioc (which saves them hours of tedious collecting in the forest, but are not at all essential to their diet). The exchanges do not stop at these basic staples, however. The Bambuti also receive from the Bantu a range of luxuries and conveniences, including all iron objects (principally arrow- and spearheads that greatly increase the efficiency of Bambuti hunting), pottery (the Bambuti have no potters), tobacco (a prized luxury), salt (another scarce and highly desired commodity) and matches (the Bambuti have no fire-making technology, and must therefore keep their fires burning and transport embers from camp to camp)—not to mention other commodities acquired by the Bantu through long-distance trade.

In addition to meat and honey, the Bambuti offer the Bantu their labor and occasionally a woman who usually becomes a junior wife of a Bantu. (Bantu women never marry Bambuti, and the unidirectionality of interbreeding clearly indicates some measure of Bambuti subordination to the Bantu. The Bambuti as a group are woman-losers, and thus their fitness is correspondingly reduced.) Turnbull describes the labor which the Bambuti furnish as desultory, unreliable and intermittent, and the Bantu regard the Bambuti as lazy (much as Belgian colonials regarded all Congolese, incidentally). For a few hours of lackadaisical work in the fields, in house construction or in manioc pounding, the Bambuti receive loads of starchy food and a few trinkets. Clearly, their labor is not essential to the village economy nor is the village food to the Bambuti. Both sides regard the transaction as a convenience more than as a necessity.

Perhaps one of the main intangible benefits that the Bambuti bring to the Bantu, and vice versa, is amusement. The Bantu regard the Bambuti as childish pranksters, good dancers and musicians, and entertainers. (In this too, their stereotypes of Bambuti closely resemble the racism of the Europeans toward all Congolese during the colonial era.) The Bambuti are, therefore, called upon to participate in Bantu festivals and are even incorporated into Bantu rites of passage, such as initiation and marriage. The Bambuti, for their part, also find the Bantu villagers amusing, pretend to play their games, act clownishly and delight in tricking them into favorable transactions. The Bambuti regard their sojourn in the Bantu village as something of a lark, a pleasant break from ordinary forest life, during which they are fed in exchange for a little work and clowning. In addition, they get some useful trade goods from it—otherwise unobtainable. When they tire of the game, they simply leave for the forest, until the fancy strikes them again. For the Bantu, too, the Bambuti are an amusing change of pace, a kind of travelling circus of dwarfs, who, in addition to being entertaining, bring meat and do a little desultory work around the house and fields.

Such a picture of ethnic relations, as is drawn by Turnbull (1965), is, I suspect, somewhat idealized, for, underlying the good-humored bonhommie of the interaction, there is clear evidence of inequality, racism and paternalism. Indeed, Bantu–Bambuti relations seem like a buffoonish reenactment of a classical colonial relationship. What saves the Bambuti from the fate of becoming a conquered people is that they have so far managed to retain a large measure of economic self-sufficiency and that their forest habitat affords them a refuge. How much longer is problematic. Changes in the environment, such as opening the forest to logging operations could drastically alter the relationship, almost certainly to the Bambuti's detriment. In other parts of central Africa, such as Rwanda, Pygmy groups, such as the Batwa, have indeed become incorporated as low-status groups into states dominated by Bantu or Hamitic conquerors, such as the Watuzi. The Bambuti way of life is doomed. Hunters and gatherers today constitute perhaps 0.02% of Africa's population. While it lasted, however, it was a reasonably good way of life.

Symbiosis: The Pastoral Fulani and their Agricultural Neighbors

Full symbiosis, i.e. an ecological system in which two or more ethnies occupy the same habitat but adapt to different ecological niches and develop peaceful, mutually beneficial relations without the establishment of a hierarchy between them, is an exceptional situation. Very commonly, one group conquers the other and establishes itself as a ruling class over them in a multiethnic state. A fair approximation to a nonhierarchical symbiosis, however, is achieved by the pastoral Fulani (also called Fulbe, Bororo or Peul) and their horticultural neighbors in a vast stretch of the West African Sudan and Sahel regions from Gambia to the Cameroon (Buchanan, 1953; Michael G. Smith, 1960; Stenning, 1959, 1960, 1965). Once more, we shall ignore the fact that since the turn of the 20th century, the whole of West Africa became incorporated in the colonial empires of Britain and France and thus the Fulani were one conquered people among many.

The Fulani number some seven million people, about half of whom are concentrated in Northern Nigeria where they share the savannah with the Hausa, Kanuri and many other sedentary groups of horticulturalists. It does some violence to historical facts to describe the relations between the Fulani and their neighbors as nonhierarchical, since the Western Sudan has been characterized by a succession of highly complex, large, multiethnic states for at least 1500 years before the colonial era. The empires of Ghana, Songhai, Mali, Kanem-Bornu and Sokoto, to name but a few of the larger ones, all included Fulani nomads, along with scores of other ethnies (Oliver and Fage, 1962). The most important of these states for the Fulani of northern Nigeria are the Hausa emirates conquered in a Muslim *Jihad* (Holy War) by the Fulani under Usman dan Fodio in the first decade of the 19th century. Some of the Fulani settled in the Hausa cities they conquered, intermarried with the Hausa and became the ruling aristocracy of a vast feudal empire under the Sultan of Sokoto. After a few generations, the town Fulani became physically and culturally almost indistinguishable from their Hausa subjects.

However, the pastoral Fulani, who concern us here, retain a distinct identity and mode of life, despite the fact that they are also conscious of their historical links with the town Fulani. The pastoral Fulani, who, like their town relatives, are Muslims and consider themselves as members of the same ethny, are the poor country cousins of the Fulani ruling aristocracy. They do not share their political power, but they are accorded higher status than the Hausa and other subjects of the town Fulani. Unlike the town Fulani aristocrats who, through polygyny with Hausa women, look physically like the more "Negroid" Hausa, the pastoral Fulani are phenotypically quite distinct from their neighbors: their skin color is a much lighter copper brown, and their facial features are more "Hamitic" than "Negroid." The pastoral Fulani stress these physical features, especially their lighter skin and aquiline noses, as a means of asserting their superiority over outsiders. One of their proverbs states, "See the nose, understand the character" (Stenning, 1965, p. 369).

The Fulani, like most other African pastoralists, have a classical patrilineal organization. The basic social groups are clans, lineages and sublineages, formed by descendance from common male ancestors. Residence is virilocal, and the smallest local groups are in fact extended families corresponding to segments of patrilineages. The size of the local groups is dictated by ecological considerations. During the rainy season when pasture is abundant and conditions permit greater concentrations of man and beast, whole clans or major sections of patrilineages may form into large dispersed encampments. In less favorable circumstances, the local group may consist of only about 20 related extended families. Extreme drought forces even greater dispersal of individual extended families.

Since the Fulani have been Muslims for centuries—indeed have produced many puritanical religious reformers who turned successful conquerors after launching Holy Wars—marriage customs reflect Islamic law. Polygyny is frequent and desired, and first marriages tend to be endogamous within the patrilineage. When the bride stays within the patrilineage, no bridewealth is paid. The preferred spouse for a young man is his father's brother's daughter or his father's father's brother's son's daughter. Subsequent marriages are often outside the lineage, including cousins through female lines, nonrelatives, non-Fulani and slaves.

Inheritance of both property and authority follows clearly the patrilineal principle. A man's heirs are his sons, his brothers, his brother's sons, his father's brothers and his male cousins in the male line—in that order. The main form of property for pastoralists is, of course, livestock, mostly cattle, but also sheep, goats and horses. Livestock ownership permits capital accumulation and thus sizeable difference in wealth between families.

The pastoral Fulani are a relatively egalitarian society, compared to their sedentary neighbors. They are stratified mostly by seniority and sex, but traditionally they had slaves, and, in addition to being more or less loosely incorporated into larger states, two types of leaders play a political role in community affairs. The *ardo* is the more traditional leader, a kind of community spokesman, mediator of disputes, presider over consensus and middleman in dealing with outsiders. The *laamiido* is more of a chief with executive functions, but he is a more recent creation of the British colonial administration, entrusted with tax collection, registration and other "dirty work" of the larger government. Traditionally, the pastoral Fulani formed very loose groupings based on patrilineal kinship, and they had no state of their own and no well-defined social classes other than Fulani freemen and foreign slaves.

Virtually the whole existence of the pastoral Fulani revolves around livestock, especially cattle. It provides the basis of the diet, either directly through meat and milk or indirectly through trading milk and beasts for grain and other crops produced by the sedentary agriculturalists. Each family group has its herd made up of sheep and goats, but above all cattle: a stock bull, milking cows, heifers, calves and pack oxen. The Fulani are strictly nomads. Their cattle keep them continuously on the move. They set up flimsy temporary camps, but have no place they can call home, no territory they own, no concept of ownership of space. They are always on someone else's land.

Strict ecological conditions dictate the Fulani's moves. Their lives are a perpetual search for pasture and water for their livestock and their annual migrations are fine-tuned to the cycle of rainy and dry seasons. Precipitation determines not only the availability of pasture but, just as importantly, the distribution of the tse-tse fly. Along with the anopheles mosquito (the vector of malaria), the tse-tse fly (carrier of sleeping sickness) is one of the great scourges of Africa. Cattle cannot survive in tse-tse-infected country, which is also the wetter country, but cattle also need grass, and grass needs water. The trick consists of staying one jump ahead of the tse-tse fly, which, like green pastures, extends its range with the onset of the annual rains. The Fulani maximize the use of that narrow niche, moving northward to drier lands closer to the Sahara during the rainy season, and again southward toward the denser savannah when the tse-tse fly retreats during the dry season. The whole operation requires a multiplicity of risky guesses based on the best available intelligence and experience of weather and local conditions, but also of social conditions imposed by the sedentary land users.

Survival for the pastoral Fulani thus requires not only fine tuning to local ecology but also good ethnic relations. The latter are based partly on trade. The Fulani frequent towns and markets where they acquire grain, metal goods and numerous other goods produced by their sedentary neighbors in exchange for milk and livestock. Milk is sold by Fulani women who carry it on their heads in large calabashes and sell it in towns and villages, door-to-door or on public marketplaces. Live animals are sold by men, often to Hausa merchants who transport and resell the beasts to butchers, several hundred miles to the south, in the tse-tse infested forest belt where the cattle can only survive a couple of weeks but where there is a brisk demand for meat.

In addition to trading with their sedentary neighbors, the pastoral Fulani must also negotiate their access to pasture and water during their annual cycles of transhumance through other peoples' land. This involves a lot of diplomacy and careful control of animals, so that no damage is done to crops. Cattle are allowed over fallow land (and, as tropical agriculture requires long fallows, much land is under fallow in any given year), or over land which has just been harvested and when it can feed on maize and other cereal stubble. In exchange, the dung left behind provides the agriculturalists with fertilizer. With careful management and good manners, everybody is happy.

CONCLUSIONS

Two main conclusions can be drawn from these brief accounts of systems of ethnic relations that stop short of full integration into multiethnic states. One is that these systems very easily tip over to the fourth stage where one of the ethnies asserts its political dominance and starts exploiting the others, transforming symbiosis into parasitism. In fact, nearly all contemporary systems of ethnic relations are of this kind, to which I shall turn in the next chapter and devote much of the rest of this book.

The other conclusion is that ethnicity is not always an all-or-none concept. Ethnic boundaries are not always sharply drawn, although they can be, especially if they correspond to phenotypical differences. Commonly, however, ethnicity is a matter of *degree of relatedness*. People typically form both alliances and cleavages, and grade the violence and destructiveness they inflict on each other on the basis of their real or perceived degree of relatedness. That is, both cooperation and conflict in human societies follow a calculus of inclusive fitness, which, in man, is often at least partly conscious, but which need not be conscious to be operative.

Since relatedness is a matter of degree, it is frequently the case that different levels of ethnicity may be activated by conflicts, depending on the relatedness of the main parties to the conflict and on the groups of kinsmen which each side can muster. This phenomenon has been closely studied by Chagnon among the Yanomamö (Chagnon, 1977; Chagnon and Bugos, 1979) and has been noted in other societies as well. For example, this was clearly the case in the ethnic politics at the Nigerian university I studied (van den Berghe, 1973a). If the contenders to an academic post were, say, Ibo and Yoruba, then political alignments would tend to follow these large ethnic cleavages. If, however, the competitors were both Yoruba but from different regions, then major ethnic subdivisions of the Yoruba would align against each other—and so on down to the level of the local town and the lineage group and subgroups.

This multitiered system of ethnic competition produces a system of fission and fusion analogous, indeed homologous, to the ones described by anthropologists in their discussion of segmentary lineage systems (Evans-Pritchard, 1940). By now, this should not surprise us, since we have seen that ethnicity *is*, in fact, an extension of kinship.

We have also seen how kinship and marriage ties between parties to a dispute inhibits violence or, at least, restrains its destructiveness. This was the case in Maori warfare as previously noted; Chagnon (1977) reports the same for the Yanomamö; Evans-Pritchard (1940) notes that the Nuer do not kill women and children in wars between different Nuer clans but kill them when fighting the Dinka. To use an example closer to home, there was a blatant difference in the level of ferociousness of American soldiers in the Pacific and European theaters during World War II. According to American notions of racism, the Germans were misguided relatives (however distant), while the "Japs" or the "Nips" were an entirely different breed of inscrutable, treacherous, "little yellow bastards." This was reflected in differential behavior in such things as the taking (versus killing) of prisoners, the rhetoric of war propaganda (President Roosevelt in his wartime speeches repeatedly referred to his enemies as "the Nazis, the Fascists, and the Japanese"), the internment in "relocation camps" of American citizens of Japanese extraction, and in the use of atomic weapons. It is doubtful that atomic bombs would have been dropped over, say, Stuttgart or Dortmund, but hardly a whisper of protest was heard about Hiroshima and Nagasaki.

SUGGESTED READINGS

There are a number of general statements on human ecology by sociologists (Hawley, 1950), economists (Boulding, 1978), anthropologists (Steward, 1977) and others, but none is specifically focused upon ethnic relations. Several monographs and collections of articles, however, deal extensively with the ecological dimensions of ethnic relations; such are Aguirre Beltrán (1979), Fredrik Barth (1969), Collier (1975), Shahrani (1979) and van den Berghe and Primov (1977).

ETHNICITY AND COERCION:
THE POLITICS OF HIERARCHY

In the previous chapter, I surveyed the first three stages of interethnic relations based on the regulation of competition for scarce resources by means of territoriality and specialization. I now turn to the most complex, fourth stage, where coercion and hierarchy begin to play a salient role in ethnic relations. For all practical, contemporaneous purposes, the entire world is now in stage four and, therefore, I shall devote a disproportionate amount of space to it. Indeed, much of the remainder of this book will deal with it.

DOMINANCE AND COERCION IN ANIMAL SOCIETIES
Coercion and its resulting hierarchies are not unique to humans. Many social animals establish what ethologists call "hierarchies," "dominance orders" or, in birds, "pecking orders." There is considerable discussion among students of animal behavior about the nature of hierarchy (E. O. Wilson, 1975). Some animals establish linear hierarchies; others do not. In some species, there are separate male and female hierarchies; in others, the order of dominance varies depending on the resource competed for; in others yet, an animal's condition (e.g. oestrus and lactation) changes its relative position. There is much disagreement on how best to measure hierarchy, or on whether hierarchy is a unidimensional concept. Many ethologists measure hierarchy, indeed *define* hierarchy, as order of access to resources, especially food or, for males, receptive females; yet others focus on rituals of submission and dominance (which, among many primates, frequently take pseudosexual forms such as mounting or presenting the genitalia); some stress "displacement behavior" (i.e. the yielding space to an approaching animal); some insist that, among primates, "attention structure" (who pays attention to whom) is crucial (Altmann, 1962; Chance, 1967; Chance and Jolly, 1970; E. O. Wilson, 1975, Chapter 13).

Underlying all these interesting disagreements, differences of emphasis and fine points of methodology and measurement, however, students of animal behavior broadly agree that dominance or hierarchy is a concept abstracted from the observation of animals competing for access to resources. In the last analysis, what defines the hierarchy of a group is an order of access to resources. The master paradigm explaining how resources are distributed in a social group is, again, maximization of individual inclusive fitness. The strongest do not always get all; in fact, they seldom do. Animals predisposed to eat their helpless young, for instance, would not reproduce successfully! Yet there clearly is an important element of coercion, or the threat thereof, in the establishment, maintenance and challenge of hierarchies. Outside of the context of kin selection (especially parental care) and reciprocity (especially between mated reproductive adults) animals maximize their fitness by outcompeting others for resources, directly or indirectly. Speed and deceit play a role in that contest, but coercion, i.e. the use of force or the threat thereof, is the main method by which dominance is exerted, maintained and indeed challenged.

Indeed, it is safe to generalize that there is no hierarchy without underlying coercion. Coercion is the use of force or its threat to increase the fitness of the dominant animal at the expense of subordinate ones. The more or less stable result of their multiple contests over resources is what we call the dominance order of a group of social animals.

HUMAN DOMINANCE SYSTEMS: COERCION AND DECEIT

Complex as dominance is among nonhuman animals, it is nothing compared to what hierarchy has become in the human societies of the last few millenia. Human hierarchies are vastly more complex than anything found in other species because of the following:

1. Humans form not only individual dominance hierarchies, as do other animals, but also establish *group* hierarchies. So far, nothing beyond small, unstable coalitions of two or three individuals has been found in the more intelligent nonhuman mammals such as baboons. Only human societies are organized on the basis of stable group hierarchies and, even in our species, this is a relatively recent development of the last few millenia.
2. Humans have the capacity to magnify, indeed to reverse, through an increasingly lethal technology of violence, biological inequalities of strength or intelligence between individuals. Biological differences of strength based on age and sex still explain human dominance orders within small groups, such as families or gangs, but human group-based hierarchies are explainable almost entirely in terms of social organization of the technology of violence. Socially oppressed groups are not necessarily made up of weaker or dumber individuals. Indeed, typically they are not. Instead, they are composed of individuals who owe their inferior

position to technological and/or organizational inferiority in using the means of violence.

3. The human capacity for conscious deceit (through ideology, *inter alia*) further enhances our species' capacity for group inequality beyond anything known in other species. Human systems of group inequality, especially the ones perpetuated by all large, centralized states, are almost invariably bolstered by an ideology that disguises the parasitism of the ruling class as either kin selection or reciprocity. Subjects are told that they are ruled (i.e. exploited) in their own best interests, either by a benevolent despot who claims some kind of fatherly interest in them and who supposedly saves them from their own greed and ineptitude, or through a supposedly freely entered social contract wherein the rulers are held to be chosen representatives and servants of the people entrusted with promoting the common good and arbitrating and regulating individual conflicts of interest.

The first type of ideology used to legitimize the status quo—paternalism—is the most common one in preindustrial societies. It has been repeatedly reinvented in countless monarchies of Europe, Asia and Africa, in defense of colonialism and chattel slavery in the Americas and Africa—indeed almost everywhere powerful agrarian states developed. The second and more recent justification for tyranny and exploitation—often misnamed "democracy," either of the liberal or of the socialist "people's" variety—is characteristic of industrial societies since the French Revolution.

This is not the place to trace the development and analyze the operation of complex systems of group coercion and exploitation in human societies, as that would take us too far afield. I shall largely confine my remarks to tracing the relationship of group coercion to ethnic relations. Nevertheless a few preliminary observations are in order:

1. Group stratification is a relatively recent phenomenon in human evolution; it accompanied the so-called Neolithic Revolution, that is, the domestication of plants and animals that greatly increased human population density, led to sedentarization into more permanent settlements and made possible the accumulation (and, hence, the appropriation) of surplus production.
2. Group stratification co-evolved with the state. The essence of the state is intraspecific—indeed, intrasocietal parasitism. The state is the coercive apparatus used by the few to exploit the many. The state *is*, in fact, the ruling class organized to extract surplus production through the use of deceit or violence or the threat thereof. By parasitizing the exploited classes through control of labor and its products (forced labor, slavery, taxation), members of the parasitic class convert, in effect, organized coercion into higher fitness for themselves at the expense of the exploited. Plunder and predation *between* human societies existed long before the rise of states. With the emergence of the state, however, parasitism was extended *within* societies.

3. Ideology will be treated as a form of organized, collective deceit whereby parasitism is disguised—usually as either kin selection or reciprocity. To say that ideology reflects class interests is not to say that it is unimportant. Some forms of deceit are successful—successful, that is, in terms of consequences for fitness—and are therefore important.

The reader will readily see that the above formulations on the nature of the state, stratification and ideology, while formulated within the general paradigm of maximization of individual inclusive fitness, is fully congruent with Marxist class analysis and, indeed, owes a great deal to it.

ETHNICITY AND THE STATE

Innumerable authors have stressed the fundamental distinction between nation-states and multinational states (Connor, 1978; Deutsch, 1966; Deutsch, and Foltz, 1963; Emerson, 1960; Francis, 1976; Geertz, 1967b; Leo Kuper and Michael G. Smith, 1969; Michael G. Smith, 1965a; Schermerhorn, 1970; Young, 1976; Zubaida, 1970, 1978). Certainly many of the key words used by social scientists in the analysis of domestic and "international" politics rely implicitly or explicitly on that distinction: state, nation, nation-state, nationality, nationalism, subnationalism, communalism, internationalism, tribe, tribalism, ethnicity, colonialism, imperialism, plural society, multiethnic state, multinational state, ethnic nationalism and so on. Yet the literature on these subjects is so hopelessly muddied by inconsistent and, indeed, blatantly conflicting usages of these terms that the urge to create neologisms is almost irresistible. In an effort to clarify the muddle without introducing new terms, I shall set forth a few straightforward definitions.

A *state* is a collectivity headed by a group of people who exercise power over others (who are neither kinsmen nor spouses), in order to extract surplus production for their own individual and collective benefit.

A *nation* is a politically conscious ethny, that is, an ethny that claims the right to statehood by virtue of being an ethny. Such a ideology is called *nationalism*.

A *nation-state* is a state made up almost exclusively of a single nation.

A *multinational state* is a state made up of two or more nations.

A *multiethnic state* is a state made up of two or more ethnies that do not claim statehood.

Imperialism is the domination of one or more ethnies over others.

Colonialism is long-distance imperialism, usually over noncontiguous territory and over culturally unrelated ethnies.

These simple definitions may not solve all problems, but at least they eliminate much of the needless confusion that arose from such careless usage as calling multinational states like Nigeria, Zaïre or India "nation-states." If "nation-state" is to be used synonymously with "state," then the term is superfluous. Similarly, "ethnic nationalism," by our definition, is a redundancy. Terms like "tribe" and "tribalism" become altogether superfluous since they really mean "nation" and "nationalism" and are used mostly invidiously to refer to Africans. (Why should the Hausa or the Zulu be tribes, but not Danes or French Canadians?)

Now let us return to the distinction between state and nation. Why is it important? At the outset, it is obvious that the two are far from being coterminous, despite the pious fictions of international conferences where delegates pretend that all states are "United Nations." We know better, of course. Only about 10% of the "United Nations'" 150-odd states are genuine nations or at least come close to it by the criterion of having 90% or more of their population speaking mutually understandable dialects of the same language. The remaining 90% are multinational or multiethnic states, some of which may still hope to become nation-states, but many of which do not even try or have long since given up the attempt.

Conversely, many nations are divided between several states and may thus be called multistatal nations: Kurds, Armenians, Germans, Basques, Koreans, Yorubas and Ewes, to mention but a few examples on three continents. The extent to which these multistatal nations are nationalist and irredentist varies enormously—both from place to place and cyclically. Nationalist movements are volatile and highly responsive to historical opportunities such as wars, revolutions and the breakdown of imperial systems.

One thing is clear: the real nation-state is a rare entity. But, rare though it is, it seems to be seductively attractive as a basis of political organization. Much bloodshed has accompanied the efforts to create nation-states. In every age since the recorded history of states, nationalism has inspired masses of people to veritable orgies of emotion and violence. Nationalist conflicts are among the most intractable and unamenable to reason and compromise. The problems of political integration and legitimacy, while present to some extent in all states, are compounded in multinational states. In short, it seems that a great many people care passionately whether they are ruled and exploited by members of their own ethny or by foreigners. Where many grudgingly put up with the former, they lose little opportunity to rebel against the latter. Why?

On the face of it, it should make little difference whether one is fleeced by people who speak one's own language or a foreign tongue. Yet, it clearly does make an important difference—often the difference between passive, reluctant acquiescence and sometimes suicidal rebellion. I have already suggested the answer as to why the nation-state is a more viable political entity than the multinational state. The nation-state is legitimated by kin selection—the most fundamental basis of animal sociality. Conversely, that basis of legitimacy is not available to the multinational state. Queen Victoria could cut a motherly figure in England; she even managed to proclaim her son the Prince of Wales; but she could never hope to become anything except a foreign ruler of India. Similarly, the fiction that the Emperor of

Japan is the head of the most senior lineage descended from the common ancestor of all Japanese might convince the Japanese peasant that the Emperor is an exalted cousin of his, but the myth lacks credibility in Korea or Taiwan.

THE NATION-STATE

Before looking at the systems of ethnic domination imposed on multinational states, let us look more closely at the emergence of the nation-state and at the legitimation of rule in the nation-state. There are basically two ways in which primary states are formed: externally through conquest and internally through centralization of power.* That is, an ethny can conquer its neighbors, impose itself as a ruling class over them and thus create a multiethnic state. Alternatively, within an ethny, an individual or group can gradually assert authority over the rest of the ethny, thus giving rise to a nation-state. Though the two processes are distinct, they are often complementary. Centralization of power within the ethny, as it typically gives rise to a more cohesive political and military organization, often facilitates enlargement by conquest. Conversely, if the fruits of conquest are to be reaped, the conquering group must develop a system of permanent domination, and this fosters the development of centralized power within the conquering group. In practice, then, states are typically seen to emerge out of a double process of external conquest and internal centralization of power.

When political (and, indeed, other social) scientists think of nation-states, they generally tend to project the European experience since the Renaissance. This is unfortunate since nearly all European states for the last 2000 years or so are secondary formations that fragmented or emerged from previously existing states. Many European states, including some comparatively small ones (e.g. Yugoslavia, Czechoslovakia, Belgium and Switzerland), are multinational states—not nation-states. As for those European states that come close to being real nations, they were created either through the political and military consolidation of multistatal nations (e.g. Germany and Italy in the 19th century) or through the disintegration of multinational empires (e.g. The Netherlands in the 16th century, Poland, and Hungary and, briefly, Latvia, Estonia and Lithuania in the 20th century). In both cases, the nation and the state had coexisted for centuries, but they were not coextensive. Either the nation was split up into a multiplicity of squabbling statelets (as in Germany, Italy and, earlier, France) or a multiplicity of captive nations were ruled by large empires dominated by one or more ethnic groups (such as Austria-Hungary, Russia, Ottoman Turkey and Spain).

Except for Switzerland, a loose confederation that grew from within over the last seven centuries, and a few statelets left over from the Middle Ages like Monaco, Andorra and San Marino, all contemporary European states

---

*Secondary states can be formed from existing states through secession, of course.

emerged as complex bureaucratic machines from other complex states. Belgium, for instance, a relatively new state born in 1830 out of the collapse of the Napoleonic Empire and the shambles of the Congress of Vienna, was, from the outset, a full-blown, modern, bureaucratic state (but *not* a nation), and in barely over half a century, it launched on a vast colonial adventure in the Congo.

Clearly, then, Europe in recent centuries is a poor exemplar of either the nation-state or, much less, of how nation-states first developed out of stateless societies. Africa, which until recently still had many stateless societies and where a number of states had recently emerged or were emerging at the time of the European conquest, is much more instructive in this respect. States start in agricultural and/or pastoralist societies, usually from modest and inconspicuous beginnings, at the village level. Indeed, the core unit around which state institutions slowly emerge is typically small enough to be a subethny, a single local community within an ethny. Certain basic conditions have to be present before a state can emerge: sedentary villages, agriculture and/or livestock raising, some storable surplus production, and the beginnings of inequality in status and access to resources between adult men.

From these general background conditions characteristic of many tropical horticulturalists, the embryonic state typically develops around village chieftaincy. An individual, because of luck, skill, political acumen, manipulation of religious functions or simply the help of a large group of kinsmen, begins to assert his authority and to claim privileges over villagers other than his wives or junior kinsmen over whom his domestic authority would extend in any case. The germ of chieftaincy is thus the assertion of authority and privilege *beyond* the domestic sphere of marriage and kinship relations that characterize all human societies, including stateless ones, and which are based principally on sex and seniority. If an individual claims and is granted authority over people who are not related to him by blood or marriage, that group has an embryonic state.

The specific bases of chieftaincy vary somewhat from society to society, but the basic ingredients of it are few and repeatedly found. One is *religious charisma*, as noted long ago by a number of social scientists (James G. Frazer, 1890; Mauss, 1924; Weber, 1968, first published in 1922). A person acquires power by performing religious functions and by claiming special powers of healing, divination or witchcraft. Theocracies and divine kingships are very common. Indeed, the notion of totally secularized power is quite recent (barely 200 or so years old) and, even today, seldom realized in practice. The king is typically a priest (and magician as well) and his power hinges on the gift of grace and the magical properties (especially fecundity) attributed to him. Monarchical power rests almost invariably on a basis of religious ideology. When that basis of legitimacy is extended from an individual to his kin and is hereditarily transmitted, then a clear transition occurs from incipient chieftaincy to an established monarchy.

Another frequent component of incipient chieftaincy is the principle of *seniority* inherent in kinship organization. This is especially effective in unilineal descent societies (either patrilineal or matrilineal) in which one line of descent (male or female) is stressed, thereby giving rise to large, cohesive kin groups, known as lineages and clans. In nearly all human societies, authority over kin is allocated on the basis of seniority (often qualified by mental competence). A man has authority over his junior relatives. If a lineage is numerically important in a village, its head obviously has a political advantage over heads of smaller lineages and may use that advantage to extend his authority over them. This extension of authority over nonkin often becomes institutionized through a claim (often mythical) that a particular clan or lineage is *collectively* senior to other clans and lineages—for example, by representing the descent line of the *eldest* son of the mythical founding ancestor. When the principle of seniority is extended from individuals to descent groups, the kinsmen of the chief automatically acquire an aura of superiority; they begin to constitute a royal clan on which the power of the king rests and from which his successor will be chosen.

A third common, indeed practically universal, feature of emergent chieftaincy is *polygyny*. Polygyny is also found, on a limited scale, in stateless societies, but the scope of it is greatly extended in politically centralized societies. One of the very first privileges and benefits accruing from political power is access to reproductive women. This occurs long before marked differences in lifestyle, diet, dress, consumption, housing and so on develop between rulers and ruled. Even in small-scale village-level societies where the chief lives much like everyone else, he already has more wives. Power, in short, is immediately converted into fitness, i.e. reproductive success.

Since political power is predominantly wielded by men, our discussion of it is in the male gender. But it must be noted here that there is a simple biological reason why polygamy is a uniquely *male* reward of power. A man can greatly increase his fitness by having several wives; a woman does not derive a comparable advantage by being polyandrous.

Polygyny, and thereby reproductive success, is not merely a reward of power. It is also a means of consolidating and perpetuating it. This is done in two ways: first, by producing more kinsmen and thus enlarging the size of one's kin group and, second, by establishing ties of alliance and reciprocity with other kin groups through marrying off one's daughters to other groups and taking wives from other groups. The king, through matrimonial politics, can thus easily become father-in-law, son-in-law or brother-in-law to many of his subjects and be at the hub of a network of matrimonial alliances. Indeed, fertility is frequently associated with kingship. The king is expected to have many children, and his powers of fertility are, by extension, assumed to be magically related with the well-being of the nation, so that his continued potency is a prequisite to his retention of political office. Regicide of aging kings is a common feature of many monarchies (James G. Frazer, 1890).

Since the setting within which states emerge is typically a sedentary agricultural village, the state originally encompasses a single ethny or, indeed, only a section thereof. Ethnic homogeneity is, of course, one of the facilitating conditions in the emergence of states. To the extent that the ethny or subethny is already conceived of as an extended kin group, chieftaincy itself is seen as a mere extension of the preexisting authority structure within the corporate kin group. The village chief is not yet an exploiter: he is merely a *primus inter pares* among lineage or family heads—a kind of superfather of a superfamily. At that embryonic level, there is not yet a clear stratification between rulers and ruled, although many such societies already have one variety or other of domestic slavery. There is not yet any systematic exploitation (except of slaves who are generally outsiders), not any taxation, not any appropriation of surplus production by the few, and not any evident signs of wealth, status and hierarchy between free men. The chief is still mainly an influential leader, a mediator and an adviser, rather than a boss, a judge or a policeman. His authority is still bound by custom and relies on consent rather than coercion.

This embryonic state of affairs can last a long time if there are no strong pressures toward further centralization of power (such as endemic warfare sometimes fosters), and if the system of production limits the amount storable surplus and thus the exploitability of human labor. Where wealth is created in substantial, storable and stealable quantities (which can happen in pastoralist societies and in the more intensive forms of tropical horticulture), states can develop, consolidate and expand quite rapidly. Villages on the road to chieftaincy often have an organizational advantage in warfare and can thus establish hegemony over neighboring communities, giving rise to loose confederations of villages. At this level, we are still typically within the confines of a single ethny. We are witnessing in fact the birth of a nation-state.

Loose village confederacies headed by a nominal priest-chief can in turn coalesce into a full-blown statelet headed by a real king with executive powers of life and death, and with a retinue of wives, relatives, courtiers, appointed officials and bodyguards. His powers may still be limited by custom and checked by a council of elders, but he is now a genuine monarch who gives orders, passes judgement, distributes rewards and punishments, accepts and collects tribute. In short, the king now exercizes a definite amount of coercion, derives direct material benefits from his rule and relies on a circle of supporters who constitute the germ of a ruling class and who are the beneficiaries of the king's favors.

So long as all this takes place within the ethny, the problems of legitimacy are still mitigated by an ideology of extended kin selection. The growth of national consciousness that accompanies this process of political centralization is usually fostered by a myth of common origin in which the king is the living head of the royal clan, which, in turn, is only one branch of the descendants of the common ancestor.

The ideology of kingship is one of extended kinship. The king is a paternal figure, a superfather of a superfamily, tied to his subjects by multiple bonds of blood and marriage. He is, in fact, often looked upon as the living symbol of the nation, the embodiment of its collective spirit, the last incarnation of the common ancestor and the symbolic father of the nation. Kingship is merely the political expression of the nation. With even considerably more justification than Louis XIV, the king can truly say, *L'état c'est moi* or, better yet, *La nation c'est moi*.

Because of its ready-made ideology of extended kinship, the ethny is, one might say, the natural matrix of the nascent state. Political institutions of kingship find a ready justification so long as they grow within the confines of a preexisting ethny. An embryonic state can extend without much difficulty to the outer boundaries of the ethny and assimilate neighboring groups that speak mutually understandable dialects, share similar traditions and see each other as, somehow, related. However, where conquest crosses an ethnic boundary (that is when the state becomes multinational), a whole new order of problems of legitimacy arises, and a set of important thresholds are crossed. The multiethnic or multinational state is a qualitatively different entity from the nation-state. It necessarily grows out of external conquest; it lacks prima facie legitimacy; it rests on naked coercion; it results in a sharp group hierarchy; and it leads to visible and resented exploitation by foreigners. While, in the nation-state, coercion and exploitation are both blunted and concealed by the preexisting ideology of extended kinship that underlies the concept of ethny and nation, the multiethnic state stands naked as the instrument of the ruling group, typically the conquering ethnic group as a whole, or a smaller group drawn overwhelmingly from it.

Let us illustrate this sharp contrast with two "traditional," i.e. precolonial, African states: Swaziland in Southeastern Africa and Rwanda in the very heart of the continent. Although Rwanda covers twice as big an area as Swaziland, and has ten times it population, the two states share some broad similaries of ecology, technology and social organization. They occupy roughly the same type of habitat (mountainous tropics or subtropics, in a warm, well-irrigated setting). They both have much the same economic level. They are both patrilineal, virilocal, polygynous societies with a broadly similar type of kinship and family organization. Even their political institutions resemble each other in their broad features and have much the same antiquity: both are hereditary monarchies, with an interesting and uniquely African balance of authority between the king and queen mother. Both have existed for several centuries before European rule, and both regained their political sovereignty in the 1960s after a colonial interlude of three generations.

The overwhelmingly striking difference between them, however, is that Swaziland is a genuine nation-state, one of the few in Africa, while Rwanda was, until the revolution of 1959–1963, a multiethnic castelike society dominated by Tuzi conquerors. It is to this sharp contrast, and to its dramatic recent consequences that I now turn.

SWAZILAND

Swaziland is a mere speck on the map of Africa—some 15,000 square kilometers in size, or about half the size of Belgium. Sandwiched between the Republic of South Africa and Mozambique, it was drawn into the competing imperialisms of the Boer and the British and, though never conquered by arms, it first became incorporated into the sphere of influence of the Transvaal Republic, and then it became a British High Commission Territory (in effect, a protectorate) after the Boer defeat in the War of 1899–1902. After some three generations of colonialism, it regained its formal political sovereignty in 1968, and became one of a handful of genuine African nation-states. The present population of the kingdom is approximately 300,000, some 7% of whom are non-Swazi, mostly people of European origin (numbering about 8000) or closely related Bantu-speakers from neighboring territories. Perhaps another 100,000 Swazi live in the Republic of South Africa (Hilda Kuper, 1947a, 1947b, 1963, 1978; Marwick, 1940).*

Unlike many states that are members of the United Nations, but have yet to become nations, the Swazi have been a nation long before they received international recognition as such. The ruling Dlamini clan traces its genealogy back about 25 generations, and the kingdom emerged about 200 years ago out of an amalgam of closely related Nguni and Sotho clans (subgroups of the "Southeastern Bantu") which was gradually welded together into a nation under the Dlamini dynasty. European contact in the late 19th century accelerated this process of monarchical centralization under the Dlamini. Swazi is a name given to them by Europeans after a corruption of the name of a 19th century king, Mswati, but they refer to themselves as the "people of Ngwane" or the "people of Sobhuza," two important 19th century kings, of whom the present reigning monarch, Sobhuza II, is a descendant (and, incidentally, the longest-reigning monarch in the world). Details about the origins of the kingdom are lost in the night of time, but it emerged around one clan, the Dlamini, from which every king must come. It grew by cultural absorption of native San groups and of immigrants and refugees, and by conquest of neighboring groups of closely related language and culture, who were gradually assimilated into a unitary state through diplomacy and matrimonial alliances with the royal clan.

In social organization, the Swazi resemble the other Southeastern Bantu. They have patrilineal descent; marriage is virilocal (i.e. the bride goes to live with her husband and his male kinsmen) and sanctioned by payment of a large bridewealth in cattle (lobola). Divorce is permitted but rare. Polygyny is desired and is the rule for older men of high status. Authority

---

*The problem of the "ethnographic present" plagues much anthropology insofar as descriptions of "traditional" systems have often attempted to freeze an ever-changing reality into a static structural framework. Often, several time-frames have been compressed into one "ethnographic present." My second-hand account, drawn from ethnological work stretching over 30 years, is no exception. The following account describes a "traditional" system that developed before European conquest and continued to exist in modified form thereafter. The very label "traditional" is misleading for it implies that the pre-European system was static. In fact, it was continuously evolving, thus eluding description as an ideal model. Yet, European contact did constitute an important discontinuity in Swazi history, so great a discontinuity that many contemporary analysts (including Heribert Adam on reading this account in manuscript form) would largely discount the relevance of the past for the present. The emphasis here is not on an understanding of contemporary Swazi politics, but on the evolution of the "traditional" system. All the problems of trying to freeze a changing reality into a static account of a "traditional" system also apply to my account of Rwanda.

within the large, virilocal, polygynous, extended families is exercised by the oldest male who is the head of the localized lineage segment. Inheritance of property (mostly cattle) is in the male line, but the relative rank of co-wives in polygynous households determines which of the sons is the main heir of his father.

The Swazi economy is based mainly on hoe horticulture of maize, millet, groundnuts, beans, gourds, pumpkins and other crops, and animal husbandry, principally of cattle, but also of goats, sheep and poultry. Hunting and gathering play a subsidiary role. Women do the bulk of the agricultural work, while men tend the livestock. Land tenure is communal and land cannot be sold or alienated. It is held in trust by persons in political authority and allocated for agricultural use to individual families, according to their needs. Wives, in turn, are allocated individual gardens by their husbands. Grazing lands are used in common. Cattle, the principal form of wealth and necessary to the acquisitions of wives, are owned by individual men, with the king as the largest owner (some 3000 heads out of 334,000 for the Swazi as a whole, in 1936). Except for a few ritual specialists (medicine men and diviners), there is little division of labor beyond age and sex.

The central political institution of the Swazi nation is the kingship, of which the incumbent king is but the living representative. The king symbolizes the spirit of the Swazi nation; called Ngwenyama (Lion), the king is a lineal descendant of the founder of the dynasty and is at the apex of a system of graded prestige between lineages and clans, whose relative ranking is determined by closeness of filiation to the king. The 70-odd clans in the Swazi nation are divided into four broad categories of prestige depending on the number of kin and marriage links with the king and the royal Dlamini clan, and the number of political offices bestowed by the king on clan members.

There are no sharp differences in wealth between clans, not even between the royal clan and the others, and thus the Swazi do not have social classes in the usual sense. They do not even have slavery. However, substantial wealth differences (principally in the form of cattle ownership, converted into polygyny) existed between individuals. Some of the older men in politically important positions have hundreds of cattle and a number of wives. As the distribution of political offices, such as district chieftaincies, is controlled by the king and is openly nepotistic, close relatives of the king are much more likely to be rich and powerful than members of commoner clans and to have many more wives and children. But there are no clear differences in lifestyle between the Dlamini and the other clans. Only the king himself stands out as the biggest cattle owner, polygynist and father of the kingdom.

The king is not an absolute monarch. His power is held in check by the countervailing weight of the queen-mother, who holds her own separate court and has certain traditional functions. In addition, the king has to abide by the opinions of two councils, a smaller inner council of about 20, composed of senior members of the Dlamini clan (a kind of House of Lords) and a much larger house of commons made up of nonroyal chiefs, headmen and lineage heads. The two councils must achieve consensus, and the king, who is the last to speak, cannot safely overrule his councils. In case of disagreement between the two councils, the king should try to resolve the issue, but if he is unsuccessful, the matter is shelved.

There is no strict primogeniture in succession to the throne. Instead, the heir is born to the royal wife of highest rank and to avoid competition for the throne, it is preferred that the main royal wife bear the king only one son. The king's mother on accession of her son to the throne becomes the second most important personage in the kingdom. When the king's mother dies, a classificatory mother, such as a mother's sister, is substituted to play that role. The classificatory mother must belong to the same clan as the king's mother, and may even be a king's wife from that clan (Hilda Kuper, personal communication).

The Swazi monarchy is buttressed by religious ritual that continuously legitimizes the kingship as the symbolic incarnation of the nation. As the king is strong and fertile, so is the nation. The great ritual of kingship and fertility (Incwala) is at once a first fruits ceremony and a renewal of the kingship and the nation. It constitutes the core drama of Swazi national solidarity and is celebrated every year when there is an adult king on the throne.

Clearly, the Swazi are a politically conscious ethny—a unitary nation. The symbol of that unity is the king who stands in the position of a super-father to a superfamily. This is true in a triple sense. As an extensive polygynist with scores or hundreds of children, he literally sires a large progeny. But he is also the head of the prolific and powerful royal clan, a clan whose size is constantly increased by the polygyny of the king's kinsmen. Since the king's favors are nepotistically dispensed, the royal clan he heads is a superclan in terms of wealth and reproductive success.

Finally, the extensive polygyny of the king allows him to play a complex game of matrimonial alliances linking him to the commoner clans through multiple ties of blood and affinity. The king deliberately marries women from the various clans of his kingdom; indeed, he has a moral obligation and is expected to do so. In turn, he gives away his many daughters in marriage to favored chiefs in other clans. The king as superpolygynist thus finds himself a father-in-law, brother-in-law or son-in-law to the leaders of most commoner clans and through his female relatives has nephews and grandchildren scattered to the four winds of his realm. Conversely, many commoner clans have kin through females in the royal Dlamini clan.

Hilda Kuper, who through her masterly biography of King Sobhuza II has established herself as the foremost authority on Swazi kingship, states it well:

> The Swazi say, Inkosi kabili (a king is king twice). He is king not only of the nation but also of his own kin, the Malangeni (children of the sun); the two are interwoven. . . . When Sobhuza's people talk of him as "child of the nation" and "father of the nation," they are not using meaningless metaphors (Hilda Kuper, 1978, p. 118).

The king is thus clearly the hub of a vast network of nepotism that extends over the entire ethny. The children of kings and the senior branches of the Dlamini clan are called "children of the sun," constituting a social and political elite. More distant relatives are less exalted but still receive the royal title of Nkosi. The king's in-laws also receive royal favor. Obviously, not everyone in a nation of 300,000 can be a kinsman of the king; but, thanks to polygyny, enough people belonging to enough commoner clans can trace a tie of blood or marriage to the king or one of his predecessors to weld the entire nation into a vast system of kin selection, a grand extended family with the king as its superfather in a real as well as a symbolic way. The king is the nation and the nation is the king.

It must be noted that, despite "modernizing" influences, the Swazi monarchy has survived well over a decade of formal political independence. Indeed, since independence from Britain in 1968, the Swazi rejected the Westminster-style constitution that the British thought would appropriately "democratize" and "modernize" the nation, and reverted to something closer to their traditional system. British-style parliamentary elections were found divisive of national solidarity. King Sobhuza II dissolved Parliament in 1972. New elections were held; a new Parliament unanimously declared the Constitution unworkable, and called on the king to resolve the crisis. In 1973, the King-in-Council formally repealed the Constitution to the loud approval of a crowd of his loyal subjects. It remains to be seen whether the Swazi monarchy, surrounded as it is by republican regimes of the right and left, can survive its present king; but even if it does not, the political change is unlikely to degenerate into the orgy of genocidal violence which engulfed Rwanda.

RWANDA

Rwanda is about twice the size of Swaziland (26,000 km^2) and its population of three million is about ten times bigger, giving it an extremely high population density for tropical highlands (about 115 inhabitants per square kilometer). Not surprisingly, famines recur every few years when the rainfall is inadequate. Rwanda is more tropical than Swaziland since it lies only 2° south of the equator, but its higher elevation (mostly between 1200 and 2500 m) gives it a mild climate. The hilly landscape interspersed with lakes is among the most beautiful in the world.

As we already noted, there are a number of broad similarities between Swazi and Rwanda society (d'Hertefelt, 1965; de Heusch, 1966; Lemarchand, 1970; Maquet, 1957, 1961). Both rely on an intensive form of hoe horticulture for the bulk of their food. The main crops in Rwanda are beans, peas, sorghum, millet, maize, sweet potatoes, cassava and bananas, and the bulk of the agricultural work, as in Swaziland, is done by women. The same domesticated animals constitute the livestock of both countries: mostly cattle (the principal source of wealth and the main source of bridewealth necessary to acquire a wife) but also goats, sheep and poultry.

Like the Swazi, the Rwanda live in clusters of beehive-shaped houses scattered over hillsides. The basic residential unit in both cases is the virilocal, extended, polygynous family, and descent is traced patrilineally. Authority within the lineage is exercized by seniority in the male line.

The clans and subclans are exogamous, and marriage is by bridewealth, usually of a cow and subsidiary gifts. Poor people without cattle can substitute goats, hoes or even bride service for the cow. Divorce is possible but relatively infrequent. Polygyny is preferred and is the rule among older men of wealth and status.

Even the Rwanda monarchy, with its balance of power between the king and the queen-mother and its quasisacred conception of kingship, bears a broad similarity with that of the Swazi and many other kingdoms of Eastern Africa. This is scarcely surprising as numerous waves of migration down Eastern Africa, from the Nile Valley and the Ethiopian highlands southward, led to the diffusion of many culture traits over the entire area.

One thing, however, that Rwanda clearly lacks is nationhood. Rwanda is a sharply hierarchized society divided into three quasicaste groups: the dominant Tuzi who, until the revolution of the early 1960s, made up some 17% of the population, the Hutu peasantry with some 82%, and a small Pygmoid group, the Twa, making up 1% of the total. The monarchy, established by the pastoralist Tuzi conquerors who came down from Ethiopia in the 16th century, was entirely the political instrument of the Tuzi as an ethnic ruling elite. The traditional political system was maintained through a regime of "indirect rule" during the German and then Belgian colonial interlude. The European colonial administration kept the traditional Tuzi chiefs in place so long as they collaborated with the colonial authorities and ruled through them. For purposes of syntaxic consistency, the political and social system I shall describe will be referred to in the present tense, even though it was destroyed in 1960 by a violent Hutu revolution.

The Tuzi, who are Nitotic pastoralists similar in physical features to the Galla and other peoples of Ethiopia, are a racially and socially self-conscious ruling group, deliberately using the state machinery they monopolize (except at the lowest village level), to dominate and exploit the Hutu peasantry. They developed a genuine racist ideology, taking pride in their slender, tall stature (some 15 cm taller than the Hutu, and 30 cm taller than the Twa, on the average) and their distinctive facial features (such as their aquiline nose) and looking down on both the Hutu and Twa as coarse, ugly and inferior. The Pygmoid Twa in particular are regarded by both Tuzi and Hutu as apelike and barely human and treated with a kind of amused condescension. The Tuzi regard themselves and are regarded by others as intelligent, astute in political intrigue, born to command, refined, courageous and cruel. The Hutu are viewed by their Tuzi masters much as peasants are all over the world. They are seen as hardworking, not very clever, extrovert, irascible, unmannerly, obedient and physically strong. As for the Twa, they are considered gluttonous, loyal to their Tuzi masters, lazy and lacking in restraint (Maquet, 1961). These attributes are regarded as inherent in the nature of each group, though somewhat modified by learning; i.e. Rwanda developed a genuine brand of indigenous racism.

Each group has its fixed, ordained place in the social order. The Twa are a small pariah caste of hunters, potters, iron-workers and archers in the Tuzi army. They are strictly endogamous and are looked down upon by both Hutu and Tuzi. The Hutu till the land, tend the cattle owned by the Tuzi and are the source of the surplus production on which the Tuzi live parasitically. The Tuzi, headed by the *Mwami* (king), are the ruling aristocracy. They specialize in warfare and administration, despise manual labor and endeavor to spend as much of their lives in conspicuous leisure as possible. Tuzi women spend their time playing music, weaving fine artistic baskets and supervising domestic servants. Both Tuzi men and women avoid even walking long distances; instead they are carried in basketry litters by their Hutu or Twa servants. (So, incidentally, were often Belgian colonial officials on inspection tours before the advent of the automobile.)

"Passing" from one group to the other is difficult due to the rather strikingly different phenotypes of the three groups, but, of course, considerable miscegenation took place over generations, as Tuzi men regularly take on Hutu women as concubines (although seldom as regular wives). Marriages between Twa and Hutu are also rare and stigmatized, and a Tuzi woman would almost never condescend to marry "down" to a Hutu man. Nevertheless, there are a number of people whose fathers are Tuzi and mothers Hutu and who, over time, gradually insinuate themselves into the lower ranks of the Tuzi aristocracy. The Twa are close to being a genuine self-enclosed caste, but the boundaries between the Hutu and the Tuzi, though highly rigid and hierarchical, allow *some* upward mobility for the Hutu through miscegenation. These two groups are thus best described as quasi-castes.

The basic relationship between Tuzi lord and Hutu peasant is a feudal, paternalistic one. Underlying the entire political structure, there is, much as in medieval Europe or Japan, a vast network of patron–client ties that link individuals in private contracts where protection is exchanged for loyalty. These ties extend up and down the social hierarchy, between the Mwami and his highest courtiers, between aristocrats of different ranks and between Tuzi aristocrats and Hutu peasants and Twa servants. In the case of the Hutu peasant, he receives, besides the protection of this Tuzi master (mostly against abusive treatment from other Tuzi), one or more head of cattle to care for. In exchange for being allowed to till his fields and to keep the milk and the male offspring of the Tuzi-owned cows, the Hutu client owes his Tuzi master loyalty, banana beer and other agricultural tribute, and any labor services his patron may request. The Tuzi, in addition, keep property of the cows and all female calves.

The central political institution of this complex system of feudal exploitation is the monarchy. Unlike the Swazi king who incarnates the spirit of the nation, the Mwami of Rwanda is the head of the Tuzi nobility and the supreme ruler of the Hutu and Twa subjects. The state is not the political expression of the nation as it still is to a considerable degree among the Swazi, but the exploitative instrument of the ruling ethnic elite. The Mwami, like his Swazi counterpart, is also highly polygynous, but his polygyny reflects more his preeminent royal *droit de cuissage* than a careful policy of allying himself through marriage with commoner lineages and clans, as is the case with Swazi kings.

In theory, the Mwami's power is absolute. He possesses a preeminent right over all the land and cattle, and a right of life or death over his subjects. He appoints his heir from among his younger sons, subject, however, to official announcement by court ritualists and violent challenge by ambitious half-brothers of the heir. Finally, his person and office are surrounded by a quasidivine aura and dramatized by the careful keeping of sacred regalia, such as the royal drums to which blood offerings are regularly made, and onto which are attached the genitalia of defeated foreign rulers (d'Hertefelt, 1965).

In practice, however, the power of the Mwami is not as absolute as the Rwanda theory of divine right would have it. Royal power is counterbalanced by that of the queen-mother and her court, by the hereditary offices and privileges of his powerful Tuzi vassals, and by ritual dignitaries in charge of secret codes and rites considered essential to the continuation of the kingship (including announcing the king's heir on his death). It must be noted that such restraints as exist on royal power emanate almost entirely from the Tuzi nobility, not from the people as a whole. There is no representative organ or even informal channel for the expression of opinion for the Hutu or the Twa as there is in the Swazi "House of Commons." Hutu and Twa are governed without even a fiction of consent.

The Rwanda monarchy, in short, had not only achieved a greater measure of centralized power at the time of European conquest than was the case in Swaziland, but it was also far more coercive, exploitative, arbitrary and absolutistic. Rwanda was a multiethnic state run for the benefit of the Tuzi aristocracy. Swaziland is a genuine nation-state where royal power is subject to a wide measure of consent, hemmed in by genuine representative institutions.

The lack of legitimacy of Tuzi power on the part of the Hutu became immediately apparent when political independence from Belgium was imminent. During the Belgian trusteeship period, a new elite of Western-educated Hutu had graduated from Catholic mission schools, and it was these *évolués*, as the Belgians called them somewhat invidiously, who led the challenge against Tuzi domination. Nevertheless, they found immediate, enthusiastic and nearly unanimous support among the Hutu peasantry who saw an unprecedented opportunity to overthrow Tuzi rule. The Hutu revolution broke out in November 1959 with outbreaks of local peasant jacqueries against their Tuzi overlords (Leo Kuper, 1977). Tuzi chiefs were killed and their property burned and looted; the Tuzi retaliated. Several elections took place in 1960 and 1961 under Belgian and then United Nations supervision, and Hutu-dominated parties polled about 80% of the votes and rejected the monarchy by the same margin. (Not coincidentally, that figure corresponded closely to the Hutu percentage in the Rwanda population.) The Mwami and many Tuzi followers fled Rwanda into neighboring countries, and a "democratic republic" with a presidential regime was established in July 1962.

The new regime did not put an end to anti-Tuzi hostility, however. Hutu politicians organized campaigns of terrorism against the Tuzi, and Tuzi refugees (some 130,000 of them by the end of 1963) retaliated by mounting guerrilla raids from neighboring territories. In total, perhaps about 12,000 people, overwhelmingly Tuzi, were massacred in 1962–1963, in an escalating orgy of arson, pillage, rape, torture and mutilations characteristic of ethnic conflicts. By now, Tuzi rule over Rwanda has been completely broken, and most Tuzi are in exile. As a counterpoint to the grim story of Rwanda, independence in Burundi (another Tuzi-dominated kingdom to the south of Rwanda) was also accompanied by a genocidal orgy, but there the Hutu were the principal victims.

COERCION AND LEGITIMACY IN MULTINATIONAL STATES

Clearly, multiethnic states face a problem of legitimacy that is incommensurable with that of nation-states. It is true that the larger, the more bureaucratized, the more centralized and the more exploitative a nation-state becomes, the thinner the fiction of common kinship wears, and, thus, the more problematic legitimacy becomes. Still, common nationhood, so long as the fiction of common descent retains the appearance of plausibility, remains a powerful rationale for state power. Being plucked by people who speak your language, share your customs and values, and are, however vaguely and remotely "your people" is more tolerable than being exploited by foreign conquerors.

Perhaps the soundest reason why foreign conquest and domination are so deeply resented is that they almost invariably represent a direct threat to the biological fitness of the conquered. The very reproductive success and, hence, biological survival of the conquered group is at stake. It is no accident that military conquest is so often accompanied by the killing, enslavement and castration of males, and the raping and capturing of females for purposes of enhancing the fitness of the conquerors.

Even when conquest is relatively mild and not openly genocidal, the subordinate group in an ethnic hierarchy almost invariably "loses" more women to males of the dominant group than vice versa. Hypergamy (mating upward for women) is a fitness-enhancing strategy for women, and, therefore, subordinate-group women do not always resist being "taken over" by dominant-group men. But subordinate-group men lose fitness by loosing potential mates from their group without any hope of access to dominant-group females. It is not accidental that the most explosive aspect of interethnic relations is sexual contact across ethnic (or racial) lines; nor is the asymmetry of the resentment surprising. No group is concerned about gaining women; every group resents losing women.

Conquest and domination mean, in the first instance, a fitness loss. The loss is felt both at the individual and at the collective level. Collectively, since the offspring of subordinate-group women who mate with dominant-group men are generally "lost" to their maternal group, the subordinate group suffers a decrement of reprodutive power. Over several generations, this loss can be reflected in serious demographic changes in ethnic group ratios. Dominant groups tend to grow disproportionately. Individually, there is only a fitness reduction if the circulation of women between groups is asymmetrical, as it almost invariably is. Through the suction of women into the upper group (without getting women in return), the pool of mates for lower-group males is correspondingly reduced and, therefore, so is their fitness. Females of the subordinate group also indirectly lose fitness through the lowered fitness of their male relatives. *Individual* females who choose the hypergamous strategy, however, can *gain* fitness if their children become assimilated to the ruling group and gain access to upper-group privileges (including polygyny). This sex asymmetry in fitness strategies in ethnically stratified societies often creates tension *between* the sexes, *within* subordinate groups. The female option of fitness maximization through hypergamy is deeply resented by subordinate-group males.

How do multiethnic states, or "plural societies" as they have also been called, cope with this problem of legitimacy? The range of solutions is limited, and is determined by two main variables: (1) the degree to which one ethny (or coalition of ethnies) monopolizes power and privilege to the exclusion of all others, and (2) the degree to which citizens of plural societies are incorporated into the state as individuals or as members of their respective collectivities (Leo Kuper and M.G. Smith, 1969).

On the first variable, some multiethnic states, like traditional Rwanda or contemporary South Africa, represent one extreme where one ethnic (or racial) group single-handedly monopolizes power and actively excludes other groups from participation. These polities are classic cases of imperial conquest states or colonial societies, in which the state is the political arm of the ruling ethnic group. At the other extreme are a few polities like Belgium or Switzerland, where several ethnies coexist according to some negotiated modus vivendi, but where none dominates the others. Such states, called "consociational democracies" by Lijphart (1968a) or "proportional democracies" by Lehmbruch (1967), are actually relatively few. Since they are not held together by coercion, the maintenance of a working political compromise between ethnies is always a delicate and chancy endeavor. In between these extremes are a number of states where one ethny or a small coalition of ethnies plays a preponderant role in the state, but is more or less willing to share power with other groups or, at least, to coopt the elites of some of the other groups. Ethiopia, the Soviet Union, the United States and Israel are a few examples.

The second variable is one of state policy and jural status, and its importance has often been underrated, although it has been of central interest to the scholars in the "plural society" tradition (Leo Kuper, 1957, 1965, 1974; Leo Kuper and M. G. Smith, 1969; Lowenthal, 1972; Schermerhorn,

1970; Michael G. Smith, 1965a; Smooha, 1975, 1978; van den Berghe, 1973b). The key criterion here is whether the state and the legal system give official recognition to group membership or not. Some states, for example France, incorporate their citizens purely on an individual basis. They distinguish between citizens and foreigners, but all citizens are equal in the eyes of the law, subject only to qualifications of age (e.g. children are disfranchised), mental competence, criminal record and, until recently, sex. The state, at least in principle, does not care whether you are Catholic or Protestant, white or black, noble or commoner. There are no provisions in the legal system giving special status to any ethnic, religious, linguistic or racial subgroup of citizens within the state; all citizens (with the above qualifications of age, mental competence and so on) have equal rights and obligations; their relationship to the state is *legally* identical. Any racial or ethnic distinctions that may exist are supposed to be ignored by the state and all of its agencies.

The opposite case is, of course, that of states that officially recognize different communities within it and entrench that recognition in legislation giving different groups different rights and obligations. This differential incorporation according to group membership within the state can be more or less extensive in scope, more or less discriminatory or benign in intent and practice, and more or less imposed by force or achieved by consensus and negotiation. The mere official recognition given by the state and its legal organs to collectivities within the state, whatever its intent, has profoundly different implications and consequences from those that flow from a legal system based purely upon individual rights.

Actually, most states resort, to a greater or lesser extent, to differential incorporation by criteria of group membership. They include nearly all colonial and imperial regimes, most settlers societies like Australia, South Africa and the United States, and most multinational states like Belgium, Nigeria, India and the Soviet Union. Soviet internal passports have a space for "nationality" (meaning not "Soviet Citizen"—but "Armenian," "Jew," "Russian," "Ukrainian" or whatever); the United States still treats American Indians for some purposes as members of foreign nations with special land tenure, fishing, hunting and other rights determined by treaty; South Africa makes "race" the basis of a vast system of legal discrimination known as apartheid; Israel pigeonholes its citizens into different religious communities and forces people to abide by Islamic, Christian or Jewish religious law regardless of whether one is even religious; Belgium forces its citizens to opt for one language group and categorizes people and municipalities as either Flemish or Walloon (with a bilingual option for Brussels); India recognizes Harijans ("untouchables") as a special group deserving reserved seats in Parliament and special protection because of past discrimination, and so on.

The list of countries whose legal system entrenches differential incorporation is quite long; it would probably include at least two-thirds or three-fourths of the members of the United Nations. In some cases (such as South

Africa), group discrimination is both malign and all-encompassing; in others it only affects small minorities and circumscribed aspects of life, and it is supposedly benign in intent. However, the sheer official recognition of group differences in rights, privileges and relationship to the state tends to perpetuate (even to create) pluralism and to exacerbate political conflicts between ethnic groups. The case against differential incorporation has been argued eloquently by Glazer (1975) for the United States, by Srinivas (1969) for India, by Leo Kuper (1957, 1965, 1974) for South Africa and by many thoughtful and well-meaning people all over the world. However benevolent its stated intent, "affirmative discrimination" (to use Glazer's phrase) typically boomerangs because it reinforces the ethnic boundaries it supposedly tries to erase.*

THE THREE TYPES OF MULTIETHNIC STATES

If we dichotomize the two variables of degree of ethnic monopolization of power (ethnically exclusive or inclusive) and mode of incorporation into the state (individual or collective), and if we combine the two variables into a single schema, we end up with the two-by-two figure of Schema I. A striking but trivial feature of Schema I is the emptiness of Cell A. In theory, a ruling group could remain ethnically exclusive and retain a monopoly of power and yet treat everyone equally as individuals and on the basis of merit. It could do so if it managed to define merit in such a way as to maintain a monopoly of it. In practice, no ruling group manages to do so, though some go quite far in trying. The practical options of an ethnic group ruling a multiethnic state are to retain a monopoly of power by officially and legally discriminating against other groups, and thus to form a classical imperial or colonial system (Cell B) or to move, however slowly, reluctantly, and gradually toward a Cell C or Cell D situation. The logical end-result of the latter option is the end of ethnic domination by one group, though sometimes that process can be slowed down through astute and well-tried techniques of cooptation and selective assimilation of elites from subordinate groups, of fomenting conflict between subordinate groups, and so on.

Let us briefly examine each of the three types of situation represented by Cells B, C and D. Cell B is the classical colonial or imperial system in which one ethny dominates the others. I shall examine this type of polity in greater detail in Chapter 5, for there are a number of basic similarities in the way colonial or imperial societies are organized. If we define colonialism as long-distance imperialism over noncontiguous territories, then we find that colonialism is really an extreme case of imperialism.

---

*It has been eloquently argued by the theorists of "consociationalism" (Lehmbruch, 1967; Lijphart, 1968a, 1977a) that the institutionalization of ethnic (or racial) criteria of group membership by the state need not be discriminatory and invidious, and can lead to stable and successful democratic pluralism. In this respect, the consociationalists clash with the "conflict pluralists" (Leo Kuper, 1974; Leo Kuper and M. G. Smith, 1969; M. G. Smith, 1965a; Smooha, 1975; van den Berghe, 1973b) who tend to be pessimistic about the possibility of democratic pluralism. We shall return to this central issue in Chapter 9.

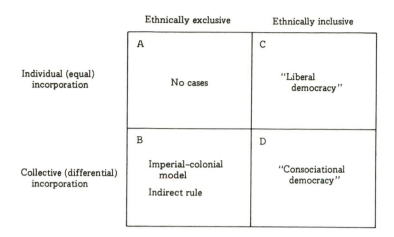

SCHEMA I. Ethnic exclusiveness and mode of incorporation.

Since colonialism is usually imposed on ethnies that are very different both physically and culturally from the conquerors, the social gulf between rulers and ruled is all the greater and the more unbreachable, and the restraints on exploitation are practically nonexistent. In addition, colonialized societies are typically smaller-scaled (stateless or small states) and/or at a simpler level of technology than their colonial masters; otherwise they would not have been conquered. Therefore, colonial regimes are maximally coercive and exploitative.

The techniques for ruling empires and colonies are basically the same all over the world and have been independently rediscovered many times. Conquered populations can either be assimilated to the conquering group, selectively at the elite level or in toto, through persuasion or coercion, gradually or brutally; or ethnic separation can be tolerated, encouraged or maintained by force, and conquered groups can be administered through a system of indirect rule. Native institutions are modified to suit the conqueror, but otherwise left as undisturbed as possible; religious, linguistic and cultural diversity is tolerated; and the local elite is allowed to keep some of its privileges in exchange for becoming auxiliaries of the imperial regime. The native ruling class, if such existed before, is allowed a small share of the spoils for doing the dirty job of running the empire cheaply for the benefit of the conquerors. Where no such native ruling class existed before the conquest (as in stateless societies), the colonial regime often created "native chiefs" who, in time, came to form a pseudotraditional system invented in the conqueror's image of what a native society ought to be like.

The term "liberal democracy" applied to Cell C of Schema I is, of course, a misnomer. No state, whether precapitalist, capitalist or socialist, is a real democracy, however much it may claim that label. Nor is the ideology of individualism that underlies this concept of the state a monopoly of 19th-century European liberalism. However, the misnomer is so firmly entrenched in common parlance and in our political thinking, that no satisfactory alternative term exists. (The Marxist term, "bourgeois democracy," to distinguish it from "people's democracy" is no more satisfactory. It merely doubles the number of misnomers, for a "people's democracy" is no more a democracy than a bourgeois one.)

The type of society in Cell C is one composed of several ethnic groups, but where two basic conditions prevail:

1. The ruling group is a *class* drawn from several ethnies; that is, no ethny has a monopoly or near-monopoly of power.
2. The state officially recognizes only individuals; it may either actively promote "national integration" or tolerate cultural and linguistic pluralism; but it does nothing to give pluralism official recognition, to grant certain communities special rights or to entrench pluralism in legislation.

In pure form such situations are rare, first, because historical circumstances usually give one of the ethnic groups in the state a disproportionate if not exclusive share of power, and, second, because the state is often forced, or finds it convenient, to recognize the reality of ethnic differences and to accede to demands for separation and special treatment.

Sometimes it is the dominant majority that seeks to maintain a measure of exclusiveness; more often minorities seek special status out of fear of assimilation. Contrary to classical colonial societies where the dominant ethnic group is a minority (often a very small one of less than 10% or even less than 1% of the total population), in a "liberal democracy," if there is a dominant ethnic group, it is a numerical majority.* A dominant ethnic majority can therefore claim that it rules not by virtue of ethnic exclusivism but according to "democratic" principles of majority rule. Such a claim leaves the minorities with little option other than to join the majority by assimilation (if they are permitted to do so) or to claim special protection and special rights to retain their separateness (and thereby also their subordination as a minority group).

Even though, in most "liberal democracies," the state takes some steps in recognizing ethnic diversity (such as enumerating people by ethnic, religious or language group in its population census, giving state subsidies to ethnically, linguistically or religiously segregated schools), there has long been a general trend in Europe, Latin America and other states under European influence, to move away from recognition of ethnicity (and religion). This was part of a trend toward individualism, universalism and secularism

*In much of the U.S. literature on race and ethnic relations, the terms "majority" and "minority" are used as synonyms for "dominant" and "subordinate," respectively. Since many, if not most, dominant ethnic groups have been small minorities and subordinate groups are often overwhelming majorities, the use of this terminology is confusing and ethnocentrically American. Therefore, when I speak of minority and majority, I shall refer only to numerical proportions and not to relative power positions.

that gained momentum since the French Revolution in the late 18th century. Various groups, such as Jews in Europe, the Burakumin in Japan and slaves in the Western Hemisphere, which had hitherto been subject to a discriminatory legal status were "emancipated" as a result of the Englightenment. Assimilation into the rest of the population did not necessarily follow emancipation, but, at least, the legal possibility of assimilation now existed, and the expectation generally was that assimilation would come in the end. The ideal of the liberal state is assimilationist.

Recently, that is, since the 1960s, there seems to have been a resurgence of ethnic sentiment in many countries that were long thought of as fairly unitary or at least on an irreversible course of assimilation. Such was the case, for instance, with the various ethnic racial and ethnic movements started by "Black Power" in the United States. Even textbook examples of nation-states, like France, now experience separatist or, at least, regionalist movements in Corsica, Brittany, Occitania and the Basque country. Whether this reversion to more ethnic pluralism is a temporary fad or a longer-range process of disaggregation of multinational states remains to be seen. The states that seem to be in the most trouble, such as Lebanon, Canada, Britain (with Northern Ireland) and Belgium belong in Cell D, as we shall see presently.

Few states, then, qualify as pure "liberal democracy"—pure in the sense that they give no official recognition whatsoever to ethnic, racial, religious or language groups within their borders. The states, however, that lean in the liberal assimilationist direction also tend to be the ones like the United States (for whites), Israel (for Jews), Australia (for whites) and Brazil, whose aboriginal populations are small and/or have been extensively wiped out or expelled, and whose main ethnic groups are territorially dispersed immigrants of fairly recent origin. Such, at least, is the typical matrix for a successful melting pot.

By contrast, societies in Cell D are often, though not always, characterized by the fact that their principal ethnic groups are both indigenous and non-sympatric. They share a single state apparatus, but each ethnic group has its own turf. Switzerland, Belgium, Yugoslavia, the Soviet Union, India and Nigeria are a few examples. There are, however, some would-be consociational democracies where the territorial separation is not as clear-cut, and where the constituent ethnic groups are immigrants rather than indigenes. Lebanon, Trinidad, Guiana and Canada are cases in point.

The immigrant-indigenous distinction, while useful up to a point (Lieberson, 1961), breaks down in the end, because if one pushes it back far enough, everyone is an immigrant, or, conversely, every group regards itself as indigenous vis-à-vis groups of more recent arrival. However, the degree to which ethnic groups are sympatric or not is extremely important in terms of practical consequences. The more territorialized ethnic groups are, and the larger and more economically viable ethnic territories are, (1) the less the existence of separate ethnic groups can be ignored by the state; (2) the more ethnic boundaries are likely to be self-perpetuating; (3) the less likely the groups are to assimilate or melt together; and (4) the less reason they have to stick together in a single state.

"Consociational democracies" have in common with "liberal democracies" that, though made up of several ethnies, the ruling group is a class drawn from several ethnies rather than overwhelmingly from a single ethny. The ruling group is a grand coalition of elites sharing power and distributing spoils to their ethnic constituencies. Consociational democracies also share with liberal democracies a façade of representative and parliamentary institutions, elections, political parties and the other paraphernalia of states (capitalist, socialist or Third World) that make a pretense of being "democratic." Unlike liberal democracies, however, consociational democracies *institutionalize* ethnicity in the political and jural structure of the state. They officially recognize ethnies, accord them proportional representation in state organs, run segregated school systems, draw internal boundaries according to linguistic lines, categorize their citizens by ethnic affiliation, and grant each group a special legal status. Indeed, they go a long way in forcing everybody to fit willy-nilly into one of the cells of the multiethnic mold.

Most states that embark on such an official policy of recognizing and entrenching ethnic pluralism are quite fragile. Switzerland is perhaps the one successful example, for reasons to be examined in Chapter 9, but the unfortunate cases of such states that have exploded in violent conflict or that constantly seem to be on the brink of doing so are many: Nigeria, Lebanon, Cyprus, Pakistan-Bangladesh, Sri Lanka, Guiana, Canada, Zaïre and numerous others. The reason for the instability of consociational democracies is simple. When confronted with escalating demands for ethnic separatism, the state faces the basic options of repressing such demands by force (and thereby damaging its democratic façade) or of yielding to these demands (thereby encouraging their further escalation, and taking another step toward the dissolution of the multinational state).

Now it is time to take a closer look at different types of multiethnic states and at the problems they present.

SUGGESTED READINGS

Much of the literature on race and ethnic relations deals with inequality. Among the best general treatments of the subject are the texts by Francis (1976), Mason (1971), Schermerhorn (1970) and Shibutani and Kwan (1965).

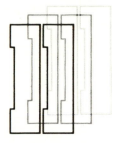

SOME
RECURRENT
SITUATIONS

COLONIAL EMPIRES

Colonialism is a special form of imperialism. It is imperialism over distant peoples who usually live in noncontiguous, overseas territories and who therefore look quite different from their conquerors, speak unrelated languages, and are so culturally alien to their colonial masters as to provide little basis for mutual understanding. In addition to all these factors that make for a maximum gap between conquerors and conquered, the latter are typically at a strong technological disadvantage (otherwise they would not as easily have been conquered), and this disadvantage readily becomes translated, in the ideology of the conqueror, as proof of inferiority and as a justification for continued domination.

All these characteristics of the "colonial situation" (Balandier, 1963) make the colonial form of imperialism an extreme one, not only in terms of brutality of conquest, exploitation and domination, but also in terms of social distance between masters and subjects, rigidity of ethnic boundaries, bipolarity of living standards and elaboration of self-serving ideologies. Colonialism is imperialism writ large; imperialism without the restraints of common bonds of history, culture, religion, marriage and blood that often exist when conquest takes place between neighbors. Colonialism is imperialism set in the concrete of a rigid, castelike system of ethnic relations.

In the last analysis, what make for the special character of the colonial situation is the perception by the conqueror that he is dealing with totally unrelated, alien and, therefore, inferior people. Colonials are treated as people totally beyond the pale of kin selection and as complete strangers whose very humanity is sometimes called into question, but toward whom, in any case, feelings of sympathy, solidarity and commonness of history and destiny seem ludicrously inappropriate. "They" are simply not like "us." Even the most fundamental appeals to common humanity seem to need qualification in colonial situations. "They," supposedly, do not have the same needs as "we" do; "they" feel differently, "they" are, in short, a separate, and inferior, breed—different from "us" in *nature*. A saying of Andean Mestizos concerning Indians puts it well: *El índio es al animal que mas se parece al hombre.* ("The Indian is the animal which most closely resembles man.") Not unexpectedly, racism is the ideology of colonialism, *par excellence*, although racism is not confined to colonial situations, nor are all colonial regimes equally strongly and explicitly racist.

TYPES OF COLONY AND COLONIALISM

At this point, we must clear up a terminological confusion. The terms "colony" and "colonialism" have two very different meanings—one much older than the other. By far the older meaning of "colony," and one which is still in common usage, both in ecology and in common parlance, is a group of organisms that have spread to a new habitat. Thus, we say that a plant "colonizes" an island. By extension, in reference to humans, a colony has long meant a branch of an ethny that has "hived off" and established a new residence, e.g. the German colony in Nebraska or the American colony in Paris. In these cases, no conquest is implied: merely residence apart from the parent population in the midst of people from different ethnies.

A colony, in the sense of a political dependency of a "mother country" (note the kin terminology) acquired by a process of both settlement and conquest, is a special meaning that became more widespread with the maritime expansion of Europe, starting in the late 15th century, although it is also used in reference to antiquity (e.g. the Greek colonies of Italy) and the renaissance (e.g. the Venetian colonies in the Adriatic). Even then, a distinction came to be made between the "colonies of settlement" and "colonies of exploitation," with the terms "colonialism" being reserved for the system prevailing in the latter.

"Colonies of settlement" such as the English and French colonies of North America, Australia and New Zealand were principally nontropical territories with climatic and ecological conditions favorable to European settlement but marginal to their aboriginal populations of hunters and gatherers and simple horticulturalists. The latter were, therefore, sparse and often nomadic, and could be easily displaced or exterminated to make room for European settlers with a more advanced military, medical and agricultural technology favoring rapid demographic growth and economic development. Colonies of settlement thus gradually became mere extensions of Europe, which in time became politically independent of their "mother countries" but still retained many economic, social and cultural ties with them.

Even before colonies of settlement became politically sovereign, their European populations were treated quite differently from other "colonials." White colonials may have chafed at what they considered to be discriminatory taxation, and exclusion from top political positions; they may have resented being regarded as country bumpkins isolated from the main center of "high culture." But, however "unfairly" treated, they remained kith and kin of the home population—cousins in the diaspora, *not* subjects to be exploited. The relationship between the colonial office at home and settlers in the colonies always remained fundamentally different from those between the colonial office and dark-skinned natives. With white colonials, relations were always of the intraethnic type, and exploitation and domination were restrained by law, custom, religion and countless civilities. There prevailed, in fact, a system of extended kin selection that survived even the most extreme tests of rebellion. The American War of Independence, for instance, was fought with remarkable civility, chivalry and restraint compared to, say, the Zulu Wars or the Ashanti Wars. There was much bitterness between loyalists and rebels, to be sure, but it was the bitterness of family quarrels—the bitterness of a divorce settlement followed by the necessity of reconciliation because of the common children.

None of these considerations prevailed in the relationship between colonial office and natives, nor indeed between natives and European settlers. "Colonies of exploitation," as the term indicates, were meant to be exploited. The principal restraints were those imposed by poverty and lack of resources of the colony, by difficulties of access, by inefficiency of administration, by astuteness of natives in evading exactions and, occasionally, by long-range considerations of depletion of colonial assets. Even long-range self-interest of the colonizer was not always a guarantee against ruthlessly destructive plunder, as the history of most Spanish American colonies shows.

Correspondence between local Spanish colonial officials and their superiors in Spain complaining about a gradual decline in annual tribute payments from Indians stresses one recurrent theme: *Se están acabando los indios*. ("Indians are being finished off.") Yet, the appalling conditions of forced labor in the silver and mercury mines, the textile mills and the plantations, which were emptying vast stretches of territory of their Indian population, were never substantially ameliorated. Only at the very end of the Spanish colonial period, in the late 18th century, did the Indian population begin to recover from colonial depredations. The colonial orange was squeezed dry with little concern about long-range depletion.

The Catholic Church repeatedly tried to intervene, pleading that Indians too had immortal souls, but to little avail. Indeed, monasteries themselves became prominent exploiters of Indian labor, under the guise of saving souls. With or without souls, Indians were clearly *not* kith and kin, as far as the Spaniards were concerned. Inhuman treatment was routine, and Indian uprisings were repressed with ruthless ferocity, compared to the rather genteel fighting that characterized the wars of independence against the creoles in the 1810s and early 1820s.

THE ECOLOGICAL, DEMOGRAPHIC AND TECHNOLOGICAL CONTEXT OF COLONIALISM

Whether a colonial territory becomes a colony of settlement or a colony of exploitation hinges principally on a set of ecological and technological conditions. The typical colony of settlement, as far as the expansion of

Europe since the 18th century is concerned, has had one salient characteristic: it has been *nontropical*. From a biased, Eurocentric perspective, the
broad "temperate zone" between the Arctic and the Tropics seems to present
such obvious advantages as to make its desirability self-evident. In fact, the
opposite is true. Man is, by nature, a tropical or subtropical animal. Like
all other primates, the first three or four million years of hominid evolution
took place in a tropical or subtropical environment, and the ability to survive
in colder climates had to await the development of more advanced technologies.

However, several thousand years of cultural and biological adaptation put
the exploding European population at a competitive advantage, relative to
the indigenes, in the nontropical parts of the world. Much of that advantage
was technological. European societies, by the turn of the 16th century, and
increasingly thereafter, were the most advanced in the use of animal traction
and wind and water power, in the development of metallurgy, weaponry
and navigation, and in intense plow agriculture of nontropical lands. Only
China and Japan could have competed with Europe in the early phase of
colonial expansion (up to the 18th century), but, for complex historical
reasons, they did not expand their territories as Europe did. (However, in
China, there was a lot of agricultural colonization of new lands, permitting
rapid population increase.) Admiral Cheng Ho's expeditions in the first four
decades of the 15th century proved that China could have conquered much
of the world then, but it did not (Braudel, 1973). Nor, be it noted, were
China and Japan conquered by Europe. It is certainly no accident that the
only major part of the world that escaped European conquest was much like
Europe in both climate and technological level. That is, it was inhabited by
a densely settled population of advanced, nontropical agriculturalists with
a sophisticated technology. This was a setting in which Europeans were at
little or no competitive advantage until the 19th century.

An advanced technology of production made possible an entire complex
of interrelated developments which, in combination, gave Europe a tremendous competitive edge over much of the rest of the world. In the late
Middle Ages intensive deep-plow agriculture with crop rotation and fertilization combined with increasing use of wind and water power and an
advanced iron metallurgy to create a series of social transformations. These
included a population explosion, a production surplus, a centralization of
power in states of increasing size and complexity, a vast improvement of
military and naval technology, the growth of cities as centers of long-distance trade and handicraft production, in short, the human and material
resources and the technological skills to expand and conquer (Bloch,
1939–1940; Cipolla, 1965; White, 1962).

Culture and technology, extremely important though they were, tell only
part of the story of the colonial expansion of Europe. Biology also played
a role. Specifically, Europeans were biologically adapted to nontropical
climates. In tropical areas, they often were at a biological disadvantage in
relation to better-adapted natives. Skin pigmentation for protection against

skin cancer and the gene for sickle-cell anemia conferring some protection against malaria in heterozygotic carriers are two examples of human genetic adaptation to the tropics. Until the advent of the late 19th century medicine, the tropics were, literally, a white man's grave.*

In the Western Hemisphere, however, Europeans had a tremendous advantage. They unwittingly, and sometimes even wittingly, carried with them bacteriological warfare, being vectors of diseases such as smallpox, influenza and measles, to which European populations had become largely immune but against which Amerindian populations were unprotected (McNeill, 1976). A history of human migration and colonization must therefore include an important ecological and epidemiological component.

European settlers, when they emigrated to temperate climates, came biologically and culturally equipped for successful competition against aborigines for whom the habitat was marginal, given their level of technology. An advanced agricultural society permitting high population densities could (and did) easily swamp thinly settled nomads who were typically hunters and gatherers, or primitive agriculturalists. In such environments (e.g. Canada, the United States, Australia, New Zealand, the extreme southern tip of Africa and the southern half of South America), the European settlers multiplied through immigration and successful reproduction, while the natives were virtually exterminated through imported disease and warfare or pushed back to the least-desirable areas. The demographic expansion of Europeans was doubly easy and rapid in the Western Hemisphere through the selective impact of epidemic diseases.

Looking at European expansion in ecological terms, the Europeans were suddenly able, through the development of reliable ocean navigation, to fill a vast *empty niche*. Luckily for them, there was a vast area in North America, and, in the Southern Hemisphere, in Australia, the Southern tip of Africa and the Southern half of South America, which was very thinly settled by nomads or seminomads who were either hunters and gatherers, or very marginal horticulturalists. Equipped with a technology of nontropical, advanced plow agriculture, European settlers could explode demographically in that favorable habitat. The demographic success story of the French Canadians in the 19th century is a case in point of how reproductively successful a population can be when it suddenly encounters an empty niche. With relatively little immigration from Europe, the French population of the Province of Québec multiplied thirteenfold (from 92,000 in 1771 to 1.2 million in 1871) in the century after British conquest. And it did so in a situation of complete labor self-sufficiency. It produced its own food, shelter and other necessities without any slave labor. Even the servant class was of European stock.

---

*The bark of a Peruvian tropical tree later called cinchona was chewed as a malaria preventative since around 1630, but the commercial mass cultivation of a strain of cinchona producing a medically effective quinine was first successfully accomplished by the Dutch in the East Indies, in the late 1860s, barely a decade before the European scramble for Africa.

The Chinese, Koreans and Japanese would probably have been equally successful in filling that empty niche, had they crossed the Pacific. Their ships and navigational techniques in the late 15th century were only slightly inferior to those of Europe. The Europeans accidentally stumbled into the empty niche while looking for a new route to Asia, and it was not until the 17th and 18th century that they really began to fill it—and not until the mid-19th century that the expansion process was virtually completed. By the 17th century, European naval and firearms technology had vastly outstripped that of the Far East (Cipolla, 1965).

COLONIALISM IN THE TROPICS

In the tropics or subtropics, the story was quite different. There Europeans were at a biological disadvantage, especially in the Old World tropics where they were highly susceptible to a wide range of tropical diseases such as malaria, sleeping sickness and yellow fever, without the advantage of carrying with them diseases capable of devastating native populations. Migration within the Old World had been sufficient to create roughly comparable levels of immunity to the great epidemic killers that ravaged Amerindians, mostly influenza, measles and smallpox. In the Old World tropics, Europeans could not rely as much on racially selective bacterial allies as they could in the New World tropics.

Besides the epidemiological barriers to European settlement in the tropics, there were also major cultural barriers. By and large, Europeans had an overwhelming superiority in the means of violence through the possession of firearms, but this advantage was greatly mitigated by three major factors:

1. The European presence was always demographically precarious. On the one hand, Europeans had such a high mortality rate in many tropical areas that their fitness was sharply reduced. In tropical Africa, for instance, even with the great medical advances of the 20th century, the European population never achieved replacement levels of reproduction. Europeans were constantly replenished through immigration, and very few European women successfully reproduced in the African tropics. On the other hand, many parts of the American, African and Asian tropics and subtropics were densely settled when Europeans arrived. It was thus very difficult for Europeans to overcome their position as a small minority, often of less than 1% of the total population.
2. In many parts of the tropics and subtropics, the Europeans encountered highly organized state societies running into hundreds of thousands or even millions of members who, therefore, could often put up stiff resistance to European conquest. Europeans overcame part of that disadvantage by relying extensively on native troops equipped with firearms, but these native auxiliaries often rebelled and the wide distribution of firearms almost inevitably meant their spread among native societies. Indeed, in many cases (such as West Africa and New Zealand), it was

European trade that introduced large numbers of firearms, sometimes with devastating consequences to native societies that started using firearms in fighting each other. In any case, Europeans in much of the tropics were not only vastly outnumbered, they also faced cohesively organized societies of considerable size, often capable of fielding armies of thousands of disciplined, trained soldiers.

3. The competitive advantage of European production technology was seriously reduced by tropical conditions. The two main forms of colonial production, mining and plantation agriculture, remained entirely dependent on vast quantities of non-European labor. European agricultural technology was ill-adapted to tropical conditions, and the main contribution of Europeans in subsistence agriculture was the carrying of food crops from one part of the tropics to another. Transportation technology was revolutionized by European conquest, but the European impact on basic agricultural production was much less dramatic. By the 20th century, European preventive medicine and hygiene produced a population explosion, but the main beneficiaries of it in terms of fitness were the tropical natives, not their colonial masters. As for the ability of Europeans to survive in the tropics with their own technology and *labor*, it seems to have been quite limited.

Attempts at creating self-sufficient European colonies in warm climates generally failed, at least until the advent of modern medicine in the 20th century. Costa Rica is the only New World tropical country that is of predominantly European stock. Even in a relatively favorable, quasi-Mediterranean climate, such as that of the Cape Colony at the southern tip of Africa, the success was only partial. Whites managed to expand demographically and displace the native Bushman and Hottentot nomads, but within six years of their initial settlement in 1652, they were importing slave labor (De Kiewiet, 1941; Marquard, 1962; van den Berghe, 1965).

It might be argued that the availability of native or slave labor saved Europeans the trouble of trying very hard, but, outside the tropics, European settlers (who could also have imported and used slave labor) managed to do quite well. Yet, almost nowhere in the tropics, with the exception of Costa Rica, did a self-reliant European colony develop. When the aboriginal population was wiped out, as in the Caribbean Islands, slaves or indentured labor was imported from other tropical areas. Attempts at using European labor in the tropics or subtropics (as in Hawaii) were uniformly unsuccessful.

In short, European colonialism in the tropics was characterized by the following:

1. an inability of the European population to reproduce to replacement levels, much less to expand demographically at the expense of the natives;

2. European political control obtained largely through a superior technology of violence and of transportation;

3. complete reliance on the labor of tropical populations, native or imported, for the exploitation natural resources (mining, timber and agriculture).

In the last analysis, European colonialism in the tropics hinged on the availability of a supply of labor from people acclimatized to work hard in hot weather. Without such a supply, colonial exploitation was impossible. The two most desirable properties of labor were cheapness and docility, each of these being determined in turn by a multiplicity of factors. Nevertheless, certain generalities emerge from the wide variety of local conditions. Basically, there were two broad types of tropical colonies of exploitation: colonies in which the bulk of the labor force consisted of natives and colonies relying on an imported slave or indentured labor force.

The first type was most successful where the native population was already sedentary, agricultural and relatively dense at the time of conquest and, preferably, where it was already a peasantry—i.e. the exploited primary producers of a stratified, state-organized society. When the Europeans conquered complex native states with an established peasantry, their principal difficulty was the conquest itself. Once political domination was achieved, however, the rest was relatively easy, for two basic ingredients necessary for effective exploitation were already in place:

1. an administrative machinery to collect tribute, organize labor for public works, and so on;
2. a peasant population with the following attractive qualities:
   a. easily controllable by being sedentary and attached to the soil;
   b. cheap, since it was abundantly available for the taking, without having to be bought or transported, and since it fed and reproduced itself;
   c. docile, since it was already used to being taxed and exploited by native rulers and subject to domination by a ruling class; and
   d. productive, since it was acclimatized to hard work under local conditions.

Such a situation characterized the highlands of Meso-America and the Andes, much of North, West and Central Africa and nearly all of tropical Asia. As I shall show presently, these conditions led to the more or less independent development of very similar systems of domination, to what may be considered the prototypical "colonial situation" (Balandier, 1963; Lugard, 1929; Maunier, 1949).

Slavery (or indenture, the 19th century substitute for chattel slavery) led to a substantially different type of colonialism to which I shall devote the next chapter. All the colonies based principally on chattel slavery have a general family resemblance—long noted by many students of slavery (Freyre, 1964; Genovese, 1965, 1969a, 1974; Patterson, 1967; van den Berghe, 1967). Basically slave colonies developed where there were not enough natives to supply labor demand, or where the natives were unavailable or unsuitable to the tasks required of them. Only then did the conquerors resort to the more expensive expedient of importing and buying its colonial labor force. Slaves not only had to be captured or bought and transported (often with high risk of mortality and morbidity), but they also had to be fed and sustained, and they frequently did not reproduce to replacement levels. In the Western Hemisphere, only in the English colonies of North America, i.e. outside of the tropical zone, were slaves sufficiently reproductive to increase their numbers without continued massive importation well into the 19th century.

Slavery, then, was an expensive solution, and thus a last resort. It was only developed when natives were unavailable or unsuitable, and that meant basically where they belonged to nomadic or seminomadic societies of hunters and gatherers, primitive stateless horticulturalists or, occasionally, pastoralists. These modes of production sustained only low densities of population (often well under one inhabitant per square kilometer), and thus natives were few to start with. In addition, nomadism meant that such aborigines as existed were mobile, elusive and difficult to control. They typically had a vast hinterland into which they could escape labor exploitation.

Even when expeditions were mounted to catch them (as the Portuguese tried in Brazil, for example), they so frequently escaped, committed suicide or died of disease that these attempts soon proved abortive. Furthermore, nomads typically are unused to being exploited since their own societies are often relatively egalitarian, ill-adapted to steady hard labor and lacking in the skills useful to colonial exploiters (as cultivators, for example). They are, in short, lovers of freedom and make very poor colonial underlings. Not unexpectedly, they are regarded by their conquerors as lazy, shiftless and unreliable, as an obstacle to development and as a nuisance to be displaced. The dictum of the American frontier, fondly quoted by President Theodore Roosevelt, expressed that attitude succinctly: "The only good Indian is a dead Indian."

CLASSICAL COLONIALISM

What we may call classical colonialism—the exploitation of native, tropical populations by small European minorities—developed principally in three areas of the world: first in tropical America, especially in the Spanish colonies and principally in the densely settled highlands of Meso-America and the Andes; then in Asia, from India to Indochina and Indonesia, and lastly in Africa where it only came in the late 19th century but quickly engulfed nearly all of the continent.

The historians, accustomed to steeping themselves in the detailed peculiarities of a given place and time, and to stressing the uniqueness of each, may shudder at the thought of lumping together 16th-century Peru and 20th-century Nigeria, 18th-century India and 19th-century Angola. Much has been written about the differences in colonial policy between the main colonial powers. The Latin Catholic colonizers (Portugal, Spain and France) were, on the whole, more racially tolerant, more assimilationist and more rigidly centralized than their Protestant rivals (England, Holland and Germany) who were more openly racist, made fewer attempts to impose their language and culture, and tended to rule more pragmatically, according to local conditions.

Native cultures ranged from complex, stratified, imperial structures like those of the Moghuls in India and the Inca in the Andes, to village-level, stateless, egalitarian societies like the Ibo of Nigeria, and the Masai and Kikuyu of Kenya—with chieftaincies and states of all sizes and degrees of complexity in between. Climatic conditions ranged from relatively benign for Europeans, for example in the Kenya highlands and in the high-altitude regions of Mexico, Peru, Ecuador, Colombia and Bolivia, to lethal—until the use of quinine against malaria—such as the coast of West Africa. (Kwameh Nkrumah, leader of the Ghana independence movement, jokingly suggested that Africans should erect a monument to the anopheles mosquito, the vector of malaria.)

These differences, and many more besides, help explain differences among colonial territories, and, of course, a detailed understanding of any one of them presupposes an intimate familiarity with its history, its indigenous cultures, its ecological conditions, its economic base and the policies of the colonial power. Nevertheless, underlying these considerable differences from colony to colony, certain uniformities can be detected that justify speaking of classical colonialism as an ideal type. Our concern here is not with explaining the details and the idiosyncrasies, but with discerning the commonalities.

Since the purpose, often explicit, of keeping a colony was to exploit it, the relative success of the enterprise hinged on securing and controlling native labor (for without it exploitation was well-nigh impossible, or, at any rate, much costlier) and keeping the cost of that control as low as possible. The basic solutions to this twofold problem of cost of administration and control of natives were few and simple and, therefore, independently reinvented time and again. The basic set of colonial equations was

European = dear

Native = cheap

To it, the entire political, economic and social structure of the colonial territory could be reduced. It followed from it that successful administration of a tropical dependency had to be done with as *few* Europeans as possible. Europeans were expensive to bring in and to maintain at the princely level to which they quickly became accustomed in their colonies; they were notoriously susceptible to disease and alcoholism, and they were allergic to hard work. Therefore, the fewer the Europeans, the more cheaply the territory could be managed. Europeans, therefore, must be saved strictly for key positions of command and supervision that could not be entrusted to natives and retained at a minimum of posts requiring technical expertise and for which natives could not readily be trained. The classical colony was run with a skeletal crew of highly paid, highly privileged and often highly skilled Europeans who invariably constituted a more or less closed ruling caste.

European colonials in the tropics adopted a palatial lifestyle, far superior to what most of them could have hoped to have achieved back home. Typically lodged and furnished at government or company expense in manicured, segregated, gilded ghettoes, Europeans were exempt from all manual labor. The typical colonial family had a retinue of at least six servants: a cook and his assistant, one or two "house boys," a gardener, a laundryman, sometimes a coachman or chauffeur. Their social life was entirely limited to their own kind. Contacts with the natives were limited to utilitarian ends and almost solely of a hierarchical, master–servant type. Intermarriage was almost totally nonexistent, although concubinage between white men and native women was frequent, though sometimes semiclandestine. Native concubines were excluded from European social life and so were in most cases their "half-breed" children, although in the more assimilationist colonies of Spain and Portugal mulattoes and mestizos gradually infiltrated the dominant group. Elsewhere they often constituted a group of intermediate status, as on many West Indian islands (Lowenthal, 1972).

The extent to which notions of European superiority were based on race or on culture varied somewhat from country to country. British, Belgian, Dutch and German colonizers tended to be more openly racist, ascribing the supposed shortcomings of the natives to innate, genetic disabilities. The Latin colonizers (Spain, Portugal and France), however, were openly ethnocentric and automatically assumed that their language, religion and culture were superior to those of the natives, but they tended to grant the latter a greater ability to acquire these superior attributes. That is perhaps why, being less racist, the Latin colonizers were often more intolerant of native culture and of native failure to embrace their civilization with alacrity. The English or Dutch, who believed that the African was intellectually incapable of turning into a European, could then afford to be condescendingly tolerant of indigenous culture as best adapted to the supposedly inferior mentality of the native. The Frenchman or Spaniard, who granted the Indian or the African the capability of becoming a European and a Christian, was tempted to see any failure on the part of the native to become an *évolué* (as the French colonial terminology described Europeanized Africans) as an act of defiance or perversity.

Whatever the detailed modalities of European colonial ideology, social relations across the color line were subject to a rigid etiquette of dominance and subordination—rationalized through a complex ideology legitimating European rule. In the early Spanish–Portuguese phase of colonial expansion, the legitimation was religious: Europeans went out to save benighted heathens from eternal damnation. Later, the ideology increasingly took a secularized form: Europe had a "civilizing mission" to lead primitive peoples out of their savagery. In either case, the model of social relations was paternalistic. Natives were considered to be irresponsible, incapable of ruling themselves, backward grown-up children who could not fend for themselves. It was therefore in their own best interests to be ruled by Europeans who had a sacred trust to lead them to a higher level of spiritual and material existence. The latest incarnations of that paternalistic ideology, revamped to suit the rhetoric of political independence, was the U.S. Peace Corps, the French *Coopération* and the British Volunteer Service Overseas. According to Albert Schweitzer, the African was his brother, but his younger brother.

What political and economic reality did this façade of benevolent despotism hide? Basically, the system of domination was designed to achieve as cheaply as possible the measure of control necessary to produce optimum exploitation. Where the main resource was land, as was the case outside the tropics, the indigenes were simply swept aside, giving rise to colonies of settlement.

Where trade was the object and where goods could be obtained profitably, cheaply and safely without territorial conquest, Europeans confined themselves to small, fortified, coastal settlements defended more against each other than against their native neighbors and partners in trade. Thus, for well over three centuries, Europeans and West Africans collaborated in a thriving slave trade with only minimal territorial encroachments (Davidson, 1961). It was too risky and costly for Europeans to pursue directly themselves a commodity that Africans vied with each other to produce at low cost. The same was true of trade in spices and other luxury goods in the Orient. In fact, the more "progressive" capitalist European powers launched their colonial adventures as chartered semiprivate trading companies. The Dutch, French and British all founded state-sponsored but privately owned East and West Indian companies which, during much of the 17th and 18th centuries, combined the functions of an import–export firm, a shipping line and a colonial government.

Often these chartered trading companies grew into colonial empires and were eventually taken over by the government of their respective countries. This was the case, for instance, with the British in India, the Dutch in Indonesia and, later, the British in Nigeria. The political take-over of large tropical territories was often initially resisted by European governments who feared the trouble and expense of maintaining a land empire. The British in South Africa, for example, always sought to contain the expanding European settlers (who admittedly were Boers rather than British, and thus colonial rivals), and to minimize its administrative responsibilities over the hinterland, until the discovery of diamonds in 1867 and of gold in 1886 (De Kiewiet, 1941).

Therefore, Europeans only conquered colonial territories when they thought it would pay to do so, and when health conditions gave a fair chance of survival. In the case of much of South and Central America, these conditions were met soon after initial contact at the turn of the 16th century. The Spanish and Portuguese intended to plunder, not to trade, and climatic and epidemiological conditions in the American tropics were considerably more favorable to the Europeans than in Africa or even Asia. Altitude put vast stretches of the American tropics well beyond the reach of the great tropical killer diseases (malaria, yellow fever, sleeping sickness and bilharzia) and imported European diseases (measles, plague, smallpox and influenza) conveniently decimated native populations already demoralized by the extraordinarily swift and brutal conquest of Cortes in Mexico and Pizarro in Peru. Indeed, some epidemics even spread from the Caribbean to the Andes so swiftly that they *preceded* Pizarro by a few years (McNeill, 1976).

In the Asian and African tropics, conditions were far less favorable for conquest. Native societies were often large and powerful, and indigenes (except on isolated Pacific islands) were often as immune as their would-be conquerors to European-borne diseases. Conversely, the local climate was often dangerous and debilitating to Europeans who were thus scarcely in a position to mount military expeditions into the interior. They were only safe, both militarily and healthwise, in their coastal forts and on their ships (Cipolla, 1965; Davidson, 1961). Finally, goods could often be obtained cheaply through peaceful trade.

Over time, however, improvements in military and naval technology steadily increased the power disparity between Europe and the rest of the world in the 17th, 18th and 19th centuries, and medical breakthroughs, such as the use of quinine as a malaria preventative and curative drug, made it increasingly tempting for the Europeans to eliminate the native middleman in trade and to take over themselves.

CONTROL OF NATIVE LABOR

European expansion in the tropics was not only a question of controlling trade at the source, however. Of greater significance, it increasingly became a question of *organizing production* of raw materials through the control of *native labor*. By the 17th century the more dynamic regions of Europe, especially England, France and the Low Countries, were experiencing a population boom made possible by economic and technological development, and they became more and more voracious in their demand for tropical products, both raw materials like hardwoods for ships and windmill gears, and luxury goods like gold, silver, spices and sugar. Capitalism thrived and, by the late 18th century, the Industrial Revolution was on, with its multiple needs for a vast range of new raw materials (iron, copper, cotton, jute and oil to lubricate the machinery). Rising standards of living also greatly increased the demand for tropical luxuries: coffee, tea, cocoa and cloves. Furthermore, the vast population of the tropical colonies increasingly became not only a source of labor to produce raw materials but consumers of finished products made in Europe.

It is possibly an overstatement to claim that industrial capitalism would not have been possible without colonial exploitation, but it certainly thrived on it. After the mad scramble for Africa in the last quarter of the 19th century, virtually the whole surface of the earth, except for China, Japan, Korea, Thailand, Ethiopia and a handful of other isolated states, had come under European hegemony and had become incorporated into what Wallerstein (1974) has called the "capitalist world system." Western Europe expanded overseas, and Russia expanded over its vast Siberian hinterland. The whole world was cut up into European spheres of influence and markets.

Many of the colonial raw materials required in Europe, whether minerals or plantation crops, demanded an *organization of production* which the natives, left to themselves, were unwilling to provide. It is hard to convince a tropical peasant, or indeed anyone, to work ten or 12 hours a day cutting sugar cane or digging gold. Unless forced to do so, they naturally preferred not to do monotonous, back-breaking, dangerous and unhealthy work for long hours, for low wages, under a blazing sun and while badly fed. This unwillingness earned them the reputation for "laziness" with their colonial masters, who themselves shunned *all* manual labor in the tropics. In short, the running of plantations and mines required European supervision—indeed, coercion.

This is how classical colonies of exploitation developed. The problem was to maximize output while minimizing overhead. Since output required supervised and coerced native labor, the overhead was mostly of a political nature. European colonial governments had to create and maintain political conditions such as to produce a reliable, steady supply of docile and cheap labor. And they had to do it at minimum cost. This meant, first of all, using as few Europeans and as many natives as possible. The more natives could be used as instruments of their own oppression, the less expensive the colonial operation became. Specifically, this meant mostly two things: the use of native troops under European officers as ultimate enforcers of colonial "law and order," and a system of indirect rule through native chiefs.

Both of these techniques are worth some attention since they had profound implications for ethnic relations in the colonies. The use of native troops in the control of native populations is almost universal in the European colonial experience. The only notable exception is South Africa, a subtropical territory, half colony of settlement and half colony of exploitation, where the European settlers were numerous enough to provide the armed forces, and where they jealously (and successfully) guarded their monopoly of firearms. Where Europeans were few (i.e. nearly everywhere in the tropics, especially in Asia and Africa), they could only provide the officer ranks of the armed forces—typically less than 5% of the men under arms.

Colonial armies did not need to be the most efficient and technically competent. Basically, colonial troops were made up of quickly trained, cheaply equipped infantrymen whose main skill was an ability to shoot down unarmed civilians and to burn and loot villages. To be sure, colonial troops were occasionally used to repress well-organized insurrections (including sometimes mutinous, armed units of the colonial army), and even to fight their masters' wars on different continents. Their main task, however, was to prevent local populations from rebelling by their intimidating presence, to guard European installations and prisons and to repress revolts.

There were inherent dangers in arming native troops, and mutinies were common—occasionally quite serious, as, for example, the Great Indian Mutiny of 1857 (Mason, 1974). However, these dangers could be greatly mitigated through a judicious policy of dividing and ruling by playing up ethnic antagonisms within the native population. The favorite formula was to form ethnically homogeneous units at the company, batallion or even regimental level to create esprit de corps within the unit, and rivalry and competition between units. Units, always under European officers (and sometimes even noncommissioned officers), would then be posted far away from their home territory—preferably among their traditional enemies. If a unit mutinied, it could not count on the sympathy of the local population, and units from different ethnic groups could be relied upon to wipe them out.

Ethnic stereotypes also played a role in the recruitment of native troops, who were generally picked from what the British called "martial races." This often meant ethnies with a record of military success in precolonial days and therefore especially hated by their neighbors. The loyalty of native troops was also often fostered by granting them inexpensive privileges, such as good food and quarters, a colorful uniform, a small but regular income in cash and the implicit right to molest, pilfer and exploit in a small way the local population, thereby reinforcing the already existing antagonisms.

INDIRECT RULE

The term "indirect rule" is generally attributed to Lord Frederick Lugard, who served as British governor of Northern Nigeria at the turn of the 20th century, and who wrote extensively on the subject of how best to rule natives (Lugard, 1929). The practice, however, long antedates him and is found not only in all European colonial empires, but also in other imperial systems such as the Ottoman and the Moghul Empires. The Nazis even tried to create an indirect rule system by appointing a *Judenrat* (Jewish Council) in the Polish ghettoes, while implementing the Final Solution. Even under such extreme circumstances, the system worked to a remarkable extent.

The reason for the popularity of indirect rule and its independent reinvention by many colonial rulers is that it constitutes the simplest and cheapest way of running a colony. Stripped of its fancy rhetoric of noblesse oblige, civilizing mission and similar ideological claptrap, indirect rule boils down to this: if the native society you conquered already had a ruling class, strip it of ultimate power and keep it under close watch, but rule through it; that is, let it do the dirty work of tax collection, *corvée* labor gathering, police, and so on, for you. In exchange for being your puppet, allow the native ruler to keep the trappings of power and those privileges that do not interfere with your ultimate control. So as not to antagonize the people needlessly, do not disturb local law, custom and religion, especially as these generally tend to support established authority, allowing the maximum degree of local autonomy compatible with your interests as the colonizer. In short, rule through native chiefs; give them a free hand so long as they behave; and do not gratuitously interfere with local customs.

Indirect rule had two drawbacks, however. It was easy enough to implement where a centralized state had existed before, and where, therefore, an entire administrative structure was already in place. This explained Lugard's success in Northern Nigeria, which for several centuries had consisted of large feudal states and had been welded into an empire by the Fulani a century before the British conquest. The latter was merely the latest episode in a long history of conquest by various ethnic groups. Lugard merely put a label on a solution that obviously imposed itself. Where the conquered people belonged to a stateless, classless society, however, there was no obvious political structure to use, and indirect rule had to be created from scratch. Native chiefs, if they did not exist, had to be created; but this was often more easily said than done, since they would not be obeyed. Indeed, sometimes natives played jokes on the colonial administration, pretending that a very low-status person or the village simpleton, was their chief, making him and the colonial administration the butt of ridicule. In Southeastern Nigeria, for instance, inhabited by stateless, village-level, egalitarian societies like the Ibo, the British policy of indirect rule was never effectively implemented.

The second limitation of indirect rule is that its effectiveness rests on a give-and-take basis and thus puts limits on what the conqueror can do. The role of native ruler in a system of indirect rule is a very delicate one. If he becomes entirely the stooge of the colonial regime, he looses all credibility and legitimacy with his people and thus ceases to be effective, for his actions will be resisted and sabotaged, and his orders ignored. If, however, he sides with his people and resists too openly the colonial administration, he is likely to be replaced by someone more pliable. The native chief is thus perpetually performing a balancing act between the colonial rulers and his subjects. The former must see him as a useful collaborator; the latter as a buffer and protector against "excessive" exploitation. That posture, in turn, can only be maintained if the colonial power is content with the status quo and does not seek to alter radically the system of production and to intensify the exploitation. In short, indirect rule is ideal in state-organized societies where the colonial power is content to be only moderately exploitative and to leave the status quo largely undisturbed.

The extent to which indirect rule was applied varied considerably. The system was most consciously developed by the British in India, Burma, Nigeria, the Sudan, and by the Dutch in Indonesia. The Spaniards and Portuguese, who were determined to transform and convert to Christianity the societies they conquered and to exploit them to the maximum with little regard even for the life of the Indian labor necessary to the entire colonial enterprise, used much more direct methods of rule. Even the Spaniards, however, used Indian *caciques* or *curacas* (chiefs) when they found it convenient to do so, granted them special privileges and went to the trouble of educating them in Spanish and Catholic ways in special schools. The

French, too, who were supposedly more assimilationist than the British in their colonial policies and more centralist in their administration, instituted, in fact, indirect rule systems in Morocco, the Western Sudan and Indochina.

Colonial theories diverged more than colonial practices. Even the Jesuitical dogmatists and the Cartesian apologists of the *mission civilisatrice* were driven to expediency in practice. Conversely, the British pragmatists erected their sensibly flexible practices into the pseudotheory of indirect rule. In actual fact, every colonial power was trying to run its empire on a shoe-string budget. That, inevitably, meant letting the natives become partners in their own subjugation, at the very least at the local village level and sometimes at all levels but the highest. The more indirect rule, the cheaper the administration, and the more invisible the foreign conqueror. The native chief was at once a useful auxiliary, an alibi for failure and a scapegoat for the hostility of the natives. Colonialism thus exploited not only preexisting ethnic rivalries but also such class conflicts as existed in precolonial societies.

The simple schema of colonial rule sketched above was often complicated by the presence of groups other than colonial rulers and native subjects—and by conflicts of interest within the colonial elite itself. Sometimes, two European ethnies competed for colonial control over a native population—as happened in the old triangular Boer–British–Bantu conflict in South Africa (Marquard, 1962; van den Berghe, 1965). Sometimes different sectors of the colonizer population had divergent interests. Conflicts between church and state frequently came to the fore in the Spanish and Portuguese colonies.

All these complications and local differences notwithstanding, the political structure of classical colonialism was both remarkably simple and remarkably similar in its essentials from country to country and from period to period. So was the rigidly hierarchical system of ethnic relations that flowed from that political structure. We now examine the colonial system of production that was made possible by this social and political order.

THE COLONIAL SYSTEM OF PRODUCTION

All colonial economies were premised on the same conception of their function. They were seen as part of an integrated whole that included the more developed economy of the "mother country" or *métropole*, the needs of which they were meant to serve. Colonies existed to produce raw materials (timber, minerals, cotton, jute and oil) for European industry and agricultural commodities (many of them luxury items such as tobacco, sugar, rum, coffee, tea, cocoa and spices) for European consumption. They also served as a market for cheap European manufactured goods.

Two cardinal economic policies followed logically from this conception. One was an attempted monopolization by the métropole of all trade with its own colonies, to the exclusion of rival colonial powers. The other was the deliberate fostering of economic dependency of the colony on the métropole.

As concerns the monopolization of trade between colony and métropole,

Great Britain was the exception. Starting in the late 18th century, and increasingly in the 19th, Britain became the champion of free trade; but it was in its interests to do so. Indeed, by then, Britain had become the first shipping nation in the world, the leading industrial economy, the supreme naval power and the largest colonial country. In effect, the advocacy of free trade by Britain was little more than a disguised request for free commercial access to the whole world, including, of course, its rivals' colonies. Some of the weaker colonial powers, such as Belgium, had no option but to accept the "opening" of its colonies to free trade, but most resisted strenuously.

The fostering of economic dependence of the colony on the métropole meant principally the prevention of self-sufficiency. This could be achieved negatively by discouraging the development in the colonies of industries that would compete with home industries. In the 19th century, for example, Britain, despite her advocacy of free trade for other countries, was concerned with Indian competition for the British textile industry, trying everything to stifle it. Positively, economic dependency of the colony was fostered through highly specialized development of a few products for export. In the aggregate, the colonial world produced a wide range of goods, but the monoculture of cash crops often prevailed in individual colonies: sugar and its by-products in the Caribbean, cocoa in the Gold Coast (now Ghana), groundnuts in Senegal, sisal in Tanganyika (now Tanzania), and so on. Monoculture meant extreme dependence since the crop in question was rarely a basic subsistence crop and was scarcely ever consumed locally in significant amounts. The French, for example, produced wine in Algeria, a Muslim country where religion forbids alcoholic beverages. After nearly a quarter century of "independence," Ghana, the world's leading producer of cocoa, still imports most of the little chocolate it consumes from Britain!

Not only were colonial cash crops not consumed locally, but they also took away much land from subsistence agriculture, thereby leading oftentimes to a decline in the native standard of living and a deterioration in the quality of the diet. High-yield, low-quality root crops such as manioc and yams, for instance, were substituted for more varied and protein-richer cereal and bean crops. In extreme cases, such as in the West Indies, food had to be massively imported because nearly all available arable land was in sugar cane. Dependency thus generally meant impoverishment as well. Paradoxically, the more "developed" a colony was in terms of export productivity, the worse the diet of its population. Black South Africans, for instance, have one of the highest incidences of *kwashiokor*—a nutritional disease caused by a starchy diet—even though their country is by far the most highly developed industrial power on the African continent, with one of the continent's highest per capita income.

An additional source of dependence of colonial economies was that the few commodities, whether mineral or agricultural, in which they specialized were highly susceptible to extraordinary price fluctuations on the world market or, alternatively, were produced under conditions where the colonial power artificially imposed by force a very low price. Most of the economic imbalance and dependence created during the colonial period still adversely affects Third World countries today. This continued economic dependence of formally independent countries on the capitalist (and to some extent on the socialist) countries is now referred to as "neocolonialism."

THE CONTROL OF COLONIAL LABOR

Within the colony the detailed modalities of the system of production varied according to local conditions and to the commodity to be produced. Mining generally required large-scale organization with a large, reliable, disciplined but fairly unskilled labor force. Some crops, such as cocoa, could be efficiently produced by small independent farmers. Others, such as sugar cane, which required factories for immediate processing, were most practicable under a large plantation system. Each commodity favored a particular system of production. Nevertheless, there were a number of commonalities in the internal organization of colonial economies.

The key factor, of course, was the control of labor. The first problem to be solved was to create a *supply* of labor. Initially, lack of labor supply often presented a serious obstacle to exploitation. Self-sufficient subsistence peasants with only minimal exposure to a market economy and to its artificially created needs for manufactured products could not easily be convinced to work long hours for low wages under strenuous, dangerous, unpleasant conditions that typically took them away from home and family for long periods of time and exposed them to accidents and diseases.

However, the problem of labor supply was easily solved through the simple device of the head tax. Every adult man in the colony was forced to pay an annual tax *in cash*; the alternative was often a specified term at forced labor—in effect a labor tax in lieu of cash. Since the main ready source of cash in still largely unmonetized colonial economies was working for Europeans, the imposition of a head tax was a simple way of instantaneously creating a labor supply where none or little existed before. The only requirement was a system of coercion capable of collecting the tax or, alternatively, imprisoning the evader and supplying him as forced laborer to his colonial employer. Even a highly industrial economy like South Africa still relies on the simple device of the head tax (imposed only on blacks and misleadingly called "poll tax," even though blacks are disenfranchised) to create a steady supply of cheap labor (Horwitz, 1967; van den Berghe, 1965).

Once labor supply was initiated by taxation, it usually became self-perpetuating. Natives having been exposed to a market economy quickly developed a desire for the manufactured goods it produced, which entailed more and more wage work. As more and more able-bodied men entered the "modern" sector of the colonial economy, the "subsistence" sector declined in relative and sometimes in absolute importance. Labor supply could also be enhanced by simply dispossessing the natives of their land to "open up" the area for large European-controlled ranches, haciendas and plantations.

Land dispossession, the development of nonfood cash crops and manpower shortage in the subsistence sector could quickly reduce the latter to sub-subsistence, transforming the able-bodied men into permanent serfs or wage workers attached to European plantations and mines.

Having secured a supply of labor through the more or less direct use of coercion, colonial governments and private employers next faced the problems of ensuring that native labor would remain cheap, docile and reliable. Four basic systems of labor exploitation were developed to these ends. Naturally, there were many local variations, and sometimes a single colony simultaneously adopted features of more than one system or gradually evolved from one type of labor to another; nevertheless, there are four discernible patterns, each with its own features. In ascending order of severity, they were (1) the quota system, (2) the migrant labor system, (3) the hacienda system and (4) chattel slavery. The last type was so extreme and had so many unique features that I shall reserve Chapter 6 to discuss it. Here, I shall confine myself to a brief description of each of the other three types.

The Quota System

The quota system was, on the whole, the least ruthless, largely because it was instituted mostly in territories, such as West and Central Africa, where Europeans were fewest and where their control was most tenuous. Natives were induced, through various blends of coercion and persuasion to cultivate certain crops or to collect certain wild products (e.g. rubber and timber) and to furnish fixed quantities of it for a fixed price under some kind of quota system: so much per man or so much per village. Initially, ruthless terror was sometimes used to fill these quotas. The Belgians, for example, in the early days of the "Congo Free State" (another quaint misnomer), liberally cut off the hands of quota delinquents as a production incentive. Naturally such extreme methods were counterproductive and typically did not last long.

More liberal versions of this method of induced production of cash crops were used by the French and the British in West Africa. Production of cocoa, coffee or groundnuts was left to individual small farmers, but the government would act as a monopsony, i.e. it would monopolize the purchase and marketing of the produce, impose arbitrary (and low) prices and often collect an excise tax on production in addition. Sometimes the price was just high enough to be a production incentive by itself. Failing that, colonial governments often forcibly imposed the cultivation of cash crops on reluctant villagers (sometimes with ecologically catastrophic results).

By and large, however, the quota system was the mildest form of exploitation, insofar as the worker retained some control of production (if not of marketing), worked more or less at his own pace and generally could stay at home among his family and friends. From the perspective of the colonial masters, the system was suboptional and was only introduced where they lacked the means to impose a more stringent form of exploitation.

The Migrant Labor System

The migrant labor system marks a clear shift in the level of intensity of labor exploitation. Practiced widely in Africa, Asia and increasingly in postcolonial Latin America, it is based on contract wage labor. A worker obligates himself for a specified period of time for a specified wage (often plus rations and a few trade goods such as a blanket or a cooking pot, given as an initial incentive to sign up). The duration of the contract varies but is typically fairly short (a few months). Not only are wages low but so is overhead for the employer, for the worker comes alone, leaving his family at home and is, of course, strictly prevented from organizing to improve his work conditions. The labor force is rotated frequently, thereby preventing the worker from striking any roots and making any demands.

Control of the work force is easy since the worker is typically housed in barracklike camps provided by the employer and under the control of company police. Sometimes, workers are locked up at night; they are generally cut off from the surrounding society (where the workers are often strangers), and they are utterly dependent on the employer for food, supplies (in company stores) and medical care (if any). For the duration of the contract, in short, the worker surrenders nearly all his freedom and, except for the fact that his obligation is for a limited time and that he is paid wages, the system is not all that different from slavery. Indeed physical conditions are sometimes worse than under slavery, since the employer has less of an incentive to keep him healthy.

For all its numerous advantages, the migratory labor system has one drawback: because of rapid turnover, it is unsuited for any operation requiring highly skilled labor. Plantations and mines, however, require mostly unskilled workers who can be trained in hours or at most days, and agriculture and mining are the main employers of migratory labor. The few skilled workers needed can, of course, be paid and treated better; in some cases, Europeans are hired for the purpose, especially in colonies like Algeria and South Africa where whites are (or were) numerous enough (10 and 17%, respectively, of the total population) to provide much of the artisan class. Elsewhere (as was the case in the copper mines of the Belgian Congo) the policy was to stabilize part of the African labor force by offering family housing to skilled workers.

A key prerequisite for the operation of a migrant labor system is the existence of a rural hinterland from which the workers are drawn, to which they return between contract periods and where the remainder of the population lives. In many parts of the colonial world, virtually the entire country is a vast labor reservoir. In some of the more complex systems of labor migration, entire territories serve as labor reservoirs for more "advanced" ones, e.g. Upper Volta for Ghana and the Ivory Coast, or Malawi and Mozambique for South Africa. Migrant labor systems incorporate vast regions into a single complex economic system.

The largest such system on the African continent is the one created by the vast industrial complex of South Africa. It was initiated a little over a century ago with the development of diamond and gold mining. It still exists there, virtually unchanged since its inception, and there it has achieved its ultimate perfection as a system of rational exploitation and control of colonial labor. A more detailed analysis of South Africa will be reserved for Chapter 8, but a word must be said here about the "native reserve system," as it represents the ultimate impoverishment of the rural hinterland necessary to a migrant labor system.

Where this process of land dispossession was extensive, as in South Africa, the Kenya Highlands, and other areas attractive to European enterprise, the remaining land, often the poorest, was declared to be "native reserves," a kind of rural slum, often incapable of supporting its population. Able-bodied men were forced to work in the European sector for wages to support their families, and the native reserve became a vast holding pen for reproductive women, children and old people past their economic usefulness. The native reserve then had a double advantage: it was poor enough to force the economically productive to work in the European sector; at the same time, it raised just enough food to keep women reproductive and to relieve the European employers of the burden of feeding their workers' dependents. The native reserve was thus literally a labor reservoir from which workers came and to which surplus laborers could return. It was also a labor nursery, the breeding ground for the next generation of cheap laborers. Finally, it was a convenient dumping ground for the unfit, thereby further contributing to the cheapness of labor by reducing the overhead of providing accommodations and feeding the nonproductive population.

The Hacienda System

The hacienda system was most characteristic in Spanish America, hence its name, and in many countries such as Guatemala, Ecuador, Peru and Bolivia it still exists or was only recently abolished through land reform. The hacienda shares many characteristics with the slave plantation: it is a little self-contained feudal world in which masters and servants live in an intimate, stable, life-long but highly unequal relationship. In a sense, a hacienda is like a slave plantation run with indigenes who did not have to be bought and brought in because they were already there.

A number of circumstances, besides nominal, legal freedom, made the lot of the hacienda serf considerably less abject than that of the plantation slave, however. The hacienda serf belonged to an established community of kinsmen, in-laws and friends; he was generally given a plot of land to cultivate for his own use and often owned some livestock; usually about half his time was his own; he frequently had the theoretical right to leave (even though he often had no other place to go, except another hacienda); finally, the power of the owner was often contrained by custom or limited by the fact that he was often an absentee who preferred to live in town.

The Spanish hacienda system evolved over time. It began as a grant of the crown (*encomienda*) to meritorious conquistadores. The grantees initially did not own the land nor were their privileges hereditary; they merely had the right to collect tribute (and keep part of it for themselves) from the Indian population settled on the land, in exchange for converting them to Christianity and making them faithful subjects of the king. Over time, these grants became increasingly hereditary, and Spanish settlers claimed more and more legal ownership of the land. The peasants living on these estates gradually became serfs—much as the peasants of Medieval Europe.

The typical arrangement was one of "labor tenancy." In exchange for labor furnished by the male head of the peasant family, he and his family were entitled to live on the estate, to cultivate a plot of arable land for his own use and to pasture a specified number of livestock on hacienda land. Detailed conditions such as a number of days of service, size of individual plots and number of animals permitted varied greatly, but the general arrangement was much the same and so was the paternalistic system of ethnic relations prevailing between masters and serfs.

The hacienda was like a feudal fief: a little self-contained, self-sufficient world, where generation after generation of peasants were born, lived and died in the shadow of the "big house" and its dependencies (chapel, cemetery, storerooms, stables and so on). The owners were often absentees represented by a caretaker, but even then the model of ethnic relations was one of paternalism. This was symbolized by the fact that the owner was often the godfather of most of his serfs. Some masters were relatively humane and imbued with a spirit of condescending benevolence while others were ruthlessly exploitative.

The hacienda system was less *rationally* exploitative than the migrant labor system, and was often economically inefficient and archaic. However, the serf was continuously under the control of his master—a control from which there often was no escape since the serf's only home was the hacienda. Haciendas were owned incidentally not only by private individuals but also by the Catholic Church and its various religious orders. The typical Indian mission was often a hacienda. Some of these mission stations, such as the vast estates of the Jesuits in Paraguay and Brazil, became in fact little self-contained theocracies within the larger Spanish and Portuguese empires.

This crude typology of colonial systems of labor exploitation is little more than a gross way of putting some order into complex reality. In fact, systems of colonial exploitation often overlapped and shaded off into one another. For example, the "indenture system," whereby East Indian contract laborers were imported for five-year terms into British colonies (often to replace African slaves after Abolition in 1834), combined features of the slave plantation for which it was a substitute form of labor and of the migrant labor system described above. It was originally conceived as a kind of long-term, long-distance (intercontinental) migrant labor system, but it typically gave rise to permanent populations in the "host countries," largely because it permitted the immigration of women. Repatriation to a desperately poor home country was not an attractive prospect to the workers after completion of indenture, so most stayed in Fiji, Trinidad, Guiana, Kenya, South Africa, Mauritius and so on—often to become "middleman minorities."

CONCLUSION: COLONIAL RACE AND ETHNIC RELATIONS

Of course, the extreme forms of exploitation and domination described in this chapter led to rigidly hierarchical ethnic relations. The fundamental social premise underlying the colonial society was that rulers and subjects are so different in physical appearance and in culture as to share virtually nothing. Racism was often invoked to begrudge them even humanity. *Macaque* (Rhesus monkey), for example, was a favorite epithet of Belgian colonials in referring to Africans. Even when common humanity was conceded, it was immediately qualified. The natives had a primitive mentality; it would take them thousands of years to reach the European level of civilization; they did not feel like Europeans (and, therefore, could be mistreated); their needs were less (and, therefore, low wages were quite adequate), and so on.

The whole of colonial society was suffused by a double standard of justice, ethics, behavior, pay and privilege. To be European meant automatic inclusion in the ruling caste, automatic enjoyment of an extremely high standard of living and automatic entitlement to a privileged legal and political status. To be a native meant political disenfranchisement, legal treatment as an incompetent minor subject to special statutes, low wages for hard work, discriminatory taxation and exploitation, exposure to arbitrary treatment without effective legal redress, and automatic subordination in all contacts with Europeans.

Some colonial powers exempted a few selected natives (*évolués*, in the Belgian and French terminology, *asimilados*, as the Portuguese called them) from some legal disabilities, but, even then, the social barrier often remained. Over time, after much interbreeding, the rigid racial distinction often broke down or, at least, became blurred and mitigated. This clearly happened in the Spanish and Portuguese American colonies (Mörner, 1970; van den Berghe, 1967). Complex processes of decolonization would require a chapter to themselves. Even as rigid a social system as colonialism could not remain forever frozen. In fact, colonialism rested on fragile foundations, often crashing down quickly and violently. While it existed, however, it gave the impression of a frozen society, changing at only a glacial pace; of a strangely stilted, archaic society unlike the rest of the world, and of a society in which everyone is wearing masks and playing strained, unnatural roles (Fanon, 1971).

Naturally, this enormous political, economic and social barrier that separated European rulers and colonial subjects made for a sharp dichotomization of social roles depending on whether one interacted within the ethny or across ethnic boundaries. Colonialism was an extreme case of ethnic relations designed to maintain not only inequality across ethnic lines but also strangeness, incomprehension and lack of empathy. Both rulers and subjects were type-cast in stereotypic roles and attitudes, so that it was extremely difficult to penetrate the ethnic role-taking and get at the individual behind it. "Knowing the natives," for Europeans meant little else than having accepted the stereotypes and norms of the colonial society. The recently arrived European was ridiculed as unknowledgeable and naive because he had not yet developed the trained incapacity to have a normal human relationship across ethnic lines.

The psychological effects of this strained play-acting were numerous and much has been written about them (Bastide, 1950; Fanon, 1963, 1965, 1971; Mannoni, 1964; Mason, 1975; Memmi, 1965, 1968). Colonialism was dehumanizing for rulers and ruled alike. The colonial master had to bear the strain of living up to the superman image he had created of himself and of being surrounded by sullen, hostile people whom he feared and mistrusted but on whom he was totally dependent. He often found solace in alcohol. The native had to bear the constant burden of discrimination, exploitation, injustice and humiliation. In addition, his principal defense was often to "work within the system," i.e. to pretend to be what his masters thought he was and by doing so, to manipulate, evade and deceive to maximum advantage. Indeed, deceit is the last resort of the weak in oppressive situations. But it has its costs too. The role of the "good native" ascribed to the colonial subject was demeaning and robbed him of human dignity; furthermore, by playing it, he reinforced the stereotype that created the role in the first instance and thereby helped perpetuate the system. However, the penalties for rejecting the type-cast roles were high, both for colonizer and colonized. The former was socially ostracized as a traitor to his race; the latter was branded an "uppity nigger," "cheeky kaffir" or whatever the local phrase was, often inviting violent retribution.

In one domain, however, colonialism did not manage to repress all expressions of common humanity. It could not prevent interbreeding. To be sure, the interbreeding was highly asymmetrical, in the hypergamous direction, as is true in nearly all hierarchical systems. It was overwhelmingly dominant-group males who mated with subordinate-group females. In some of the more puritan Protestant colonies of Holland and Britain, this form of interethnic contact was severely frowned upon, while the Catholic colonizers tended to be more tolerant of concubinage with native women. Whether condoned or condemned, it took place.

Interbreeding was no indication of racial or ethnic tolerance, as it has sometimes been interpreted to be. Rather, it took place despite intolerance. It shows that even the strongest social barriers between human groups cannot block a specieswide sexual attraction. The biology of reproduction triumphs in the end over the artificial barriers of social prejudice. The implications of "miscegenation" (as interbreeding is called in racist societies) are even more important for slave societies than for colonial societies. Some colonial societies managed to survive for centuries despite extensive interbreeding. This was the case, for instance, in the Spanish American colonies, where the caste system gradually broke down, but where the political and economic institutions of colonialism lingered on. In slave societies, the opportunities for interbreeding were even greater than in colonial societies, but the threat it presented to the slave system was also much greater. To this topic I now turn.

SUGGESTED READINGS

Some classics on the colonial situation are Balandier (1970) and Mannoni (1964) on Africa, Boeke (1953) and Furnivall (1948) on Asia, and Aguirre Beltrán (1979) on Latin America. Mason (1971) is an excellent general text with much material on colonial societies, and the Wallerstein (1966) reader contains many excellent articles. Influential indictements of colonialism and appeals for its overthrow are found in Fanon (1963, 1965) and Memmi (1965, 1968).

SLAVERY

Like "colonialism," the word "slavery" evokes strong emotions and has been used in a wide range of meanings. However reluctantly, we must start with a definitional exercise. In Western societies, "slavery" calls to mind gangs of blacks picking cotton or cutting sugar cane under a white overseer on horseback. Depending on one's politics, that vision comes either in a liberal *Roots* version of cruel master and oppressed slaves—or in a conservative *Gone With the Wind* image of stately mansions, mint juleps, smiling mammies and spiritual-singing field hands. Much of the historical debate over what the southern United States euphemistically called the "peculiar institution" centers around which of these two images comes closer to reality. The current ideological fashion is to give greater credence to the liberal version, and any revisionism in the other direction—indeed even any attempt to remove the debate from the moral arena to the empirical one—encounters furious attack (Fogel and Engerman, 1974; Gutman, 1976).

I shall return to Western "chattel slavery" presently and devote most of this chapter to the very peculiar brand of slavery that flourished in the European colonies of the Western Hemisphere for roughly three-and-a-half centuries, especially in Brazil, the Caribbean and the southern English colonies of continental North America. Before I do, however, I shall examine other, very different, types of slavery, for, without this comparative overview, it is impossible to appreciate the peculiarity of Western chattel slavery.

DEFINITIONS OF SLAVERY

First, there is the issue of definition. The word is bandied about with a bewildering array of meanings and qualifiers. One hears of "chattel slavery," "debt slavery," "wage slavery," being a "slave" to love, to one's work, to one's habits, to television and so on. Obviously, in its loosest meaning, slavery implies some surrender of free will, either internally or externally generated. Here, we are not concerned with these loose usages, nor with usages which are obviously laden with ideological overtones, as when Marxists talk of "wage slavery." (Since slavery normally means unpaid work, "wage slavery" is no great addition to the arsenal of analytical concepts!)

Within the narrower definitions of slavery, two main traditions are discernible. One stresses the legal aspects of slavery and defines slavery principally in terms of deprivation of certain rights of free adult men or of a general status subject to specific disabilities and restrictions not imposed on free adult men. The qualification of freedom by age and sex is necessary here because in all human societies, children are deprived of many rights of adults and are often treated as a species of property of their parents; and in the vast majority of societies women do not have equal rights with men. Yet, to extend the definition of slavery to women and children, although it might please some feminists, child-rights activists and other champions of good egalitarian causes, would dilute the concept well beyond its optimum analytical usefulness.

The second tradition in the definition of slavery stresses the economic aspects of the institution and defines slavery as compulsory labor without remuneration—as complete alienation from the product of one's labor. Here, too, one must exclude parental and marital relations, for, within the domestic family economy, there is much compulsory, unremunerated work that can only be called "slavery" through an unhelpful stretch of the concept.*

Both types of definition of slavery leave unresolved a number of ambiguous or marginal cases. Does imprisonment for a crime constitute slavery? Some authors have argued that it does, or at least that the two have much in common (Sellin, 1976), but most definitions of slavery imply moral blamelessness on the part of the slave. By that criterion the millions of political prisoners in the Soviet and Nazi concentration camps of the 1930s and 1940s were slaves, a definition broadly congruent with other forms of state slavery in antiquity. Surely, there was no fundamental difference between the Soviet inmate of the Gulag Archipelago digging a canal, the Jew or the Communist loaned out to Krupp by the SS concentration camp, the Slav or Moor pulling the oar of a Venetian galley, or the Nubian building a pyramid for King Cheops. But, what of compulsory military service? Legal attempts at having it declared "involuntary servitude" have consistently failed, for readily understandable reasons, even though the "wages" involved are often nominal.

Serfdom and "debt peonage" are often marginal cases. A serf may be nominally free to go, but what if he has no other place to go? A peon or sharecropper may receive cash, but what if the wages are below subsistence

---

*As I was writing, for example, I just told my reluctant son to rake the grass I had cut the previous day. I do not intend to pay him for his work; and as he is still a minor he does not have the option of escaping my paternal authority. Yet, he is not, in any meaningful sense, my slave.

and are in fact designed to keep him in perpetual debt so as to prevent his departure?

Legal definitions of slavery are also difficult to apply cross-culturally. A strictly legal definition would clearly exclude serfdom and debt peonage, for instance, but it would raise difficult problems of where to draw the line between slavery and other types of unfreedom. Many societies give special legal status and impose disabilities to certain categories of persons who are not generally considered slaves. Indenture for a specified term of service is certainly a significant infringement of freedom and can easily be converted into outright slavery as blacks experienced in the early days of the English American colonies, but it is not normally considered slavery. A similar institution is "pawning," a practice in a number of central African societies where the labor of a junior relative could be alienated to a creditor, both as collateral and interest for a debt. The situation was temporary and nonstigmatizing and probably does not qualify as slavery, though it did entail a loss of jural rights.

Rather different from these situations are the cases of stigmatized, outcaste groups that suffer distinct disabilities, such as being forbidden to marry outside their group, to live outside certain areas, to participate in political life, to engage in any except a few defiled occupations, and so on. Examples of such groups are numerous: blacksmiths and storytellers in many West African societies, Jews in most of Europe until the 18th century, untouchables in India until the 20th century, the *Eta* or *Burakumin* of Japan until the 19th century, black South Africans to this date, and blacks in the southern United States until the 1950s. Despite the stigma and often crippling economic disabilities attached to these groups, they are better described as *castes* rather than slave groups.

Our attempt to arrive at a workable concept of slavery leads us to a composite definition incorporating elements of both the legal and the economic tradition. Let us define slavery as unremunerated, forced labor and legal exclusion from political participation and civil rights by right of purchase or capture—irrespective of age, sex or criminal behavior of the victim. The definition may seem unduly restrictive, but extending it presents more problems than it solves and generally leads one to a situation where all or nearly all human societies have "slavery." Thus, if one removes the exclusion of sex, any of the hundreds of societies where wives are acquired by bridewealth and have little choice of husband becomes, by that token, a slave society.

The above definitional exercise may strike some readers as sterile and arbitrary, especially if they have ideological axes to grind. It leads, however, to an interesting and unpremeditated result. In an endeavor to arrive at a definition of slavery that made sense cross-culturally, I came very close to restricting the concept of slavery to *interethnic* forms of unfreedom and, therefore, to equate slavery with a particular form of ethnic (or race) relations.

Slavery is a form of unfreedom and disability that is largely restricted to ethnic strangers—to people who are defined as outside the solidary group. Consequently, forms of unfreedom, disability or exploitation imposed on ethnic outsiders are qualitatively different from those that befall a fellow ethnic. A fellow ethnic may be deprived of freedom as punishment for a crime, but that is not slavery, for slavery seldom implies the notion of punishment. A fellow ethnic may be despised because he belongs to a low-status lineage, but this is not slavery either, for slavery is more than low status. In fact, slavery is not entirely incompatible with a high status. Some West African societies, for instance, had a "slave nobility"—certain important political and military posts reserved for slaves or descendants of slaves (Nadel, 1942). Slaves in Imperial Rome, in Ottoman Turkey and in China could occasionally rise to powerful positions by becoming the King's favorite. A fellow ethnic may be economically exploited and politically disfranchised because of age or gender, but no society regards its young or its women as slaves, however mistreated these categories of people may seem to an outside observer.

SLAVERY AS A FORM OF ETHNIC RELATIONS

What then makes the slave? Surely being an outsider, a foreigner, is not enough, for not all outsiders are enslaved. Slavery is an important form of ethnic relations but by no means the only one. Conquered indigenous groups may be dominated and exploited, as we have seen in the last chapter, but they are typically not enslaved. Nor are voluntary immigrants into a society, however lowly, despised, penniless or powerless they may be on arrival—and however discriminated against they may remain for a long time. I shall examine examples of such immigrant pariah groups when I deal with middleman minorities in the next chapter.

A slave, then, is most likely to be not only an outsider to his master's ethny—but an *immigrant* and an *involuntary* immigrant. But not even all involuntary immigrants are enslaved. Sometimes imperial powers have forced entire conquered groups to relocate. It is true that such situations have been called slavery, as with the Jews in Egypt and Babylonia. I suspect, however, that so long as the basic kinship and social structure of the conquered group was left standing, such collective "captivity" resembled colonial status more than slavery. Certainly, many types of forced population transfers within or between states had nothing to do with slavery. Between states, population transfers often take the form of swapping of ethnic or religious minorities, each group joining the main body of its ethny. Examples are the Muslim–Hindu transfers between India and Pakistan after independence in 1947 or the transfers of Germans, Poles and other central Europeans after World War II. Within states, imperial powers have often summarily moved entire populations groups; the Incas, for instance, regularly did so to colonize distant areas with groups of proven loyalty and to bring unassimilated groups under closer control near the center of the empire. These groups, known as *mitimae*, were certainly not slaves.

The only additional condition making for enslavement, besides foreign and involuntary immigrant status, is *isolation*. The slave is, at least initially, the atomized individual torn out of his social group—the person without kinsmen, without a lineage, without a group to call his own. The slave is, first and foremost, a person *torn out of his network of kin selection*. He is not only involuntarily among ethnic strangers in a strange land; he is there alone, without his support group of kinsmen and fellow ethnics. Even if there are fellow ethnics among other slaves, he is prevented by the circumstances of his enslavement to reconstitute an ethnic support group. *He is on his own.*

The next question is this: What circumstances create slaves? There are basically two: capture (through war or kidnapping) and purchase, followed by long-distance travel outside one's ethnic territory. This basic scenario describes equally well the most commercialized forms of capitalist chattel slavery practiced by European countries in the New World and the most primitive forms of slavery between small stateless societies all over the world. There are vast differences of scale, of economic rationality and of organizational complexity between these slave-holding societies, but the basic story of individual capture or purchase followed by removal from home territory in the great common denominator of slavery.

DOMESTIC VS CHATTEL SLAVERY

Western literature on slavery is heavily ideological and moralistic. Since the 18th century, and even before, the ethical tradition of the West has put the institution on trial, even while it was still widely practiced and while it was being revived on a vast scale. Thus, the rebirth of large-scale slavery in the West since the 16th and, increasingly, in the 17th, 18th and 19th centuries was accompanied by an outpouring of literature attacking and defending slavery. This reached a crescendo with the abolitionist movements of the 18th and 19th centuries, especially in Britain, the United States, France and Brazil, and from the late 18th century the apologists for slavery were clearly on the defensive.

In hundreds of societies where slavery existed over several thousand years, slavery was taken for granted and required no apology. The peculiar desire in the West to apologize for the existence of slavery had far-reaching and paradoxical consequences, the most important of which was the florescence of racism. The virulent form of racism that developed in much of the European colonial and slave world was in significant part born out of a desire to justify slavery. If it was immoral to enslave people, but if at the same time it was vastly profitable to do so, then a simple solution to the dilemma presented itself: slavery became acceptable if slaves could somehow be defined as somewhat less than fully human.

I shall return to that theme later, but even today, nearly a century after the abolition of slavery in the last major Western country (Brazil in 1888), the scholarly literature on slavery is still saturated with guilt and moralism.

Slavery and the Holocaust are probably the two monumental events of modern Western history that the conscience of the Western world cannot live down. Unfortunately, moralism often interferes with scholarship, so that today when someone suggests, for example, that the *material* conditions of slavery in the United States were on the whole no worse than those of many free workers—and far superior to those prevailing in Brazil or the Caribbean (Fogel and Engerman, 1974), he is sure to elicit passionate dissent because he is immediately seen as a rehabilitator of slavery. The vast bulk of the historiography on slavery has stressed the dehumanizing nature of slavery, more particularly of the Western brand of chattel slavery, and most especially of slavery in the English colonies.

The main ideological thrust of the slavery literature has been to document how horrible slavery was, and the *comparative* literature has mostly compared degrees of badness (Freyre, 1964; Tannenbaum, 1947). The consensual outcome has been that, while all slavery is bad, Western capitalist "chattel" slavery was considerably worse than the "domestic" slavery practiced in many precapitalist, non-Western societies, and that of all the brands of chattel slavery the one imposed by the Protestant powers, especially England, was more ruthless and dehumanizing than the Catholic, especially the Iberian, variety.

This exercise in guilt expiation of Western, particularly Anglo-Saxon, scholars has not been fruitful. Degrees of evil are difficult to measure, and the outcome differs radically depending on the criteria chosen. For example, even if one accepts the Tannenbaum (1947) thesis that the Catholic, Latin legal and religious tradition made for a more benign and less dehumanizing conception of slavery in Ibero-America than the Protestant, English tradition in the United States, by *material* criteria the United States comes off much better. Slave mortality was *much* higher in Brazil and the Caribbean than in the United States, which was the only major slave society where the slave population grew by natural increase rather than importation.

One of the legacies of this guilt-expiating tradition has been the dichotomy between "domestic" and "chattel" slavery. By chattel slavery is generally meant the rational, systematic exploitation of slave labor in vast capitalist enterprises, mostly plantations and mines, producing commodities for the world market. By contrast, domestic slavery is defined as the small-scale slavery prevalent in hundreds of precapitalist (and often preliterate and even prestate) societies, in which slaves often became incorporated into the extended family structure of their owners and, in time, became assimilated into their captors' society.

Unquestionably, there are crucial differences in types of slavery, but any simple dichotomy of depraved capitalists and noble savages simply will not do. The differences between "domestic" and "chattel" slavery are largely differences of scale and complexity of society, and of mode of production, rather than differences in degrees of badness. It is true that in a number of non-Western societies slaves were treated more or less as poor relatives and were gradually assimilated, especially if they were females. But the horror stories also abound and easily match anything that a Mississippi cotton plantation can offer. Male slaves were frequently castrated in Muslim societies, sometimes under such brutal conditions that 80 to 90% died of the operation (Bovill, 1958, pp. 244–245; A. G. B. Fisher and H. J. Fisher, 1971). The funeral of a king in Dahomey was accompanied by mass executions of slaves who were buried with him (Herskovits, 1938). War captives and slaves were systematically humiliated and often tortured to death in some North American Indian societies. Among some South American groups of the Amazon Rain Forest, slaves were well-fed, but only in preparation for a cannibalistic feast preceded by a mock battle in which the slave would be clubbed to death (Magalhães de Gandavo, 1922, first published in 1575). The Tuareg of West Africa kept Bela slaves to work in salt mines under conditions probably far worse than those prevailing in any American plantation. Miner (1965, pp. 40–41) writes of domestic slavery in Timbuctoo:

> Many aspects of the old system of slavery were not particularly harsh and a household slave was probably in a more favorable position than a poor freeman today.

But in the very next paragraph he describes the Tuareg slave-holding system in much less benign terms:

> Probably the most vicious aspect of the old system of slavery was the ruthlessness with which families were broken up. The Tuareg made a practice of separating children from their parents, which may account for the almost complete acculturation of Bela to Tuareg ways of life. Some work, such as that in the salt pits at Taodeni, was literally killing. There men worked all day in terrific heat with their legs in salt water. The only drinking water was also salty.

What distinguishes Western chattel slavery from domestic slavery is not greater moral depravity, but greater *economic rationality* born out of a capitalist mode of production oriented to a world market and consciously profit-maximizing. Before I turn to the slave regimes of the Western Hemisphere, however, I shall briefly examine domestic slavery.

SLAVERY IN PRECAPITALIST SOCIETIES

From contemporary ethnography, we can reconstruct the moment of human evolution where slavery appeared. Slavery is part of the set of transformations that accompanied the domestication of plants and animals some 10,000 years ago, in the so-called Neolithic Revolution. It clearly antedates the rise of states, for many contemporary stateless societies already had slavery, but it came after the development of agriculture and livestock breeding.

To a hunter and gatherer, a slave is worthless. Why should a stranger be fed and watched over in a society that produces little or no surplus and where labor is not the scarce factor of production? The difference between abundance and scarcity in hunting and gathering societies largely originates in ecological conditions such as rainfall. When times are good, food is readily gathered without any need for additional labor; in periods of scarcity, extra labor is even more useless as it represents a net drain on scarce resources. Female slaves would, of course, produce children for their male owners, but the hunting and gathering mode of production puts severe ecological constraints on polygyny. The cost of slave keeping is not only one of providing food and bare necessities, but also that of supervision. A slave, being a stranger, can, by definition, not be trusted and, therefore, must be prevented from running away, doing mischief and, if male, impregnating the captors' women. Unless the value of the slave's labor more than equals both sustenance and custodial costs, slavery is not a viable institution.

Agriculture is clearly the critical threshold where slave labor is economically exploitable because, with agriculture, labor becomes a scarce factor of production, and surplus can be accumulated. Even the simplest kind of agriculture—tropical swidden horticulture—is much more labor-intensive than hunting and gathering. Slave labor can mean surplus production. With surplus production, more extensive polygyny also becomes possible. Wealth can be converted into wives through payment of bridewealth, an institution very common among tropical horticulturalists, and women are put to work in the fields creating wealth (as well as children) for their husbands.

In simple horticultural societies, women make far more desirable slaves than men. They often not only do the bulk of the agricultural labor, but they also increase the fitness of their male owners by producing children. Also, to capture a woman spares her captor the cost of the bridewealth he would have had to pay for a woman from his own ethny. Furthermore, female slaves are more easily controlled than male ones, especially when burdened with young children. Male slaves, on the other hand, are much freer to run away and, unless castrated or closely watched, present a constant threat to the fitness of their masters. They are often still more trouble than they are worth. That is why many societies that regularly capture and take in women from other ethnies, keep few, if any, male slaves and then often keep them for relatively short periods of time (such as a few weeks of fattening before eating them).

By contrast, the control and incorporation of captured women is so easy that it often does not even require real institutionalized slavery. Captured women, after an initial "breaking in" period in which they may be gang-raped, have their children killed and be otherwise ill-treated, become gradually incorporated as junior wives in polygynous households and, after a while, are often treated much as native women. (Some might argue that captured women do not have to be given a special slave status, as *all* women in their societies are "enslaved"; this, again, extends the definition of slavery.) In any case, their children are typically completely assimilated into the captor group.

The regular use of male slave labor is found in some of the more complex stateless societies. Stateless but stratified nomadic societies like the Tuareg kept slaves to work in agriculture and in salt mines and even engaged extensively in the trans-Saharan slave trade (Nicolaisen, 1963). But, of course, they were in constant contact with large state societies to the north and south of them, and they long acted as trade intermediaries between them. Large-scale exploitation of slave labor and slave trading are more characteristic of state-organized societies. In fact, relatively few preindustrial states did *not* have some variety or other of slavery.

In the great majority of state-level societies that were both patrilineal and polygynous, the assimilation of female slaves and their offspring within one or, at most, two generations was the rule. The female slave would simply be taken in as junior wife in the polygynous household of her master, and her children by him would, according to the rule of patrilineal descent became free members of their father's lineage. Thus, while the institution of slavery was permanent, the status of slave was often relatively impermanent, at least for women and children.

Male slaves were another matter. Their reproductive success was frequently seriously impaired by slavery—in extreme cases through castration, a practice almost ubiquitous in Muslim societies and not infrequent in a number of other societies ranging from China in the Far East to the boys' choir of the Sistine Chapel in the West. (Indeed, castration was not always linked to slavery.) Furthermore, those who had children had no easy way of securing the emancipation and assimilation of their offspring, especially not in patrilineal societies. In the latter, they sometimes gave rise to slave lineages, set apart from the lineages of commoners and nobles and given special hereditary functions (such as forming the king's bodyguard in the Hausa Kingdoms), even after their members were legally emancipated (M. G. Smith, 1960). The formation by male slaves of hereditary slave descent groups did not preclude in some cases humane treatment and even access to some positions of power and wealth. Indeed, some of the Islamized societies of West Africa even had a slave nobility (Nadel, 1942). Certain political offices were reserved for members of slave lineages. But the slave status of descendants of male slaves was much more likely to become hereditary than in the case of descendants of female slaves.

The main difference, of course, in the position of male and female slaves, even in matrilineal or bilateral descent societies, is in the option of hypergyny open to women but not to men. In virtually all slave systems, the female slave can improve her position and that of her children by mating with her master or one of his kinsmen. Even if emancipation does not result, at least improved conditions can be expected, and her sexual and reproductive value to her master make the hypergynous strategy a likely possibility for almost any nubile female slave. However, the male slave is generally debarred from access to free women. Some clandestine unions may take place but are typically not acknowledged and institutionalized, nor do they markedly improve the conditions of the slave. Indeed, they may expose slaves to the danger of retribution from free men who compete for access to these free women. Male slaves are thus frequently allowed to mate only with slavewomen, and their offspring often inherit slave status.

Such hereditary slave groups, when they constitute themselves into established communities, often become transformed into caste or serf groups, but, even then, they find it difficult to escape their underprivileged or pariah status. An important feature of slavery is its *individual* nature. It is exceptional for real slave *communities* to develop, without becoming transformed into something rather different from slavery. Slavery can long endure as an *institution* in a given society, but the slave status of individuals is typically only semipermanent and nonhereditary. Slaves seldom develop a sense of community; they seldom become a corporate group—a *Klasse für sich* (to use Marxist terminology). Rather, they are much more commonly unstructured congeries of atomized individuals. The institution of slavery may persist, but the personnel rotates. Unless a constantly renewed supply of slaves enters a society, slavery, as an institution, tends to disappear and transform itself into something else.

Basically, this happens in two ways: the predominantly female way of emancipation and assimilation through concubinage with masters, and the establishment of slave families and communities that gradually or abruptly transform themselves into other types of groups (e.g. pariah castes, serf groups, tribute-paying communities or share-cropping tenants). In the former case, slave status seldom survives longer than two generations. In the latter, some kind of inferior status tends to become hereditary, but within a few generations it typically ceases to be real slavery.

The nub of the problem is, again, kin selection. An essential feature of slave status is the condition of being *torn out of one's network of kin selection*. This condition generally results from forcible removal of the slave from his home group by capture or purchase. Being literally alone against the world and being a stranger are the essential conditions that remove restraints on domination and exploitation of the slave. These conditions make him, at least initially, a dehumanized commodity, but, by definition, they cannot last indefinitely. The longer the slave lives in his master's society, the less of a stranger he becomes; the more ties are established—the less alone and atomized. Since the most powerful and basic ties are those of blood, the reconstitution of a kin network *both* with the master group and within the slave group gradually transforms the very nature of slavery. The great internal contradiction of slavery is, thus, kin selection. The only safe way of perpetuating pure slavery is systematically to split up all kin groups among slaves and to prevent their reproduction.

Slavery is often said to have disappeared or to be incompatible with industrialization, but that is a liberal (and socialist) myth. Slavery was massively revived in the Soviet and Nazi concentration camps, and it was harnessed to industrial systems of production—one socialist, the other capitalist. Slavery knows no ideological boundaries. In earlier epochs, this "ideal-type" of slavery was also approximated in massive forms of chattel slavery practiced by states. Many larger states of antiquity used massive quantities of slaves in galleys, in salt mines, in the construction of pyramids, irrigation systems, roads and other public works, and in plantation agriculture.

The simple dichotomy between domestic and chattel slavery, examined earlier, is of limited use, hiding many differences between societies where slavery has existed. The usual identification of chattel slavery with the capitalist mode of production—and of domestic slavery with precapitalist societies—breaks down on closer scrutiny. There is a clear difference of scale and of "economic rationality" between chattel and domestic slavery. The former is characterized by large-scale organization of labor in highly complex, centralized states that engage in trade and produce for export markets. But these conditions already existed in precapitalistic states, such as Ancient Greece, Rome, Persia, Egypt and China, and continue to exist in socialist societies, as shown by the existence of the Gulag Archipelago.

There are two interesting Marxist traditions in the treatment of slavery. The "classical" Marxist tradition sees slavery as a precapitalist, indeed, prefeudal, mode of production. The Neo-Marxist tradition sees chattel slavery as characteristic of agrarian capitalism. Both conceptions are wrong. Slavery appears as soon as labor can be profitably exploited—that is, as soon as the products of labor can be stored. Slavery increases in scale and tends to become more systematically and rationally exploitative as productive technology improves, as trade develops and as states become increasingly large and centralized. The extent to which a system of slavery approaches the "ideal type" of totally rational, dehumanized chattel slavery, where the slave is reduced to a pure economic commodity, is determined mostly by the power of the state and of the individual members of the ruling class rather than by the system of production *as such* or, much less, by ideology.

Of course, it takes a relatively complex and differentiated system of production to produce a state powerful enough to have chattel slavery and to make the latter profitable. Chattel slavery requires either a state able to maintain public works and fleets of galleys, or a trading economy sufficiently developed for large-scale mining and agricultural exports. This generally means agrarian societies, i.e. societies relying on a complex agricultural technology with use of animal traction, the wheel, the plow, and wind and water power. Some societies of western Africa, which are just below that technological threshold, already had large-scale slavery before European conquest. Some Hausa nobles owned hundreds of slaves, and the slave population of some West African cities like Kano is estimated to have ranged between one-fourth and one-half of the total (A. G. B. Fisher and H. J. Fisher, 1971; Miner, 1965; M. G. Smith, 1960). These highly stratified, complex horticultural societies, however, did not yet have genuine chattel slavery.

Chattel slavery is sometimes associated *exclusively* with agrarian societies and is thought to be incompatible with industrialization. This notion is invalidated not only by the 20th-century concentration camp systems in both their Fascist and their Communist variant, but also by the use of slave labor in 19th century factories in the United States and in Brazil (Goldin, 1975; Karash, 1975). What is needed to maintain or recreate slavery in a modern industrial economy is a totalitarian state. The Nazi concentration camps, such as Auschwitz, were surrounded by industrial out-stations especially constructed to make use of cheap labor rented out to industrialists by the S.S. (Kogon, 1950).

SLAVERY AMONG THE HAUSA

Before turning to the slave regimes of the Western Hemisphere that are usually considered to be the type-cases of chattel slavery, let us examine more closely the more "domestic" type of slavery in a complex horticultural society of Africa, the Hausa of Northern Nigeria. Our account will be based principally upon the Emirate of Zazzau and the city of Zaria, studied by Michael G. Smith (1960), and upon Mary F. Smith's (1954) biographical account of a Hausa woman. The Hausa are one of the largest ethnies of Africa; they number at least 15 million people, occupying much of Northern Nigeria and Niger. Islamized some 500 years ago, they have a long tradition of centralized, hierarchical states with a literate ruling class (M. G. Smith, 1965b).

The Hausa live in the savannah environment of the Western Sudan and engage in intensive swidden agriculture, based principally on cereal crops (sorghum, millet, maize and rice), though many other plants are cultivated as well. Stratified into a ruling aristocracy, an urbanized middle class (traders, priests—teachers and artisans organized in specialized guilds), a mass of peasants and slaves, they have, for at least five or six centuries, had important cities, taken part in long-distance trade across the Sahara and been part of large conquest empires of which the British Empire was but the last. In short, the Hausa have long been organized in complex societies of the feudal type, comparable in many respects to those of medieval Europe or Japan, though not quite as technologically advanced.

Zazzau is one of the Hausa states conquered by the Fulani in 1804 and incorporated in a vast feudal empire dominated by a mixed Hausa and Fulani aristocracy. Inequality pervades the entire social structure. Not only are people stratified in broad strata with specialized functions: noblemen with political offices, priests and teachers, merchants, artisans, soldiers, prostitutes, ordinary peasants and large numbers of slaves, but they are also linked by *personal* relationships of patron to client, based on the exchange of loyalty and services for protection. Clientage is clearly distinguishable from slavery, since patron—client ties link not only free men and slaves, but also free persons of unequal status, including noblemen of different rank—all the way up to the king and his direct vassals.

When the British imposed their control over the Hausa States through military conquest in 1902–1903, they sought to abolish slavery and the slave trade, which they found to be well-established institutions. Their efforts met with only very partial success, as people continued to be identified as exslaves or descendants of slaves, and relations of master to slave continued as clientage or serfdom. Slaves were permitted to declare themselves free, but fewer than 10,000 had done so in the whole of Northern Nigeria by 1920 (M. G. Smith, 1960, p. 223). While the capture and sale of slaves was largely abolished after British rule, the institution of slavery itself lingered on, and abolition was very gradual.

In traditional Hausa society slavery was a legal status that could be ended for both sexes through manumission, purchase of freedom and, for females, through bearing a child for their master. Female slaves typically became their master's concubines in this polygynous, Islamic society and thus had a relatively quick escape from slavery if they were fertile. For men and their descendants, slave status was often hereditary. A basic distinction was made between slaves acquired through capture who were strangers and generally non-Muslims, and those born into slavery who were raised as Muslims and could not legally be sold. Captives were, however, sold and used by vassals in payment of taxes to the king.

Muslim slaves born in slavery were better treated than captured pagans. They were acculturated to the language and customs of their masters, often lived in their master's household, called their master and his kinsmen by their terms such as "father" and "brother," had "joking relationships" with their master's children, took part in the religious life of their master's family and had their marriage (sometimes to a free woman) arranged by their master. All the same, even the privileged Muslim slaves had facial scars to identify them as slaves, were legally and politically dependent on their masters, passed on slave status if male to their children and could not dispose of their property at will. The descendants of a male exslave continued to be identified as such and to inherit inferior status, menial jobs and dependence on the descendants of their ancestor's master. That is, even after a person was emancipated, his dependence and that of his descendants continued in the form of clientage or serfdom to his master's descendants. Occupationally, slaves were concentrated in menial jobs, principally in agriculture and domestic service, but the king's slaves often became professional soldiers, and favorite slaves of high-ranking noblemen could rise to positions of considerable power and wealth. Some rose to relatively high military or civilian rank among the royal office holders and came to constitute a kind of privileged, hereditary slave nobility. Slaves or exslaves could even become slave owners in their own right and could marry free persons. However, a master inherited his slave's property. A Hausa proverb justifies this practice, as well as hereditary slavery: "If you buy a hen and a rooster in the market and they have chickens, to whom do the chickens belong?" (M. G. Smith, 1960, p. 259).

While many slaves lived in the intimacy of their master's extended family and were treated as family retainers, as concubines or almost as poor relations, others were definitely exploited in a more systematic manner. Wealthy aristocrats owned entire villages of slaves who cultivated their lands for them; some forms of slavery thus verged on hereditary serfdom. Accounts by 19th-century European travelers estimated the slave population of some districts of Hausaland as ranging from one-third to one-half of the total (M. G. Smith, 1960). Obviously, such a large servile population played an important role in the system of production.

Besides the slaves proper, Hausa society also had other social groups distinct from the mass of free men. Some occupational groups (hunters, blacksmiths, butchers and tanners) were ascribed low status and constituted endogamous pariah castes. Castration was also practiced, and eunuchs constituted a status group by themselves, distinct from both slaves and freemen in that they shared some of the disabilities of the former and some of the privileges of the latter. Their status was, in the nature of the case, irreversible (unlike slaves who could be freed), but they had privileged access to some important political positions.

As can be seen from this one example of slavery in a complex preindustrial, precapitalist society, the word "slavery" is merely a convenient label covering a wide range of statuses and situations, with considerable variation even within a single society, let alone cross-culturally. The general conclusions arrived at earlier are supported by the Hausa case, however. Female slaves are more easily assimilated than male ones. The prototypical slave is the stranger who is torn out of his kinship network. To the extent that the slaves live and reproduce in their "host society," they either gradually assimilate as individuals (especially so in the case of females), or distinct slave groups begin to form which, in time, acquire more the characteristics of caste, serfdom or clientage than of slavery proper.

THE SLAVE REGIMES OF THE WESTERN HEMISPHERE

Europe inherited the institution of slavery from Rome, but slavery was gradually replaced by serfdom in much of Europe during the Middle Ages. However, it never completely disappeared, especially not in the Mediterranean area, where the extensive use of galleys created a continuing demand for slaves. The sudden expansion of Europe in the American tropics, in the 16th century, revived and extended European slavery on a scale hitherto undreamt of. By the time the transatlantic slave trade was effectively ended in the middle of the 19th century, an estimated 12 to 15 million Africans had crossed the ocean in chains (Curtin, 1969; Davidson, 1961). The loss of human potential to Africa caused directly or indirectly by the transatlantic slave trade was much greater. Between 10 and 20% of the slaves (and comparable proportions of the European crews) died of disease in transit (Curtin, 1969), and vast numbers were killed as a result of the innumerable raids and wars between African nations, fostered by the European demand for slaves. Estimates of total deaths range from 50 to 200 million, but even the lower estimates qualify the transatlantic slave trade as the greatest crime in human history. (The Nazi Holocaust and Stalin's Gulag Archipelago are the only serious contenders.)

The trade continued to grow from small-scale beginnings in the late 15th century (Table I). Until 1600, less than a million slaves were exported from

TABLE I. Estimates of Slave Imports into the Americas

1500–1525	12,500
1525–1550	125,000
1550–1600	750,000
1600–1650	1,000,000
1650–1700	1,750,000
1700–1750	3,000,000
1750–1800	4,000,000
1800–1850	3,250,000
TOTAL	13,887,500

Source: Dunbar (1861).

Africa. In the 17th century, the volume of trade tripled to some 2,750,000. In the 18th century, the "golden age" of the traffic, some 7,000,000 slaves were transported to the Americas. The 19th century marked the first attempts by the British Navy to halt the trade, at least in West Africa, and by the 1850s, transatlantic slaving was over. Yet, another 3 to 4 million Africans crossed the ocean in the first half of the 19th century—at a rate comparable to that prevailing in the 18th century.

The history of the Atlantic slave trade reveals a complex business partnership between Europeans and Africans. It pitted Africans against each other, and European slaving nations against each other, much more than Africans against Europeans (Davidson, 1961). Any reading of the enterprise as one of blacks against whites is a gross distortion of a much more complex reality. Most slaves were captured by Africans and sold by Africans to Europeans. Extensive slave trading had existed inside West Africa and across the Sahara, long before the European demand developed, but there is no question that the establishment of slave colonies in the Western Hemisphere greatly increased the traffic and intensified warfare between African nations (Bovill, 1958; Davidson, 1961; A. G. B. Fisher and H. J. Fisher, 1971; Oliver and Fage, 1962).

The constellation of circumstances created by European colonial expansion in tropical and subtropical America made slavery practically inevitable and made the western coast of Africa, from Senegal to Angola, the most likely source of supply. First the Spanish and the Portuguese, then the English, French and Dutch, found themselves in control of tropical territories that they could not successfully settle with large numbers of Europeans, and where the indigenous population was initially sparse and inaccessible (in the case of the Amazonian jungle) and quickly decimated by epidemics (especially in the Caribbean).

After they discovered that these territories were suitable for the cultivation of certain crops for export to Europe, the development of colonial economies hinged on the importation of cheap, docile labor, i.e. of slave labor. A glance at a map of the world shows that the west coast of Africa was destined to be the source of slaves, for these reasons:

1. The West African coast was the nearest source of labor acclimatized to the tropics. Slaves were taken mostly from West Africa to the West Indies, and from Angola to Brazil.

2. The transatlantic slave trade fitted in nicely with the sailing circuit across the North and South Atlantic established by the trade winds. The slave trade thus became the notorious "Middle Passage" of a vast triangular journey that brought European manufactured goods (firearms, textiles, brandy, glass beads and metal wares) to Africa in exchange for slaves; then sold slaves in exchange for tropical crops in the Americas—mostly sugar and its derivatives (molasses and rum) but also tobacco, coffee, indigo, cotton and others; and finally traded their colonial wares in Europe for manufactured goods with which to buy new slaves. The risks were substantial but so were the profits.

3. The relatively advanced societies of West Africa sustained high enough population densities to provide a continuous supply of slaves for well over three centuries. Contrary to general opinion, Africans were so successfully enslaved, not because they belonged to primitive cultures, but because they had a complex enough technology and social organization to sustain heavy losses of manpower without appreciable depopulation. Even the heavy slaving of the 18th century made only a slight impact on the demography of West Africa. The most heavily raided areas are still today among the most densely populated.

4. Africans were especially valuable as a source of labor because they were not only acclimatized to the tropics, but also because they were relatively immune to the European diseases that decimated American Indians.

5. Most African slaves came from agricultural societies. This meant that they were used to hard work in hot climates, and also that they had a number of useful skills as experienced peasants, blacksmiths and so on.

The prototypical slave unit in the New World was, of course, the plantation, but not all African slaves worked on plantations. In Brazil, mining (of diamonds and other precious stones) consumed vast numbers of slaves, if only because mortality in the mines was extremely high. In the highlands of Spanish America, where Indian labor was cheaper and more abundant, African slaves often became prized house servants and artisans, living in cities. Even on the West Indies islands, whose economies were almost exclusively based on sugar cane plantations, a minority of the slaves were house servants and craftsmen, living in towns. Nevertheless, the mass of slaves in the colonies that relied most heavily on slave labor consisted of field hands on plantations.

Of the crops produced by slave plantations, sugar was by far the most important. The Spanish saying stated it well: *Donde hay azucar, hay negros.* ("Where there is sugar, there are blacks.") Successful sugar cultivation is both capital- and labor-intensive because the sugar cane, once cut, must be crushed and converted into sugar and molasses before it ferments. This requires a fairly large scale of production. Each unit of production must have ready access to a processing mill, and although it was possible for several smaller plantations to share a mill, the ideal setup was a plantation of several hundred hectares with its own mill and a slave labor force of 100 men or more, and with continuous, year-round cane cutting and processing. A sugar plantation was a complex operation requiring a large supply of disciplined, robust workers driven to cut cane, an animal transport system to bring the cane to the mill, and skilled craftsmen to run the mill and keep the machinery in good repair. The sugar plantation, in short, was a little self-contained rural industry, relying on coercion to squeeze maximum profit from an unwilling labor force.

A breakdown of the destination of slaves in the New World clearly shows the paramount importance of sugar as the main crop of the slave plantation system. Between 1701 and 1810, at the height of the system of plantation slavery, British North America imported a mere 348,000 slaves—about 3,000 a year. By comparison, the Spanish colonies imported 579,000 (mostly in Cuba, Santo Domingo, Puerto Rico and the coastal strips of Mexico, Venezuela, Colombia, Ecuador and Peru); the British Caribbean islands, 1,401,000; the French Caribbean, 1,358,000; the Dutch islands, 460,000; and Brazil, 1,891,000 (Pescatello, 1975, pp. 47–48).

These figures reveal how marginal to the slave trade the southern United States were. They were in fact the only major slave plantation area devoted to crops other than sugar cane (first tobacco, then cotton), the only non-tropical area and the only area where slave plantations co-existed with yeoman farming (not in the exact same location, to be sure, but in closely contiguous zones). Since tobacco and cotton did not have the same complex technological requirements as sugar making, southern United States plantations could be, and indeed typically were, much smaller than the sugar plantations of the Caribbean and Brazil. In 1860, on the eve of emancipation, there were about 350,000 slave owners in the United States—1.3% of the country's whites. Among them, they owned some 3,952,000 slaves, for an average of only a little over 11 slaves per owner.

Only one-fourth of the slaves lived on plantations of over 50 slaves; only 2,600 United States plantations had more than 100 slaves. Below size 50, one may question the appropriateness of the term "plantation" (Genovese, 1974, p. 7). Roughly half of the slaves lived in productive units of less than 20 to 50 slaves. By comparison, the average late-18th century Jamaican plantation had 240 slaves (Craton, 1975, p. 252). That is, many slaves in the American South lived either on medium-size farms rather than real plantations, and quite a few even lived as servants and craftsmen in cities. The plantation regime was really marginal to the North American economy and was only one of the economic sectors of the American South.

Of course, one of the main reasons why so relatively few slaves were imported into the English North American colonies, is that the life expectancy of slaves in North America was much higher than in the rest of the slave colonies. This was a result both of a healthier climate, free of most tropical diseases, and of better diet and work conditions (Fogel and Engerman, 1974). Indeed, the North American slave population was the only one in the Western Hemisphere that increased more by reproduction than by immigration. In the 50 years between 1810 (after the slave imports were halted in the United States) and 1860, the "Negro" population more than tripled from 1.4 to 4.4 million. To be sure, these figures involved many people of mixed descent, but since very few "blacks" were born to white women, the increase still reflects a good measure of the reproductive success of black *women*. Considering that this period antedates the advances of preventive medicine in the latter part of the 19th century, such a rate of population increase is quite remarkable. It was undoubtedly one of the highest in the world at that time and is comparable to the reproductive success of French Canadians—a proverbially prolific group—during the same period. Between 1815 and 1865, the population of Québec (which was overwhelmingly French and, after the British conquest, increased almost exclusively by natural increase) grew from 265,000 to 980,000, a multiplication factor of 3.7 compared to 3.1 for U.S. blacks (Urquhart and Buckley, 1965).

THE GUILT ASCRIPTION GAME: WHOSE SLAVERY WAS WORSE?

Such a conclusion seemingly contradicts much historiography that has depicted the North American variety of chattel slavery as especially ruthless and harsh (Freyre, 1963, 1964; Tannenbaum, 1947). In fact, that tradition based its conclusions principally on the *legal* status of slaves and the frequency of manumission. The latter was indeed much more infrequent and difficult in the United States than in Brazil, and even in the West Indies where a large middle class of free mulattoes gradually emerged on most islands (Lowenthal, 1972). As Genovese (1969b) points out, any comparison of slave regimes must clearly distinguish between (1) material conditions of life (work, diet, housing, clothing, hygiene), (2) social conditions (family security, religious life), and (3) access to freedom and citizenship. Revisionist historiography has established that, even in the second respect, North American slavery was not as destructive as it had long been depicted to have been (Gutman, 1976). Only on the third basis of comparison does North American slavery come out unfavorably.

The main differences between the American slave regimes become understandable in materialist terms, without invoking cultural differences in degrees of benevolence or malevolence. In North America, the legal inportation of slaves was stopped in 1808 (20 years after the U.S. Constitution was adopted) and, thereafter, the supply of slaves became, but for a little contraband, entirely internal. Prices rose to about $1,800–$2,000 for young adults (a figure to be multiplied at least sixfold in today's dollars), and high prices made it profitable to protect the investment through good diet and medical care—and to promote reproduction. Even before the importation of slaves was stopped, slaves cost more in North America than in the West Indies, because they generally went through middlemen, usually in Jamaica, where they were kept to be "seasoned" and to recover from the Middle Passage before resale for profit on the continent.

Until the 19th century, the demand for slaves in North America was not very great. Since slaves took well to the mild climate of the American South, owners discovered that it was more profitable to keep their slaves strong and healthy and to encourage slavewomen to reproduce than to rely on fresh stock from Africa, who often arrived sick, who had to be broken into slavery, who had to be trained from scratch and who were often seditious and escape-prone. The premium was thus on satisfaction of the demand for slaves through internal reproduction and on long-range exploitation of a high-quality labor force born to slavery (hence, more docile), acclimatized to local conditions (and therefore healthier), culturally assimilated to their masters (and therefore easier to handle) and skilled in a wide diversity of tasks ranging from field work and domestic service to the full range of specialized crafts like needlework, blacksmithing and carpentry.

Once established, this system of breeding your own slaves created an approximately equal sex ratio that further facilitated reproduction. As for material conditions, the more diversified agriculture of North America made it possible to feed slaves an adequate diet inexpensively. Food was locally produced, often on the plantation itself or nearby. In short, in North America, where slaves were expensive but where conditions of survival were good, the emphasis was on long-range productivity: slaves were not only worked, they were also systematically bred. Slave breeding became a special kind of animal breeding, especially developed in the "Old South," to supply the growing labor demands of the larger cotton plantations of the "New South" after the 1830s (Sutch, 1975).

These rational considerations made for relatively good *material* treatment of slaves, but they also discouraged manumission. Since slaves were such a large investment and skilled slaves were so expensive and difficult to replace, manumission was correspondingly costly. The owner thereby lost considerable productive capital, and the slave or exslave had little chance of accumulating enough money to buy his own or his relatives' freedom. Therefore, manumission was infrequent and discouraged. Only about one-tenth of the "Negro" population of the United States was free in 1860. A greatly disproportionate number of them were mulattoes, and, thus, presumably often blood relatives of the master who emancipated them or their ancestors. The only other slaves who were regularly emancipated were old people past productive and reproductive age, so as to avoid the cost of feeding the aged and infirm. This was such a problem that several southern states passed laws requiring slave owners to post a large bond when they manumitted slaves, so as to forestall the danger of old freedmen becoming a public burden.

My argument, in short, is not that North American slave owners were more humane than elsewhere, but that conditions in North America favored keeping slaves strong and healthy and, therefore, productive and reproductive. By contrast, conditions in Brazil and the West Indies were radically different. The climate was tropical and thus mortality was higher. Slaves were principally in sugar cane plantations and secondarily in mines. In both cases, work conditions were extremely strenuous; in mines, they were downright lethal. Slaves were cheaper than in North America because the West Indies and Brazil were closer to the source of supply. However, providing slaves with an adequate diet was more difficult, especially in the West Indies where agricultural land was scarce and allocated almost exclusively to the monoculture of sugar cane. Staple foods had to be imported, and they tended to be low-quality starches. Slave reproduction was hampered not only by disease, poor diet and high mortality but also by a high masculinity ratio. Since the demand was principally for strong field or mine workers, many more men were brought in than women. Women took nearly as much space on slave ships and fetched a lower price on arrival, unless they were particularly attractive.

Jointly, all these conditions dictated a different optimum solution in the utilization of slave labor. Except for a small elite of skilled house servants and craftsmen, maximum productivity was achieved by working slaves to an early death (often in a few months in the case of the Brazilian mines, in a few years in the West Indian sugar plantations), and then by replacing them with fresh imports. The motivation was cold profit maximization unaffected by moral considerations (Fogel and Engerman, 1974; Engerman, 1975). On the positive side, since slaves were cheaper, more expendable and more easily replaceable, it followed that manumission was relatively easier and more frequent than in North America. Thus, the seeming paradox in the relative "benevolence" or "malevolence" of slave regimes is resolved. The material conditions of slavery and the ease of emancipation vary *inversely* with each other—and for basically materialist reasons. It is as meaningless to compare slave regimes in terms of how humane or inhuman they were as it would be to debate whether the Soviet concentration camps were more humane than the Nazi ones, or whether Buchenwald was better than Dachau.

Chattel slavery is, first and foremost, a system of production adapted to a set of ecological and social conditions. Its modalities are understandable much more in terms of an ecological model of fitness maximization (or—what is substantially the same—an economic model of profit maximization) than in terms of an idealist model ascribing causality to ideological and cultural superstructures. Least enlightening of all in understanding the nature of slavery is the moralistic game of guilt ascription or expiation. Indeed, the blanket ascription of collective racial guilt for slavery to "whites" that is so dear to many liberal social scientists is in itself a product of the racist mentality produced by slavery. It takes a racist to ascribe causality and guilt to racial categories.

PATERNALISM, HYPERGAMY AND KIN SELECTION

A feature of slave plantations that has been extensively stressed is pater-nalism or patriarchy (Freyre, 1963, 1964; Genovese, 1969a, 1974; van den Berghe, 1978a). Descriptions abound of the slave plantation as a self-con-tained, self-sufficient microcosm under the patriarchal authority of the owner, as a kind of big unhappy family, so to speak. All chattel slave regimes developed a legitimating ideology of paternalism. Apologists for slavery depicted the slave as a kind of irresponsible, immature, impulsive, emo-tional, happy-go-lucky, grown-up child who could not fend for himself and in whose best interest it was, therefore, to be taken care of by a benevolent master. The latter was, in turn, described as a father figure having the welfare and happiness of his unwilling charges at heart. Some authors went as far as to interpret the master–slave relationship in turgid psychoanalytic terms, such as a complementary sadomasochistic relationship rooted in pseudo-oedipal conflicts (Freyre, 1963, 1964). Others simply dismissed the pater-nalistic façade of the slave plantation as a self-serving ideological superstructure to justify slavery (Cox, 1948; Genovese, 1969a, 1974).

Once again, the issue is not how benevolent slave owners *really* were, or what the proportion of "good masters" was. There is no question that pa-ternalism *was* a self-serving apology for slavery. One also does not need to search far to see that the paternalistic etiquette of dominance and subser-vience, including the "Sambo psychology" of slaves (pretending incom-petence, childish delight and grateful sycophancy), was a ritualistic façade masking real attitudes. Indeed, this paternalistic etiquette of ethnic relations is not unique to slave regimes: it is found wherever two groups live side-by-side in a situation of great inequality combined with close spatial prox-imity and emotional intimacy. The parent–child model of interaction, which also has these properties, is easily extended by analogy to the master–slave relationship.

It does not take far-fetched psychoanalytic concepts of oedipal conflicts and sadomasochism to understand why paternalism is so popular a model for tyranny. Where a parental–filial relationship *does* exist, kin selection ensures that the interaction, however unequal, is mutually beneficial in most cases. That is, the real father does have an interest in the fitness of his children and does generally discipline them "for their own good," because their own good is also his own good. Their genes are also his. Where the parentage is fictive, so, we may assume, is the benevolence. Paternalism uses the fiction of biological relatedness to make tyranny appear just. It uses the deep-rooted symbols of kin selection as a political mystification to justify parasitic exploitation and to hide the coercive nature of the political system that perpetuates that exploitation.

But what if masters and slaves were in *fact* relatives, as they frequently were? We know that all slave systems, chattel and domestic alike, are great genetic melting pots. It is precisely the nearly complete control of the master over his female slaves that makes for the high rate of interbreeding characteristic of all slave regimes, and which differentiates slavery from other types of ethnic subordination such as ordinary conquest, pariah caste status or even serfdom. Under slavery, male slaves are virtually powerless to prevent their masters from mating with "their" women. Slavewomen also lack effective power to resist and, furthermore, they can gain appreciable advantages by *not* resisting.

Therein lies the fundamental asymmetry of male and female slavery. The mating system of the slave plantation was both polygynous and hypergynous. The owner, his sons and the overseer were polygynous since they had access not only to white women whom they married—but also the pick of young slaves whom they took as concubines. Concubinage with slaves was somewhat more clandestine and hypocritical in the English and Dutch colonies than in the Spanish, Portuguese and French territories where it was brazen, but there is no evidence that the actual *incidence* of interbreeding was any higher in the Catholic countries. It is safe to assume that, since control over slaves was about equal, the opportunities for mating with slaves were also similar, and that most such opportunities were taken since they combined business with pleasure. Mulatto slaves were generally worth more than black ones, and therefore masters had a financial incentive to encourage interbreeding if not by themselves, then by their overseers or guests (who were often offered the sexual hospitality of a slavegirl).

From the standpoint of the slavewoman, mating with an owner or overseer was a form of hypergyny. It gave her a chance for a better job in the big house, for better diet and clothes for herself and her offspring and perhaps the hope of emancipation, or at least favorite treatment, for her children. In all slave regimes, there was a close association between manumission and European ancestry. In 1850, in the United States, for example, an estimated 37% of the free "Negroes" had white ancestry, compared to about 10% of the slave population. The southern free Negro population was even more disproportionately mulatto (Genovese, 1974, p. 414). In the West Indies, too, the free people of color were predominantly mulattoes and quadroons, so much so that, on many islands, they came to constitute a clearly distinct middle class in a three-tiered hierarchy of color (Craton, 1975). This hierarchy survived slavery, existing to this day. The elite is white; the middle class is brown; and the mass of peasants and workers is black (Lowenthal, 1972). Obviously, nepotism often resulted in manumission of relatives.

Even if the slavewoman wanted to resist her master's attentions, she was seldom in a position to do so; consequently, she often had little option but to make the best of a bad bargain and bear her master's children. This was often a better option than mating with another slave with little opportunity of bettering her children's life chances. In either case, the product of her reproductive investment was the property of her master. In either case, she increased her fitness, but, through the hypergynous strategy, her chances of improvement for herself and her offspring were better.

Conversely, the male slave's fitness was greatly diminished by slavery, much more than the fitness of the female slave. He was denied access to white women, often under penalty of death or castration. The economics of most slave regimes, by creating a considerable surplus of male over female slaves, imposed celibacy or polyandry on the male slave, thus further reducing his reproductive success. Of the slavewomen, the younger and more attractive ones were often preempted by the white owners and overseers. He was thus left with the older, less fertile ones.

Even then, his choice of mates was often curtailed by his master. It is not true that slave owners systematically broke up slave couples (Genovese, 1974; Gutman, 1976). On the contrary, it was often in their interest to foster stable slave families, for the sake of morale, and to discourage escape. Sometimes, slaves were sold or exchanged to permit a valued slave to live with the woman of his choice if she belonged to another plantation. Again, benevolence is not the question here, but interest. There were not enough slavewomen to permit stable monogamy for most male slaves in most slave regimes. Those who were stably mated often had to be content with older women. Many had no permanent mate at all, had to share women with other slaves, and had their sex lives reduced to irregular, unstable relationships. All this translated into low average reproductive success for male slaves.

The first significant consequence of this hypergynous, polygynous mating system of the plantation was, thus, a great sexual asymmetry in the reproductive impact of slavery for men and women. Slavery drastically reduced the fitness of male slaves; it had little or no such adverse effect on the fitness of female slaves whose masters had a double interest—financial and genetic—in having them reproduce at maximum capacity.

This sexual asymmetry of reproductive strategy for male and female slaves had as a consequence frequent conflicts of interest between slavemen and slavewomen. In particular, the men resented both their inability to protect their women from sexual contact with whites and the women's greater opportunities for improved status and treatment. Also, many male slaves did not have the consolation available to almost all slavewomen—of procreating and raising their own children.

At a group level, these conflicts between the sexes within the slave population were an important factor militating against the formation of group cohesion and solidarity among slaves. Slaves were effectively prevented from forming an effective solidary community, not only because they came from a great many different origins and were often uprooted by sales, but also because of these sex conflicts. Slavery was much tougher on men than on women. No wonder that so many black women emerged from it as towers of strength, compared to their male companions. They had an easier time of it. It is perhaps not far-fetched to suggest that, even today, much of the ambivalence in relations between black men and women in America (including the stereotypes of female strength and male weakness) has its roots in the highly asymmetrical mating system of the slave plantation.

The second fundamental consequence of the polygynous, hypergynous system of plantation mating was that it undermined the institution of slavery itself by continuously creating ties of blood between masters and slaves, and between whites and blacks. That is, kin selection operated across racial lines, so that the plantation was in fact a breeding system—a big family of sorts, albeit a rather perverse exemplar thereof.

After several generations of interbreeding, a complete phenotypic continuum between African and European was created, making the categorical *racial* distinction that underlied Western slavery increasingly tenuous and untenable. If the rationale for keeping a person enslaved was that he was black and therefore inferior, near-white slaves were a constant embarrassment and a living reproach. And, if these mulattoes and quadroons were, in addition, your children, your grandchildren, your half-siblings, your cousins, your nephews and nieces, your uncles and aunts, the embarrassment became even more acute. You had to admit that the blood you shared with them enobled them; but if that were so, then how could you justify retaining them as slaves?

Obviously, nepotism operated between masters and slaves as it did within the two groups. The biological basis of kin selection was too deep to have been completely overridden by such a recent and arbitrary cultural arrangement as slavery. Slaves who were kinsmen were treated preferentially and often freed. Slave mothers could not hate their master's children if the latter were also their own. Inevitably deep bonds were created between masters and slaves, making for multiple strains within the system of slavery itself. To the extent that the plantation was an enclosed breeding unit, a reproducing population in the genetic sense, the chasm between master and slave was at least partially bridged, and the rudiments of a genuine extended family, of a clan, or a micro-ethny were laid.

Paternalism was thus not entirely a myth. The plantation was always an *incipient* family and therein was its deepest contradiction, a contradiction that it could not, in the long run, survive. Chattel slavery was a system of ruthless, parasitic exploitation, serving the interests of the masters. But if slaves become kinsmen you cannot exploit them without indirectly exploiting yourself. Yet slavery, by making the slavewoman widely available to her master made this paradoxical outcome inevitable. Western slavery thus literally contained the genetic seeds of its own destruction. A slave system can only perpetuate itself by continuously replacing its personnel. A *breeding* slave system cannot persist very long. Slavery makes for quick acculturation and interbreeding. Assimilation in the second or third generation is almost irresistible.

EPILOGUE

Ironically, while all the slave plantation regimes of the Western Hemisphere bore an air of family resemblance, they gave birth after their demise to very different societies with radically distinct types of race and ethnic relations (van den Berghe, 1978a). Even a relatively small area like the Caribbean shows a bewildering internal diversity of systems of race, ethnic and class stratification.

At one end of the spectrum are the societies, principally Spanish-speaking, where the descendants of slaves are almost totally assimilated to, and undistinguishable from, the rest of the population. Mexico is a case in point. It has approximately the same percentage of its population as the United States who are of wholly or partially African descent (Aguirre Beltrán, 1946). Yet, today, there is no group of people in Mexico who consider themselves or are considered by others as blacks, Africans or in any sense distinct from descendants of Amerindians or Europeans. If one travels to Vera Cruz, one encounters many people who bear clear traces of an African ancestry, but they are completely assimilated in the rest of the population. They seemingly do not even tend to be endogamous.

At the other end of the continuum, the United States stands out as a rigid racial-caste society. There, strangely, as slavery was abolished, racism—the underlying rationale for slavery—survived. The ideological mystification survived the economic institution. Whites who, for over two centuries, had lived and interbred with blacks in situations of intimate and continuous contact suddenly shuddered at the thought of living with them as equals. Masters and slaves had created a common culture and were in the process of welding themselves into a new hybrid race. Suddenly, whites discovered a concern for the purity of their blood and rent asunder what was being forged together. They created a system of racial segregation that confined all those tainted with the stigma of African blood to pariah status, including in many cases their own relatives (Woodward, 1955).

In between these extremes are countries like Brazil, Cuba, Jamaica, Puerto Rico and other Caribbean islands where people are still conscious of a color continuum that broadly correlates with social class distinctions, but where there are no distinct, corporate racial groups. People tend to marry partners of adjacent shades on the color spectrum and tend to associate certain "somatic norm images" (Hoetinck, 1967) with certain descriptive racial labels, but there are no breaks in the spectrum, no barriers between groups, no rigidity or racial self-consciousness in interaction. Those societies are racially conscious but not racially segregated.

Clearly, the association between slavery and racism that is so often taken for granted is merely an accidental artifact of the history of Western expansion. Slavery has often existed without any trace of racism. Conversely, racism can develop and persist in the absence of slavery. That Western racism became a convenient ideological underpinning of slavery was simply a result of the fact that slaves were fetched from far away and, consequently, looked very different from their masters. The history of the United States since 1865 shows that, unfortunately, racism can long survive slavery. In fact, the present system of endogamous racial castes in the United States is more likely to perpetuate racism than the system of slavery that preceded it.

SUGGESTED READINGS

The literature on slavery is not only voluminous but much of it is excellent. For accounts of slavery and the slave trade in traditional African societies, see Bovill (1958), A. G. B. Fisher and H. J. Fisher (1971) and Miner (1965). On the transatlantic slave trade, Curtin (1969) and Davidson (1961) are mines of information—the former on the transportation and distribution of slaves in the New World and the latter on the complex trade partnerships between Europeans and Africans in Africa. The plantation regimes of the Western Hemisphere have been abundantly described and analyzed, but a few works stand out as classics. Tannenbaum's (1947) comparison of the legal status of slaves in the English and Iberian colonies, Freyre's (1963, 1964) accounts of Brazilian slavery, Mellafe's (1975) little introduction to slavery in Latin America, and the works of David B. Davis (1970), Elkins (1968), Fogel and Engerman (1974), Genovese (1965, 1969a, 1974) and Stampp (1964) on North American slavery are all extremely informative. There are edited collections by Foner and Genovese (1969), Engerman and Genovese (1975) and Pescatello (1975)—all three of which contain papers on several countries of the Western Hemisphere.

MIDDLEMAN MINORITIES

Every country, it is often said, has "its Jews." Turkey has Armenians and Greeks; West Africa has Lebanese; East Africa has Indians and Pakistani; Egypt has Copts; Indonesia, the Philippines, Malaysia, Vietnam and Thailand have the Chinese. The list of these "Jews of . . ." is a long one and so is the bibliography of works concerning them (Blalock, 1967; Bonacich, 1973; Delf, 1963; D. P. Ghai and Y. P. Ghai, 1970; Gary Hamilton, 1978; Schermerhorn, 1970; Turner and Bonacich, 1978; van den Berghe, 1975a). What makes such culturally unrelated groups appear so similar to each other in a wide range of societies? What do they share to make them behave in such seemingly like ways?

There are three main, possible sources of similarity:

1. The intrinsic characteristics of these groups themselves.
2. The nature of the larger societies in which they live.
3. The particular economic niche which these groups occupy in their respective societies.

Before I try to answer the puzzling question of why culturally diverse groups tend to behave similarly in many different societies, I shall try to identify the main features of the middleman minority and, thereby, to construct an ideal type of the social situation in which middleman minorities find themselves. In doing so, we must keep in mind that an ideal type is not an accurate description of any particular situation but rather an analytical distillation of the common elements of a whole range of situations. From these empirical generalizations, interrelationships and causality are then inferred.*

---

*Any list of characteristics of an ideal type raises the problem of empirical approximation of actual groups to the ideal type. Often, a given group lacks, or only imperfectly represents, one

(continued)

AN IDEAL TYPE OF THE MIDDLEMAN MINORITY SITUATION

As a general definition, I shall call a "middleman minority" (MM) any ethnically distinct group that specializes in the selling of goods or skills. Such a broad definition tells us practically nothing about the conditions that bring such groups into existence. Indeed, there is a cluster of characteristics that are remarkably uniform from society to society—conducive to the formation of middleman minorities. I shall group these characteristics into the three categories suggested earlier:

Characteristics of Middleman Minority (MM) Groups

1. MMs are not native to the country or area where they reside. They arise from immigration, not conquest, and they are usually voluntary immigrants. MMs do not generally come from groups that have been enslaved, although they are not uncommonly descendants of indentured laborers. Often they come of their own free will, attracted by economic prospects in the country of destination or propelled by destitution out of their country of origin.
2. MMs are characterized by strong extended families, usually of the patrilineal, virilocal type. The authority structure of these families is strongly patriarchal and seniority-based, and networks of nepotism are extensive and actively maintained, even over long distances. It is not uncommon for familistic ties to be maintained even across oceans.
3. As the very term indicates, MMs constitute a minority of the population of their host country, often a small minority (less than 10% or even 5% of the total).
4. MMs tend to be endogamous.
5. MMs tend to be culturally enclosed with their own set of institutions (voluntary associations, places of worship and entertainment, merchant and artisan guilds, schools, etc.).
6. MMs are often spatially segregated in urban ghettoes.
7. As a consequence of characteristics 2, 4, 5 and 6, MMs generally assimilate and acculturate more slowly into their host societies than other immigrant groups.
8. The class status of MMs is generally that of an urban petty bourgeoisie, appreciably better off than the majority of the population, though often far from wealthy.

(continued)
or more of the characteristics of the ideal type. For instance, while MMs are generally not indigenous, the Copts of Egypt are. Sometimes most members of a MM do not engage in the classical MM occupations (retail trade, skilled crafts, specialized labor-intensive services), but are instead peasants or ordinary workers. Such is or was the case of South African Indians and of Armenians in Turkey. Yet, when a visible minority of them are found in middlemen occupations, the MM stereotypes are readily extended to all members of the group, irrespective of occupation. Visibility (through cultural distinctiveness and residential segregation) of a MM is at least as important in determining its treatment as its occupational distribution. Stereotypy is as readily extended to "positive" traits as to "negative" ones. For instance, not all Jews are smart, but the overrepresentation of a minority of Jews among intellectuals, academics and professionals easily gives the impression that Jews tend to outsmart Gentiles. This stereotype, incidentally, is generally shared by both Jews and Gentiles. "Polish jokes" in the United States originate in Eastern European Jewish jokes stereotyping local Gentiles (often Poles) as stupid. Slyness, cunning, and intelligence are qualities often attributed to MMs, and accepted by MMs as part of their self-image.

9. Politically, MMs are often powerless because of their minority status and their cultural marginality and therefore vulnerable to attack. Such wealth as they have is not readily convertible into power.
10. MMs often possess certain skills, such as specialized crafts or mercantile organization, which are scarce in the rest of the population.
11. MMs frequently exhibit values that Weber (1958) associated with the "Protestant Ethic": frugality, thrift, hard work, postponement of gratification and lack of ostentation.

Characteristics of the Host Societies

1. MMs tend to immigrate into complex, stratified, agrarian societies.
2. The economy of these societies is one of mercantile capitalism with well-established markets, money circulation and trade. Indeed, the best opportunities are found in a market economy in the process of expansion into hitherto unmonetized primitive exchange economies.
3. MMs usually find themselves in plural societies, i.e. societies containing sharply distinct ethnies, each with its own set of autonomous institutions but linked in a common polity and economy (Furnivall, 1948; Leo Kuper and M. G. Smith, 1969; Schermerhorn, 1970; M. G. Smith, 1965a; Smooha, 1975; van den Berghe, 1973b). MMs constitute merely one group in a congeries of ethnies.
4. As in the case in most plural societies, MMs typically find themselves ruled by an autocratic government dominated by one ethnic group. Such are colonial societies or other imperial states that have grown from conquest.
5. The state frequently imposes a set of special legal restrictions on MMs. Laws governing immigration, land ownership, access to high-status positions, taxation and trade often discriminate against MMs.
6. MMs are generally the object of much hostility in their host society. They are subject to a "competitive" type of prejudice and are despised by both the ruling class above them and the masses of natives below them (van den Berghe, 1978a). They are accused of being clannish, underhanded, dishonest, sly, disloyal, greedy, avaricious, exploitative and unassimilable—in short, dangerously clever and perilously alien.

Characteristics of the Economic Niche Filled by MMs

1. As indicated by the term, MMs are in a middleman position. They are typically much poorer than the ruling class, but much richer than the mass of natives. Their function is to act as intermediaries in a market economy, as sellers of specialized services and finished products, as buyers of raw materials, as importers and exporters of goods, as money lenders and so on. They tend to fill intercalary positions opened up by a market economy between rulers and ruled.
2. MMs are especially likely to fill occupations that require only a modicum of capital (since their material resources are typically limited, at least initially), but that are labor intensive and require special skills scarce in the majority of the population. Among these skills are specialized crafts catering to luxury goods (goldsmithing, jewelry making), literacy, bookkeeping, an understanding of market forces and organi-

zation of trade, distribution and credit—not to mention the complex skills of manipulating customers and political masters developed through urban experience.

3. MMs owe much of their success to their ability to harness nepotism in the service of capitalism. Their economic organization is based on the systematic mobilization of unpaid family labor in family businesses and of nepotism in employment, extension of credit, supply and distribution of goods, and so on. The success formula of applying kin selection to mercantile capitalism is not unique to MMs. The family firm is found in many other groups as well. But the cultural and physical enclaving of MMs facilitates the extension of nepotism from the extended family to the wider network of the MM as a whole.

THE MIDDLEMAN'S PREDICAMENT: WHOSE FAULT IS IT?

So far, I have simply listed the main recurrent features of MM situations without suggesting any order of precedence or causality between them. The predicament of MMs is obvious. No other type of ethnic group is in such a perilous, vulnerable and defenseless position as the MM. No other groups are as frequently the victims of pogroms, expulsions, confiscations of property, discriminatory taxation and even wholesale genocide. In the catalogue of human bestiality to man, MMs almost invariably appear as victims: Jews in Europe, Armenians in Turkey, Indians in Uganda, the "boat people" of Vietnam (who are mostly ethnic Chinese), the Chinese in Indonesia and many other such MMs have been repeatedly victimized throughout human history.

Indeed, the MM is the ideal scapegoat. It is defined as alien and therefore beyond the protective sphere of extended nepotism that includes the native population. MMs are often exterminated or mistreated without a whisper of protest in the general population and, indeed, often with active support. The small size of the MM makes it powerless and therefore safe to attack, especially when it is concentrated in vulnerable urban ghettoes. MMs are often wealthy enough to excite the envy of the masses and to make their plunder profitable to the rulers—yet too poor to capture the reins of power. In fact, they are *pariah capitalists*, hated for their wealth, mistrusted for their alienness, despised for their weakness, excluded from politics, rejected from civil society and tolerated only as long as they serve a need.

A MM can do no right. If it retreats into the protective cocoon of ethnic isolation, it is accused of clannishness. If it seeks assimilation, it is pushy. If it attempts to demonstrate its loyalty to the state, that behavior is ascribed to opportunism. If it keeps out of politics, it is disloyal. Economic success, thrift, hard work and family loyalty, which are deemed admirable qualities in others, are considered sins for MMs. What is good management, fair profit, fair return on investment, initiative and free enterprise in the native capitalist becomes greed, usury, unfair competition, underhandedness and exploitation in the pariah capitalist.

MMs are invaluable to ruling classes because they create capital, offer a range of valuable services that other groups are either unwilling or unable to provide as cheaply, are a source of taxation, credit or bribery money, modernize the economy and extend markets for goods, and generally energize the economy that the ruling classes parasitize. At the same time, the hostility directed at them by the masses makes MMs ideal scapegoats for anything that goes wrong. Jews in medieval Europe, for example, have been accused of committing not only economic crimes, like usury, hoarding and speculation, but also civil and religious crimes, like ritual murders, the poisoning of wells, witchcraft, the spreading of plague epidemics and the like. To the Nazis, the Jews were involved in a worldwide conspiracy that was at once Bolshevik and capitalist. The "Elders of Zion" were an international consortium of banquiers, bent on spreading atheistic communism. Where a MM can be implicated, prejudices are so blinding that no amount of absurdity detracts from credibility.

Inevitably, moralistic judgments about MMs have invaded the social science literature. The sympathies of many liberal social scientists have often gone to the MMs as defenseless groups, and the behavior of these groups has widely been interpreted as adaptive reactions to the severe constraints under which MMs have found themselves (D. P. Ghai and Y. P. Ghai, 1970; van den Berghe, 1975a). Thus, cultural encapsulation, clannishness, nepotism, deviousness, failure to assimilate, divided loyalties and other alleged sins of MMs have been widely interpreted as defensive reactions against hostility and discrimination in the host society. Some more radical social scientists, however, disturbed by the capitalist features of MMs, have suggested that the hostility of the host society to MMs is, at least, in part attributable to the values and the behavior of these groups, such as their "sojourner mentality" (Bonacich, 1973).

As usual, moralism does little to advance understanding of complex behavior. Little purpose is served by ascribing guilt and judgments of guilt or innocence change with shifts in ideological fads. Thus, the proverbial "failure to assimilate" of MMs is a sin in countries dominated by an assimilationist ideology and a virtue where pluralism is the official line.* Clearly, the behavior of MMs and of other groups in their host societies are interrelated (Turner and Bonacich, 1978). In the last analysis, individuals act in the furtherance of their interests, and differential behavior at the group level is a function of differential group position in the society's political and economic structure.

Applied to MM situations, this simple utilitarian paradigm explains both the treatment and the behavior of MMs principally in terms of the economic niche they occupy. Structural conditions of the host society create the niche for a foreign entrepreneurial class, while structural characteristics of certain ethnies predispose certain groups to occupy MM roles. Given the existence of the niche and the presence of a group with the necessary skills and attributes to fill it, the "competitive" type of ethnic relations characteristic

---

*Incidentally, an ideology of cultural pluralism is not necessarily associated with a liberal, tolerant political regime, nor assimilationism with intolerance and tyranny. South Africa, for instance, has a clear policy of cultural pluralism, despite being one of the world's most racist and illiberal regimes.

of MM situations is highly likely to develop irrespective of the specific values and ideologies of either the host society or the MM group.

When they find themselves in MM situations, Jews, Chinese, Lebanese, Armenians, Indians, Pakistanis, Greeks and Ibos develop surprisingly similar traits. Conversely, the same groups put in different situations begin to behave in ways radically distinct from their previous stereotypes. Jews in the diaspora, for instance, frequently remark how "un-Jewish" Sabras (Israeli-born Jews) are. The same group of Askenazic Jews will drastically modify its behavior depending on whether it lives in a *stetl* in Poland or a *kibbutz* in Israel. The difference is one of being a despised minority in a hostile country or a triumphant conqueror in a state one dominates. In both cases, individuals behave so as to maximize their fitness. Different settings dictate different strategies and produce drastically different outcomes.

HOW THE ECONOMIC NICHE CREATES MIDDLEMAN BEHAVIOR

Let us look more analytically at the dynamics of the MM situation. First, let us define more precisely the nature of the economic niche filled by MMs. Basically MMs interpose themselves between a ruling class and the mass of the population by performing roles that the upper class does not want to perform and for which the lower class lack special skills, capital or other advantages. Those roles are often, but not always, mercantile. They frequently involve providing, distributing and marketing goods and services in a preindustrial economy with an expanding market and monetary system. Classical MM occupations are the import–export trade, retail and wholesale shopkeeping, money lending, buying and reselling of cash crops, specialized craft production in owner-operated cottage industries, specialized labor-intensive services such as restaurants and laundries and the provision of transport facilities (mule trains, buses and trucks). Most of these forms of entrepreneurship are started with little capital and are initially very labor-intensive. With time, some MMs become wealthy and control larger, better capitalized businesses such as banks, large import–export firms, chains of wholesale and retail businesses, shipping or bus lines and warehousing, milling or manufacturing establishments, but large-scale capitalism is the exception. Labor-intensive, limited-capital, petty entrepreneurship is the rule.

Another set of roles sometimes occupied by MMs are clerical, administrative and technical ones in expanding public and private bureaucracies, such as railway employees, petty civil servants and the like. Both these bureaucratic occupations and the more traditional entrepreneurial ones become a monopoly of MMs only to the extent that they are not desirable to members of the ruling class or accessible (for lack of skills, capital or opportunities) to the lower classes.

The most fertile ground for MMs are colonial or imperial systems in which the ruling class, which is often a non-native conquering group, extends its domination and its market system over a native population that initially lacks the skills to fill a broad middle range of occupations. If the conquering group is too small to fill these intermediate-level occupations from its own ranks or finds the rewards of these occupations too meager and the work too hard, it welcomes MMs to fill the niche. The native population is often initially unsuitable for a variety of reasons: it is not literate; it is not urban and therefore lacks familiarity with a monetized market economy; it lacks capital and access to credit; it cannot effectively draw on the unpaid work of relatives; or it does not possess the requisite linguistic skills to act as middlemen.

MMs can also successfully infiltrate settled societies where the ruling class is native, especially if they bring in new skills or products, but in settled societies, the middle tier of service and mercantile occupations is much more likely to have been gradually filled by natives. Therefore, opportunities for MMs are much more limited, unless the native population imposes on itself some self-inflicted restrictions such as the prohibition of usury in medieval Christianity and Islam that created a niche for Jews. The expanding conquest society with an alien ruling class and a multiplicity of native subjects is a much more likely prospect for a MM, especially if the conquered societies had no native merchant class before their incorporation into the new imperial system.

It must be emphasized that, initially, commercial opportunities for MMs are often quite marginal. The native population is typically extremely poor, produces little surplus, has little or no cash and is geographically inaccessible. There are great difficulties of climatic adaptation, of transport and communication, of learning new languages and of obtaining credit. The overhead costs of inventory are high, and the volume of trade is low and erratic. Customers expect credit and are slow to repay. Many businesses can only be kept afloat through long hours of hard work by all the members of the family.

If the familistic mode of production often makes the difference between the success or failure of these precarious small enterprises, it follows that groups with a strong network of extended family ties and with a strong patriarchal authority structure to keep these extended families together in the family business have a strong competitive advantage in middleman occupations over groups lacking these characteristics. This explains the prevalence of groups with patrilineal, virilocal, extended families and strong seniority-based authority in MM roles and, conversely, the absence in these roles of groups where kin ties have been disrupted by a history of slavery, or of groups characterized by a high degree of individualism, by small nuclear families and by a relatively egalitarian family structure.

Indeed, the nepotism so crucial to the success of the family firm is often extended to the entire ethny. In their precarious position, MMs have to make the best possible use of resources and, therefore, extensively resort to ethnic nepotism as sources of employment, credit, transport facilities, intelligence about market conditions and so on.

MMs are generally welcomed, at least initially, by ruling classes of plural societies because they perform cheaply many useful functions. They often extend trade beyond the urban areas and thereby open up new markets for manufactured goods produced by the colonial power. They modernize transport, stimulate the economy and bring the native population into closer control by, and into dependence on, the colonial government. They help staff cheaply and efficiently the lower ranks of the bureaucracy and provide a pool of useable skills before these can be developed in the native population. Most importantly, they serve the useful function of deflecting the hostility of the subject population from the rulers. Since MMs deal more directly and frequently with the masses than the upper class, and since many of these encounters take place in a context of cultural differences and misunderstandings and involve conflicts of interest, it is little wonder that MMs become primary targets of hostility by the native masses. The MMs are generally seen as the most direct exploiters and cheats and are blamed for the system of domination they did nothing to create.

To the extent that MMs become more successful and expand the scope of their economic activities into domains where they begin to compete with the ruling class, they also become the object of virulent prejudice from the top. In a sense, the more economically secure a MM becomes, the more politically precarious its position grows. If it grows wealthy, it becomes the target not only of envy from the bottom, but also of confiscation, discrimination, expulsion or even extermination from the top. Success is thus frequently fraught with danger, and it must be hidden. MMs basically survive by keeping a low profile, by remaining as inconspicuous as possible, by being unostentatious about wealth, by staying out of politics (at least overtly), and by adopting a conciliatory, nonaggressive stance.

THE VICIOUS CIRCLE OF ETHNIC RELATIONS IN MIDDLEMAN MINORITY SITUATIONS

It is easy to see how the very nature of the economic niche and its resultant pattern of interaction creates "typical" MM behavior. The latter in turn reinforces stereotypes and heightens hostility against MMs by host populations. Hostile reactions further accentuate MM behavior, and an almost inescapable vicious circle of ethnic relations ensues. Alien merchant communities often grow slowly and inconspicuously at first. A few enterprising sailors and merchants arrive in a foreign land. They discover an opportunity for trade and settle down. If they survive the first trial period, they send money home to bring wives, children and relatives. Little by little, the word spreads at home that so and so is doing well in a distant land and more undertake the journey. On arrival, they naturally turn for help to relatives, friends or friends of friends. Soon the nucleus of a little ethny-in-the-diaspora is formed. Fellow ethnics stick together for protection, mutual aid, comfort and sociability. Where else can one turn in a strange land?

Little ghettoes quickly and easily form, because a trading community has no better place to locate than at the heart of urban settlements, in harbors, on crossroads and so on. Trade dictates location, and economy, convenience and safety make for combining the place of business and the place of residence. Since money is scarce, there is a strong premium for relying for help on the unpaid labor of wives and kinsmen. Since the shop is run as a family business, what better arrangement than for the family to be housed behind or above the store? You save on housing, are close to your place of work and are protected against theft. Since trade attracts more trade, shops locate close to each other and, if most traders happen to belong to the same alien ethnic group, you have the nucleus of an MM ghetto. Add a schoolhouse and an exotic-looking temple or community hall, and the place acquires a strikingly alien character that heightens the visibility of its population.

Trading anywhere, but especially in poor and foreign countries, is a chancy proposition, and success in it requires a combination of complex skills. One must learn the local language and culture, understand the economics of the marketplace with all the intricacies of supply and demand, credit, interest, risk, overhead, inventory, volume of trade, profit margin and so on. One must meet competition; correctly assess (and often create) demand for goods; adapt to the purchasing behavior of the natives; know when to extend credit and when not; deal with government officials whom one must learn how and when to bribe, cajole or manipulate; negotiate one's way through the bureaucratic red tape of trade licences, import duties, sales taxes, health and fire regulations, building permits, zoning laws, and so on. All this requires skills of literacy, bookkeeping and reckoning, considerable astuteness and acumen in understanding both the market system and the intricacies of social relationships, and great adaptability to local diet, climate and customs. Even though the MM may not assimilate to the host society, it must learn a great deal about it to survive, and, therefore, it must be quite adaptable.

Frugality, thrift and industriousness are initially imposed by the very difficulty of starting a business and of gradually accumulating capital for inventory and expansion. When success comes, it is good public relations to remain as inconspicuous as possible and to hide one's wealth. Nobody likes to see the rich alien merchant flaunting his affluence in a poor country. In dealing with the natives, it is best to be blandly affable but to hide one's feelings and opinions. With the powers that be, one is best subservient and sycophantic. Toward all, except fellow ethnics, one must be coolly calculating, ever alert and watchful, because one is always acutely aware of the precariousness of one's position. One feels caught between the fury and envy of the poor from whom one lives and the rapaciousness and whim of the powerful on whose sufferance one depends.

Against these multiple dangers, one develops nepotism as self-defense; one hedges one's bets by sending money abroad in case of emergency; one keeps one's ties with home and with other kinsmen in the diaspora as a safety net; one bribes for protection and then tries to evade taxes to be able to afford bribery; and one adapts sale tactics to the customers' behavior. For instance, one raises asking prices in expectation of haggling, one uses short weights because one knows that customers like to think they are getting something for nothing, and therefore expect a "gift" on top of their purchase, and so on.*

All these adaptive behaviors earn one a reputation for stinginess, dishonesty, clannishness, deviousness, disloyalty and unassimibility. But one had no real choice. Even if one wanted to assimilate, one would be rejected. Attempts to do so would be regarded as "cheekiness" or "pushiness" by those above and insincerity or opportunism by those below. Participation in open politics is also a closed avenue. If the government is autocratic, MMs are excluded by virtue of being alien, or represented only through a system of indirect rule which reinforces their marginality by giving them separate communal status. If there is a parliamentary democracy, MMs are either disfranchised by citizenship or outright racist legislation—or too small in numbers to prevent discriminatory treatment. In short, it is extremely difficult to assimilate into a society that rejects you, to demonstrate loyalty to a state that discriminates against you, and to show trust and confidence in people who hate and threaten you.

Even MM groups that do achieve a large measure of assimilation are not safe from persecution, as shown by the tragic history of German Jewry. The majority of German Jews felt so German and so assimilated that they were long lulled into a sense of security. Notwithstanding some acts of desperate last-minute resistance in the Warsaw ghetto, in the Sobibor, Treblinka and Auschwitz concentration camps, and in a number of partisan groups (Steinberg, 1978), hundreds of thousands of people walked into the gas chambers, not believing that such a thing could ever happen to them.

Similarly, all protestations of loyalty to the United States did not save second- and third-generation Americans of Japanese descent from being sent

*Any attempt to characterize the behavior of a group inevitably raises the problem of the validity of ethnic group stereotypes, and invites accusations that the writer accepts such stereotypes. I am not for a moment suggesting that MMs are any more clannish, nepotistic or deceitful than anyone else. Rather, I am suggesting two things. First, because MMs tend to be ostracized, powerless minorities, their general human propensity to behave selfishly in the furtherance of their individual interests is socially reinforced by a greater need for self-defense. Second, because MMs are generally alien and visible, behavior that is generally human and situationally elicited will tend to be stereotyped and ascribed to ethnic peculiarities.

Thus, the propensity to cheat (in the general sense of seeking to maximize benefits through deceit) is universal in an intelligent animal like man, and is certainly rampant in business transactions, but, when the MM merchant cheats, his behavior will be "explained" in terms of ethnic stereotypes. The issue, therefore, is not the validity of the stereotype. Most stereotypes have some experiential basis. Of course, members of MMs cheat, are nepotistic, and so on. They would not be human if they did not behave that way. The essence of stereotypy and prejudice is not the falsity of the belief, but the misattribution of the observed behavior to particularistic rather than universalistic causes.

Incidentally, the sociobiological approach to human behavior, developed here, far from supporting racism or ethnism as it is often alleged, explicitly resorts to a more universalistic level of explanation than is generally practiced in the social sciences. It seeks to explain behavior in the broadest possible terms, which means at least in pan-human terms, and quite often at an even broader level (e.g. at the levels of primates, mammals, vertebrates or all animals). Thus, sociobiology, through its reductionist strategy of seeking explanations for behavior at the most general level, is the very antithesis of racism or ethnism.

to concentration camps and despoiled of their property. The supposedly "democratic" nature of their government did not protect them against the most blatant forms of racial discrimination. MMs are not safe under any political regime. Wealth is not a source of security. "Weak money" is one of the characteristics of MMs who are not allowed to convert their wealth into power. Wealth makes MMs, if anything, more vulnerable to exploitation, confiscation or expulsion. It can be used for bribery or ransom, but often MMs can do little more than buy their way out of discrimination, confiscation or even annihilation as some Jews did in Nazi Germany or more recently ethnic Chinese in Vietnam.

ASIANS IN EAST AFRICA: A CASE STUDY

The saga of Asian immigrants to the former British territories of Kenya, Uganda and Tanganyika (now Tanzania) is well documented and represents a type-case of the MM situation (Bharati, 1972; Delf, 1963; D. P. Ghai and Y. P. Ghai, 1970; Gregory, 1971; Hollingsworth, 1960; Mangat, 1969; Morris, 1956; van den Berghe, 1975a). Asians have had both political and trade contacts with the entire coast of East Africa from the Horn to Mozambique for approximately 3000 years, and the Arab influence was dominant on that coast and its off-shore islands, such as Zanzibar and Pemba, for several centuries before European conquest. Indeed, in the early 19th century, the East African slave trade made Zanzibar the capital of a large empire ruled by Arabs from Oman. Those Asians, however, were a ruling class—not a middleman minority.

It was European conquest at the turn of the 20th century that turned the Asians into a MM. The great bulk of the 350,000-odd Asians who, until the 1960s lived in the three territories of former British East Africa, came after 1895. This was the date when the British started building the Uganda Railway to link Mombasa, Nairobi and Kampala. Local African labor was deemed "unreliable," so the British government brought in some 32,000 "coolies" from India on indenture. About 2500 of them died, principally of blackwater fever; some 23,000 returned to India and some 7000 settled in East Africa (D. P. Ghai and Y. P. Ghai, 1970). During the construction of the railway, some Indians began to come in as merchants and to establish *dukas* (shops) along the railway, initially to cater for fellow Indians. After the end of the railway construction, that merchant immigration from India continued until, by the 1920s, virtually the entire retail trade of East Africa was monopolized by Indians.

Many of the indentured Indians who remained became railway employees, petty government clerks and skilled craftsmen, as they possessed many skills as yet scarce in the native African population and useful to the rapidly expanding British colonial administration. Many Indians were literate, spoke some English and were somewhat familiar with Western culture through prior exposure to British rule in India, were accustomed to urban life and a market economy, and were knowledgeable about machinery and industrial technology. Those were all signal advantages that gave them a great competitive advantage over the Africans.

Except along the narrow coastal strip where the natives belonged to the urban, literate, Muslim culture of the Swahili speakers, East African nations were either nomadic pastoralists like the Masai, the Somali or the Turkana, or horticulturalists like the Kikuyu, the Baganda, the Luo and many others. The centralized kingdom of southern Uganda (Bunyoro, Ankole and Buganda) were more complex societies than those of the interior of Kenya and Tanganyika, and in Uganda the Indian monopoly over trade and middle-echelon clerical and craft occupations was not as sweeping as in Tanganyika and Kenya. Nevertheless, for about 50 years, Indians came to control nearly all of the trade and of the middle-level occupations and thus to constitute an urban bourgeoisie and petty bourgeoisie in a rigid three-tiered colonial society.

A brief sketch of the classical colonial society of British East Africa is necessary here to place the Indian community in its total context. At the apex of the social, political and economic pyramid were the Europeans (overwhelmingly British after the German defeat in World War I when Tanganyika passed from German to British administration). The Europeans monopolized the senior ranks of the civil service and the officer ranks of the colonial army, i.e. all the command posts of the colonial regime. In addition, they occupied, at least initially, most of the university-level posts in the professions (engineering, law and medicine) and the key managerial positions in large transport and business undertakings (banks, railways and export–import firms). In the Kenya Highlands and in some parts of Northern Tanganyika, there were also some white settlers with large ranches and plantations of sisal, tea, coffee and other tropical export crops, using an African labor force. These settlers, although they never numbered more than a fraction of 1% of the East African population, intended at one stage to make Africa their permanent home, therefore clashing with the British Colonial Office after World War II when it became increasingly clear to metropolitan Britain that independence was inevitable.

This thinly scattered European minority, numbered barely 90,000 out of a total East African population of some 25.1 million in 1962, i.e. just before (for Kenya) or after (for Tanzania and Uganda) independence. More than half of them (56,000) lived in Kenya, mostly in and around the capital of Nairobi, center of the "White Highlands," but, even there, they were outnumbered by Africans at least 20 to one. Europeans lived in a gilded ghetto of their own making. In every city of any size, they reserved for themselves segregated residential areas where they built large, comfortable villas and were served by African domestics. They send their children to all-white schools, staffed by white teachers. They imposed racial segregation in hotels, restaurants, bars, public transport, cinemas, theaters—in every conceivable facility, public or private. Indeed, social apartheid, at least in Kenya, was as rigid as in South Africa. Europeans also had a privileged legal status, and the entire governmental and legal apparatus buttressed the racial supremacy of the whites, whether colonial officials or private settlers. For example, in the colonial councils advisory to the governors, the Europeans, like the Asians and later the Africans, were represented as a separate community, but in numbers vastly disproportionate to their percentage in the population. In 1945, for example, the Legislative Council in Kenya had 41 members of whom 33 were Europeans, 5 Asians, 2 Arab and 1 African (Tandon, 1970).

Economically, the standard of living of Europeans was so vastly greater than that of the Africans that there was virtually no overlap in their income or wealth distributions. The poorest white was still richer than all but a handful of Africans. There are no accurate figures for that period, but European per capita income in East Africa was at least *20 times* that of Africans ($50 to $75 a year is an approximate estimate of the latter in late colonial times). To be white meant to live in a modern masonry house with several rooms, extensive furniture and appliances, a staff of three to five African servants and, generally after World War II, a motorcar, electricity (supplied by one's own engine in the rural areas) and other modern amenities. Even in the rural areas where some of the amenities were lacking, white farmers lived baronially, if not royally, on estates of hundreds of hectares, surrounded by entire villages of African workers and servants.

Naturally, the European community was almost totally endogamous, although white bachelors often took black mistresses. The latter were completely excluded from European society, however, as were their mulatto children. These liaisons were socially frowned upon and were tolerated only for bachelors. Most Europeans came to East Africa with their wives and children, especially in Kenya where the highland climate was considered ideal for European settlement.

Leisure-time activities were also entirely segregated by race. The whites attended their tea parties at Government House, their Sunday afternoon horse races, their polo, cricket and bowling matches, their classical music concerts, their steeple chases and so on, among themselves, although always served by a numerous staff of African domestics. In Nairobi and environs, the British minority even managed to stamp out local vegetation and introduce a tropical version of the English countryside—fake Tudor manors, manicured lawns and all. Indeed, much of Nairobi and the Kenya Highlands still bear the stamp of a tropical, Victorian England, graceful and aristocratic but incredibly incongruous in the African landscape.

At the bottom of the social pyramid of East African colonial society were, of course, the Africans. They made up about 98% of the region's 25 million inhabitants in 1962, and over 90% of them were either pastoralists moving across vast stretches of semiarid savannah with their flocks of cattle and goats, or poor subsistence farmers eking out a meager livelihood from small plots cultivated by swidden agriculture. Overpopulation grew worse and worse throughout the colonial period, as some groups, especially the Kikuyu, were dispossessed by the white farmers, and as European preventive medicine caused a population explosion. Up to one-tenth of the African population gradually migrated to the urban centers and the white farms to become mostly a poorly paid urban or rural proletariat. In the cities, they established vast overcrowded, unsanitary, racially segregated shanty towns where they erected flimsy corrugated iron shacks that often lacked all public amenities like electricity, running water and sewers. A few were lucky enough to be housed somewhat better by their European or Asian employers, but most lived under abject conditions, far worse because of overcrowding, filth, unemployment and crime, than many of the rural areas from whence they came.

Yet the cities were a magnet because only there (and on the white farms) could one work for wages with which to pay taxes and to buy goods (including food) that increasingly became necessities. As subsistence agriculture declined in self-sufficiency because of overpopulation, and as the entire economy became increasingly monetized and opened up to trade goods, Africans became increasingly dependent on the "modern" sector of the economy controlled by Europeans and Asians. But, in that modern sector, their social mobility was almost totally blocked by both the European and the Asian population. Even semiskilled occupations, such as clerical and artisanal jobs, which in other colonies without MMs were open to natives, were often preempted by Asians in East Africa, especially in Kenya. So urban Africans were almost entirely confined, if they could find employment at all, to menial jobs as domestic servants in European or Asian households, stevedores and day laborers, unskilled construction workers, and policemen, night-watchmen and soldiers in the colonial army. Local industry was limited to a few small firms, mostly Asian owned, and offered little employment.

Entrepreneurial outlets were almost entirely closed by Asian competition, so African trade was practically limited to the selling of fresh produce, small-scale hawking and peddling and some illegal brewing of beer. Opportunities for Africans were somewhat better in Uganda and Tankanyika where the European and the Indian population were proportionately about half as large as in Kenya, but, even there, Africans constantly felt that their "advancement" was blocked. Even though they were the victim of a colonial system imposed by Europeans, the man who was directly perceived as doing the blocking and the exploitation was, almost invariably, the Indian immediately above the African, rather than the lofty, distant European.

A few Africans, lucky enough to attend mission schools and become literate in English, gradually entered the lower reaches of the professions, mostly as teachers and nurses, catering to other Africans, for racially discriminatory pay, in segregated institutions. Until shortly before independence, the social apex that an African could hope to reach was to be an underpaid teacher in an African school. From that small mission-educated class came the leadership of the independence movements that eventually overthrew the colonial regime. Kenyatta, Nyerere and Obote were all products of mission schools.

Thus, this was the colonial matrix into which Indians implanted themselves as an intermediate stratum. In 1962, Indians numbered some 90,000 in Tanzania, 80,000 in Uganda and 180,000 in Kenya (Bharati, 1972). In East Africa as a whole, they outnumbered Europeans by about four to one, but they were still a bare 1% of the population of Tanganyika and Uganda, and 2% of that of Kenya.

It was, of course, their relatively small number that permitted East African Indians to be as economically successful as they were. East Africa could not have produced enough surplus to keep a much larger Asian merchant population, but it did produce enough to secure for its middleman minority a standard of living some *six times* greater than the African mean, though three times lower than the European mean (Delf, 1963; D. P. Ghai and Y. P. Ghai, 1970). On the eve of Kenya independence in 1962, only 0.5% of African taxpayers reported incomes of more than £400 per annum, compared to 68.4% of the Asians and 92.2% of the Europeans (D. P. Ghai, 1970, p. 109). Most *dukawallas* (as the owners of the ubiquitous rural dry goods stores were known) lived frugally and modestly by European standards. They were typically housed in crowded back rooms or above their stores, in quarters that Europeans would have considered cramped, dark and unattractive. Yet, seen through African eyes, they were affluent. They live in large masonry buildings, often employed a couple of African servants, and frequently owned such luxuries as a kerosene refrigerator or a motor car, which would be totally inaccessible to any but a handful of Africans.

Some Asians were wealthy indeed, sufficiently so to excite the envy even of Europeans, and, in time, a growing number of Asians began to compete with Europeans in the professions. By far the greater number, however, were just moderately successful retail traders who had rural dry goods stores in distant villages, small urban shopkeepers and craftsmen or modest clerks and petty bureaucrats on limited salaries. In short, most Asians were far too poor (and too discriminated against) to compete seriously with Europeans, but, in African eyes, Indians always seemed to occupy all the positions to which an ambitious African with a moderate amount of Western education and a little starting capital might aspire.

Despite their relatively small numbers, East African Asians were, for several reasons, highly visible. Their skin pigmentation, appropriately intermediate on the colonial scale of color prejudice, set them off from both Europeans and Africans. So did their distinctive style of dress, the smell of their cooking, the sound of their language and music broadcast over the radio, the architecture of their mosques and temples—in short, their entire culture that was so odorously, colorfully and audibly exotic—clearly neither African nor European.

In addition to their culture and phenotypic visibility, Indians lived in highly conspicuous places where everybody went, namely, in the very heart of towns. Nearly all the buildings in the main commercial streets of East African towns, except for a few official buildings like the post office, the police station, the jail and the court building, would be Indian-owned stores and workshops, typically two stories high, with the extended family of the owner living upstairs and the kitchen and toilet facilities in the backyard.

Also in the commercial heart of the town would be the temples and mosques, frequently the most colorful and attractive buildings to be seen in a wide radius. Even the *dukawallas* who tended distant rural shops lived in a conspicuous place, usually a row of masonry buildings with corrugated iron roofs alongside an open market place. Their dwellings were obviously much bigger, better and more expensive than the mud and grass huts of native architecture.

It is not true that Asians were inadaptable in East Africa. Nearly all Indian men learned to speak English, and, by the second generation, both sexes had become fluently Anglophone, while continuing to use their native tongue (mostly Gujarati, Cutchi, Punjabi or Hindustani). Most Indians also learned the upland Swahili pidgin which is the trade language of East Africa; while few spoke the "correct" coastal Swahili, their fluency in "kitchen Swahili" was often superior to that of the Europeans. The more rural Indian shopkeepers did indeed become somewhat Africanized, while the urban Indian became more Anglicized.

Yet, Indians lived mostly among themselves, for various reasons: they chose to as a matter of ethnocentrism and felt culturally if not racially superior to Africans; their economic niche led them to concentrate in the commercial centers of towns; they were prevented by Europeans from gaining entry into the white elite; and they were hated and rejected by Africans, at virtually all class levels. East African Indians were literally encysted as a foreign body in the African landscape. Partly, they wanted it that way; but even those who did not had no option. They were forced to go to their own schools because the European schools would not admit them, and the African schools were dominated by Christian missionaries who exerted strong pressures to convert and were for the most part of very low quality. Their religions (Hinduism, Sunni and Ismaelite Islam, Sikhism and Jainism) also cut them off from both whites and blacks.

For entertainment, social life and welfare and medical services, the Asians were also forced by colonial indifference and neglect to organize their own voluntary associations on a communal basis. Indeed, the British colonial administration did everything to encourage Indian communalism, as it was compatible with their policy of dividing and ruling. The British, for example, gave official communal representation to Asians on the advisory councils to the British governor. In keeping with the British view of the Asians as racially inferior to themselves but superior to the Africans, Asian representation, too, was proportionately smaller than the European, but greater than the African one. Despite this representation in advisory bodies, Indians were, of course, almost totally excluded from power in the three British territories, even more so than the Africans to whom the Colonial Office recognized at least a theoretical right to eventual self-rule. The Indians, in British eyes, were mere interlopers.

Although, to both Europeans and Africans, Asians looked like a homogeneous group and a single community, they were nothing of the sort. It is true that the vast majority of them came from the northwestern corner of the Indian subcontinent, mostly from Gujarat and the Punjab, and thus could be expected to be fairly homogeneous. Nevertheless, they represented in microcosm the Indian kaleidoscope, with its multiple religious, linguistic and caste divisions, well described by Bharati (1972). Even the gross division into Hindu and Muslim, largely recognized by Europeans, only began to scratch the surface of the complex splintering of Indians into tightly endogamous little subgroups of only a few thousand members each. East African Asians thus shared little more in common than a broad geographical origin and membership in a despised, powerless, vulnerable, defenseless group of pariah capitalists.

Not only were Indians a tiny minority of the 25 million people of East Africa. They were an almost infinitely divided and subdivided minority. One must see the adaptation of Indians to the MM situation against the backdrop of this diversity and splintering. Their commercial success was due, in good part, like that of other MMs, to their systematic application of nepotism to a rapidly expanding market economy. They literally brought capitalism into the vast interior of East Africa, and they did so through complex and multiple networks of kin selection. This was not true at a broad pan-Indian level. Indeed, there was almost no feeling of pan-Indianness among East African Asians. Even the Indian independence movement did not bridge the social chasms between caste and religious groups; quite the opposite, it widened the Hindu–Muslim gulf.

Indian enterprise was a matter of kin helping kin; extended families setting up small family businesses and, little by little, expanding into little chains of stores owned by kinsmen; uncles hiring nephews, cousins lending each other money and so on. Beyond the extended families, the network of nepotism incorporated the endogamous caste and/or religious group of a few hundred—or at most a few thousand people. Typically, the same caste or religious subcommunity (e.g. the Patels, the Goans and the Sikhs) would maintain much closer ties with their small group in other parts of Africa or even in India, than with their Indian neighbors from other groups. Patterns of endogamy perpetuated this situation.

East African Indians vividly demonstrate how tight networks of nepotism not only can survive in complex, urban societies but can be made to serve adaptive needs in a highly capitalistic system which is supposedly inimical to such "irrational" constraints. Not only are kin selection and capitalism not incompatible; the former is demonstrably a formula for success in the latter.

EPILOGUE: THE CRISIS OF INDEPENDENCE

East African Asians were not only a type-case of MM when they successfully adapted to the economic niche created by the European conquest of the area. Their misfortunes since independence in Kenya (1963), Tanzania (1961) and Uganda (1962) also poignantly illustrate the "weak money" syndrome characteristic of pariah capitalists. With the outbreak of the Kenya

War of Independence (the so-called "Mau Mau Rebellion" of British history books) in the early 1950s, the handwriting on the wall was clearly to be read for both Europeans and Asians: African political independence was inevitable. The prospect was far from enchanting for Europeans, but most of them had really little to lose except a little prestige and, if worse came to worse, their farms. At least in Kenya, the British managed to install a conservative, capitalist, neocolonialist regime led by Jomo Kenyatta, whom they had, a few years earlier, framed as a terrorist leader and imprisoned. Most Europeans stayed, retaining their privileged economic position. Once they got over the shock of sharing their favorite bars, restaurants, hotels, cinemas and schools with a few members of the new African political elite and of having to "watch their language" in talking publicly to and about blacks, they could continue their life of genteel affluence in an ideal climate. Indeed, the white population of Kenya increased after independence, and today Nairobi is one of the most chic and cosmopolitan European cities of Africa, chock-full of *Wabenzi* of all shades of skin pigmentation.*

The Indians did not fare so well. Indian leaders shifted from the traditional, prudent attitude of staying out of politics, to supporting the African nationalist movements, both verbally and with money. A few intellectuals even openly identified with African aspirations and took an active part in politics, but most leaders of Indian organizations simply repeated pledges of allegiance to the new governments and bribed politicians, while always expecting the worst. Anti-Indian feelings in the African population were rampant, and these prejudices could and were in fact exploited by African politicians. At regular intervals, Asians were admonished in speeches by African ministers or members of parliament that they had better curb their rapaciousness and stop being leeches on the body politic, or dire things would happen to them.

A survey that I conducted in sociology classes at the Universities of Nairobi, Kenya, and Makarere, Uganda, in 1967–1968, indicates the depth of anti-Asian prejudices, even in the most highly educated and articulate segment of the African population, the very elite that now governs these countries. Of a group of 129 African students, 44% regarded the contribution of Asians to East Africa as "mostly negative," 49% regarded it as "mixed" and only 7% as "mostly positive." Over three-fourths (77%) advocated racial discrimination in employment in favor of Africans, irrespective of citizenship. At the same time, 71% denied that there was any racial discrimination against Europeans and Asians in East Africa. (Interestingly, of the 24 Asian students in the same sample, 88% thought they *were* being discriminated against on racial grounds.) Asked in two separate questions what the positive and negative traits of Asians were, 52% of the African students mentioned only negative traits or explicitly stated that Asians did not have any positive traits. Only two positive traits were reported by more than 10% of the

---

Wabenzi, the plural of *Mubenzi*, is a Swahili neologism referring to drivers of Mercedes Benz motor cars. This is a term of hostility and derision directed at Kenya's neocolonialist ruling class.

sample: business ability and contribution to economic development. However, 42% accused Indians of exploiting Africans, 27% of dishonesty or deceit, 32% of clannishness and unwillingness to mix with other groups, and 19% of superiority feelings vis-à-vis Africans.* Even the "positive" responses were sometimes indirectly negative. Thus, one student said, "some are honest."

Politically, East African Asians were given one option at independence. They could either apply for citizenship of their country of residence or get British citizenship. Approximately one-third of the Kenya and Uganda Indians, and about 80% of the Tanzania Asians chose local citizenship in the hope of avoiding discrimination (Tandon, 1970). In the end, the option turned out to be illusory. Those who chose African citizenship were accused of opportunism and soon discovered that race rather than citizenship was the basis of much government policy (as in the granting of trade licences, hiring and promotion in the civil service and so on). At least this was the case in capitalist Kenya, which increasingly adopted a policy of racial discrimination, called Africanization, to squeeze Asians out of trade and out of clerical, managerial, technical and civil service jobs. First, Asians were pushed out of rural areas; then the discrimination shifted to the urban areas. There, the squeeze was slow and gradual because Asians were not only merchants, but also occupied some 30 to 40% of all the key managerial, clerical, technical, professional and skilled manual jobs. They were not easily replaceable, and Kenya did not want to jeopardize its reputation for being a neocolonialist, capitalist paradise. Yet, political pressures to phase the Indians out of trade and middle-echelon jobs were irresistible.

In socialist Tanzania, President Julius Nyerere generously proclaimed that all Tanzanians were equal, and that racial discrimination was totally unthinkable in a socialist country, but so was capitalist exploitation. Consequently Asians found themselves squeezed out qua capitalists, rather than qua Asians, an ideological nicety that was, no doubt, lost on most of them.

In both Kenya and Tanzania, Asians are thus being pushed out gradually, but as quickly as can be done without disrupting the economy too seriously. In Uganda, the outcome was more drastic. When the semiliterate thug and army boxing champ, Idi Amin, took over the country in 1971, he was not much concerned about either ideology or economic development. He simply expelled all Asians irrespective of citizenship. In 1972, about 80,000 Asians were forced to leave Uganda in a few weeks' time—without their assets. In the end, it turned out that Idi Amin was giving them preferential treatment, because he butchered an estimated quarter of a million black Ugandans before he was overthrown by a Tanzanian military invasion in 1979.

What about those Asians who opted for British citizenship? That strategy turned out to be disadvantageous as well. Asians thought that a British passport, if worse came to worse, assured them entry into Britain. They

---

*Percentages add up to more than 100, because a number of students gave multiple responses. The questions were entirely "open," i.e. the subjects did not check off a list of adjectives but answered in their own words.

knew they would encounter considerable racial discrimination there, too, but they felt that a mature and prosperous "democracy" like the United Kingdom was a reasonable assurance against the Idi Amins of this world. Unfortunately, these eminently prudent considerations were foiled by the democratically elected British Parliament. By 1968, the denial of work permits and trading licences to Asians with British passports was creating an exodus to Britain that was itself in the throes of racist agitation against "Commonwealth immigration." In anticipation of Britain closing its doors, Asian emigration out of East Africa accelerated, and the British Parliament responded by passing a piece of legislation restricting Asian immigration. A new law declared that there were really two classes of British passports: those held by people with a British grandfather and others. Only holders of the first kind of British passport had an automatic right of entry into Britain; others would be let in on a quota basis only and would have to queue up. The oldest "democratic" parliament in the world had used racial criteria to deny entry to its own citizens!

Where pariah capitalists are concerned, formal democracy is no protection. Ethnic sentiments can be instantaneously mobilized in the defense of interests or even hysterically whipped up in response to imaginary threats. Conversely, middleman minorities have little else than nepotism on which they can rely for self-protection in a hostile environment.

SUGGESTED READINGS

Middlemen minorities have been written about extensively in articles (Bonacich, 1973; Gary Hamilton, 1978; van den Berghe, 1975a), in textbooks (Blalock 1967; Shibutani and Kwan, 1965) and in a number of monographs and collections of papers dealing with a single group (Delf, 1963; Hilda Kuper, 1960), but there is no good general book on the subject. On East African Asians dealt with in this chapter, the best sources are Bharati (1972), Delf (1963), D. P. Ghai and Y. P. Ghai (1970) and Mangat (1969).

CASTE

The concept of "caste," like that of "slavery," covers a wide range of meanings and of social phenomena, human and nonhuman. Entomologists use the term "caste" to designate functionally and anatomically discrete morphs of the same species of social insect (Oster and Wilson, 1978; E. O. Wilson, 1971, 1975). Thus, they speak of workers and soldiers among ants or termites as "castes." Apart from the social insects, however, the term "caste" is usually reserved to human societies, and, clearly, the overlap of meaning between the entomological and anthropological use of the term is limited to a single feature: specialization in the division of labor.

Insect castes lack basic elements of what is usually called a "caste" in human societies and, conversely, possess characteristics not found in human castes. Caste status among social insects is not inherited, since most members of an insect colony are sterile and reproductive queens can typically produce all castes characteristic of a given species. Such environmental factors as diet, presence or absence of a queen or fertilization versus non-fertilization of the egg will determine whether a bee, a wasp, an ant or a termite becomes a worker or a queen, sterile or reproductive, and female or male. Individuals can, and sometimes do, change their caste status within their own lifetime. Morphologically, insect castes are characterized by distinct differences in gonadal activity, body size, mandible shape and size, and so on, which make them particularly suited to their functional specialization in the colony to which they belong. In short, insect castes are not even good analogs, much less homologs, of human castes.

THE TWO TRADITIONS IN THE DEFINITION OF CASTE

However, whereas entomologists have a clear idea of what they mean by "caste" in the "eusocial" insects (i.e. those that have sterile castes), social scientists cannot agree on what they call "caste" in human societies. Many books and articles have been written on human caste societies, but, the more one reads, the more confused the issue seems to be (Berreman, 1960; Cox, 1948; de Reuck and Knight, 1967; De Vos and Wagatsuma, 1966; Dumont, 1970; Ghurye, 1952; Hsu, 1963; Hutton, 1946; Karve, 1961; Smythe, 1952; Srinivas, 1969). So, inevitably, we must begin, as we did in the chapter on slavery, by clarifying some of the confusion.

Basically, there are two traditions in the use of the term, "caste": there are those, often Indianists, who would prefer to reserve the term for the peculiar social groupings found on the Indian subcontinent, principally among Hindus, but also in other religious communities who have been influenced by surrounding Hindus (Cox, 1948; Dumont, 1970; Ghurye, 1952; Hutton, 1946). The irony of their position is that the word caste, which they would want to restrict to India, is in fact European in origin. It comes from the Spanish and Portuguese *casta*, a term applied by the Iberian colonizers in the New World to designate phenotypically distinct "racial" groups: European, Amerindians, Africans and their intermixtures: *mestizos, mulattos* and *zambos*.

Why (East) Indianists are so eager to restrict the concept of caste to a society where the very word is alien is puzzling. After insisting that "caste" in all its complexities (which they delight in expounding) is unique to the Indian subcontinent, Indianists immediately face a serious problem. They cannot quite determine whether by caste, they mean *varna* or *jati*, two very different concepts. The term *varna* (which means "color" in Sanscrit, but probably never referred to skin color) is used to designate one of the four broad status categories mentioned in a number of Hindu religious writings such as the Baghavad Gita. In descending order of status, the four *varna* are the Brahmins, the Kshatriyas, the Vaishyas and the Shudras. The *jati*, however, are the thousands of groups and subgroups into which Indian society is subdivided and to which most Hindus are conscious of belonging. While most *jati* can be assigned broadly to one of the four *varna*, many groups do not fit (e.g. the *harijans* or "untouchables," who are below the four *varna*, and the "tribals" who are altogether outside the system). It is the *jati* or the sub*jati* that is the effective social group for most purposes. The four *varna* are little more than a rigid, static, oversimplified scheme superimposed by religious literati on a much more complex, dynamic, locally diverse reality.

To be sure, the Hindu caste system is unique. The religious concepts of *karma*, of *dharma*, or reincarnation and of ritual purity and defilement used to rationalize it; the multiple precepts and prohibitions concerning inter-caste contacts, marriage and commensality; the division of labor; the multiplicity of divisions and subdivisions between groups all make India quite unlike any other society in the world. Indeed, to an outsider it seems more than a little mad; even to an insider, it is so complex that no one can gain a coherent overview of it, much less construct a rational model of it. Where else do 600 million people divide and subdivide themselves *ad infinitum* into supposedly air-tight but interdependent little groups bound by such a multitude of rules that one is never quite sure whom one may or may not touch, drink or eat with, marry or whatever. One must first ask to what group a person belongs! And even then, it is not clear what one should do because there are simply too many groups, too many rules and too many disagreements.

To describe in any detail this monument to human folly and perverse ingenuity, known as the Hindu caste system, is beyond the scope of this book. We would have to explain why it is all right to accept fried but not boiled food from some people, both kinds of food from others and neither kind from some; why one must bathe if the shadow of an untouchable falls on one; why a lower-caste person should hire a high-caste Brahmin as cook; why different wells have to be used by different people in the same villages; why upper-caste people should be vegetarians while only lowly untouchables would touch a juicy beefsteak; why virtuous upper-caste widows should throw themselves on their husband's funeral pyre, while women from some low castes are hereditary prostitutes; why everything you do is virtuous so long as you follow the rules, and so on. Clearly, the word, "caste," is inadequate to convey all these complexities.

THE MINIMUM DEFINITION OF CASTE

This brings us to the second approach to the use of the term. Many scholars, principally anthropologists and sociologists who are not Indianists, have used "caste" to characterize a broad type of rigid social groups. Kroeber (1948), Warner (1941), Alison W. Davis and the Gardners (1941), Myrdal (1944) and many others have proposed what has been termed the "minimum definition of caste." They advocated the use of the term to designate any group exhibiting three features:

1. endogamy, i.e. compulsory marriage within the group;
2. ascriptive membership by birth and for life, and, hence, hereditary status;
3. ranking in a hierarchy in relation to other such groups

By this definition, caste is an analytical construct that applies to the Hindu caste system but to a number of other systems as well. One of its most frequent applications outside India has been to racial groups in countries with a rigid racial hierarchy and clear definitions of racial boundaries, like the United States and South Africa (A. W. Davis, B. B. Gardner and M. R. Gardner, 1941; Myrdal, 1944; van den Berghe, 1965, 1978a). In these cases, the term is often qualified and specified, and people speak of "racial caste." This usage has been severely criticized by scholars who have argued that race relations in the United States or South Africa bear only superficial resemblance to caste relations in India (Cox, 1948).

The issue, however, is not how closely India resembles the United States or other "caste" systems, but whether there is any analytical value in having a term to designate an ideal-type of social group characterized by extreme rigidity and permanence of membership, absence of intermarriage and invidious distinction vis-à-vis other such groups. Certainly, the objection to applying "caste" to racial groups is of dubious validity since *casta* in the original Iberian-American usage was applied to phenotypically distinct groups. The *casta* system of classifying people, in the Spanish colonies in particular, was never so rigid as to constitute a real caste system in the modern analytical sense just defined. Interbreeding quickly blurred *casta* distinctions and undermined any attempt to classify people according to a racial taxonomy. Nevertheless, the original Spanish *casta* system was meant to be a hierarchical classification of racial groups. It was even based on a notion of *limpieza de sangre* (cleanliness of blood), not all that unlike Hindu conceptions of ritual purity.

Interestingly, the concept of "race," as used in North America to designate a phenotypically distinct group, was imported into Asia by some scholars who applied it to a situation best described in terms of caste. The *eta* or *burakumin* of Japan have been described by De Vos and Wagatsuma (1966) as an "invisible race." Thus the terminological confusion has come full circle. Some phenotypically distinct racial groups have been called "castes" by analogy with the Hindu system. Conversely, some physically undistinguishable caste groups have been called "races" by analogy with North American society.

Where does all this semantic imbroglio lead us? I personally think that it is useful to have a special analytical term applicable to a wide range of societies to designate that particular combination of class and ethnicity by a special term. "Race" will not do for that purpose, since only some of these systems are based on phenotypical distinctions. Furthermore, not all societies that do make phenotypical distinctions have the degree of rigidity and racial endogamy that one associates with caste. Examples of such race-conscious but relative flexible social systems are Brazil, most Caribbean islands, Hawaii and others (Lind, 1955; Lowenthal, 1972; van den Berghe, 1978a). "Race" has utility as an analytical concept to designate phenotypically distinguished groups but *not* as a synonym for "caste." "Race" can be a special case of caste but also a special case of more flexible social orders.

CASTE AND STIGMA

Here, I shall use "caste" to refer to those rigid social orders in which people are assigned by birth and for life to compulsorily endogamous groups that are, furthermore, *stigmatized*. We are, therefore, adding the additional element of *stigma* to the minimum definition of caste. "Hierarchy" is too weak a term to describe this element of caste. To be sure, castes are in a hierarchy, but what makes caste peculiarly invidious and demeaning is that the lower group or groups in the system are not simply regarded as socially inferior. They are also viewed as morally debased, ritually impure, genetically inferior (or whatever the rationale for their invidious treatment) by accident of birth—and for reasons quite unrelated to individual merit, behavior or actions.

As the stigma is believed to be immutable, there is nothing which the stigmatized individual can do to escape it, except "cheat" (that is, avoid detection through deceit, e.g. by "passing" or by changing a caste name) or work for the destruction of the status quo. Hinduism provides, of course, a third supernatural "solution" through the notion of reincarnation. "Good" behavior in one's present existence, defined as "knowing one's place" in the caste order and acting accordingly, ensures caste promotion upon rebirth in the next life, until achievement of perfection brings Nirvana, the end of the cycle of rebirths, the loss of separate identity and the fusion of *atman* (soul) into the universal godhead. However, we are concerned with ideo-logical superstructures here only insofar as they affect behavior and thus regard Hindu theology as a means of perpetuating caste, not as a way of escaping its consequences.

Caste, in short, means stigma for those at the bottom. It means ascriptive group membership but to a group that everyone despises. It means hierarchy, but a particularly demeaning type of hierarchy, a hierarchy supposedly based on immutable inferiority. It means endogamy but not the usual kind of preferential endogamy. The endogamy of caste is not one of choice; it is imposed by the contempt of others. You must marry "your own kind" because nobody else will have you.

Of course, stigmatization is not limited to caste (Goffman, 1963). A stigma can be individual, nonhereditary and acquired. The criminal, for example, is stigmatized because of his own behavior, and therefore his stigma is justified and merited according to that society's moral code. Stigma only becomes caste when it attaches to entire groups, when it is transmitted hereditarily and when it is totally divorced of any notion of individual responsibility. (Again, the Hindu notion of responsibility for one's action in previous reincarnations does not count; it is merely an ethical dirty trick invented by Brahmins.)

Since castes are endogamous, and since membership is acquired by birth and for life, castes quickly became descent groups, and since we have seen earlier that the basis of ethnicity is common descent we could simply define caste as *stigmatized ethnicity*. This simple definition has problems, how-ever. For one, it would immediately provoke a chorus of protest from the Indianists who would, quite rightly, point out that caste (*jati*) in India is not looked upon by most people as a stigma. A person's *jati* is a positive reference group. It is the group within which one finds all of one's relatives and many of one's closest friends, acquaintances and associates; it is the all-encompassing matrix within which one lives one's life. Since the whole society is organized in caste groups, one's caste membership is all-important. Outside of it, there can be no social life. It is only modern ideology that has emphasized the negative aspects of caste, the Indianist would say, but tra-ditionally caste was also a positive thing, a solidary support group of kins-men and associates that performed specialized functions in a vast, complex, interdependent society. Most people had caste groups above and below them, but those hierarchical relations were secondary to the positive rela-tions of connubium, commensality, reciprocity and sociality *within* the caste.

All of this is true, and constitutes one more reason why the term "caste" is so inadequate to describe Indian reality. Better, caste, as just defined, describes not the *whole* system of *varna* and *jati* in the traditional Hindu system but only one small part of it, namely, *untouchability*. Indeed, by the traditional Hindu definition of their position, *harijans* ("children of god," the pious euphemism coined by Mahatma Gandhi to refer to the "untouchables") are *outside* the Hindu "caste" system. They are so debased that they have no place in the hierarchy of the four *varna*; their subgroups are so much below every one else that they even have the "privilege" of being exempted from virtually all moral injunctions of Hinduism. They are "free" to eat beef, kill animals and remarry—in short, do all things abhorrent to Hindus.

CASTE SOCIETIES VERSUS SOCIETIES WITH CASTE GROUPS

To resolve this apparent problem, I suggest that the most fundamental respect in which the Hindu "caste" system is so special is that the *entire society* is divided into rigid endogamous *jati*, not just some pariah groups. This is so much the case that even the 17% or so of India's population who practice supposedly noncaste or even anticaste religions, like Islam, Sikhism, Jainism, Zoroastrianism, Buddhism, Christianity and Judaism, are themselves, for the most part, subdivided into caste or quasicaste groups. Through a process known as "sanscritization" (Srivivas, 1969), Hinduism reabsorbs, behaviorally if not theologically, the minority religious groups, and high-caste practices filter down the Hindu caste hierarchy.

Only one other society has attempted to construct an equally all-encompassing caste system—South Africa. Far more common are the societies in which some groups, usually minorities, are treated as hereditary, endogamous pariahs, but where the rest of the population is not casted. In short, there have been very few *caste societies*, but there have been a sizeable number of *societies with caste groups*. In the former category, I would unequivocally place only India and South Africa; while in the latter are Japan (with the *burakumin*), the United States (with Afro-Americans) and a number of traditional West African societies, where blacksmiths, storytellers and, in the case of the Ibo, devotees of a special cult are endogamous pariah castes (Tuden and Plotnicov, 1970). Clearly, then, when one compares, say, the whole of Indian society with the entire United States, one is struck much more by the differences than by the similarities. However, if one restricts the comparison to the *pariah groups* of, say, the United States, Japan and India, the number of similarities increases dramatically (De Vos and Wagatsuma, 1966).

Let us return to our tentative short definition of caste as stigmatized ethnicity. There is more than just stigmatization that makes caste a very special case of ethnicity. First, caste is, at least in part, externally imposed on the bottom groups by the group or groups at the top; the top groups police and enforce the group boundaries. This does not preclude feelings of solidarity in the bottom groups, but that solidarity is often the solidarity of degradation. Pariahs stick together only because they do not have the option of joining other groups. In fact, stigmatization often has the effect of making the pariahs internalize feelings of their own inferiority. The solidarity of pariahs is often fairly low, precisely because it grows not out of internally generated feelings of ethnocentric pride, but out of externally imposed denigration. Even when pariah groups develop "ethnic pride" movements, the ideology of these movements is typically laden with ambivalence and is reactive to the dominant group's ideology of stigmatization. The solidarity of pariah groups is typically the negative solidarity born out of desperation. It makes a profound difference whether one belongs to a group by choice, or whether one is forced to. This makes a critical difference both in terms of the collective definition of the group and in terms of individual identity and self-evaluation. Pariah caste situations typically foster assimilation ideology in the bottom groups, not ethnic pride.

Second, the basis of caste differentiation is structural, not cultural as is usually the case in "ordinary" ethnicity. Pariah castes typically share two characteristics: they perform despised but essential roles in the division of labor, and they share the same general culture, language and values with the rest of the population. Pariah groups, unlike other ethnies, are not set apart because of a past history of autonomous existence symbolized by a separate language, culture and, often, territory. They are set off because they have been ascribed an inferior role in the division of labor. Precisely because they lack a history of autonomy, of separate territory and of a distinct cultural identity, pariah castes typically share the same basic culture, religion and language with the unstigmatized groups. Furthermore, since they perform specialized roles in an interdependent economic system, pariah castes lack even the option of establishing a separate, autonomous, self-sufficient ethnic entity. Nationalism is not a realistic possibility to them.

CASTE, CLASS, SLAVERY AND ETHNICITY

Pariah castes have the worst of all possible worlds. Caste status shares with *class* the feature of specialization in the division of labor but without the option of changing jobs according to supply and demand in the labor market. Caste status shares with *slavery* the stigma of low status, the political disability of powerlessness, the drudgery of hard work and the burden of economic exploitation, but without the possibility of individual escape from that low status through flight or emancipation. Caste status shares with *ethnicity* the feature of common descent, but it lacks the realistic option of nationalism because it lacks a positive ethnic identity, a territorial basis, distinctive cultural traditions and an autonomous basis of subsistence.

Short of suicide, exile or, sometimes, surreptitious "passing," pariah castes members can only hope for the demise of the system that keeps them apart, that is, for the disappearance of the stigma and, therefore, of their group identity. Of all the ethnic groups, castes are the only ones which, if given an opportunity, would commit "auto-ethnocide," that is, which would gladly shed their separate identity and join the main body of the society whose culture they share. If they fail to do so, it is not because they do not want it, but because the persistence of the stigma prevents them from doing so. Notwithstanding fashionable ideologies to the contrary, this is equally true of *harijans* in India, of *burakumin* in Japan or of Afro-Americans in the United States.

THE CASTE SITUATION: AN IDEAL TYPE

Let us retrace our somewhat circuitous and laborious steps in the attempt to arrive at a concept of caste useable for purpose of comparative analysis. We started out with India, not because India, in its complex entirety, is typical of anything beside itself, but because that is where most discussions of caste start—implicity or explicity. We, then, examined the other tradition that developed around the concept of caste, namely, the attempt by sociologists and anthropologists to construct a "minimum definition" of caste applicable to a number of societies besides India. Finally, we refined the analysis to arrive at an ideal type of caste, the point at which we are now.

A *caste situation* may be said to exist to the extent that the following conditions are found:

1. presence of one or more hereditary descent groups with membership ascribed at birth and for life;
2. imposition of prescriptive endogamy on these groups;
3. attribution of an immutable collective stigma to some of these groups, irrespective of individual behavior of their members;
4. ascription of specialized functions in the division of labor to these groups;
5. economic interdependence of these groups on a common society;
6. absence of large-scale territorial separation between these groups, but numerous attempts to enforce both spatial and social barriers to various forms of intergroup interaction between them;
7. relative cultural (including linguistic and religious) homogeneity between the groups, at either the societal or the subsocietal level.

To the extent that all or nearly all members of a society belong to caste groups, we can speak of a *caste society*. Where only a minority of pariahs belong to caste groups, we shall speak of a *society with caste groups*. Thus, India and South Africa are caste societies, whereas Japan and the United States are societies with caste groups.

CASTE IN INDUSTRIAL SOCIETIES

It has frequently been asserted that caste is a social formation incompatible with an industrial mode of production. Caste produces rigidity in an economy that requires a mobile labor force capable of changing occupations and acquiring new skills. If, as functionalists like Kingsley Davis (1942) suggested, caste is a way of ensuring that jobs (passed on hereditarily) will be done tolerably well, it is also a recipe for conservatism. A rapidly changing industrial economy presumably requires something more adaptable than hereditary occupations.

Yet, of the four larger contemporary societies where features of caste are still most prominent, two (the United States and Japan) are among the world's most hyperindustrialized; one (South Africa) is the most highly industrialized country in Africa, and the fourth (India) is undergoing a rapid process of industrialization. The counterargument is that all four of these societies show signs of moving away from caste organization, in conformity with the functionalist prediction. To this, in turn, it can be said that two of these societies (South Africa and the United States) developed many features of their racial caste system in the late 19th century as they were entering their first phase of rapid industrialization (Myrdal, 1944; van den Berghe, 1965; Woodward, 1955). Furthermore, both of these countries were tardy, reluctant and only moderately successful in dismantling their caste systems. In the United States, the process only started in earnest in the 1940s, and in South Africa it has barely begun and then only with the greatest reluctance on the part of the whites—with all deliberate slowness. As for Japan and India, legal abolition of caste disabilities seems to have had only a slow and marginal effect on behavior (Srinivas, 1969; De Vos and Wagatsuma, 1966).

On balance, then, the functionalist argument that caste is incompatible with an industrial economy seems partly valid but overstated. On the one hand, it underrates the nonrational aspects of human behavior, especially when some form of ethnic or "racial" sentiment is involved. On the other hand, it underplays the adaptive capabilities of humans who do not stop at creating economically cumbersome, costly and complex adjustments if they feel threatened. To anticipate our answer, the ultimate measure of human success is not production but reproduction. Economic productivity and profit are means to reproductive ends, not ends in themselves. Therefore, a dominant group, like South African whites, can be expected to sacrifice a great deal of economic efficiency if it perceives that alternative policies threaten its survival. The ultimate justification given for apartheid in South Africa is the Afrikaners' right to survival as a separate ethny.

Of the four countries under consideration, India and Japan developed their caste institutions over many centuries of their existence as complex agrarian societies. The limited success that both have experienced in the 20th century in eliminating the disabilities of *harijans* and *burakumin*, respectively, can be ascribed to social inertia. Old prejudices and habits die hard, it is said. Actually, this is hardly an explanation, because humans are capable of changing their behavior very quickly when it is in their interest to do so. Japan supposedly emancipated the *burakumin* in 1871, and yet, to this date, private detective agencies make a living investigating the family backgrounds of prospective spouses and employees for possible *burakumin* ancestry (Hayashida, 1976). Four or five generations would seem a long enough time to change attitudes, especially when we know of numerous instances where one generation is quite enough (e.g. in sexual mores).

However, let us grant that the traditional caste systems of India and Japan are less problematic than those of the United States and South Africa, because they were developed in the kind of society where one would expect them to arise—namely, in complex agrarian societies. Let us, therefore, turn to South Africa and the United States.

SOUTH AFRICA

South Africa is a country of such extraordinary complexity that we can only attempt the barest summary description of the long sequel of historical events that led to its present form. Fortunately many books cover the subject adequately (Adam, 1971; De Kiewiet, 1941; Marquard, 1962; Sheila Patterson, 1953, 1957; Walker, 1957). The "race problem" of South Africa is, of course, predominantly a creation of its European settlers and should be called the "white problem." It began with Dutch settlement at the Cape in 1652 and quickly led to the growth of a little slave colony in and around Capetown. Until the abolition of slavery by the British (who in 1806 conquered the Cape from the Dutch) in 1834, rural districts around Capetown were occupied by small slave farms producing wine, fruits, vegetables, cereals and other fresh produce, mostly to resupply the sailing ships on their way between Europe and Asia. During these two centuries, the interbreeding of white settlers with slaves from Madagascar, Mozambique and the Dutch East Indies, and with aboriginal "Hottenhots" (Khoikhoi), led to a distinct group of people known today as the "Coloureds" (or, according to more recent, fashionable terminology, "browns").

These Coloureds are a close homolog, incidentally, to Afro-Americans in the United States, in that they are principally immigrants of mixed ancestry with a history of slavery, but are linguistically, culturally and religiously almost completely Europeanized. Except for a small minority of Muslim "Cape Malays," South African Coloureds are, but for skin pigmentation, poverty and stigmatization, virtually undistinguishable from South African "whites." Indeed, a good many of the latter are Coloureds who have "passed" in previous generations. In South Africa, as in the United States, there are those who argue that the Coloureds (and American blacks) have a culture distinctly their own, but empirical evidence for that assertion is equally scanty in both cases. The case for a separate *cultural* identity of these two groups rests almost entirely on a combination of regional and class differences, plus a history of racial discrimination. The outstanding difference between South African whites and Coloureds is not culture but the *caste* line that separates them.

Starting in the 18th century, but at a rapidly accelerating pace after the 1830s, Dutch settlers (first called "Boers," the Dutch word for "farmer," and later "Afrikaners," the Dutch word for "Africans") began to migrate into the interior of Southern Africa. They first came into violent contact with "Hottentots" (Xhoi-Xhoi) and "Bushmen" (San), and later with the various south-eastern Bantu nations (the Sotho, Xhosa, Ndebele, Zulu, Venda and others). The descendants of these Bantu nations are now known as "Africans" or "blacks" (not to be confused with the "Afrikaners" who are whites of Dutch descent).

The saga of the Boer expansion into the South African interior forms the central episode of the historical myth of white (and especially Afrikaner) South Africa and parallels in many ways the saga of the western frontier in the United States. The Boers had to fight on two fronts, however: against the black nations which were finally subjugated in the 1870s but which were too numerous and too well-organized to be wiped out, and against the British who repeatedly attempted to contain Boer expansionism.

The Boers established a series of more or less ephemeral whites-only republics in the Orange Free State and the Transvaal, but the discovery of diamonds in Kimberley in 1867 and then of gold near Johannesburg in 1886 spelled their doom. The Boer Republics became attractive targets for British imperialism, and after an abortive attempt in 1880, Britain finally defeated them in the 1899–1902 Anglo-Boer War.

The fourth major "racial" group in the South African kaleidoscope (besides the whites, the Coloureds and the Africans) are the Asians. They are overwhelmingly East Indians who first came in 1860 to work as "coolies" on the sugar plantations of coastal Natal, a British colony. Later, these indentured laborers were joined by Indian merchants, and South African Indians came to acquire many of the characteristics of a middleman minority.

In 1910, in the aftermath of the peace negotiations after the Anglo-Boer War, the Union of South Africa was established by joining the British Colonies of the Cape and Natal with the former Boer Republics of the Transvaal and the Orange Free State. The Union of South Africa was to be a "self-governing" state (later called "dominion" within the British Commonwealth of Nations). The term "self-governing" appears in quotation marks, however, because, except to a limited extent in the Cape Province, only the whites had the right to vote and to govern themselves. South Africa became in effect a white-ruled state with an internal colonial empire of "native reserves" (Marquard, 1957). After about 40 years of coalition governments in which English and Afrikaner whites shared the spoils of ruling the non-whites, the Afrikaner Nationalist Party won the 1948 elections, and immediately proceeded to implement its program of *apartheid* or "separate development."

So much for a bare outline of South African history. At present, there are 25 million South Africans, of whom 17% are whites (roughly 10% Afrikaner, 7% English); 10% Coloureds; 3% Asians, and 70% Africans. Each of these "racial" groups is subdivided by language and religion, so that there are in fact many more ethnies than racial groups. The four racial groups, however, are loosely analogous to the four *varna* of the Hindu system, each subdivided into smaller ethnic communities, loosely analogous to *jati*, although much more flexible. To complicate matters further, South African Indians have imported a miniature version of the Hindu caste system that continues to operate (albeit in greatly simplified form and affecting only marriage to any significant degree) within their own group and subgroups. In fact, the barely one million South Africans of Indian origin are divided among three main religious groups (Hindus, Muslims and Christians), five language groups (Hindi, Urdu, Gujarati, Tamil and Telugu) and a multiplicity of caste groups.

There is much discussion in the South African literature on the extent to which the Nationalist program of apartheid was something new, or merely an attempt to consolidate an apparatus of white domination and exploitation that had been in place since the end of the 19th century. Certainly, all the main features of the system had long existed. The "native reserve" system was instituted in the 1840s, restricting African rural land occupancy to 13% of the total area of the country (for 70% of the population). The infamous "migratory labor system" (whereby male workers are virtually imprisoned in military-style barracks for the duration of a labor contract at the end of which they return home to their native reserves) was the cheap solution to the exploitation of the diamond and gold mines and was put in operation late in the 19th century.

"Pass laws" to control the movements of Africans by means of a "reference book" to be produced on demand by the police date back to old 18th-century vagrancy laws applied to Hottentots. The "Immorality Act," making sexual relations between white and nonwhite a criminal offense, goes back to 1927. Racial discrimination in wages and employment and the creation of a split labor market, with supposely skilled white workers being paid up to 12 times as much as supposedly unskilled black workers, were also primarily creations of the mining industry in the second half of the 19th century. Numerous forms of racial segregation in urban housing, public transport, places of worship and entertainment, public buildings, rest-rooms, hotels, restaurants, hospitals and so on had all long been "customary" nearly everywhere in South Africa (though slightly less so in the Western Cape with its old paternalistic, slavery tradition).

What, then, was new about apartheid? The answer is this: the attempt to transform what had hereto been merely a highly exploitative, tyrannical and racist brand of settler colonialism into a full-fledged racial caste system, entrenched in law and frozen for all time. The apartheid program called for, and soon tried to implement, the principle of maximum segregation between airtight racial groups in every sphere, except the economic one where non-white labor was essential to the prosperity of the white-dominated economy. The white group was made *compulsorily* endogamous by the Prohibition of Mixed Marriages Act (1949) and a beefed-up Immorality Act (amended in 1950 and 1957). Surreptitious "passing" of Coloureds for white was stopped by the Population Registration Act (1950), providing for the official racial classification of all South Africans and the issuance of racial identity cards.

What little residential mixing had taken place in a few urban areas was undone by the Group Areas Act (1950, amended in 1952, 1955 and 1957) which provided for the massive displacement of people (overwhelmingly nonwhite) to create racially pure residential zones. The education of blacks was taken away from missionaries suspected of liberalism and assigned to the newly created Ministry of Bantu Education under the provisions of the Bantu Education Act (1953). The three English-speaking universities that had accepted a few nonwhite students (albeit in a segregated way) were henceforth prevented from doing so by the Extension of University Education Act (1959), and completely segregated "universities" were created for each of the nonwhite racial (and in some cases, ethnic) groups.

Politically, too, the incipient scrambling of the racial omelet was undone. The Act of Union of 1910 gave Coloureds and blacks in the Cape Province a limited franchise (qualified by property requirements) on the common voters roll. A series of laws whittled down that representation, minimal as it was. First, the franchise was extended to white women but not to nonwhite women, thereby halving the nonwhite representation. Then, Africans were removed from the common roll and allowed instead to elect three white MP's (out of 153) to represent them. Then the Coloureds were taken off the common roll and allowed to elect four white representatives. Finally, both Coloureds and Africans lost even this vestigial representation through whites in a common parliament and were given instead puppet institutions of their own. The "native reserves" were revamped as "Bantustans," which, one-by-one, are now given nominal political independence while remaining under white control. The Coloureds and Indians supposedly rule themselves through puppet councils of their own.

The Reservation of Separate Amenities Act (1953) not only legalized the creation of racially segregated facilities in every walk of life, public and private, but it also explicitly allowed *inequality* in the provision of these facilities. This list of racially discriminatory acts is by no means exhaustive, but it gives a fair idea of what apartheid is all about: the perpetuation of white supremacy through the imposition of a racial caste system that would freeze the status quo for all time. H. F. Verwoerd, a former Prime Minister, could not have stated it better when, in 1964, he reasserted, "We want to make South Africa White. . . . Keeping it White can only mean one thing, namely White domination, not leadership, not guidance, but control, supremacy."

Naturally, such a program was not unopposed. Black underground organizations, such as the African National Congress and the Pan-African Congress, have been active for many years, and there were two large-scale but abortive rebellions in 1960 and 1976. Both of them were repressed in bloodbaths. The South African Army and Police are armed and trained primarily for counterinsurgency. The state has virtually unlimited powers of arrest and search without warrant, detention without trial, censorship, banning, exile and so on, under laws with names such as the Suppression of Communism Act, the Public Safety Act, the Sabotage Act and the like. When that fails, the police shoot down peaceful demonstrators in the streets (including hundreds of boys, aged 12 to 18, in 1976) and torture and assassinate political prisoners in jail (such as, in 1977, Steve Biko). South Africa also has the dubious distinction of being the hanging capital of the world: it *legally* executes between one-half and three-fourths of the total death penalties for all noncommunist countries. Blacks who make up 70% of the population account for 82% of the executions (Lever, 1978).

All of this is done, let it be emphasized, in a relatively highly urbanized and industrialized country, with one of the highest per capita income and literacy rates in Africa (Horwitz, 1967). Not only that, but the systematic attempt to transform an exploitative but pragmatic form of settler colonialism into a dogmatically rigid caste society was done rather late in South Africa's industrial development. It took place during the post-World War II boom.

Why did white South Africans, and the government which represents them, invest such a vast amount of energy and resources into creating such a monstrous society that seems so widely at variance with what one expects from a modern industrial economy, whether capitalist or socialist? Several answers have been suggested. The orthodox Marxist answer is that apartheid ideally suited the kind of dependent, peripheral capitalism represented by South Africa, especially in the mining industry (Johnstone, 1976; Wolpe, 1970). As proof of their thesis, Marxists point to the spectacular rate of postwar economic development. There is no question that the migratory labor system was indeed highly suited to the extractive industry, and that initially the main impetus for capitalist development came out of diamond and gold mining. By World War II, however, secondary industry had far outstripped both agriculture and mining in importance; each of the latter contributes about one-tenth of the South African GNP compared to one-fourth for manufacturing. In secondary industry, apartheid did impose artificial shortages of skilled labor and other uneconomic restraints that many industrialists have done their best to circumvent. The Marxist thesis somewhat explains the genesis of some features of the system in the late 19th century, but it is not a satisfactory explanation of post-World War II apartheid. All the same, it is true that white South Africans have been able to have both their butter and their guns, and that apartheid served them well. This is true, however, not because apartheid is the handmaiden of capitalism, but because it represents the interests of a settler minority.

Another thesis is that Nationalist apartheid policies represented the interests not of the capitalist class (which is predominantly English) but of the white "aristocracy of labor"—the highly paid, skilled, white workers who are protected from black competition by racial legislation. This creates a split labor market that benefits mainly the privileged white working class, predominantly Afrikaner. This is the class that elected the Nationalists to power (Bonacich, 1979). The split labor market thesis of apartheid has, of course, considerable merit. Many events in South African history point to a conflict of economic interests between capitalists and white working class—a conflict resolved at the expense of black workers. There was even an abortive white labor revolt against the mining companies in 1922 over the issue of displacement of whites by cheap black workers. The slogan of the socialist strikers was "Workers of the world unite for a white South Africa!" The fact remains, however, that the Nationalist Party is an ethnic party of the Afrikaners, not a class party of the white working class. Voting statistics show clearly the ethnic character of the party that invented and implemented apartheid.

A third explanation is that the Afrikaner Nationalists, far from being racial dogmatists bent on transforming South Africa into a rigid caste society, are in fact a flexible, pragmatic oligarchy of politicians ready to compromise not only with their Afrikaner electorate and with the English business interests but, if need be, win with the "moderate" leadership of the nonwhite groups that it is ready to coopt, bribe and cajole into acquiescence (Adam, 1971; Adam and Giliomee, 1979). There are some recent developments that lend some credibility to this view, and, of course, it would be ridiculous to claim that the government has always been totally unbending to practical considerations. Nevertheless, the South African government has, on numerous occasions, shown considerable alacrity in paying a considerable economic price to implement various apartheid schemes that made no sense except within the framework of apartheid ideology. The creation of segregated colleges for the various nonwhite groups is a case in point. The maintenance of a huge police and paramilitary apparatus to enforce the pass laws is another.

What can we conclude? Despite its costs, apartheid served the interests of the Afrikaners and, more broadly, those of the whites, quite well, at least up to the present. In real terms, the standard of living of white South Africans is among the highest in the world, especially if one takes into account the low cost of services, housing and food. These are heavily subsidized by artificially low nonwhite wages; whites also enjoy the shelter of high wages and racial privileges that they could not sustain in the absence of a systematic system of racial discrimination. It is no mean achievement for a group of 4.5 million people to sustain a level of collective affluence that, depending on the criteria selected, is five to eight times higher than the 20 million people who are black or brown. This kind of group disparity, sustained over several centuries, does not happen "naturally" in a free-market economy. It develops through concerted discrimination, and it can only be maintained through continued discrimination.

Therefore, the question is not whether apartheid was most conducive to the optimization of output under a capitalist mode of production. It obviously was not, though it also proved itself not to be as *incompatible* with industrial capitalism as some would have predicted. Rather, the question is whether apartheid was an optimal policy for the defense of the interests of the group that advocated and implemented it.

The answer is by no means obvious. Perhaps in the short run it is positive and in the long run negative. Time will tell, and there are signs that we shall not have to wait much longer for an answer, for apartheid is rapidly coming unstuck at the seams. But more of that later. Let us look at the Afrikaners as a highly politically conscious ethny, and at the options they had as a group, given their objective situation. English-speaking whites acquiesced in and benefited from apartheid too, but they were less directly involved, since it was the Afrikaners and their Nationalist Party who were the main architects of apartheid.

If any group of people on earth qualify as an ethny, the Afrikaners do. All analysts are in agreement here (Adam, 1971; Adam and Gilionee, 1979; Moodie, 1975; Munger, 1967; Sheila Patterson, 1957). The Afrikaners regard themselves not so much as white settlers, capitalists, a working class or European colonials, but as a people with a sense of destiny forged through three centuries of struggle against great odds, as a nation with a heroic tradition and an origin myth (the Great Trek), as a vast descent group of kinsmen who share the same blood and as the "white tribe of Africa." Like countless other ethnies, they regard themselves as superior to their neighbors—vastly superior in their case because they think of themselves as being racially, morally and culturally above the "pagan barbarians" around them. (The Biblical "chosen people" theme from the Old Testament comes in as a handy parallel here, notwithstanding considerable anti-Semitism among Afrikaners.)

The ultimate defense of apartheid to which Afrikaners resort, after all the ideological claptrap of "separate development" has been disposed of, is the right of survival on African soil. That is, Afrikaners, like other people, ultimately reduce the problem to stark fitness considerations. Here, there are four main alternatives:

1. *Emigration.* But claiming no other home, where would they go?
2. *Individual survival as equals in a color-blind, integrated society.* This solution is abhorrent because it implies loss of ethnic identity and, ultimately, the unspeakable taboo of "miscegenation." Integration is rejected because it is seen as a process of moral, cultural and racial degradation.
3. *Collective survival as a separate ethny but without the right to boss others.* This solution is probably more acceptable to many Afrikaners than the first two, but its logic implies territorial partition and a much reduced "whitestan," probably in the Western Cape Province. Even that they would have to share with brown Afrikaners, thus facing a new color problem, albeit on a reduced scale. So the third solution would be very costly—only to be considered as a last resort if everything else fails.
4. *The status quo, but systematically refined to its ultimate conclusion, namely the transformation of a settler colonialism into a racial caste society.* In short, apartheid.

It is not difficult to understand why Afrikaners opted for the fourth course. They realized it might be catastrophic in the end, but they firmly believed that the alternatives would be far worst, far sooner. In 1948, when they embarked on that course, hardly anyone would have predicted the collapse of European colonialism in Africa within a decade. Even in 1960, when prospects suddenly turned much gloomier things still looked far from desperate for South African whites. In fact, it would take another 20 years for white control to be relinquished in all the territories to the north of South Africa. Certainly, the intervening events elsewhere in Africa gave South African whites little reason for a belated change of course. Zaïre, Algeria and, later, Mozambique, Angola and Zimbabwe, proved unhealthy places to stay in for their excolonial whites. So what realistic option did the Afrikaners have, as a group, but to dig in so as to postpone the inevitable?

In so doing, the Afrikaners, and by extension English-speaking whites as well, behave no differently from other groups in similar situations. Now, the inevitable is at their doorstep. By defining themselves in racial and ethnic terms, they have also defined the terms of the confrontation: five million whites perched precariously at the tip of a continent inhabited by 400 million blacks, with no friends in sight. No matter what happens, South African whites stand to lose heavily, perhaps their very lives, or at least their place under the African sun they love so much. Even if allowed to stay on equal terms, for most whites those equal terms will mean a drastic reduction of their present standard of living, so drastic in fact that most would probably find it intolerable and choose emigration instead.

The edifice of apartheid shows numerous cracks that herald its impending crash. The "Bantustan" scheme with is sham independence to African mini-states satisfies nobody and fails to solve the problem of a rapidly growing urban African population. The Coloureds show increasing signs of militancy and rejection of their pariah status. The puppet councils of the various nonwhite groups have no legitimacy. Industrial apartheid is being increasingly breached as the demand for skilled labor forces employers to upgrade nonwhite workers. The "black consciousness" movement is achieving an unprecedented level of solidarity between Africans and Coloureds.

In response to mounting pressure and international embarrassment, the government is belatedly jettisoning one aspect of "petty apartheid" after another. Apartheid signs are gradually disappearing from buildings. Luxury hotels and restaurants are opening up to nonwhites to accommodate diplomats and distinguished foreign visitors and to project a better image overseas. Interracial sports and cultural events are cautiously being introduced in response to international boycotts and as an internal safety valve. All this has to be done cautiously, because the government must avoid alienating its all-white electorate. The government is now even daring to discuss abolishing the ultimate racial taboo, by repealing the Immorality Act and the Prohibition of Mixed Marriages Act. All these measures are taken with the hope that the racial caste system can be dismantled without affecting the substance of white political power and economic exploitation. Perhaps the government also hopes that it can thereby co-opt the growing African middle class and appease the fury of the nonwhite masses by taking the racial sting out of exploitation.

Some analysts view these recent changes as evidence of the South African government's flexibility and ability to weather storms by trimming its sails. It is clear that the attempt to perpetuate a racial caste system in South Africa has failed. The likelihood of preserving a deracialized colonial system through symbolic concessions is also extremely low. The system is so unequal and iniquitous that it is not amenable to concessions and compromise. Past experience with decolonization elsewhere in Africa, especially in Zimbabwe (which was in almost every respect a miniature version of South Africa), seems to indicate that the end of white domination is in sight. The only question is whether it will take the form of a prolonged civil war, a negotiated partition or a frantic white exodus. The odds favor, I think, a long escalating war of attrition accompanied by a gradual economic winddown and a growing white emigration.

In retrospect, although apartheid failed in the end, it was a rational course for the Afrikaners to take, given their collective aims, and it probably did postpone the day of reckoning by about 30 years. The Afrikaners simply tried to push to its ultimate conclusions the logic of settler colonialism. They did so because they could not accept the alternative, universalistic logic of a shared, integrated society along liberal lines. Having forged a powerful ethnic identity through 300 years of historical vicissitudes, they became prisoners of their narrow racial definition of ethnicity. In this, they are far from unique. Without the pressures of a European colonial office to restrain them, they had the courage of their narrow, bigoted convictions, and they tried to apply consistently and to the bitter end the best possible program for the maximization of their fitness. And they had the saving grace of not being hypocritical about it.

THE UNITED STATES

Clearly, the United States never was a caste society by our definition. However, for the better part of a century, it was a society with one relatively large caste group. After the abolition of slavery, Afro-Americans became a pariah caste and, in some respects, remain so to the present. After the Reconstruction period, especially between 1890 and World War I, the southern states developed through their Jim Crow laws a genuine regional caste system (Woodward, 1955). In the rest of the country, the caste system was less developed, but, even there, important features of it existed in many states, for example, antimiscegenation laws. Indeed, free blacks began to be treated as pariahs in the northern states long before the abolition of slavery (Litwack, 1961).

One thing is clear about the United States: the position of blacks is quite unlike that of any other minority group. While they are, on the average, about twice as poor as whites and while racial discrimination has a strong negative impact on their standard of living, the predicament in which blacks find themselves is not *in the first instance* economic. There are more poor whites than poor blacks, and other minority groups such as American Indians and Chicanos are, on the average, much poorer than blacks. Yet, other poor groups, unlike blacks, are not pariahs. Conversely, even the black middle class is not spared all the consequences of racial stigmatization, although there is now a substantial trend toward destigmatization (William J. Wilson, 1978).

Amerindians

Let us briefly compare blacks to other ethnic and racial groups in the United States. At the bottom of the economic totem pole are Amerindians. By a rather wide margin, they have the lowest family and per-capita income of any group, the lowest level of educational achievement, the highest infant mortality rates, the lowest life expectancy and so on. By almost any objective criterion, they are the worst off. Yet, they are not a pariah group like the blacks, and they lack nearly all the characteristics of a caste. For example, far from being endogamous, they have long had a high rate of intermarriage with practically every other ethnic and racial group around them: Anglos, Hispanics, blacks and Asians.

Rather, Native Americans are classical conquered groups. They have retained the vestiges of territoriality in their reservations, and they are officially recognized as special groups with special treaty rights. Though many are highly acculturated to the dominant Anglo-American culture, some groups, especially in the southwest, still speak indigenous languages and have retained their own separate cultures. Individual Indians, however, who want to leave the reservation and exercise their rights as American citizens, can do so with little resistance. Many of them can easily "pass" for white or assume some other ethnic identity such as Hispanic. Typically, Indians who leave the reservation do not form Indian ghettoes in towns but become dispersed individuals who quickly sink into the "hobo" lumpenproletariat, intermarry or melt into the mainstream.

The Indians' relationship to the Federal government clearly follows the model of internal colonialism. The Bureau of Indian Affairs is a colonial government within a government, with special jurisdiction over groups legally defined as having different rights (recognized in international treaties), which imply separate nationhood and extraterritoriality vis-à-vis the rest of the country and the population. The situation of Indians, in short, has all the hallmarks of a classical colonial situation. Amerindians have at least the residues of territoriality, of separate nationhood and of distinctive languages and cultures. They are conquered micronations, engulfed in a huge neo-European representative government that treats them as a microcolonial empire.

European Immigrants

The situation of European immigrant groups in the United States is characteristic of what happens to voluntary immigrants who come to settle in an established society and who come neither as a middleman minority nor as a conquering group. I shall analyze that situation in detail in Chapter 10. Here, let us simply characterize it as the classical "melting pot," in which the immigrant group typically enters the labor market in the urban proletariat but gradually, over two or three generations, becomes almost undistinguishable in language, culture and class distribution with the "mainstream" population (which can be either native or, more frequently, itself the product of earlier waves of immigration). Clearly, those groups are not stigmatized, though they often encountered considerable prejudice and discrimination initially. Their "foreignness" was often resented, but they were always offered the option of becoming "Americanized." Indeed, they often had to, as the price of acceptance.

Non-European Immigrants

Immigrants from Asia and Latin America often found themselves, at least initially, in a position intermediate between the European immigrants and the blacks. They shared their "foreignness" with European immigrants, but they also suffered, for the most part, from the stigma of not being "white." Therefore, their assimilation into the mainstream was, on the whole, much slower and more difficult. Hispanics are in a somewhat anomalous twilight zone between race and ethnicity. A minority among the immigrants from Latin America can pass for white, and their position is little different from that of European immigrants. The "success story" of the Castro refugees in Florida is a case in point: they were mostly light-skinned members of the Cuban bourgeoisie who came with skills and capital and were fairly readily accepted.

Some Latin American and Caribbean immigrants are phenotypically black (including a number of Puerto Ricans, who, technically, are not immigrants) and therefore share much of the stigma of Afro-Americans. Among them, a number of West Indians (e.g. Haitians and Jamaicans) have done relatively well, because they often came with skills and because they had not been traumatized by the American caste experience. A number of West Indians, for example, have become prominent professionals, artists and intellectuals, but they have been forced to gravitate to the black community. Most immigrants from Mexico and Central America are, of course, Indian-looking and therefore also racially stigmatized, though not nearly as much as blacks.

Hispanics, through large regional concentrations in southern California and the southwest where they constitute large and increasingly vocal and politically organized minorities, have a great chance of perpetuating their cultural pluralism for several generations and perhaps indefinitely. In New Mexico, the Spanish language has acquired official status, and there is some possibility of Hispanics constituting a genuine nation, separate from the Anglo mainstream. Certainly, of all the sizeable minorities in the United States, they are the only group for which such a potential is realistic.

The Asian minorities are too culturally diverse, numerically small and geographically dispersed to have any realistic alternative to assimilation.

Initially, between the late 19th century and World War II, they were subjected to virulent racial prejudice, leading, in the case of the Japanese, to internment in concentration camps. Indeed, up to World War II, their status in the western states, especially California, was barely better than that of the blacks. However, their position drastically improved after World War II. Japanese-Americans were especially successful in terms of education and entry into the middle class, but the Chinese, too, began to disperse from their traditional ghettoes and be increasingly accepted. Successive waves of Korean, Philippino and, most recently, Indochinese immigrants all show signs of fairly rapid acculturation to, and fairly easy acceptance by the white population. Rates of intermarriage are quite high for most Asian groups, not only between Asian groups, but also with whites.

Afro-Americans

No other group in the United States approaches blacks in degree of stigmatization. Blacks are stigmatized because of their "race," not primarily because they are poor and lower class. At least one-third of the black population belongs in the middle class by educational and socioeconomic criteria, and other groups (Chicanos, Amerindians) are on the average much poorer. Blacks are not ostracized because they are foreign. Indeed, most are of older American stock than most whites. It has become fashionable in the 1970s to claim that blacks have a distinctive culture and language of their own, but that claim is largely ideological and romantic. By almost any objective standards, American blacks share the language, religion, values and so on of their white counterparts. To use a colorful Caribbean phrase, they are culturally "Afro-Saxons."

The romantic search for survivals of African culture is elusive (Herskovits, 1958). When one controls for region of origin, social class and rural–urban residence, most of the alleged cultural differences between whites and blacks "wash out." Ghetto lumpenproletarian blacks in Chicago, Detroit or New York may seem to have a distinct subculture of their own compared collectively to their white neighbors, but the black Mississippi share-cropper is not very different, except for skin pigmentation, from his white counterparts, nor is the San Francisco black physician from his white colleague. The case for "black culture" rests thus largely on the northern ghetto lumpenproletariat, a class which has no direct white counterpart. Even in that group, however, much of the distinctiveness is traceable to their southern, rural origins. The remaining differences are not African survivals but adaptations to stigma.

In short, notwithstanding much recent ideology to the contrary, Afro-Americans are as Anglo as anyone is in America. Blacks are rejected not because they are poor or foreign but because they are black. There is considerable evidence that the stigma has been diminishing over the last 30 years (W. J. Wilson, 1978), but a great deal of it still remains as shown by the continued high rate of endogamy. Interracial marriages are still taboo, and there is even considerable resistance to the interracial adoption of blacks. The caste system is slowly being eroded, but, W. J. Wilson's (1978) conclusions are still premature and overly optimistic.

How did the American social caste system develop? Broadly, as a substitute for slavery. It was the supreme irony of American democratic ideology that, in order to reconcile slavery with democracy, black slaves had to be defined as less than fully human. How else could slaveowners like Washington, Jefferson, Madison, Monroe and many other founding fathers loudly proclaim that "all men are created equal" except by implicitly excluding their human livestock from their definition of humanity? Slavery, however, as shown in Chapter 6, was not a caste system. Master and slaves lived in intimate proximity and interdependence; they interbred and formed other close affective bonds. Even though their relations remained highly unequal, neither whites nor blacks formed an autonomous, inbred community. Slaves were largely prevented from forming autonomous black communities. The social life of blacks under slavery was a truncated one (Genovese, 1974). The real community of slavery, perverse though it was, was the plantation, an interracial community, at once hierarchical and intimate, socially distant but spatially and biologically close.

Racism was developed to rationalize the subjection of blacks. The black was "all right" so long as he stayed "in his place," that is, so long as he remained a slave. As a slave, he was a perpetual minor, a dependent, a grown-up child without any claims to autonomy or political rights. Had it not been for the political tradition of liberalism, slavery would not have needed such an elaborate racist ideology. Many slavery systems, as we have seen, have been nonracist, and certainly in Latin America the more openly autocratic colonial regimes of Spain and Portugal were, on the whole, much less racist. Liberalism and racism were *complementary*, not contradictary, features of the American political credo and practice.

If blacks were inferior and, therefore, born to be slaves, if indeed slavery was good for them as well as for whites, then what was to be made of them if they were freed? The logic of the democratic ideology dictated enfranchisement, assimilation and equality. But, given the racist climate, this was unthinkable, even to people like Jefferson and Lincoln who were in principle against slavery. The thought of free blacks living side-by-side with whites on terms of equality was utterly abhorrent to them. For example, the 1821 quotation from Jefferson to the effect that "nothing is more certainly written in the book of fate, than that these people [i.e. blacks] are to be free" is frequently cited. But after a semicolon, he continues, "Nor is it less certain, that the two races, equally free, cannot live in the same government. Nature, habit, opinions have drawn indelible lines of distinction between them (Foley, 1900, p. 817)."

One solution, strongly advocated by many 18th century abolitionists, including Jefferson, was deportation to West Africa. The American Colonization Society, strongly supported by Jefferson, was founded for the purpose of settling free blacks in Africa, and later the American quasicolony of Liberia in West Africa was established to implement that purpose. Even long after it became clear that deportation on a large scale was not feasible, the idea of racial equality with free blacks was still abhorrent. Lincoln, the "Great Emancipator," for example, declared in 1858:

> I will say then that I am not, nor ever have been in favor of bringing about in any way the social and political equality of the white and black races,—that I am not nor ever have been in favor of making voters or jurors of negroes, nor of qualifying them to hold office, nor to intermarry with white people; and I will say in addition to this that there is a physical difference between the white and black races which I believe will forever forbid the two races living together on terms of social and political equality. And inasmuch as they cannot so live, while they do remain together there must be the position of superior and inferior, and I as much as any other man am in favor of having the superior position assigned to the white race (Angle, 1958, p. 117).

The other "solution" to the "black problem" was caste. Since blacks had to stay but could no longer be held as slaves, then they must be segregated in pariah communities, confined to menial jobs, kept in perpetual inferiority and political subjection and prevented from interbreeding with white women. (Racial mixture in the other direction was never regarded as problematic, again for reasons that sociobiology makes quite evident.) The southern states bear the brunt of the blame for creating the legal apperatus of Jim Crow, which was simply the formal expression of the caste system. Woodward (1955) documents in detail these developments after the Reconstruction period, especially after 1890. However, the outcasting of blacks was not by any means exclusively a phenomenon of the south.

Outcasting measures, such as segregation, disenfranchisement, prohibition of interracial marriages and denial of the right to bear arms were applied to free blacks in both the north and the south (Litwak, 1961). The fact that this happened to free blacks long before the abolition of slavery shows how much pariah status was clearly thought of as the only suitable alternative to slavery for blacks. The south is blamed for Jim Crow because the sudden emancipation of large numbers of blacks in the south made for the sudden elaboration of a vast legal and extralegal apparatus for keeping blacks in their pariah status. But free blacks, long before 1865, were already outcasted, about equally so in the north and the south, excepting perhaps New England where blacks were so few as not to present a "problem." As late as the 1940s, 30 states in the United States had antimiscegenation statutes on their books, and the U.S. Supreme Court did not declare those statutes unconstitutional until 1967 (Simpson and Yinger, 1972, pp. 503–504).

The heyday of the American caste system was the half-century between 1890 and 1940. To the social and legal practices of racial discrimination corresponded an elaborate pseudoscientific racism and Social Darwinism (Hofstadter, 1959). By the 1920s and increasingly in the 1930s, an antiracist reaction began to grow in the social sciences, under the influence of scholars like R. E. Park in sociology, Gordon Allport in psychology and Franz Boas and Ruth Benedict in anthropology, but its full impact did not make itself felt on policy and general attitudes until World War II.

The war itself provided numerous employment opportunities for blacks (and women) in industry and accelerated the migration of blacks from the south to the north and west and from rural areas to cities. The Federal government took the belated step of desegregating its Armed Services (which was still a Jim Crow force during most of World War II) and took the lead in prohibiting racial discrimination in firms under government contracts. The Brown vs the Board of Education decision of the Supreme Court in 1954 reversed the "separate but equal" doctrine which, since the Plessy vs Ferguson decision of 1896 had given legal sanction to racial segregation. With the growth of the Civil Rights movement in the 1950s and 1960's, the American caste system was under growing assault by a coalition of blacks and white liberals, and the country seemed to be moving, however slowly and reluctantly, toward a racially integrated society.

Then, around 1968, a curious reversal of integration took place. A section of the black leadership grew impatient with the pace of progress, angered by the unemployment, urban decay, educational decline, drug and crime epidemic and other endemic problems of the black ghettoes, and irritated by what it saw as the paternalism of its white liberal allies. It began to develop an ideology of black pride and black nationalism that struck a resonant chord on the nation's campuses and changed the entire climate of race relations. The universalistic *civil rights* movement became a particularistic *black* movement, the ideological thrust of which was an attempt to transform blackness from a stigma to a badge of pride and, thereby, to change the position of Afro-Americans from that of a pariah racial group to that of an ethnic group.

Logically, this new "militant" ideology called for racial separation and self-determination, the rejection of white liberalism, the development of racial pride and identity, the rejection of assimilation as an ideal, the creation of separate cultural institutions to sustain that "nationalist" movement and a political strategy of organizing blacks *qua* blacks. Afro-Americans were to unite and form a pressure group, seeking to gain racial representation at all levels of public life and to pressure for governmental intervention on behalf of blacks in both the public and the private sectors (especially in education, housing and employment).

The response was electrifying. Soon the whole country went on an ethnic rampage as one group after another organized (in part in self-defense *against* blacks) along ethnic or pseudo-ethnic lines. First the Chicanos and Amerindians, then the "white ethnics," ultimately even such nonethnic groups as feminists and "grey panthers" adopted the rhetoric, ideology and tactics of black militants. Facing mounting pressures from all sides for ethnic recognition, the government—a conservative government under Nixon, let it be noted—responded by re-institutionalizing racial and ethnic criteria for employment, housing, admission to educational institutions, busing of children to and from schools, promotions in the Civil Service, etc. "Affirmative action" was proclaimed as a concerted attempt to undertake special measures to overcome the accumulated effect of past discrimination, whether individual or institutional. With affirmative action came racial quotas, double standards and categorization of people by race or ethnicity rather than merit. The pros and cons of these policies are still being hotly debated, and now the political tide seems to be turning against them as their liabilities and ineffectiveness are becoming increasingly apparent (Glazer, 1975; O. Patterson, 1977).

The bulk of the evidence seems to suggest that, while "affirmative action" has indeed provided some high-level jobs to substantial numbers of college-educated blacks as token representatives of "their" group, it has also had a great many counterproductive consequences, not only to the society as a whole, but even to blacks and members of other ethnic minorities. Among other things, affirmative action has done the following:

1. It has heightened racial consciousness and thus partially reversed the trend to deracialization of American society. In order to enforce school busing, affirmative action in hiring, preferential admission of blacks to universities and so on, it became increasingly necessary to classify people by race and to reverse the previous trend toward the deletion of all racial information on all application forms and official records. Affirmative action, whatever its intent, gives the stamp of official approval on the recognition of racial and ethnic differences and on the legitimacy of treating people as members of groups rather than on the basis of individual merit. It, therefore, contains a profound internal contradiction because it necessarily entrenches what it purports to eliminate: racial distinctions. Affirmative action also legitimizes the dubious concept of collective guilt for past actions, since the rationale for reverse discrimination is that one group is to be advantaged compared to another to compensate for past discrimination.
2. Affirmative action has raised serious problems of equity and aroused a considerable white backlash against what is seen as unjust racial discrimination against whites, or more specifically as anti-Semitism or anti-Catholicism. Poor, educationally disadvantaged whites legitimately have asked why they, too, should not be the beneficiaries of affirmative action and they have begun to organize politically, often against blacks. So have other "disadvantaged" groups such as Viet Nam war veterans, the old and the physically handicapped. Among the nonwhite minority groups themselves, bitter factionalism and hostility are fanned in the competitive process of fighting over the rather meager spoils of affirmative action. In the end, nearly everybody has felt unjustly treated and has organized against competing groups. Once more, affirmative action, far from reducing barriers to integration, has created new ones.
3. Affirmative action increases the class gulf between the black middle class and the ghetto subproletariat. It clearly benefits some of the former, but does little or nothing to alleviate the very serious and worsening problems of the latter (W. J. Wilson, 1978).
4. Affirmative action demeans the groups it is supposed to help since the rationale for it implies inferiority. Its philosophy is clearly paternalist, and it often creates a quasicolonial structure for blacks (in the form of

"offices of minority affairs," "black studies programs," racially labeled scholarships, awards and positions, and the like). Many of these institutions, far from promoting integration, perpetuate the stigmatization of blacks and extend to them a governmental machinery similar in form and content to the Bureau of Indian Affairs or the Reconstruction Era's Freedmen's Bureau.

5. The more blacks (and other minorities) are given preferential treatment, the more questionable the qualifications of *all* blacks become. Affirmative action is therefore resented by many qualified, competent blacks as not only an insult to them, but an impediment to their careers. Another aspect of this problem is the perpetuation of white stereotypes of black inferiority. To the extent that some blacks have indeed been promoted above their level of competence to fill quotas and "guidelines" in a hurry, this is often interpreted as evidence of black incompetence.

As an economist (Sowell, 1972) suggested, affirmative action has had the effect in many highly skilled occupations, such as academic professions, of promoting blacks several notches above comparably skilled whites. The problem is compounded by the fact that blacks are often chosen and recruited by whites not on the basis of merit but according to political, ideological and behavioral attributes that will make them "good" tokens. Thus, a person who is competent to be, say, a professor of French in a junior college and who would stay there if he were white, finds himself at a large state university because he is black. There, he is found wanting by the standards of that institution and denied tenure after a few years, leading to bitterness all around. Similarly, a professor who would do well at middling state university may not be competitive at Harvard or Princeton, yet find himself there simply because he is black. Affirmative action, by creating artificial shortages in the labor market, also creates inequities in salary and racial discrepancies in levels of competence. For example, black sociologists, though still grossly underrepresented in terms of numbers, make about $4,000 more in average salary than their white counterparts (Lewis, Warner and Gregorio, 1979). In the past, of course, the reverse was often true. In many lower- and middle-level occupations, blacks were often better qualified and more educated than their white counterparts because of racial discrimination in the other direction. It was not uncommon for black railway porters and postal clerks, for example, to be college graduates.

The Future of Caste in the United States

Despite the temporary reversals caused by the policies of the 1970s, W. J. Wilson's (1978) prognosis of a gradual disappearance of the stigma of race in the United States seems likely to be realized. This will probably be accompanied by an increasing class polarization within the black group. Whereas the black middle class is experiencing declining racial prejudice, increasing acceptance in the area of employment and a lowering of barriers, there is little evidence that the lot of the black urban proletariat is improving. In some respects, it seems to be deteriorating. For example, at the time of publication of the controversial Moynihan Report (Moynihan, 1965) 26% of black children were born illegitimate; in 1976, illegitimacy passed the 50% mark. In 1965, 71% of black children lived with both of their parents; by 1977, under 47% did so. In 1961, 14% of black children were on "welfare," compared to 38% in 1977 (van den Berghe, 1979a). Statistics on youth unemployment and underemployment, on crime and on drug addition among ghetto blacks also point to a deteriorating situation, although, at the same time, there is increasing evidence that more and more blacks are getting a college education, and that the socioeconomic conditions of those who do are rapidly approaching those of their white counterparts (W. J. Wilson, 1978).

The overall picture, then, is one of movement from caste to class, despite the adverse effects of affirmative action. The United States situation is, of course, fundamentally different from that of South Africa. South African whites, especially the Afrikaners, are a dominant but beleaguered minority with an acute sense of ethnicity and race. They have built their entire way of life on political domination and economic exploitation and, without the artificial privileges of a racial caste system, they could not sustain themselves anywhere near the level of affluence to which they have become accustomed. In short, they draw enormous benefits from the racial caste system they erected. However, in the United States, the whites are an overwhelming majority, so much so that they cannot be meaningfully conceived of as a ruling group at all. The label "white" in the United States does not correspond to a well-defined ethnic or racial group with a high degree of social organization or even self-consciousness, except regionally in the south. The racial caste system is increasingly an anachronistic remnant of a previous age, and the benefits of racism to the whites are becoming more and more marginal. Most whites would probably now accept color-blind policies based on merit and the total abolition of all forms of institutional racial discrimination, although prejudicial attitudes linger on. They would do so because they realize that they have little or nothing to lose by universalism.

In the final analysis, the question is whether pluralism is a stable option in the United States. The answers varies, I believe, from group to group. Amerindian groups seem too numerous, too small and too dispersed to have any chance of ever forming viable autonomous nations within the United States, although they still retain many of the classical characteristics of nationhood (especially territoriality and a separate ancestry, history and culture). Demography and geographical dispersion also limit the chances of viable pluralism for Asian minorities. European immigrant groups, despite the much vaunted ethnic revival of the 1970s, show little inclination to escape the melting pot which, for them, was a prelude to social mobility and full participation in the "mainstream." Of all the ethnic groups, the Hispanics, by virtue of growing numbers, separate culture and geographical concentration, probably have the most favorable prognosis for viable pluralism in North America. After all, they are merely the northern pioneers of a vast ethny of over 200 million in the Western Hemisphere.

By contrast, Afro-Americans owe their distinctiveness overwhelmingly to the fact that they have been first enslaved and then stigmatized as a pariah group. They lack a territorial base, the necessary economic and political resources, and the cultural and linguistic pluralism ever to constitute a successful nation. Their pluralism is strictly a structural pluralism inflicted on them by racism. A stigma is scarcely an adequate basis for successful nationalism. I realize that the position I am taking here is not fashionable, but it is, I believe, realistic. Whether blacks like it or not, they have no real option but assimilation; and whether whites like it or not, they have no option but to accept blacks without any prejudice (or for that matter, preference), as fellow citizens. The alternative is the perpetuation of the festering sore of racism that has for too long plagued American society.

SUGGESTED READINGS

The Hindu caste system has been extensively described by Dumont (1970), Ghurye (1952), Hutton (1946) and Srinivas (1969). The analytical use of the concept in other societies has given rise to a large critical literature. See, among others, Berreman (1960), Cox (1948), De Vos and Wagatsuma (1966), Hsu (1963) and Myrdal (1944). The best symposium on the subject was edited by de Reuck and Knight (1967). For an interesting collection on the survival of the Hindu caste system overseas, see Schwartz (1967).

CONSOCIATIONALISM

At this stage the reader may well ask whether ethnic relations can ever be amicable. Can ethnic collectivities both retain their distinctiveness and live in peace and harmony with other ethnic groups within the same state and society? Since peace and harmony imply equality, the question really asks whether stable cultural pluralism can ever lead to a stable democratic polity, to what Lijphart (1968a, 1968b, 1977a) has called a *consociational democracy* and Lehmbruch (1967) a *proportional democracy*. The answer is a highly qualified "yes." It is possible, but only under very special conditions, which I will examine now.

A defining condition of consociationalism is that the cultural pluralism must remain stable; the ethnies in presence must remain distinct from each other. Ethnies can, of course, assimilate and loose their separate identity and culture, a situation that I shall discuss in Chapter 10. However, in many historical situations, people show neither any desire nor any tendency to assimilate or acculturate to other ethnies. Basically, to anticipate the subject of assimilation, people tend to assimilate and acculturate when their ethny is geographically dispersed (often through migration), when they constitute a numerical minority living among strangers, when they are in a subordinate position and when they are allowed to assimilate by the dominant group. *Dominant* minorities often retain their separate culture for many generations as we have seen in South Africa and many other colonial settings. Dispersed and subordinate minorities, however, typically adopt the language, culture and the religion of the dominant majority and, unless prevented from doing so by a restrictive racial caste system, they assimilate as well. Individuals, in short, acculturate and assimilate when it is objectively in their interest to do so; that is, when they see acculturation and assimilation as fitness maximizing. The specific circumstances in which they do so will become apparent later.

Here, we are dealing with situations where cultural and social pluralism persists indefinitely, despite extensive intergroup contact, because members of the ethnies in presence see no advantage in assimilating or acculturating. It is important to note here that it is not the amount of intergroup *contact* per se that determines the rate of acculturation and assimilation. Contact is merely a *necessary* but not a *sufficient* condition for these to take place. Rather, acculturation and assimilation occur, or fail to occur, depending almost exclusively on whether there are individual advantages in undergoing changes in language, religion, culture and ultimately ethnic identity. In the absence of such individual advantages to change, people overwhelmingly prefer to stay as they are, that is, to preserve their ethnic identity. We have already suggested earlier (Chapter 2) why ethnic identity is so basic: it is an extension of kinship. Therefore, we may expect an underlying conservatism and reluctance to change one's culture and ethnicity in the absence of strong incentives to do otherwise. Indeed, this ethnic conservatism is so great that it takes very strong individual incentives and very unfavorable conditions for the persistence of separate ethnicity (such as geographical dispersal) to overcome it.

Clearly, the condition of equality that is basic to an amicable system of ethnic relations is a potent predisposition for persistent cultural pluralism. If two or more ethnic groups have approximately the same relationship to the means of production and an approximately equal access to the structure of power, then no one has much to gain by joining another group. There can be some marginal incentive to become bilingual to facilitate communication, but bilingualism is typically quite limited (both in terms of percentages of population who were bilingual and in terms of degree of competence of individuals in their second language), seldom leading to either complete acculturation or, much less, assimilation.

Political, economic and social equality or near equality between ethnies sharing a common polity is thus a strong predisposing factor, making for persistent cultural pluralism. A second main condition for permanent pluralism is, of course, territoriality. The more geographically distinct ethnies are, the greater their chances of collective survival. Even very small minorities, like the Romansh in Switzerland or the Navaho in the United States, can maintain their ethnic separateness for centuries if they retain a home territory in which they remain a majority. The third condition for the persistence of cultural pluralism is a derivative of the other two. In ethnically mixed areas (often urban areas) cultural pluralism will persist to the extent that the groups in presence are in approximately equal numbers. In a sense, that third condition could be considered a specification of the first one, for, if there is great disparity in the size of the groups, equality between them is difficult to maintain.

Indirectly, I have already defined the fundamental setting for consociational democracy. The latter is found where the social and cultural pluralism between ethnies is permanent and where the groups in presence are approximately equal in access to power and economic resources. These conditions, in turn, exclude conquest, which creates ethnic inequality. This means that consociational democracies are typically established between *native* groups, or, at least, between groups that are several generations away from a conquest situation where one group is appreciably superior in wealth or power. Consociational democracies are also more likely to be found between native groups because native groups are more likely than immigrant groups to be territorialized. Canada, which in the 20th century increasingly assumed the character of a consociational democracy between Francophones and Anglophones, is an exception in that it was established by two immigrant groups, one of which conquered the other; but its ultimate success as a stable binational state is very much in doubt as we shall see later (Brazeau and Cloutier, 1977; Porter, 1965; Royal Commission, 1969; Smiley, 1976, 1977).

CONDITIONS FOR CONSOCIATIONAL DEMOCRACY

Let us now specify more accurately what makes consociational democracies (CD) work. Lijphart (1977a) prefaces his latest comparative study of such societies by saying that it is difficult but not impossible to achieve a stable democracy in a plural society. In an earlier account, Lijphart (1968a) suggested that it must be worked at very hard with a lot of goodwill and listed such prerequisites as an "ability to recognize the dangers inherent in a fragmented system," "commitment to system maintenance," "ability to transcend subcultural cleavage at the elite level" and "ability to forge appropriate solutions for the demands of the subcultures."

"These four prerequisites must all be fulfilled," Lijphart says (1968a, p. 65), "if consociational democracy is to succeed." He then adds several other "conditions favorable to consociational democracy," such as "distinct lines of cleavage between subcultures" (so as to reduce conflict and competition by reducing interethnic contact), "a multiple balance of power among the subcultures" (as distinct from the hegemony of one group, or conflict between *two* groups), "popular attitudes favorable to government by grand coalition," "external threats," "moderate nationalism" and "a relatively low total load on the system" (Lijphart, 1968a, pp. 67–72). He cites Austria, Belgium, Lebanon (an irony, it seems, after the events of 1975 and their continuing sequels, although, of course, the Lebanese crisis was aggravated by external factors, especially the Palestinian–Israeli conflict), The Netherlands and Switzerland as examples, and he concludes that they are all *small* countries, presumably another correlate of success.

In his more recent work, Lijphart (1977a) elaborates further on the conditions favorable to stable democracy in plural societies. CDs are characterized by "grand coalition" government in which each major ethnic section has a veto on important issues and is represented proportionately. Proportional representation by group is also stressed by Lehmbruch (1967) in his study of Austrian and Swiss politics. In fact, Lehmbruch makes this characteristic the defining one of the type of government he called *Proporzde-*

mokratie. Other favorable conditions discussed by Lijphart include a willingness to grant segmental autonomy to the ethnic groups under a federal structure, the presence of cross-cutting lines of cleavage (by class, religion and ethnicity), the existence of overarching loyalties that transcend narrow ethnic affiliation and a tradition of elite accommodation.

My main criticism of Lijphart's view of CD is that it is more descriptive than explanatory because so much of his analysis puts a heavy burden of explanation on the normative values of the political culture. Clearly, my bias is against treating such ideological or normative traits as "commitment to system maintenance," "ability to recognize the dangers inherent in a fragmented system" and "popular attitudes favorable to government by grand coalition" as anything but descriptive epiphenomena.

A CD exists when the *class* interests of the ruling elite in preserving a unitary multiethnic state prevail over countervailing interests to break the state down into its ethnic components. The CD is thus a special case of "bourgeois democracy," i.e. of a state run by a capitalist, technocratic and bureaucratic elite through supposedly representative institutions, elected officials and the other paraphernalia of parliamentarism. In a plural society, however, where primordial attachments to ethnic collectivities compete with class affiliation, the illusion of democracy can only be maintained if the elite itself is multiethnic and in proportions approximating those of the constituent ethnies in the general population. If that condition is not met, then the political system is perceived by the underrepresented groups as undemocratic because dominated by the overrepresented group or groups. Proportionality at the elite level is thus a key feature of CDs, for it is through proportionality that the multiethnic elite preserves the democratic fiction of representativeness and thus its own legitimacy. If one accepts the principle of ethnic representation, then the ethnicity of a member of the ruling class contains a validation of the right to rule.

An essential corollary of ethnic proportionality in CDs is the muting of class conflicts. To the extent that ethnic sentiments are politicized, class consciousness is lowered. If the main line of cleavage in a society is ethnicity (or some feature of it, such as religion or language), if the political game is seen primarily as an ethnic balancing act in the allocation of scarce resources, and if there are no glaring disparities in ethnic representation at various class levels, it follows that the significance of class cleavages within each ethny is correspondingly decreased. Under such circumstances, the class interests of the multiethnic elite are best served by a system of CD. The more politicized ethnicity becomes and the more ethnicized the polity, the more attention is deflected from class conflicts and redirected (or redefined) in ethnic terms. Therefore, the less blatant the pursuit of class interests by the elite becomes.

The possibility exists, of course, of class conflicts being expressed *within* each ethnic group. In Belgium, for example, the language group cleavage is overlaid by class-based political parties, trade unions, farmers' associations and other interest groups that are themselves compartmentalized by ethnicity. Nevertheless, to the extent that ethnic issues are salient, the probability of class alliances across ethnic boundaries is lowered, and class conflicts tend to remain intraethnic. Class conflicts, instead of being the primary, macrodivisive force that they are in more ethnically homogeneous societies (Schermerhorn, 1970), became secondary, microdivisive cleavages within each ethny. Their political potential for organization at the level of the central state is correspondingly weakened.

Lijphart (1977a) mentions "immobilism" as a "danger" of CDs, but, in fact, conservatism is inherent to the system, for the reasons just mentioned. To the extent that politics becomes an ethnic balancing act, the compromises and accommodations for which the ruling elites of CDs are justly famous all tend toward freezing the status quo. Since the *modus operandi* of the CD is to maintain ethnic proportionality, any social, economic, linguistic or whatever change that threatens the ethnic status quo is seen as menacing by one or more of the ethnic collectivities, and the multiethnic elite restores tranquility by enacting policies tending to counteract change. A mutual veto right vested in each ethnic segment of the elite often further forestalls the possibility of upsetting the status quo. "Immobilism," a euphemism for conservatism, results. Furthermore, attention is deflected from issues of class, and members of the elite are regarded not so much as a ruling class, but as representatives of their respective ethny and watchdogs for the maintenance of ethnic balance.

A pertinent observation is in order here. There has never been a successful multi*racial* democracy. The consociational model can work where the distinctions are ethnic, but seemingly not where they are racial. Some multiracial societies have attempted to present themselves as moving toward democratic pluralism (e.g. South Africa and Rhodesia), but such "multiracialism" was in fact a thinly disguised attempt to perpetuate the domination of one racial group over the others. When such societies were decolonized, as in Algeria, the sham of multiracial democracy, parallel development and the like quickly collapsed, and the society either became de facto monoracial through emigration of the former ruling minorities, or the political system became nonracial.

Equally invidious and unworkable are the attempts, often made in compromises of decolonization, to vest certain minority privileges and rights to formerly dominant racial groups. The reluctant concession of a 20% representation in the Zimbabwe Parliament opportunistically accepted by Mugabe and Nkomo in the 1980 compromise, for example, cannot be expected to survive independence under a black government very long, because it constitutes an affront to the black population.

Significantly, the platform of virtually all liberation movements in southern Africa has been nonracial and antiracist. With a few partial exceptions (such as the splinter Pan-African Congress in South Africa), these liberation movements like the MPLA in Angola, FRELIMO in Mozambique, the African National Congress in South Africa, SWAPO in Namibia and ZANU and ZAPU in Zimbabwe have advocated not *black* government but *majority* government on the principle of one-man-one-vote, *including* the expatriate minorities. The cynic might well argue that demographic reality makes such universalism totally safe, as the practical difference between black and majority government is negligible, but the principle of nonracialism is, nevertheless, politically sound.

There have, of course, been a number of countries in which people of different "racial" stocks have managed to live in relative harmony. I am not arguing that phenotypic differences preclude peaceful coexistence; far from it. What I am saying, however, is that the consociational model has never been successfully applied to multiracial societies. Those societies, like Mexico, Brazil, Hawaii and many others, where phenotypically distinct people have lived side-by-side in relative harmony have all been societies where no *political* recognition was given to race, where racial groups have not become organized as political constituencies, and where the state has legally and officially been *non*racial, *not* multiracial.

In the previous chapter, I analyzed the misguided effort in the United States to try to institutionalize a consociational model of racial representation by giving increasing official and legal recognition to racial categories, thereby encouraging racial groups to become increasingly self-conscious and organized for political action. The basic reason why racial consociationalism cannot succeed in creating a more egalitarian society is that race as a social category is always invidious and that, therefore, any policies based on the recognition of race inevitably have stigmatizing consequences. This is doubly the case in situations, such as in the United States, where objective *ethnic* differences between "racial" groups are minimal; in the nearly complete absence of *ethnic* markers between groups, racial markers become almost purely invidious. The only purpose for retaining racial markers is to be discriminatory. Even "reverse discrimination" cannot be anything but a demeaning form of paternalism since it implies inferiority.

Ethnic distinctions can be made invidious, of course, but they are not *necessarily* so. There is nothing invidious, for instance, in an Italian-speaking Swiss child attending an Italian-language school or a Franco-Canadian child a French-medium school; but there is something *intrinsically* invidious in an Afro-American child attending a black school or, for that matter, in his being accepted on *special terms* in a white school. Ethnicity can be, in special circumstances, a viable basis for CD, but race cannot. Race is necessarily stigmatizing; not so with ethnicity.*

So far, we have associated CDs with "bourgeois democracies," and indeed most examples of it have developed in capitalist societies like Switzerland,

---

*It was, of course, the implicit realization of this fundamental distinction between race and ethnicity that led to repeated endeavors by Afro-Americans to redefine themselves in *ethnic* rather than racial terms, by claiming a separate language ("black English"), religion (Black Muslims), culture ("black music"), history and so on. These attempts failed, in part because the objective basis for these cultural distinctions was tenuous and in part because the overwhelmingly dominant whites continued to define blacks as a pariah caste, not as a separate ethny. Powerless minorities find it very difficult to redefine themselves in terms of their own choosing, precisely because they are powerless.

Belgium or Canada. The model of consociationalism, however, is not incompatible with a "people's democracy." Several socialist countries, most notably Yugoslavia and the Soviet Union, have evolved toward consociational types of polity, that is, polities officially and legally recognizing ethnicity as a basis of political organization, representation and incorporation into the multinational state—ruled by a multiethnic bureaucratic and technocratic elite.

Where some nationalities were initially greatly overrepresented (as were the European and especially Russian groups in the Soviet Union), attempts were made, as the Communist bureaucracy became firmly entrenched, to co-opt underrepresented minorities into leading positions. This had the double effect of creating a Communist Party elite that transcends ethnic boundaries and perpetuates its class interests, creating the illusion of a representative democracy. Consociational mechanisms of elite accommodation are, in fact, remarkably similar in "people's" and "bourgeois" democracies, and they achieve in both cases an impressive degree of "immobilism." Consociationalism serves the elites quite well in both cases.

To recapitulate argument thus far, consociationalism is a special form of elite domination based on ethnic proportionality. It can work if it is based on ethnicity (or some special feature of it, such as language or religion), but not if it is based on race; race is intrinsically invidious and, therefore, cannot become a principle of egalitarian group association. Consociationalism seems to work equally well and remarkably similarly in both capitalist and socialist societies. The consequences in both cases seem to be conservative because it reduces class consciousness by politicizing ethnicity.

Unfortunately for the multiethnic elites whose interests CD serves, CD has its problems. To these I now turn. Indeed, there is an inherent contradiction in consociationalism. On the one hand, the elite, by politicizing ethnicity, become the arbiters of an ethnic balancing act that detracts attention from class conflicts and promotes conservatism. On the other hand, ethnicity is such a powerful sentiment that, once mobilized, it cannot always be controlled. When counterelites (often a semiprofessional petty bourgeoisie of school teachers, students and other intellectuals) arise, which have an interest in challenging the status quo, ethnicity can easily be fanned into raging separatism, escalating to civil war. The recent history of Lebanon, long considered a model CD in the Third World (Binder, 1966; Lijphart, 1977a; D. A. Smock and A. C. Smock, 1975), shows how fragile consociationalism is when challenged by nationalist counterelites, including those created by the Israeli–Palestinian conflict. The intelligentsia—frequently a disaffected, underemployed, impecunious, insecure group—often see in nationalism a means to challenge the "immobilism" of CDs, to attack the ruling elite and to substitute itself as the new elite of the nationalist movement.

What are the conditions that make for stability (or "immobilism") in CDs? More precisely, under what set of circumstances are the interests of the multiethnic ruling elite in keeping the consociational structure greatest and most difficult to challenge? The defining characteristics of CD with which I began this chapter are that the constituent ethnies not be in a hierarchy of wealth or prestige, and that their cultural pluralism remain relatively stable. If the first condition of ethnic equality or near-equality is missing, the system cannot be called democratic, and if the cultural pluralism is not permanent, the system ceases to be consociational. Given then these two defining characteristics and restrictions, the following seem to be the most important conditions favoring consociationalism.

1. *Some degree of territorial interpenetration of the ethnies.* The more people live outside their home territory, the more scattered ethnic enclaves are, and, the more people live in multiethnic cities, the more difficult territorial partition becomes. Since the practicality of partition is a main determinant in the successful creation of new ethnic states, the more chaotic the ethnic map looks, the greater the prospects for consociationalism. For cultural pluralism to persist however, the ethnies in presence must retain *some* territorial base, otherwise assimilation results and the state is, by definition, no longer consociational.

2. *Genetic interpenetration of the ethnies.* The more intermarriage there is between ethnies, the more kin ties cut across ethnic ones—and the more people of ambiguous status are created who cannot be neatly categorized by ethnicity. If there is completely random intermarriage, however, cultural pluralism itself disappears and, with assimilation, we no longer have consociationalism.

3. *Functional interpenetration of the ethnies.* The more institutions the ethnies share, the more difficult it becomes to disentangle a society along ethnic lines.

The first and second points are self-explanatory, but the third requires some elaboration because functional interpenetration takes many forms. Politically, the state apparatus itself is, by definition, shared in CDs. Therefore, the more centralized the state is, the more there is to share—and the more difficult separatism. Typically, early steps of ethnic separatism take the form of demands for greater decentralization and regional autonomy, e.g. the recent process of "devolution" in the United Kingdom. Also, the more powerful and centralized the state is, the more important and the larger its capital city. If the latter is ethnically mixed, as it frequently is, this is another contributing factor making partition difficult. A powerful centralized state is by definition in a better position to squelch separatism, and it creates a large bureaucratic apparatus with a vested interest in the status quo. The ideal political conditions for CD are, therefore, a centralized bureaucratic state with a large multiethnic capital and a large powerful multiethnic civil service and military forces.

Functional interpenetration is also frequently economic. The more economic interests straddle the ethnic fence, the more multiethnic the moneyed and industrial bourgeoisie are, and the more banking, industry and commerce cross ethnic boundaries, the better the prospects for CD. If, in short, the economic interests of the bourgeoisie coincide with those of the bureaucratic elite in maintaining a unitary multiethnic state, these economic and political interest groups will tend to coalesce to make it work. However, economic interpenetration does not stop at the elite level. Trade unions and professional associations, for example, to the extent that they stradle ethnic lines, also share an interest in the consociational status quo. In short, consociationalism is fostered by the *cross-cutting of ethnic and class lines*.

Beyond the political and economic spheres, interpenetration can be social and cultural. For example, several ethnies may share a common religion (as in Belgium), or religious groups can overlap with ethnic ones (as in Canada, where there are large numbers of both Francophone and Anglophone Catholics, though few Francophone Protestants and Jews). Two closely related cultural groups can also appreciate each other's music, art and other cultural institutions. Classical music concerts or art exhibits in Brussels, for example, are as likely to attract Flemings as Walloons. Brussels as the capital of a little Flemish state could not be the great cultural center that it presently is. Therefore, *aficionados* of "high culture" have an interest in the status quo that transcends their ethnicity.

In a sense, all these favorable conditions for CD are self-evident to the point of being tautological. Consociationalism works to the extent that the ethnic collectivities are: (1) not too different from each other to start with; (2) united by a multiple network of cross-cutting ties and affiliations; and (3) somewhat territorially mixed. Most simply put, ethnic groups stick together if the alternative is difficult, impractical, costly and painful, especially to the elite in whose interests the system is maintained. There is no magic to consociationalism—not even a sophisticated political theory. Consociationalism, for all its limitations, inefficiencies, particularisms and irrationalities, is simply the best arrangement possible in situations of permanent ethnic pluralism and interdependence where the alternatives (e.g. à la Lebanon) are too awful to contemplate.

Consociationalism thus prevails in situations of ethnic equality or near-equality; ethnic association is accepted because it does not entail ethnic domination and exploitation. Consociationalism is most likely to persist where a substantial degree of cultural pluralism is self-perpetuating, but where, at the same time, the ethnies interpenetrate and are interdependent in mutually beneficial ways. The mutuality of benefits in consociationalism also implies ethnic equality, of course. In the last analysis, consociationalism is based on reciprocity at the ethnic level (which does not preclude exploitation in class terms).

CASE STUDIES OF CONSOCIATIONAL STATES

Switzerland

Switzerland, a country of some six million inhabitants in the heart of Western Europe, is often mentioned as the oldest, stablest and the most peaceful, successful and affluent CD in the world (Dunn, 1972; Gretler and Mandl,

1973; Grüner, 1969; Kohn 1956; Lehmbruch, 1967; Lijphart, 1977a; Nordlinger, 1972; Weilenmann, 1951). It is made up of four indigenous language groups: the Germans make up 75% of the natives; the French, 20%; the Italians, 4%; and the Romansh, 1%. Postwar prosperity brought in a large influx of "guest workers," mostly from Italy and other Mediterranean countries. They now make up 13% of the total population, but they are largely excluded from political life since they are foreigners. If one includes guest workers in the linguistic breakdown, however, the Italian-speaking group more than doubles from 4% to nearly 10% of the total population, and the German group is reduced to 69% (Lijphart, 1977a).

Religiously too, Switzerland is divided between Catholics (42%) and Protestants (58%). While the Italians are nearly all Catholics, large numbers of both French and German Swiss belong to both religions. Thus, there is a substantial degree of cross-cutting cleavages between religion and language, an important condition for CD. Religious cleavages were salient during the wars of religion in the 17th century and, indeed, even up to the framing of the Constitution of 1848, but they have receded in importance since.

The great secret of Swiss success in their consociational experiment is that Switzerland is one of those rare multiethnic states that did not originate either in conquest or in the breakdown of multinational empires. Instead, it grew over a 700-year period as a loose confederation of "hill tribes" (as they would be called if they were located in Asia) that banded together for mutual defense. Like many other hill tribes elsewhere in the world, the Swiss had a dual advantage in resisting outside conquest: favorable terrain and lack of natural resources. They were simply not worth conquering. Like other hill tribes, too, they developed special ecological adaptations, providing highly specialized goods and services to their lowland neighbors. During the formative centuries of the Confederacy, Switzerland specialized in the monoculture of cannon fodder for the warring European states. Later it turned to more pacific ventures such as the manufacturing of watches and the management of shady foreigners' ill-gotten capital.

Switzerland, in short, is a very special case. It escaped conquest and was allowed by its neighbors to grow because it was difficult and unprofitable to invade and because it provided its neighbors valuable services. If it had not existed, it would have had to be invented. (Lebanon, incidentally, during its 1943–1975 interlude of CD, also provided banking services to its neighbors; but being a fragile and artificial state born out of the disintegration of the Ottoman Empire and nurtured under a French mandate, the consociational experiment ended in cataclysmic collapse in 1975, as it was drawn into the vortex of the Near-Eastern crisis and the Palestinian–Israeli conflict.)

From the very start, Switzerland satisfied the condition of ethnic equality as very few multiethnic states do. This is not to say that there are not great internal disparities in the distribution of wealth, both by region and by social class (Table I). In 1977, the richest canton, Basel-town, had 2.75 times the per capita income (34600 francs) of the poorest canton, Obwald (12600 francs). Basically, the densely populated, urbanized, northwestern third of the country (on an arc from Geneva to Zürich) is much richer than the more

TABLE I. Swiss Cantons by Income, Language and Religion[a]

Canton	Per capita income 1977 (francs)	Largest language group (%)[b]	Largest religious group (%)[b]
Basel (city)	34600	94 G	66 P
Zug	31300	98 G	84 C
Geneva	30200	83 F	57 C
Zürich	25100	96 G	74 P
Basel (country)	22000	97 G	74 P
Aargau	19900	98 G	58 P
Vaud	19500	88 F	79 P
Schaffhausen	19200	98 G	79 P
Glarus	19100	98 G	68 P
Neuchâtel	18400	86 F	78 P
Solothurn	18200	97 G	56 C
Berne[c]	17700	84 G	85 P
Thurgau	17600	99 G	67 P
Graubünden	17400	60 G	53 P
St. Gallen	16900	99 G	60 C
Ticino	16700	89 I	93 C
Nidwalden	16500	99 G	92 C
Lucerne	16400	98 G	86 C
Appenzell A.R.	16300	99 G	84 P
Uri	15200	98 G	93 C
Valais	15100	64 F	96 C
Schwyz	14900	99 G	94 C
Fribourg	14700	65 F	87 C
Appenzell I.R.	12800	100 G	96 C
Obwald	12600	99 G	97 C
Switzerland	20500	75 G	58 P

Sources: Federal Statistical Office; Union Bank of Switzerland.
[a]Citizens only.
[b]Code: G = German; F = French; I = Italian; P = Protestant; C = Catholic.
[c]Before secession of Jura.

rural and mountainous center and southeast. Regional differences in levels of development are much greater in Switzerland than, for example, in the United States, where in 1970 the richest state (Alaska) had a mean family income ($13,900) of only 1.90 times that of the poorest state (Mississippi, $7,300).

However, luckily for Switzerland, these regional disparities in income cross-cut ethnic differences. There is a roughly proportional distribution of rich and poor cantons in the Francophone and Germanophone areas. Of the ten richest cantons, three are French and seven German. Of the ten poorest cantons, two are French, seven German and one Italian. (Ticino, the Italian canton, actually ranks 16th, i.e. near the middle.) All four of the two richest and the two poorest cantons are German. Religiously, there is a distinct tendency for Catholic areas to be poorer than Protestant areas. Nine of the ten richest cantons have Protestant majorities, while nine of the ten poorest are overwhelmingly Catholic. However, as each canton has its class inequalities that cross-cut both religious and ethnic lines, the issue of religious disparities in wealth rarely became politicized, except indirectly in 1847, when it threatened to split the Confederacy between the more prosperous, liberal, urban and Protestant northwest, and the poorer, more rural, conservative and Catholic center and southeast.

Another crucial element of Swiss equality is dialectical. In most parts of the world where both "high" and "low" dialects of a language are spoken these dialects are stratified. Typically, the educated, urbanized, upper classes speak a prestigeful dialect that is identified with the standard "national" language, with the educational system, with the press and with all the institutions of "high culture." Conversely, the local, rural dialects are spoken mostly by peasants and the urban working class and are stigmatized, officially unrecognized and often unwritten.

In the German part of Switzerland, local dialects are still very much alive and are all quite divergent from standard "High German" (or *Schriftdeutsch*, as it is sometimes called in Switzerland). High German is the official language of school and urban "high culture," but local dialects are proudly spoken at all class levels without social stigma. At least in the urban areas, practically everyone is "diglossic" (i.e. speaks fluently both the standardized language and the local dialect), readily shifting back and forth between them, irrespective of social class. The upper classes speak local dialects as unself-consciously as the lower classes, and dialect is not a basis for drawing invidious class distinctions. Unfamiliarity with High German marks one as an unschooled person, but the phenomenon has become rare in the urban areas. This relative lack of association between dialect and class within the German ethny and the relative lack of dialectical differentiation within the French- and Italian-speaking population are additional factors tending to make the spoken tongue classless and thus ethnicity noninvidious.

The Confederacy was a league of hill tribes born out of mutual interest and convenience, which only in 1798, under the French-controlled Helvetic Republic, came to resemble a modern state, gradually starting to do more complex tasks such as running a railway, a post-office, an army and a diplomatic corps at the federal level. Even by the standards of other federal states, Switzerland is still extremely decentralized. Of all government revenues, the Swiss federal government spends only 61%, compared to 65% in Canada; 74% in West Germany; 77% in the United States and 84% in Austria (Lijphart, 1977a). The basic unit of political life in Switzerland is still the canton, despite a gradual growth in federal functions.

This great degree of decentralization, however, seems to contradict the condition of functional interpenetration that, I suggested, favored consociationalism. If each canton is largely autonomous, except in a few essential common services, what holds them together in the confederacy? The answer is, of course, the convenience of these common services. The ethnic diversity of Switzerland is only incidental to the federalism; *it does not constitute the basis of it*. Switzerland is a *confederation of cantons, not of ethnic groups*, and as such Switzerland does not really qualify as a true CD. The Swiss state gives no formal recognition to ethnicity as a basis of political incorporation, citizenship, legal rights and obligations, land tenure rights, allocation of resources, assignment to school systems—any of the usual bones of contention in multiethnic states. Switzerland as a whole practically shows none of the formal characteristics of a CD. The state does not need to be a CD, because, being so little of a state, there is so little at stake.

If one is to look for CD in Switzerland, one must look at the cantonal level. What does one find there? Of the 26 cantons (or more precisely, 22 cantons and four half-cantons) in the Confederation, 23 have more than 80% of their population speaking the same language and 17 are over 95% monolingual (Table I). Berne, which was officially bilingual before the secession of the Jura, was 84% German-speaking, and its official bilingualism did not prevent the French Catholic northern Jura from agitating for, and eventually achieving, separate cantonal status (Mayer, 1968). Twenty-two cantons are officially monolingual and, thus, hardly consociational. That leaves only three cantons that qualify as CDs, Valais (64% French), Fribourg (65% French) and Graubünden (60% German) (Table 1).

Religiously, there is a little more diversity at the cantonal level than there is in language. Still, the Catholics who are only 42% of the country's population make up over 80% of the total in ten cantons. On the whole, the cantons tend to be much more homogeneous, both linguistically and religiously, than the country as a whole. Most cantons are not good examples of CD. Of the few that are, one (Berne) has been beleaguered by separatist demands by its French Catholic minority in the Jura, which recently achieved the status of a separate canton. Graubünden is the most diverse canton, being trilingual and nearly equally divided between Catholics and Protestants.

In short, the success of Switzerland is not so much a success in CD as a successful adaptation of isolated, autonomous, marginal groups loosely banded together to provide very specialized services to their neighbors. Switzerland is a very pleasant country, but it is not much of a state by modern standards. Perhaps it is such a pleasant country *because* it is not much of a state. The real capital of Switzerland is not Berne, but Zürich, and Zürich life revolves not around the government but around the banks on or near the Paradenplatz. The other contender for cosmopolitanism is Geneva, a lakeside resort for bureaucrats of international agencies. Both Zürich and Geneva are, of course, overwhelmingly monolingual, and face none of the problems of consociationalism.

Belgium

With its ten million people, its high per capita income, its high degree of industrialization and urbanization and its strategic location between the great powers of Western Europe, Belgium is not quite as inconsequential as its small size (some 32,000 square kilometers) suggests. Lacking defensible boundaries, and being a rich prize and a strategic path of invasion, Belgium, unlike Switzerland, was repeatedly conquered, fought over and incorporated in a succession of larger states: the Roman Empire, the Carolingian Empire, the Grand Duchy of Burgundy, the Hapsburg Empire, France and The Netherlands. It did not achieve its present form until 1830, when it seceded from the Kingdom of The Netherlands, a shotgun wedding of Holland and Belgium imposed by the Congress of Vienna in 1815, in the aftermath of Napoleon's defeat at Waterloo (a Belgian village some 20 kilometers from Brussels, incidentally).

Economically, Flanders, the northern half of today's Belgium, had long been one of the most dynamic parts of Europe. Flemish cities like Ghent, Bruges, Ypres and, later, Antwerp and Brussels were among the most prosperous in Europe between the 14th and the 17th centuries, but that economic prosperity did not translate into political independence and overseas colonial expansion, as was the case with Holland to the north. The Revolution of 1830 was not a classical nationalist movement at all, and the state it created made neither geographical nor cultural sense. Despite a distinguished Belgian historian's massive attempt to "prove" the long-standing existence of a Belgian nation (Pirenne, 1930–1932), there was, and still is, no such thing.

Belgium has no "natural" boundaries. The plains of Flanders are wide open to the north and south into Holland and France; the rolling wooded hills of the Ardennes extend into France, Luxembourg and Germany; the main rivers run through Belgium, starting in France and ending in a vast estuary in Holland. Belgium makes no ethnic sense either. The "linguistic boundary" runs from east to west and bisects the country into a Flemish north and a Walloon south with the bilingual capital of Brussels enclosed in Flemish territory. An ethnic division should have left Flanders with The Netherlands and Wallonia with France. Belgium was not even the product of a religious cleavage, for, even though it is overwhelmingly Catholic (at least nominally so), the split with The Netherlands left millions of Catholics on the Dutch side of the border.

The bourgeoisie that led the Revolution and ruled the new country declared Belgium a constitutional monarchy, but it even had to go shopping abroad for a king, finally deciding on a German princeling, Leopold of Saxen-Coburg-Gotha who was conveniently in the market for a kingdom. (He had previously been offered the Greek crown, but declined.) The only thing that Belgium had going for itself in 1830 was a thriving economy at the forefront of the industrial revolution. The coal mines of the Meuse valley led to the early development of steel and other heavy industry in Wallonia, and, since the early 19th century, Belgium has remained one of the world's leading industrial states. Under its profligate and megalomaniacal king, Leopold II, Belgium even launched on a colonial adventure in Africa and acquired the vast, mineral-rich Belgian Congo (80 times the size of Belgium) which it kept from 1885 to 1960, first as a private domain of the King and then as a Belgian colony. Thus 19th-century Belgium had all the trappings of a prosperous and even relatively important state: all it lacked was nationhood. Its motto, *L'union fait la force* ("There is strength in unity."), is still more of a pious wish (some would even say, an ironic joke) than a reality.

Yet, Belgium muddled through 150 years of independence and survived two World Wars, in each case with a German invasion and four years of military occupation. It has thrived from conflict to conflict, and all the linguistic, class, religious and party-political quarrels and street demonstrations have yet to produce a single fatality (if one excludes the settlement of scores with collaborators after the two World Wars).

Ethnic conflicts in Belgium are poorly understood abroad because of the extremely intricate and changing relationships among class, religion and ethnicity (Clough, 1930; du Roy, 1968; Huggett, 1969; Lorwin, 1966, 1971, 1972; Outers, 1968; Petersen, 1975; Tindermans, 1971; Willemsen, 1969; Zolberg, 1974, 1975, 1977). In order to understand present day ethnic conflicts, we must trace back their history several centuries. The linguistic frontier—the invisible line that separates Flemings in the north from Walloons in the south—is roughly 1500 years old. It marked the boundary, during the late Roman period, between the Latinized Celts, who eventually came to speak modern French, and the Germanic Franks, who today speak dialects of Dutch, a language derived from low German.

That linguistic frontier does not correspond to any feature of topography. In places, it even bisects villages. Yet, it has been remarkably stable and enduring. Except for the suburban extension of an increasingly Francophone Brussels, which encroaches on neighboring Flemish territory, the linguistic frontier has barely shifted over the centuries. The most visible clue that one crosses the frontier is a shift in the language of commercial billboards and roads signs. Much to the confusion of foreign motorists, traveling, say, toward Mons, Courtrai, Tirlemont, Malines, Louvain or Liège, these cities suddenly metamorphose into Bergen, Kortrijk, Tienen, Mechelen, Leuven or Luik, or vice versa. Only officially bilingual Brussels has bilingual road signs, but during periods of nationalist fervor, rival youth gangs often spray paint over the offending language with the result that *both* languages are sometimes obliterated.

If the division were simply an ethnic one, language conflicts in Belgium would not be nearly as bitter as they have been. Unfortunately, they have been heavily overlaid with class conflicts, though less so today than before World War II. Starting in the 14th and 15th centuries, when Flanders was part of the Grand Duchy of Burgundy and when the Grand Dukes established their French-speaking court in the flourishing Flemish city of Ghent, the use of French began to spread among the nobility of Flanders. After the French Revolution and during the Napoleonic period, when Belgium was occupied by the French, the use of French as the prestige language of the ruling class gradually spread from the aristocracy to the bourgeoisie. By the time of independence in 1830, the bourgeoisie that led the revolution, although in good part of Flemish ethnic origin, was using French almost exclusively as the language of administration, higher education, justice, "high culture" and other aspects of public life. The Gallicized Flemish bourgeoisie continued for the most part to be bilingual, but, much like their Russian counterparts under the Czars, they spoke French among themselves and spoke Flemish (as the various local dialects of Dutch are known in Belgium) with their social inferiors.

The bourgeois state established by the 1830 Revolution, then, was in a sense a classical CD in that its ruling class was drawn from both the Walloon and the Flemish parts of the country, and in that the class interests of the bourgeoisie transcended any sectional ethnic interests. The main cleavage within the ruling class was not ethnic. Indeed, they all agreed on the use of French as the dominant language, caring little about ethnic nationalism. The political split was between liberals and conservatives, a cleavage which, in Belgium, revolved principally around religion.

Since Belgium has always been overwhelmingly Catholic (over 95%, not including the "guest workers," many of whom are Muslim), at least nominally so, it may seem odd that Belgians find it possible to quarrel over religion. Yet they do so with great alacrity. The perennial quarrel is between the liberals (and later the socialists) who, in the tradition of the French Revolution, advocate a complete separation of Church and State, and the conservatives who rally around the Catholic Church and oppose such a separation.

An important sector of the bourgeoisie has always been militantly anticlerical; some of them have been associated with Freemasonry (an anticlerical organization in Catholic countries), and the Liberal Party has been their political home. In the late 19th century, as the hitherto limited suffrage was extended to the working class, the Socialist Party grew in strength and joined the anticlerical camp, eventually to supplant the Liberals as the main opposition group to the Catholics (much as the Labourites gradually eclipsed the Liberals in Great Britain).

The main bone of contention in the "religious question" in Belgium has traditionally been the issue of state support for religious (i.e. Catholic) schools. The compromise is that the Belgian state supports a double system of schools: lay schools where no religion is taught, and religious schools, largely run by the Catholic clergy, who are paid salaries as teachers by the state. Except for religion, the school program is identical in the two systems, and state inspectors control curricula in both.

Over time, the conservatives became more and more reformist, and the present Catholic party, called the Social Christian Party, is in fact a welfare-state oriented Christian Democratic group much like its German and Italian counterparts. As for the Socialists, they have moved toward the right, now representing the conservative wing of the Social Democratic movement. The Liberals, now a small minority, stand ideologically to the right of both major parties, and represent the interests of the disgruntled, anticlerical bourgeoisie. Since World War II, Belgian politics, like those of other Western European states, are no longer sharply polarized along class lines. Each major party (Socialist and Social Christian) has a whole set of parallel institutions including schools, universities and trade unions, serving as a vast patronage network. The bourgeoisie gradually co-opted the labor elite, and, as the proletariat underwent a process of *embourgeoisement*, Belgium became a classical welfare state run consensually by overlapping elites made up of the traditional moneyed bourgeoisie, the trade union elite, the professionals and technocrats, the politicians and the ever-growing state bureaucracy.

Politically, Belgium has three groups or *zuilen* (Dutch for "pillars"), as Lijphart (1968a) designates these complex, multi-institutional social formations that are at once political parties, trade union movements, cultural and educational centers and social clubs for the elite: Catholics and Socialists, with a much smaller Liberal group. Differences in ideology have become quite inconsequential. Both major parties are basically centrist, welfare-state democrats. Their only residual difference of any importance is the "religious question" (i.e. the school issue), and even that conflict has become so ritualized and so deadlocked in "immobilism" as to lead cynics to believe that the two elites keep the conflict alive merely to justify their separate existence to the voters.

How does all this relate to the ethnic issue? These political cleavages and the religious question linked with them, cross-cut the Flemish–Walloon division. Although the Flemings are overrepresented in the Catholic camp and the Walloons in the Socialist and Liberal groups, large numbers of each ethnic group are present in each of the three *zuilen*. Indeed, each political party is organized into two ethnic wings, presents ethnically balanced tickets at elections and plays with alacrity the game of proportional ethnic representation. More than any other factor, it is that cross-cutting cleavage between ethnicity and other political issues that holds Belgium together as a CD.

The political and economic elite are represented in all three *zuilen* and, having reduced to insignificance their ideological differences, have an increasing class interest in keeping the ever growing and more powerful state apparatus together. Belgium always was a highly centralized state, modeled largely on Napoleonic France. Brussels is a large, affluent, cosmopolitan city and is the seat not only of the Belgian government but of a vast international elite of "Eurocrats." (Both NATO and European Common Market headquarters are located in Brussels.) Secession of either Flanders or Wallonia would spell disaster for Brussels and would not solve the "language problem," as Brussels itself, though supposedly bilingual, is in fact a Francophone island in a Flemish sea. Best estimates (Petersen, 1975) put the Dutch-speaking population of Brussels at less than 20%.

However, the rule of this multiparty, bi-ethnic elite has not been unchallenged by both Flemish and Walloon nationalists. In recent times, the separatist challenges crested in the 1968 elections when nationalist parties managed to win nearly a fifth of the seats in Parliament. A new compromise was reached, transforming Belgium into a semifederal state with two monolingual autonomous cultural regions and a bilingual capital. This compromise seems to have defused the language question—at least for the time being.

Precise figures on the ethnic composition of Belgium are impossible to obtain, for the language question is so controversial that the Belgian census has not dared to bring up the matter since 1947. The closest one can come to current ethnic composition is by region. Fifty three percent of the population lives in the Dutch-speaking part of Belgium, 31% in the French-speaking area and 16% in Brussels (du Roy, 1968). If one accepts the estimate that Brussels is about 80% French, Dutch speakers thus find themselves in a clear but not overpowering majority of 56% in the country at large. These figures correspond rather closely to those of the last linguistic census taken in 1947, when 42% reported their home language as only or mainly French; 53% Dutch, 1% German and 4% other languages. These figures, however, hide many complexities, giving only a rough idea of the ethnic situation.

We must return to the late 19th century for a better understanding of Belgian ethnic and class relations. We saw that Belgium was founded and ruled by a bourgeoisie that, although drawn from both Flanders and Wallonia, had become French-speaking and used French as the official language. The class domination of the French-speaking bourgeoisie, and hence the social superiority of French, was buttressed by a franchise that until 1893 limited voting to the propertied classes. Even then, universal manhood suffrage was diluted by plural voting for the bourgeoisie; *equal* manhood suffrage only came in 1919 (Lorwin, 1972). (Women had to wait until the 1920s.) The Belgian Constitution granted everyone the freedom to speak his own language, but French supremacy was evident everywhere. It began to be opposed in the 1840s, and, in 1856, the government appointed a commission to study the "linguistic question." In 1886, a Flemish Academy was set up, and, in 1898, an act of Parliament officially established equality of the two national languages. However, this act largely remained a dead letter until 1922, when Dutch was made the official administrative language north of the linguistic frontier and French south of it. Even then, the gains were only gradual and the bitterness remained. Not until 1930, for example, did the University of Ghent, a state university in an entirely Flemish city, adopt Dutch as the sole language of instruction. Only then, did the internationally famous Catholic University of Louvain, in the Flemish city of Leuven, begin to be bilingual; hitherto, it had been almost entirely French (Lorwin, 1972). As for the official Dutch translation of the 1830 Constitution, it had to wait until 1967 (Lorwin, 1972).

It must again be stressed that this Flemish nationalist movement, in the 19th and early 20th centuries, was much more an expression of *class* resentment against the Frenchified Flemish bourgeoisie than an anti-Walloon movement. It was not the Walloons in the south who were mostly resented, but the French-speaking bourgeoisie of Flanders that was favoring French as a tool of class domination. The Flemish nationalist movement was led mostly by the upwardly mobile, educated, petty bourgeoisie of students, teachers, lower clerics and professionals, who often came from peasant or working class origins and bitterly resented the status of French as an elite language and the indignity of second-class ethnicity *in their own territory*. Indeed, that class found itself in a bitter dilemma for, to be individually successful in their process of upward mobility, they had to learn French, but their failure to master French as native speakers exposed them to ridicule. The opportunists sought and often achieved assimilation into the Francophone bourgeoisie; the others saw in Flemish nationalism the only dignified alternative to class snobbery.*

Since World War II, a number of important changes have taken place. Largely through the efforts of Flemish nationalists, the status of Dutch has improved markedly, and the bourgeoisie of the Flemish cities no longer finds it *de bon ton* to speak French. Indeed, in large Flemish cities like Antwerp and Ghent where French was commonly heard in the upper classes, the use of French has greatly declined and English is now often preferred as a neutral second language. With the democratization of manners that

---

*If I may introduce some autobiographical recollections here, I remember very clearly from my own childhood in the 1930s and 1940s how invidious this bilingualism was. My paternal grandparents, who lived in the solidly Flemish city of Ghent, belonged to this gallicized Flemish bourgeoisie. They were fluent in both Flemish and French, but they always spoke French to their class equals and to members of the family, and looked down on Flemish as an inferior, uncultured, though earthy and colorful, peasant dialect. The two family maids spoke little French, and my grandparents always spoke Flemish with them, as they did with shopkeepers, tradesmen, workmen and their tenant farmers (some of whom were distant kin).

My grandfather, who was a physician, even segregated his patients by class. Next to the doorbell, a mirror reflected the image of the visitor to a basement window. The maid, before opening, took a quick look and, judging by style of dress or previous acquaintance, decided whether to take the patient to a sparsely furnished working-class waiting room where nothing but Flemish was spoken, or to the plush family parlor where only French was heard. My grandfather even had separate consulting rooms for his two classes of patients; his entire social and professional life was rigidly segregated, both linguistically and socially.

In fact, my grandfather whose family had become Frenchified in *his* grandparents' generation spoke Flemish less readily than my grandmother whose father was the first member of *her* family to speak French. She had many rich peasant kinsmen who were monolingual in Flemish and who regarded my grandfather as somewhat of a snob. When my father married a Frenchwoman from Paris and settled in Brussels, French completely dominated our household. My father continued to be fluent in Flemish but seldom spoke it, and I learned it in school, reluctantly, and as a foreign language. Like my father, I went to a French-medium elementary and secondary school where Dutch was taught as the "other" national language, but where social prejudices ascribed distinctly lower status to Dutch. (The official, standardized, written version of Flemish taught in the schools is called *Nederlands*, a language very close to the standard Dutch of The Netherlands.)

I remember how my Dutch teacher was treated as a social pariah by his colleagues and was mercilessly ridiculed by the pupils. There was even a form of snobbery consisting in documenting how *badly* one did in the Dutch course, which, unlike French, Latin, Greek, history and mathematics, was considered *pas sérieux*, roughly on par with physical education. Any suggestion by our hapless Dutch teacher that the great 17th century Dutch dramatist Vondel was the peer of Milton, Dante or Racine, excited peals of hilarity and merciless satire from us. The mainstay of our ridicule of him was to parody his accent in French. I also have mortifying memories of my French maternal relatives turning the tables of linguistic snobbery on me and making fun of my "Belgian accent." (Belgians in France are often the butt of what in the United States are "Polish" jokes.) My French grandfather, a distinguished biologist, professor at the Sorbonne and member of the French Academy of Sciences, obviously considered my Belgian upbringing to be culturally deficient and did his best during my vacation stays with him to "purify" my French of stigmatized *belgicismes*.

followed World War II, it is now considered bad manners in Belgium to express class snobbery through the ostentatious use of French as a prestige language. The "language question" has thus lost much of its earlier class-bound bitterness. Although some residual linguistic snobbery lingers on, it is much less openly expressed, and much less significant than it once was.

The "language problem," however, is not solved. Rather, it is becoming more clearly a genuinely ethnic problem, rather than a class problem in disguise. There are now basically three ethnic collectivities in Belgium rather than two: the Walloons, the Flemings and the largely Brussels-based *Francophones* who, whether of Flemish or Walloon origin, now use almost exclusively French as their private and public language. These three groups correspond, of course, closely to the three regions created in the 1962 and 1971 semifederal compromises. An interesting reversal in the perception of who is the underdog took place, however, simultaneously with economic changes.

The Walloons have always been in minority as compared to the Flemings, and, traditionally, the Flemings have had a higher birth rate than the Walloons. However, the Walloons had the social advantage of speaking the more prestigious (and, on the European scale, the more useful) language. Therefore, the demographic gains of the Flemings through their higher birth rate were canceled by the gradual assimilation of upwardly mobile Flemings into the Francophone group. The two groups kept in rough balance.

Now the Flemings have lost much of their demographic advantage in birth rate, but Frenchification has been greatly reduced, at least outside Brussels. So, one may ask, does not that new situation lead to another state of "dynamic stability" in which everyone is happy? Alas, no. The Flemings no longer feel like social underdogs, but they resent the increasing dominance of French in Brussels and the spread of Francophone dormitory suburbs of Brussels into Flemish territory. The Flemings won the battle to expel physically some 20,000 Francophone students from the Flemish city of Leuven (Louvain) and to dismember that famous Catholic university by forcing the latter to establish the new campus of Louvain-la-Neuve on Walloon soil. (Even the famous library was dismembered, on the basis of whether books were odd- or even-numbered.) Nevertheless, the Flemings feel that they are losing the capital, which they view as a cancerous French growth enclaved in Flemish soil. (Brussels, unfortunately, is some 12 kilometers north of the linguistic frontier.) The Gallicization of Brussels is made all the more inevitable through its increased status as the capital of the European Community and the NATO alliance. In a great international, cosmopolitan city, Dutch has no chance against French.

Are the Francophones, at least, happy? Far from it. The Walloons feel increasingly beleaguered, not only because they are a permanent minority, but because the economic developments of the last 30 years have not been kind to Wallonia. Wallonia, the traditional industrial heartland of Belgium now has an antiquated coal-mining and steel industry and a depressed economy, while the Flemish part of the country is teeming with new industrial plants brought in by massive foreign and domestic investments during the postwar "economic miracle". Flanders, the rural backwater in the 19th century, has become the prosperous and dynamic center of the economy. This trend is, of course, greatly accelerated by the fact that the main harbor (Antwerp) and the capital are both on Flemish soil and a mere 40 kilometers apart.

How about the Francophone Bruxellois? Are they not content? By all accounts, they are winning, both linguistically and economically. They live in one of the world's most prosperous, livable and cosmopolitan capitals, and it would seem that their only legitimate complaint should be the dreary, rainy weather. But they too feel beleaguered and unhappy. They are conscious of their linguistic insularity which, should Belgium break up, would leave them isolated. They also feel hampered in their urban expansion by the resistance of Flemish communes to the sprawl of dormitory suburbs, and they resent having, in some cases, to send their children to Flemish communal schools.

Both Francophones and Walloons, in reaction against the Flemish nationalist *Volksunie*, have therefore organized into dissident political groups of their own. The main Walloon group is antimonarchist and advocates annexation to France, but the Brussels Francophone group is little more than a discontented bourgeoisie.

For all its problems, there is no workable alternative to CD for Belgium. Partition would be disastrous to Brussels, leaving its Francophone population stranded. Furthermore, not every inhabitant is clearly classifiable as Francophone or Neerlandophone. Guest workers of many nationalities, but principally from North Africa and Mediterranean Europe now make up a sizeable proportion of the population, and many are there to stay. Most are still fluent in neither French nor Dutch. Then, there is a small German-speaking minority of about 1% in the southeast. (Belgium was foolish enough to annex some German territory after World War I, as a reward for having been on the winning side of the war.)

Perhaps as many as 10% to 15% of the population are so fluently bilingual that it makes little sense to ask what their home language is. (The 1947 language census gave 18% of the Belgian population as bilingual, but this did not necessarily mean that as many were *fluent* in both languages.) There is some intermarriage between Flemings and Walloons, which further blurs ethnic boundaries. Finally, as we have seen, many ethnic Flemings have become Francophones, but continue to regard themselves as Flemish in some sense. Surnames, for example, are far from a perfect indicator of ethnicity or language use.

If all these categories were added together, one would come up with perhaps one-fourth of the population who are not unambiguously either Flemish or Walloon. Whether they like it or not, Belgians are stuck with each other. The present system of CD has more than its share of conflict, uneasy compromises, inefficiencies and inanities. But the alternatives are worse.

Canada

With a population of about 24 million, the second largest land area in the world (after the Soviet Union) and with one of the world's highest standards of living, Canada can claim at least middle rank in the international hierarchy. Its classification as a CD applies only to relations between the two main linguistic groups: Anglophones and Francophones. Many other groups are, of course, included in the complex ethnic mosaic of Canada, and here we can only give the barest sketch of the situation (Brazeau and Cloutier, 1977; Burns, 1971; Driedger, 1978; Kalbach, 1978; Mc Rae, 1974; Porter, 1965; Royal Commission, 1967–1970; Russell, 1966; Smiley, 1976, 1977; Vallières, 1969).* The remnants of the indigenous population of Canada—Amerindians and Eskimos—now make up 1.2% of the total. They are widely scattered, both inside and outside reservations, and their relationship to the Federal Government bears many similarities with the situation in the United States. A long history of wars, alliances, territorial encroachments and broken treaties led to their conquest, displacement, gradual acculturation (often not accompanied by assimilation) and administration through a paternalistic system of internal colonialism.

The remaining 99% of the population are descendants of immigrants who came during the last 400 years, overwhelmingly from Europe. First to come were the French who settled along the St. Lawrence River and established the colony of New France. (Québec City was founded in 1608 and Montréal in 1642, but explorations of the St. Lawrence began in the 1530s.) The French fought and conquered the Indians, but they were also caught in a vast imperial conflict with England for the domination of the North American continent. That conflict was decisively won by the British in 1763, and the French, under the Québec Act of 1774, found themselves reduced to the status of a colonial people subject to what was essentially a system of indirect rule under the British Crown. The separate identity of the Québécois as French-speaking Catholics was protected (as were the privileges of the French clergy and upper class), but their political subordination to Britain made for a very unequal relationship.

Within 20 years of winning Canada against the French, Britain lost her 13 Atlantic Seaboard colonies to the rebellious settlers. The birth of the United States reinforced, however, Britain's hold over Canada, for some 40,000 United Empire Loyalists left the young republic to settle in Ontario, Nova Scotia and New Brunswick, thereby completing the encirclement of French Québec with a ring of English settlements. Still today, Franco-Canadians see themselves not only as a sizeable minority of 6.5 million among some 17 million other Canadians, but as a small Francophone enclave in a vast continent of some 240 million Anglos.

*The main source of information on Canadian ethnic relations, and especially on the French–English division, is the monumental *Report of the Royal Commission on Bilingualism and Biculturalism*, published in six volumes between 1967 and 1970. Unless otherwise indicated, most statistical data cited here came from the *Report*.

An abortive French revolt in 1837–1838 was followed by the Act of Union in 1840, joining Upper and Lower Canada (Ontario and Québec, respectively) into a territory with equal parliamentary representation of some 650,000 French and 400,000 English settlers. Thus Canada slowly evolved from a quasicolonial relationship to an unequal partnership. The next important step was the passage of the British North America Act of 1867, establishing modern Canada as a self-governing dominion of four federated provinces within the British Empire. The BNA Act provided for official bilingualism at the federal level and thus for a more equal relationship between French and English Canadians. Uprisings developed in 1869–1870 and 1885 in the new prairie provinces of Manitoba and Saskatchewan under the leadership of Louis Riel. The two Riel rebellions were coalitions of French-speaking *Métisses* (as mixed French–Indian fur trappers were called) and Indian groups attempting to resist European settlement, but they elicited considerable French sympathy in Québec.

Meanwhile, starting in the late 19th century, a new wave of massive immigration from Europe further complicated the Canadian ethnic picture. Some of it came from England and Ireland, but most new immigrants spoke neither English nor French. They were Germans, Italians, Dutch, Poles, Greeks, Portuguese, Scandinavians, Ukranians, Eastern European Jews and others, coming in at a rapidly increasing rate since the 1870s, peaking between 1900 and 1930, at a rate well over a million per decade. Between 1901 and 1911, European immigration added 28% to the Canadian population (Kalbach, 1978). In 1931, barely over half (54%) of the Canadian population had Canadian-born grandparents; in 1971, that percentage had risen to two-thirds (67%).

The history of these European immigrants closely parallels that of their counterparts in the United States. In one or two generations, they became acculturated overwhelmingly to the dominant English language group and assimilated to the fluid structure of an expanding society. They often had to start out at the bottom of the socioeconomic structure, unless they came with capital and professional skills, but, after two generations or so, they became largely assimilated with the rest of the population. As in the United States, there was a revival of European ethnic sentiment in the late 1960s and 1970s, and a number of ethnic group leaders began to argue that they jointly constituted a "third force" between the English and the French, but, as assimilation continues at a seemingly unabated pace, this is probably a passing fad. Currently, 58% of all Canadians speak English as their mother tongue, and 28% French, leaving 14% for the "third force" of first- and second-generation immigrants.

After a slump in the 1930s and 1940s, immigration picked up again, starting in the 1950s, at a rate of about 1.5 million per decade. In absolute numbers, these figures are comparable to those for the 1900–1930 period, but, as the total population more than tripled from 5.4 million in 1901 to 21.6 million in 1971, the impact of immigrants was correspondingly reduced. However, a new aspect of that post-World War II immigration did create a novel dimension to the problem. Until World War II, less than 1% of the immigrants came from countries outside Europe. That percentage rapidly rose from 6% in the 1955–1960 period, to 12% from 1961 to 1965, to 23% from 1966 to 1970 (Kalbach, 1978). Much of it came, and continued to come throughout the 1970s, from Commonwealth countries like Hong-Kong, India, Pakistan, Uganda (Asians), Jamaica and Trinidad.

Canada has had small "nonwhite" groups for a long time—from fugitive American slaves in the early 19th century to Asian immigrants later. But they were too few and too dispersed to elicit much racism or hostility. Now, Canada is belatedly discovering that, like Britain and of course the United States, it is developing a "race problem." In some urban centers like Vancouver, where Asian immigrant groups have become quite visible, there is considerable racism.

A detailed discussion of immigration and assimilation must wait for the next chapter. Here, we are mainly concerned over the impact of immigrants on the English–French conflict. Traditionally, the French have been anti-immigration, because experience told them that the great majority of immigrants, if they were not already English-speaking on arrival, assimilated into the dominant English culture. There were some exceptions to that general rule, such as Italian and Portuguese immigrants in Québec who tended to become French-speaking, but, generally, immigration was seen by French Canadians as diluting the French component of the population and, eventually, as threatening them with absorption into Anglo society.

These fears were further reinforced by the language statistics that clearly showed a much greater tendency for the French to become bilingual or exclusively Anglophone, than for the English to learn French. Some 13% of Canadians are bilingual in French and English, but whereas 30% of the native speakers of French speak English, only 5% of the Anglo Canadians speak French (Royal Commission, Vol. 1, 1967, p. 38). The French always resented this *bilinguisme à sens unique* (one-way bilingualism) in which the burden of learning the "other" national language is almost always put on them. The only two provinces of Canada where bilingualism in the official languages exceeds 10% are the provinces with large French populations: Québec (26% bilingual, 81% French) and New Brunswick (19% bilingual, 35% French). According to the 1971 Census, of the two national languages, 67% of the population speak only English (compared to 58% who are native speakers of English), 18% speak only French (compared to 28% native speakers of French), 13% are bilingual and 2% speak neither (Smiley, 1977). In fact, Francophones with 28% of the Canadian population, contribute 68% of the bilinguals.

As for rates of assimilation, the cross-tabulation of ethnic origin and mother tongue also shows the asymmetry of the situation and the justification for French fears of absorption. Only 1% of Canadians of British ethnic origin speak French as their mother tongue, but 10% of Canadians of French ethnic origin have become native speakers of English, a disproportion of ten to one in rates of assimilation to the other group (Royal Commission, Vol. 1, 1967, p. 23).

Despite the overwhelming trend for immigrants to be absorbed into the English-speaking group and for the French group to lose up to a tenth of its members through assimilation (especially outside of Québec), French Canadians have been remarkably successful is holding their own demographically. From 1881 to the present, Franco-Canadians have managed to remain a steady 30% of the total population. The onslaught of massive immigration brought the French percentages to a low of 28% in 1921; but by 1941, as immigration was reduced, the French had recovered their 30% share.

This extraordinary performance was made possible through a high birthrate. The phenomenon is known in French Canada as *la revanche des berceaux* (the revenge of the cradle).* In recent years, however, French Canadian natality has dropped rapidly and converges with that of Anglo-Canadians. By 1971, the French percentage had dropped to 29, with further declines anticipated (Smiley, 1977). The revenge of the cradle in losing its clout.

What all these statistics show quite unambiguously is that the immigrant situation is fundamentally different from the Franco-Canadian situation. Immigrants come from a variety of home countries and are territorially dispersed. Therefore, in a couple of generations, they acculturate and assimilate to their host country, and, naturally, they tend to assimilate to the more dominant of the two Canadian (and North American) cultures. Franco-Canadians, however, are likely to remain a separate nation. To be sure, nearly a third become bilingual because of the material advantages connected with knowledge of English, and about 10% have become assimilated into the English group. This assimilation, however, is almost totally confined to the provinces where Franco-Canadians are in small minorities.

In the *glacis québécois* (the Québec icefloat), the French hold their own quite well. There they even manage to absorb 9% of the population of English ethnic origin and many immigrants, like Italians, who speak another Romance language. Clearly, Québec is a solid territorial basis for a French nation in North America. Nearly 80% of the Francophone population of Canada lives in Québec, and 81% of the Québec provincial population are native speakers of French. There is another big concentration of Franco-Canadians in some districts of New Brunswick adjacent to Québec, where they make up 35% of the provincial population. Everywhere else, the French are small, scattered minorities, ranging from 8% in Prince Edward Island and 7% in Ontario (mostly in Southeastern Ontario, next to Québec) to less than 2% in British Columbia and under 1% in Newfoundland. Where French Canadians are dispersed minorities, they suffer the fate of the European immigrants: they become gradually Anglicized.

---

*It will be noted in passing here that these countervailing trends of assimilation and natural increase through higher birth rates, leading to stable ethnic ratios, show a "stable dynamic" quite similar to that between Walloons and Flemings in Belgium. Ironically, however, the Francophones of Belgium are in the position of the Anglophones of Canada, and the Flemings are analogous to the French Canadians.

The touchstone of Canadian consociationalism therefore revolves around three main issues:

1. The relationship of Québec to the rest of Canada: Is Québec to remain merely one province among ten, or is it to become a separate state as the French nationalists of the Parti Québécois advocate?
2. The implementation of CD at the federal level: To what extent are bilingualism and biculturalism to prevail in the organs and the bureaucracy of the federal government?
3. Anglo–French relations within the various provinces, but most particularly in Québec: Are the provinces themselves to be bilingual, make accommodations to their ethnic minorities and run themselves as CDs at the provincial level?

On all three counts, the Canadian experiment in consociationalism is showing every sign of failing. Precisely because there is a viable option to the status quo, Québec seems to be gradually sliding toward secession, a process symbolized by the passage of Laws 22 and 101 fostering the development of Québec as a monolingual French province and by the accession of René Lévesque and the Parti Québécois to power in 1976. Previous to 1974, Québec was officially bilingual and extended many privileges to its Anglophone minority. Although the Parti Québécois lost its independence referendum in 1980, the issue is not closed, and the victorious Liberal Party is committed to a renegotiation of confederation.

The scrupulous attempt by the federal government to implement bilingualism in the hiring of civil servants, the publication of government documents and the like, actually favored the French who had a much higher proportion of functional bilinguals than the English. However, this did little to defuse French nationalist sentiment, as the Federation merely perpetuates the minority status of the French and gives them solid control of only one province out of ten (albeit one of the two largest provinces). Official bilingualism of the federal level is seen by many French people as a kind of inconsequential tokenism and by many Anglo-Canadians as a source of irritation and needless expenditure.

As for consociationalism at the provincial level, it can be said that it remained a dead letter everywhere except in Québec, which was the only effectively bilingual province, both de jure and de facto. Other provinces, especially Ontario and New Brunswick, have made a few accommodations to their French minorities (mostly in the provision of French-medium schools) in areas where the French language is rather common but have fallen far short of the bilingualism and protection of minority rights which Québec, until recently, offered its Anglophone minority. Once more, the unidirectional character of this bilingualism irritated the French and fed the fire of French nationalism. In the end, Québec practically aligned itself with the other provinces and became officially monolingual in French in 1977. Ironically, official bilingualism, which was meant to be a symbol of CD, became the very opposite: a rankling mark of inequality. Anglo-Canadians expected the French to speak English and to extend them minority privileges in Québec, but overwhelmingly failed to reciprocate.

The real impetus to Québécois nationalism, however, has been a class conflict in linguistic disguise, much as in Belgium. Unlike in Switzerland where ethnic affiliation is unrelated to class, in Canada, there are appreciable differences in socioeconomic status between Anglo- and Franco-Canadians. It is sometimes argued that Québec is a poor province, a kind of Canadian Appalachia. This is not, in fact, the case. Québec is fifth among the ten provinces in per capita income, somewhat worse off than British Columbia. Alberta, Manitoba and Ontario, but far ahead of the peripheral Maritime Provinces and somewhat richer than the prairie province of Saskatchewan.

Striking class differences between the ethnic groups appear *within* provinces, especially within Québec. What particularly infuriated and humiliated Québécois was that, on their own home ground, where they make up over four-fifths of the population, they were often treated as second-class citizens by an English-speaking economic elite living in their midst and arrogantly expecting privileged status. This was glaringly obvious in the great metropolis of Montréal, an overwhelmingly French city, but, nevertheless, one where until the last few years virtually the whole of business life took place in English.

In banks, luxury hotels and fashionable shops, customers were almost automatically addressed in English unless they insisted otherwise. The elite university, McGill, was entirely English-medium, while the French had the plebeian Université de Montréal. The English-speaking economic elite, both Protestant and Jewish, lived in suburban gilded ghettoes, sending their children to elitist schools. The class split thus corresponded to a considerable degree to a linguistic and religious split. The economic elite was Anglophone and Protestant or Jewish. The French Catholics had, of course, an elite of their own, largely an intellectual, clerical, professional and political elite from which the leadership of the nationalist movement was drawn. But the rural population, the lower-middle class and the urban proletariat of Québec was almost solidly French (or of recent immigrant stock).

The Royal Commission Report (Vol. 3, Part 1–2, 1969, p. 18) reveals that, in 1961, the British minority of Québec earned 140% of the provincial mean for the male nonagricultural labor force, while the French earned 92%. Jews were even wealthier, earning 178% of the provincial average. Indeed, the French were doing worse than most recent immigrant groups like the Germans (112%) and the Ukranians (102%). Of the main recent immigrant groups, only the Italians (83%) were below the French in income.

Interestingly, the differences between Anglo- and Franco-Canadians were much bigger within the Province of Québec than in Canada as a whole, where Anglophones were earning 110% of the national mean and Francophones 88%. Thus, on their home ground, French Canadians had over twice as big an earning gap with the English (a 48-point gap between 92% and 140% of the Québec average), as they did at the federal level (a 22-point gap between 88% and 110%). The problem of class differentials between

French and English is principally a Québec problem created by the English economic colonization of Montréal.

The similarities between the Anglophone minority in Québec and the Gallicized Flemish bourgeoisie of Flanders are striking. Both groups were in fact a ruling economic elite made highly visible by its use of a foreign language. The language problem was in both cases greatly exacerbated by the class conflict, and, conversely, class conflicts were embittered by linguistic divisions. Radical French separatists, drawn overwhelmingly from the French intelligensia, lost no time in analyzing the situation of Québec in terms of internal colonialism and domination by an Anglo-capitalist elite with foreign links to the United States. Also, by analogy with the United States Civil Rights movement, Québécois were termed: *les nègres blancs d'Amérique* (Vallières, 1969). The situation was even worse than in Belgium. Whereas the Frenchified bourgeoisie of Flanders was at least of Flemish ethnic origin and remained bilingual, the economic elite of Québec was alien and made little effort to learn French.

It is against this backdrop of class conflict that Québécois nationalism must be understood. The recent political efforts to make Québec monolingually French are thus much more than acts of nationalist fervor. They are attempts by the French political, professional and intellectual elite to free Québec of foreign economic domination and, in the process, to substitute themselves as the new ruling class of an independent country.

Québec is not the only Canadian province where separatist sentiment is widespread. The Western provinces, too, especially British Columbia and Alberta, have also long had a keen sense of geographical regionalism—now bolstered, in the case of Alberta, by gushing oil wealth. Indeed, the 1980 national election that returned Trudeau and the Liberal Party to power after a brief Progressive Conservative interlude has shown a large amount of East–West polarization. The strongholds of the Liberal Party, which overwhelmingly dominated recent Canadian politics, are the populous provinces of Québec and Ontario. This means that the Liberal Party establishment has a strong stake in averting Québec secession through a flexible policy of concessions; without Québec, it could not rule the rest of Canada.

The Federal policy of multiculturalism, promulgated and promoted since the 1970s, is seen by some French nationalists as an attempt to depolarize the French–Anglo conflict by multilateralizing ethnicity and stressing the problems of the indigenous minority and the "Third Force" of more recent immigrants who are neither French nor English. The "French problem" thus becomes redefined as merely one among many and is by implication, to be solved within a consociational framework.

Some also argue that powerful economic interests, both domestic Canadian and from the United States, have an interest in preserving the unity of Canada. Certainly, the prospect of a flight of English capital from an independent Québec has been widely and as an argument (some would say, a scare tactic) against secession. Personally, I see no reason why capital, of whatever nationality, could not accommodate itself quite well to an independent Québec unless secession would be accompanied by economic radicalization. In particular, why should not United States economic interests be able to deal just as well with two client states north of the border as with one? A dismembered Canada might prove even more pliable and dependent than a united Canada. Whatever the political outcome in this complex battle of interests, the future of Canada remains clouded.

CONCLUSIONS

What have we learned from our quick survey of consociationalism in Switzerland, Belgium and Canada? Basically, that the prospects for CD are poor at best and that consociationalist regimes rest on a fragile set of conditions that can easily be upset. The Canadian experiment seems headed for failure, a failure which appears all the more probable as Québec secession is a viable alternative. The Swiss experience, while relatively successful, really does not count, for Switzerland is but a loose confederacy of largely self-governing and monolingual cantons. As for Belgium, it limps along as a binational state, not so much because the experiment is successful, but because the alternatives are worse; an ethnic split would leave Brussels (and, by implication, much of the Belgian economic, political, intellectual and cultural elite, both Flemish and Walloon) stranded. For Belgium, consociationalism is a solution of last resort; for Switzerland, it is a convenience; for Canada, it seems a failure.

The cards were deliberately stacked in favor of consociationalism by picking three prosperous and relatively peaceful countries with a long-standing reputation for being democratic and libertarian. A random sample of countries that attempted some kind of CD would have yielded such ghastly failures as Lebanon, Nigeria, Zaïre and Pakistan-Bangladesh. Of the Third World countries that attempted to institutionalize a democratic multinational state, only India has been relatively successful—miraculously so, considering its economic and social circumstances. Among the socialist countries, the Soviet Union claims success, but it hardly qualifies as a democratic state, and it has seldom refrained from crushing dissident nationalisms by force, both within and outside its borders.

Despite, all this card-stacking in favor of the hypothesis that CDs can work, our conclusions are definitely pessimistic. Success is exceptional, and when it does occur, one can legitimately ask whether one witnesses the success of democracy or simply a collusion of class interests between ethnic segments of an elite.

SUGGESTED READINGS

The main theorists of consociationalism are Lehmbruch (1967) and Lijphart (1968a, 1977a) who mainly applied the concept to The Netherlands, Austria, Switzerland, Belgium and Lebanon. The collection edited by Esman (1977) contains a number of relevant pieces by Zolberg (1977) on Belgium, by Lijphart (1977b) on ethnic conflicts in general and by Smiley (1977) and Brazeau and Cloutier (1977) on Canada. Works by du Roy (1968) and Lorwin (1971, 1972) are also quite good on Belgium. On Canada, see the recent collection edited by Driedger (1978).

ASSIMILATION

Up to now, we have examined principally situations where social and cultural pluralism among ethnic, racial or caste groups persists. This is obviously not always the case. Indeed, much of the literature on ethnic relations in the United States, developed by the "Chicago School" of sociology (Park, 1950; Wirth, 1956) around the European immigrant situation in the eastern and midwestern states, assumed that assimilation was the final stage of a four-phase cycle of ethnic relations. *Contact* was followed by a period of *competition*, which was in turn followed by *accommodation* and finally by *assimilation* (Park, 1950; Shibutani and Kwan, 1965). In popular parlance, this was the "melting pot" theory of ethnic relations. Later, this theory was refined into the notion of a triple melting pot along religious lines: Protestant, Catholic and Jewish (Olson, 1979). With the "revival of ethnicity" in the late 1960s and 1970s, the theory came under even more severe criticism (Greeley, 1974, 1979) but, when all is said and done, it is clear that, as far as European immigrants are concerned, the American experience was one of rapid acculturation and assimilation (G. J. Patterson, 1979).

Nor is the United States unique in this respect. Canada, Australia, New Zealand, Brazil, Argentina and Israel are other countries that received massive numbers of immigrants from a variety of countries, managing to weld them together into a relatively cohesive and homogeneous national culture. It is therefore necessary to examine the conditions under which assimilation takes place. Whether or not one finds assimilation ideologically attractive, there is no question that the countries where it has taken place have, by that token, solved many of the problems of political integration that plague plural societies. For purely practical considerations of policy, therefore, it is important to define the parameters of successful assimilation.

ASSIMILATION AND ACCULTURATION

Before we turn to that task, however, we must distinguish between assimilation and acculturation. I have already done so implicitly earlier when dealing with other situations, such as slavery, but here I must clarify the distinction more explicitly. The concept of acculturation developed by anthropologists like Redfield, Herskovits and Aguirre Beltrán (Aguirre Beltrán, 1957; Herskovits, 1938; Redfield and Herskovits, 1936) refers to the tendency, when distinct cultural groups are in contact, to "borrow" cultural items (words, tools, techniques, values, clothing, styles, foods, etc.) from each other. This process is recognized as extremely complex and far from mechanical. Cultural items are often "reinterpreted" when "borrowed"; that is, they often acquire different meanings and functions than they had in the culture of origin. Also, the "borrowing" is seldom entirely unidirectional: groups borrow reciprocally, so that all of the world's cultures are, to a greater or lesser degree, composite growths of heterogeneous origins.

Nevertheless, in situations where one ethnic is clearly dominant by virtue of numbers, technology, wealth, political power or a combination of these, acculturation is *predominantly* unidirectional. Subordinate (or minority) ethnies tend to adopt the language, religion and culture of dominant groups much more readily than vice versa, because doing so confers advantages in fitness. Occasionally, dominant *minorities* adopt the culture of the people they conquered, because they are absorbed by sheer numbers. The Mongols and Manchu in China, the Tuzi in Rwanda and Burundi, and the Fulani in the Hausa states of Nigeria are cases in point. Dominant majorities, however, stand in little or no danger of losing their culture.

Subordinate minorities, however, are under constant pressure to acculturate, because becoming like the dominant group almost invariably confers social advantages. The whole history of the spread of religions and languages, for instance, is best understood not in terms of ideology, conviction or natural superiority of one language or religion over another, but in simple utilitarian terms. However they might rationalize their actions, people generally convert or learn new languages if they perceive some advantages. It often pays to learn the ways of the rich, the powerful and the numerous; in the process one becomes more like them and, by that token, often becomes more acceptable to them. Conversely, only a few missionaries and anthropologists bother to learn the ways of the weak, the poor and the few, and even they do it because they derive professional advantages from it.

Generally, then, the greater the disparity in numbers, wealth, technology and power between ethnies, the more unidirectional acculturation is, and the stronger the acculturative pressures on the weak, the poor and the few. That is why slavery, for instance, almost invariably makes for rapid acculturation, as we have seen in Chapter 6.

Acculturation refers to the objective, observable markers that people exhibit in their behavior. What language do they speak? What religion do they practice? How are they dressed? What do they eat? What family structure do they have? And so on.

Assimilation, by contrast, refers not to the degree of cultural similarity between groups, but to the extent to which a group that was originally distinct has lost its subjective identity and has become *absorbed in the social structure* of another group.

Clearly the two tend to go together. Indeed, acculturation is a precondition, or at least a concomitant, of assimilation—for how can one lose one's sense of distinctiveness and be fully accepted into another group unless one becomes fluent in the language and culture of the adoptive group? However, if acculturation is a *necessary* condition for assimilation, it is not always a *sufficient* condition. There are a number of cases of groups that, even though they have acquired the culture of the dominant group, are prevented from assimilating and are kept in a subordinate and structurally distinct position.

Good examples of acculturated but unassimilated groups are the Coloureds in South Africa and Afro-Americans in the United States. These groups, even though they are virtually undistinguishable by culture from their dominant white counterparts in their respective countries, are kept socially and spatially segregated and have consequently evolved a series of parallel institutions (such as schools, churches, voluntary associations, and the like) that are almost *identical in cultural form* to the same institutions of their white counterparts, yet completely *separate in structure*. This cultural parallelism in segregation has been documented in detail by E. F. Frazier (1965) for the United States and Dickie-Clark (1966) for South Africa.

A MODEL OF ASSIMILATION

Contrary to what the American experience might seem to suggest, assimilation is not to be taken for granted. Ethnic sentiment being, as I suggested earlier, an extension of kin selection, it is deeply ingrained and, barring countervailing forces, tends to endure. Its disappearance is problematic, not its persistence. Left to themselves, people have a natural propensity to prefer the company of those like themselves in culture and appearance, and to behave favorably toward them because they are presumed to be, in some sense, kindred. Conversely, those foreign in culture and strange in appearance tend to be rejected because they are presumed to be unrelated to one.

A realistic model of assimilation, therefore, must bring in a powerful force to motivate people to behave otherwise, that is, in this case, to want either to assimilate strangers or to be assimilated by them. That powerful force, I suggest, is the maximization of individual fitness. Fitness is generally maximized by behaving nepotistically (and, therefore, ethnocentrically), but, under some conditions presently to be specified, kin selection may be superseded by other considerations that in turn lead to assimilation.

Assimilation presupposes the coexistence of at least two groups. For the sake of simplicity, let us build our model around two groups, although it can readily be generalized to a multigroup situation. If individual self-interest (ultimately converted into biological fitness) is the motivating force behind assimilation, it follows that, for assimilation to take place, the two or more groups must initially be in an unequal situation. The more unequal their relative position is, the more of an incentive members of the subordinate group have to be accepted into the dominant group. Conversely, if change of group membership confers no advantages, the incentive to do so is lacking. However, as we have seen, even extreme initial inequality (as in slavery) is no guarantee of assimilation. This is so for two main reasons.

First, it takes two to assimilate. Assimilation is sought by members of the subordinate group—granted by members of the dominant group. All combinations of these two sides are found. Some dominant groups are such eager assimilators that they force assimilation on reluctant subjects, a policy recently termed *ethnocide*, by analogy to *genocide*. (Ethnocide refers to the deliberate destruction of an ethny's culture without physical extermination of individuals.) Other dominant groups refuse to assimilate even groups that have become culturally undistinguishable from themselves and that are literally begging to be accepted. Conversely, some subordinate groups stubbornly resist pressures to acculturate and assimilate, while others are eager to lose their separate identity and to be absorbed. For assimilation to take place, therefore, it takes a convergence of desire for it from the subordinates and acceptance by the dominants. The conditions under which this concordance of goals is likely to be found will be examined presently.

Second, desire for assimilation is the outcome of two countervailing forces, the ethnically centripetal force of kin selection and the ethnically centrifugal force of fitness maximization through other means. The balance must favor the centrifugal force for assimilation to take place. A positive centrifugal balance, in turn, can be the product of either a strong pull toward the out-group or a weak pull toward the in-group. Subordinate groups may be in a heavily disadvantaged position, yet retain sufficient cohesion and solidarity to resist successfully the centrifugal pull of assimilation, and to offer their members an effective network of kin selection and reciprocity. That is, even subordinate groups can remain structually strong enough that leaving them may be a chancy proposition. An individual may have to trade off the uncertainty of acceptance into the high-status group for the certainty of support in his low-status group of origin.

The reductionist model of assimilation we have just presented purports to predict empirical outcomes on the basis of individuals making selfish cost/benefit calculations of alternative strategies of ethnic nepotism versus assimilation. The model applies both to subordinates' decisions to assimilate and to dominants' acceptance of assimilation, although, as we shall see, the considerations are rather different in the two cases. Crude and simple though the model is, it generates propositions that seem in fact to be borne out by empirical evidence.

CONDITIONS FAVORING ASSIMILATION

1. The greater the phenotypic resemblance between groups, the more likely assimilation is to take place. (All of these conditions are to be understood *ceteris paribus*.) This is so because the dominant group is readier to accept as biologically related groups that conform to its own "somatic norm image" (Hoetinck, 1967). Phenotype does not, of course, affect rates of *acculturation*, and this explains why groups that are highly acculturated but unassimilated often are phenotypically distinct from the dominant group (e.g. South African Coloureds and American blacks).

2. The greater the cultural similarity between groups, the more likely assimilation becomes. This is so for two reasons. The greater the cultural resemblance, the easier (and therefore the less costly) subordinates find it to acculturate, a precondition for assimilation. The more culturally similar the groups, the readier dominants are to accept subordinates as biologically related.

3. The smaller a group is in relation to the rest of the population, the more likely assimilation is. This is so because small groups often have fewer resources and are therefore dependent on the rest of the society. The smaller a group is, the more likely it is to interact with outsiders, especially to *intermarry*—the ultimate test of assimilation. (Concubinage is frequent in the absence of assimilation, but *marriage*, especially if it happens in both directions, that is with both men and women of both groups marrying out, is probably the best measure of assimilation.)

4. Lower-status groups are more likely to assimilate than high-status groups, because they have more to gain by it. Upper classes and middleman minorities often fail to assimilate because little or no status gain would result from it. Working classes that are ethnically distinct as well seek in acculturation and assimilation an avenue of upward class mobility and are therefore much more motivated to shed their ethnicity.

5. The more territorially dispersed a group is, the more likely it is to assimilate. Territorial dispersion interferes with intraethnic solidarity and therefore reduces the benefits of nepotism.

6. Immigrant groups are more likely to assimilate than native groups, because immigration is typically accompanied by geographical dispersal and a sharp reduction in the network of intraethnic ties (since the bulk of the ethny generally stays behind). The immigrant is also at a disadvantage vis-à-vis the native and thus is heavily reliant on the latter. Pressures to learn native ways are directly related to survival and success, whereas retention of ethnic separateness frequently has the opposite effect. The native, through experience, is generally better adapted to his habitat than the immigrant. Independently of the geographical dispersal that often accompanies migration, then, immigration puts a premium on imitating the ways of the presumably better-adapted native. Acculturation, in turn, favors assimilation.

The profile of the group most likely to assimilate is thus: an immigrant group similar in physical appearance and culture to the group to which it assimilates, small in proportion to the total population, of low status and territorially dispersed. These propositions should be tested by the method of paired comparison, holding constant, as best as one can, five of the six variables each time. My guess is that, in combination, these straightforward variables would account for most of the variation in rates of acculturation (measured by loss of mother tongue), and assimilation (measured by inter-marriage) between different ethnic groups in the same country and of the same ethnic group in different countries—or different regions of a country.

A systematic test of the utilitarian paradigm I just sketched, would take a large research grant, years of effort and a monograph of several hundred pages. Here I have only space for a few illustrations of the kind of data that led to my formulation in the first instance. I will briefly cite some evidence for each of the six propositions.

1. Phenotype clearly makes a difference for assimilation, in terms of acceptance by the dominant group. For example, blacks who have been English-speaking for several generations have been much less readily assimilated in both England (Little, 1947; S. Patterson, 1965; Rex and Moore, 1967; Rex and Tomlinson, 1979; Richmond, 1973) and the United States than European immigrants who spoke no English on arrival. Physically undistinguishable groups (e.g. the Koreans in Japan) can also be rejected and remain unassimilated, so looking alike is not sufficient condition for assimilation, but it seems to be close to a necessary condition in a number of racist countries. Phenotype seems much more salient a criterion of acceptance in some countries than others (the Japanese, for instance, seem much more racist than the Chinese, thought both are about equally ethnocentric). However, I would expect that, in any paired comparison of two matched immigrant groups, one physically distinct and the other physically like the native group, the latter would assimilate faster.

2. Cultural also makes a difference. Assimilation between two groups speaking closely related languages is much easier than between people speaking unrelated or distantly related languages: take, for instance, the assimilation of European immigrants in Québec (Royal Commission, Vol 1, 1967, p. 32). Of the major European groups listed in the 1961 census, all except the Italians tended to have adopted English rather than French as their mother tongue. (This, for reasons studied earlier, was true despite the fact that 81% of the Québec population is French-speaking.) Of the Germans, 26% had become English-speaking compared to only 15% who became French-speaking; of the Dutch, 40% versus 7%; of the Poles, 25% versus 6%; of the Scandinavians, 57% versus 15%; of the Ukranians, 21% versus 6%; of the Russians, 49% versus 4%; of the Jews, 55% versus 2%. For the Italians, however, the only speakers of a Romance language in that list, only 6% had become English-speaking, compared to 14% who became Francophone. The attraction toward the related French group was strong enough to overcome

the economic advantages of adopting English as one's home language.

3. The size of a group also matters. Compare, for instance, the fate of American Indians in countries where they constitute a small minority of the total population, e.g. in the United States (some 0.4%) or Canada (1.2%) with countries where they are much larger minorities, like Mexico (12%), Peru (25%) or Guatemala (43%). Different countries use somewhat different criteria of who is Indian, so comparisons are difficult. Nevertheless, it is readily apparent that the much smaller North American groups are also much more racially mixed and Westernized than their Latin American counterparts. Many North American Indian groups have ceased to exist as separate cultural and social entities. The same is true, incidentally, of the Brazilean Amazonian Indians, who also make up less than 1% of the national population. So the difference is not one of north versus south.

To arrive even at the low figure of 0.4%, the American Bureau of Indian Affairs has adopted a wide definition of who is Indian. It includes anyone who is "one-quarter blood" or who claims affiliation to a tribal group. This includes many people who are bilingual or even monolingual in English, who are phenotypically undistinguishable from whites, and who indeed often choose to "pass" as such. By contrast, Indians in Mexico, Peru, Guatemala, Ecuador and Bolivia are genetically overwhelmingly Indian, are generally monolingual in their indigenous language, live as peasants in distinct, self-conscious communities and are even more marginal to their respective "national" societies than their counterparts in Canada or the United States.*

4. The proposition that low-status groups have more of an incentive to acculturate and assimilate than high-status groups is well-supported by the behavior of numerous groups. For example, German, Dutch, French, Belgian, British and Japanese immigrants made little or no attempt to acculturate or assimilate to the population of the colonies they ruled. Even though they were typically very small and territorially dispersed minorities, they deliberately lived among themselves, encapsulated in small privileged ghettoes. Yet, members of these same ethnic groups, when they emigrated to countries where they were just run-of-the-mill people, assimilated much faster. The Japanese, for example, who are notoriously arrogant and stand-offish as conquerors (or even as businessmen), also have a reputation for assimilating successfully in countries as different as the United States and Brazil.

Germans who have a record of rapid and successful assimilation in the United States and Canada where their status on arrival was generally lower class or at best lower-middle class, seem to become entirely different people in South America where their status is often very high. German *hacendados*

---

*Yet, ironically, it is the much more acculturated and assimilated North American Indians who recently accompanied the other ethnic groups on their outburst of ethnic revivalism. There is no counterpart anywhere in Latin America to the American Indian Movement (AIM) or to the "Red Power" militancy shown by North American Indians. These revivalistic movements, far from indicating a failure of assimilation, presuppose, on the contrary, a good deal of it. They are attempts to reverse a process which, though not completed, is well under way.

or businessmen in countries like Argentina and Peru, for instance, are notorious for continuing to send their children to private German-medium schools and for persisting in speaking German after several generations in Latin America. Their North American counterparts, however, are often offended when one detects their German accent in English and generally avoid speaking German in public (aside from a few self-contained, endogamous communities of religious zealots, such as the Amish and the Mennonites). Immigrants find it much easier to transmit their home language to their children if the latter perceive that their foreign language is a social asset, than if they sense it to be a stigma. It is, of course, the social status of the immigrant community that determines the status of their language and, hence, their incentive to assimilate or to resist assimilation.

5. Territorial dispersal negatively affects ethnic solidarity for the simple reason that ethnics have in most cases to be in physical contact with each other in order to benefit from ethnic favoritism. Conversely, the more territorially dispersed people are, the greater the opportunities for maximizing fitness through contacts with outsiders, including intermarriage. Duncan and Lieberson (1959) have shown the inverse relationship in American cities between the index of spatial segregation and rates of ethnic outmarriage. The more territorially compact an ethny, the more solidarity it can show, holding everything else constant—and therefore the less of an incentive to assimilate. The point is so obvious that imperial powers bent on committing ethnocide have often resorted to territorial dispersal to achieve forced assimilation. The Incas of Peru, for instance, deliberately removed unassimilated groups from their place of origin and relocated them in the midst of assimilated speakers of Quechua, the official language of the empire (Rowe, 1946).

The Romans deliberately dispersed the Jews after crushing their revolt in 70 A. D. Although it is true that Jewish communities survived as small isolated minorities in many countries, there was nevertheless a clear trend toward gradual assimilation in those countries where Jews were relatively well-treated, as in the United States, Canada, Argentina, France, Britain, Holland—and even in Germany until the Hitler period. This was particularly true in Western Europe in the 18th century after several countries "emancipated" their Jews by lifting legal restrictions and separate status.

Conversely, groups that have sought to escape assimilation have frequently done so by staking out a piece of territory where they attempted to isolate themselves and to create a self-contained society. Religious groups, which in time may form ethnies, use that technique repeatedly: Mormons, Amish, Mennonites and countless communes of various religious or political persuasion; the examples are legion (Kephart, 1976). In Bainbridge's (1978) felicitous phrase, these groups undergo a process of "social implosion," whereby all ties to the outside are minimized. This strategy, in turn, calls for spatial isolation. The greater the territorial concentration is, the more chances such groups have to survive.

Countless national groups that show no tendency to assimilate themselves to their neighbors when they live in compact concentrations readily assimilate when dispersed. For example, many immigrant groups in North America underwent a two-step process of territorial dispersal that closely paralleled their process of acculturation and assimilation. They left their homeland where assimilation was often not even a realistic possibility since they were typically the majority population there. After their arrival in America, they tended to reconstitute little urban ghettoes in an attempt to recreate mutual aid networks of ethnic nepotism. This first phase of partial dispersal was already accompanied by considerable acculturation. The next step was upward social mobility and assimilation, accompanied by total territorial dispersal. The ethnic ghetto exploded outward into the final suburban melting pot, sometimes leaving only the forlorn ethnic parish church behind in a neighborhood recently "invaded" by the new wave of immigrants or by racial pariahs.

6. Immigration obviously heightens greatly the likelihood of assimilation for the reasons already noted. The more isolated the immigrant is from fellow-ethnics and the more the immigrant emigrates as an individual, the more likely acculturation and assimilation are to take place. Thus, the slave who often emigrates as an individual acculturates faster than the immigrant who comes as part of a family unit. The isolated immigrant family in turn is more likely to assimilate than the individual who migrates with a whole community. Quite apart from the territorial dispersal that generally accompanies migration, immigration fosters acculturation and assimilation for ecological and social reasons. The native usually knows best; it behooves the newcomer to learn native ways, in part because the native's adaptation to the habitat is in fact empirically tested and superior, and in part because the native is boss (if indeed the native is). The safest strategy calls for doing as the Romans, when in Rome.

An episode from my adolescence will serve as illustration. The scene is on board a liberty ship traveling from Antwerp, Belgium, to Lobito, Angola, in 1948. The trip took three weeks in relatively cramped quarters. The passengers were nearly all Belgians; the crew was also mostly Belgian, except for the catering staff of waiters and cabin attendants who were Africans from the then Belgian Congo. The Congo was the destination of the passengers, who quickly discovered that they belonged to two distinct groups of approximately equal size. There were those who had never been to Africa (or, in many cases, anywhere else outside Belgium), and those who were returning to the Congo to continue a colonial career interrupted by the war.

The newcomers were at an instant disadvantage, a disadvantage that was barely perceptible in Antwerp, but which became increasingly obvious the closer we came to our destination. Understandably, the newcomers (condescendingly called *les bleus* by the "old Africa hands") felt they were on the brink of a very adventuresome and somewhat dangerous undertaking, and felt for the most part quite anxious about climate, disease, living conditions, diet and sundry problems of adaptation to a strange tropical environment. They were, therefore, constantly approaching the old hands for

information and advice, thereby undergoing a crash course in what sociologists call "anticipatory socialization" to their role as Belgian colonials.

Anxieties mounted as the ship traveled south, and as the weather became
hotter. The newcomers were, of course, doing their best to behave as the
old hands and to disguise or hide their ignorance of colonial ways. There
was one thing that gave them away more than anything else, however,
namely their opinions and treatment of blacks. Belgium at that time had
very few black residents, and most of the newcomers had had few, if any,
experiences in dealing with blacks. They had, of course, been exposed
through mission propaganda in church and through history manuals in
schools to stereotypes of African inferiority. But the official face of Belgian
colonialism was benevolent paternalism. Initial attitudes of the newcomers
toward the black catering staff on the ship were thus, on the whole, characterized by benevolent curiosity. Behavior was uncertain because the situation was totally new and unscripted. Some reacted through "exaggerated"
courtesy, calling, for example, the waiter *Monsieur*, whereas they would
have called him *garçon* had he been white.

All this uncertainty in interaction was a source of great amusement for
the old hands, who took it upon them to coach the newcomers in racism.
Newcomers would be told their "liberalism" and "benevolence" toward
blacks would not survive two weeks in Africa. Africans were little better
than monkeys, really. If you treated them well, they would abuse the situation and stab you in the back. They were a lying, cheating, thieving lot
who had to be kept under constant watch. If you did not lock up everything
of value in your house, your servants would strip you naked in no time.
You had to be firm with them. You would soon lose your illusions about
them. And so on.

To drive these lessons in colonial etiquette home, the old hands would
behave toward the Congolese staff on the ship with the callous discourtesy
that was the daily routine of colonial life. The polite term of address for an
African, they would tell the newcomers, was "boy" or "girl," but "macaque"
got better results and was, in any case, much closer to the truth. To some
newcomers' credit, these disquisitions on the way to treat blacks were sometimes met with skepticism, but most underwent an astonishingly fast transformation of both their attitudes and behavior. In their eagerness to conform
to the norms of the prestigious old hands, the majority of newcomers had
become confirmed racists by the time the ship docked in Lobito. The few
remaining "liberals," the old hands predicted, would soon learn better.
Undoubtedly, nearly all did.

For most, the mere three weeks on the ship had sufficed to bring about
their total assimilation into the Belgian colonial role and ethic. The fear of
ridicule, uncertainty about the unknown, and the clear perception by the
newcomers that racial liberalism made one an outcast in colonial society
had all driven home colonial lesson number one: racism is adaptive in a
colonial society. The anxiety of immigration and the status uncertainty
connected with the uprooting facilitated the suspension of rationality and

critical reason. I vividly remember that one of the newcomers who eagerly adopted the epithet "macaque" in reference to blacks was a brilliant entomologist who lived to discover some 3000 new species of insects.*

THE AMERICAN MELTING POT: MYTH OR REALITY?

Between 1820 and 1930, 38 million people immigrated to the United States—32 million of them from Europe (Burkey, 1978; Olson, 1979). Since 1930, over 7 million more arrived legally, not counting several million illegal immigrants, principally from Mexico. Roughly half of that massive influx took place in the period between 1881 and 1920. Nearly one-fourth came in the first decade of the 20th century—8.5 million. The experience of immigrants, and hence the answer to the question I have just posed, did, however, differ greatly for various ethnic groups.

Broadly speaking, assimilation was easiest and fastest for the northwestern Europeans, mostly of Protestant faith, except for the Irish who came earlier. These groups included 7 million Germans, 4.7 million Irish, 3.1 million English, 800,000 Scots, 2.5 million Scandinavians and 400,000 Dutch. For the Catholic, Orthodox and Jewish groups from Mediterranean and Eastern and Central Europe, the assimilation process was somewhat more difficult but largely successful. These groups included 5.3 million Italians, 3.8 million Russians and Poles, 4.3 million from the countries of the Austro-Hungarian Empire, 600,000 Greeks, 600,000 from Spain and Portugal and 700,000 from France. The one million-odd Asian immigrants and the seven to ten million Latin Americans encountered much more prejudice and resistance in assimilation, but their situation has improved rather dramatically since World War II. For the 25 million blacks, whether descendants of American slaves who are completely acculturated and, at least, sixth-generation American, or for the million or so more recent arrivals from the Caribbean, assimilation remains as elusive as ever.

Differences in both culture and phenotype go a long way in explaining this continuum. This was primarily a continuum of acceptance (or rejection) by the dominant group, rather than a continuum of willingness to be assimilated by the immigrant groups. The more the immigrant group resembled the dominant WASPs (White Ango-Saxon Protestants) in phenotype, language, religion and values, the faster and the easier the assimilation. Indeed, the dominant ideology was drastically different depending on whether an immigrant group was defined as white or colored. White immigrants were

---

*John Stone reports similar findings in his study of white immigrants to South Africa. One of his respondents gave the following description of his rapidly changing racial attitudes (Stone, 1973, p. 159): "You pass through three phases: first, you feel sorry for the native, which lasts for a few weeks. . . . Then, for about six months when you begin to know and work with them, you dislike them more than South Africans do; finally, things even up and fit into the picture and you accept them for what they are." Stone's quantitative study of attitude change among British immigrants to South Africa shows little support for the thesis that immigrants who were initially racists selected themselves to emigrate to South Africa, and much evidence showing that they became racists quickly after arrival.

put under considerable pressure to learn English, become United States citizens and assimilate.

Within the large European contingent a clear dichotomy was made between "honorary" WASPs; i.e. Germanic and Anglo Saxon northwestern Europeans and all others, and this invidious dichotomy was clearly embodied in the immigration acts of 1921 and 1924, imposing a quota system favoring "better" immigrants from Protestant Nordic countries (Handlin, 1957). Indeed, discriminatory quotas were reaffirmed as late as the McCarran-Walter Act of 1952 (Olson, 1979). Nevertheless, the overriding principle was that white was right, and that all Europeans were basically assimilable.

Far different was the attitude toward Asian immigrants. Chinese "coolies" had been welcome to build railways in California, but, when the job was done, agitation against further Asian immigration became intense, resulting in the Chinese Exclusion Act of 1882 (renewed in 1892 and 1902). The ban against all Chinese immigration was symbolically lifted in 1943 when China was a war-time ally, permitting the entry of 105 persons per year (P. I. Rose, 1974). However, as a reversal of this outburst of liberalism, persons of Japanese descent, whether United States citizens or not, were incarcerated in concentration camps in 1942—a racist retaliation against Pearl Harbor.

Only in 1965, was the Asian immigration policy greatly liberalized. This followed a dramatic diminution in the amount of anti-Asian prejudice and a rapid increase in Asian assimilation (including, in the case of some groups such as Japanese-Americans, high rates of intermarriage) in the aftermath of World War II.

Latin American immigrants have been in a different position from Asian immigrants. Some of them are phenotypically white, finding it no more difficult to assimilate than Italians or Spaniards. The ease with which Cuban Castro refugees, a predominantly white bourgeosie, assimilated is a case in point. Puerto Ricans cover the entire color spectrum, and the darker ones find assimilation much more difficult; however, since they are United States citizens, they cannot be barred from the mainland. Mexicans, the largest Latin American group by far, find it easy to enter illegally through a long, poorly patrolled border.

Although Latin American immigrants face much racial and cultural prejudice, and thus assimilate rather slowly, many business interests (especially in agribusiness but also in small labor-intensive industries) find them a convenient source of cheap labor. Thus, business interests excercise little pressure to stop immigration, legal or illegal. Ironically but understandably, the main interest groups who want to stop illegal Mexican immigration are trade unions and established Mexican Americans, who fear competition in unskilled and semiskilled employment.

Returning to the European immigrants for whom assimilation has indeed been a reality, the conditions were favorable. They were, by and large, accepted, the more so if they resembled the dominant WASP in culture and appearance. They were largely uprooted from their home cultures by long-distance migration across the ocean (a trip of no return for most, until the easy and cheap travel of the post-World War II era). They were territorially dispersed in urban centers and surrounded by strangers. Almost wherever they went, they were in the minority as soon as they left their little urban enclaves. More importantly, they entered, for the most part, the bottom of the urban occupational structure. They made up the unskilled and semis-killed working class of the booming American industrial machine.

Not all groups assimilated with equal ease and speed. Indeed, for hardly anyone did assimilation come easily. Learning a new language and a new way of life, enduring the ridicule of making mistakes and appearing foreign, suffering the anxieties of a strange, uncertain world, being poor and at the mercy of disease, death and unemployment (Social Security is less than half-a-century old), all these were the fate of the immigrant, even of the relatively "privileged" European. Little wonder that the first generation sought to reestablish in the New World a cocoon of security, well-being and *Gemütlichkeit* in the ethnic enclave. Ethnic sentiments are not that easily discarded.

However, for the great majority, the ethnic ghetto was only a way-station in a double process of assimilation and of upward mobility. Most immigrant families stayed in the ghetto only for one or two generations. Children of immigrants typically lost their ability to speak the home language, though many still understood it. The third generation became overwhelmingly monolingual in English and began to intermarry extensively. Since assim-ilation was a virtual prerequisite for upward social mobility, assimilation and acculturation became symbols of successful attainment of middle-class status. Conversely, remaining in the ethnic neighborhood, retaining ethnic ties and speaking the "old language" became stigmas of failure and badges of working-class membership. This led, of course, to poignant intergener-ational conflicts between immigrants and their assimilated children and grandchildren, but the attraction of assimilation was well-nigh irresistible for most.

There are, of course, a number of exceptions. Some groups, usually re-ligious zealots, like the Chassidic Jews, the Amish of Pennsylvania and others, managed to retain their separate ethnic identity and to resist, indeed, actively to reject, both acculturation and assimilation. Even these groups have "lost" many of their members to "the world," but they have succeeded in surviving as separate microethnies, even under unfavorable circumstan-ces. Their methods for doing so are nearly identical in all cases. They have attempted to recreate a territorial base by encapsulating themselves in an urban ghetto or in a contiguous rural area. They impose a stern discipline (usually religiously based) on their members. They strictly enforce endo-gamy (again often scripturally based) by ostracizing those who marry out-siders. They minimize and stigmatize all contacts with the outside world, which is defined as corrupt and inferior. And they cultivate a fierce sense of their own superiority: only they know how to live right and to do right.

Short of such fanaticism, assimilation for European immigrants in America was virtually inevitable.*

This last statement has become unfashionable since the "ethnic revival" of the 1970s. An entire academic cottage industry developed lately around "ethnic studies." All sorts of books are being written, extolling ethnic heritages, discovering forgotten roots and asserting how unassimilated and un-WASP most Americans are. The politics of this "ethnic revival" (or perhaps better, ethnic fad) are complex, but nevertheless easily understandable. It all began in the mid-1960s with an attempt by Afro-Americans to redefine their situation in terms of ethnicity rather than race. A black pseudonationalist movement developed, which was doomed to failure since all the conditions for successful nationalism were missing. Blacks lack a separate and distinct cultural tradition, a contiguous territory and the necessary resource base to make nationalism work.

What blacks do have, however, is an ability to frighten whites. The spectacle of the urban riots in Watts in 1965, in Newark and Detroit in 1967 and in many cities after the assassination of Martin Luther King in 1968 led many whites to irrational panic. This panic was privately translated into an acceleration of the flight to the suburbs and of the consequent deterioration of the central cities and their public school systems. Publicly, panic was converted into a massive change of policy. Whereas the thrust of the civil rights movement in the 1940s, 1950s and early 1960s had been the elimination of all considerations of race, now all kinds of government agencies competed with each other to compel school authorities, employees and others to pay great attention to race, to allocate resources on the basis of racial quotas, to bus school children according to their skin pigmentation,† to overlook seniority rules to atone for past racial guilt and so on.

Once these government policies spread, they set in motion a series of ethnic shock waves. Since blacks had seemed successful in getting special privileges by organizing as blacks, other minority groups followed suit in self-defense: Chicanos, Amerindians and Asian Americans. But the whites were not to be left out. The feminist movement copied, with very mixed success, some of the blacks' tactics. And the "white ethnics" also became active. My point is that the white "ethnic movement" is a tactical response to the perceived threat of the black movement and does not, in any meaningful sense, constitute a reversal of assimilation—much less a failure of it.

The white "ethnic movement" is basically a conservative groundswell of

*It should also be mentioned, however, that larger numbers of immigrants opted for an alternative to assimilation; namely, they returned to their country of origin. Many Poles did so, for example. Presumably, a selective factor was at work, in this return migration: it was the older and the less assimilated who returned, thereby accelerating the assimilation of those who stayed.

†Busing for school integration incidentally is a complete reversal of the famous Brown versus the Board of Education decision of the Supreme Court in 1954. That decision said it was *illegal* to bus school children out of their neighborhood to make them attend a school other than the nearest one. The Court said that children must be assigned to the nearest school, without any consideration of race.

mostly Catholic, working-class whites who find in ethnicity a respectable banner around which to organize opposition to "affirmative action" and similar government policies (Orlando Patterson, 1977). Jewish organizations, interestingly, have overwhelmingly opposed government policies that are based on race or ethnicity, and they have advocated universalism. The Jewish reaction is not surprising since Jews in the past have often been the victim of ethnic or religious quotas and since their statistical overrepresentation in many highly skilled professional and academic jobs makes them likely victims of reverse discrimination.

In conclusion, the white "ethnic movement" is really not an ethnic movement at all. Ethnicity here is an alibi for race and for class. Since whites, unlike blacks, cannot openly organize on the basis of race without being accused of racism or fascism, ethnicity provides a respectable cover for race. As for class organization, it has a poor record of political success in the United States. Since, however, the residues of European ethnicity (such as ethnic residential concentration) are largely found in the urban working-class districts of the eastern and midwestern cities, ethnicity is also a convenient proxy for class organization.

By objective standards, the melting pot has not only been a reality for European immigrants in the past; it continues apace today, if anything, at an accelerating rate. Intermarriage rates, the ultimate tests of assimilation, are telling. As late as the 1940s, 94% of Protestants married within their religious groups (Olson, 1979). By the late 1970s nearly 40% of both Jews and Catholics married outside their faith. The triple white melting pot that some scholars thought to distinguish (Catholic, Protestant and Jewish) seems to merge into a single one (Gordon, 1964; Kennedy, 1944; Peach, 1980).

Rates of ethnic outmarriage are even higher—and climbing fast. In the 1970s, Irish and German Catholics outmarried at a rate of nearly 70%; Poles, Czechs and Italians at 50%; and French Canadians (in the U.S.) at 40%. Even some of the groups traditionally regarded as nonwhites are showing rapidly rising rates of intermarriages: about 50% for Japanese-Americans, about 40% for Puerto Ricans and about 30% for Mexican Americans (Olson, 1979). Only blacks seem permanently excluded from the great American melting pot.

ISRAEL: SETTLER COLONIALISM OR INGATHERING OF THE EXILES?

Every people claims to be unique, and in some sense, of course, the claim is true. But some are more unique than others. During some 5000 years of recorded myth and history, the Jews have emerged as a people from the Sinai desert in the second millenium B.C., survived Babylonian captivity in the sixth century B.C. and preserved their ethnic identity during 1900 years of diaspora (after the destruction of the Temple in Jerusalem by the Romans in 70 A.D.). After losing about one-third of their numbers (six million out of approximately 18 million) in the Holocaust of World War II, Jews recreated a state and a nation in their historic homeland, reviving their ritual language, Hebrew, in the process. Then, this new little state (some 600,000 Jews in 1948; 3 million in 1973) victoriously fought four wars (1948, 1956, 1967 and 1973) against combined Arab forces that outnumbered them more than 20 to one. (There are some 140 million Arabs now; in 1948, they numbered about 70 million, although less than half of them belonged to the front-line enemies of Israel: Egypt, Syria, Lebanon, Iraq and Jordan.) To be sure, it did so with the material, political and military help of the United States, then the most powerful nation on earth. Still, with that kind of historical record, it is little wonder that the Jews have a sense of destiny and make a claim to special divine attention.

Even while in the diaspora, Jews have, considering how few they were, made extraordinary contributions to both Arab Muslim and European Christian civilization, producing much more than their share of philosophers, artists, intellectuals, statesmen, entrepreneurs and other leading figures. Other peoples have survived through centuries of territorial dispersal, e.g. the Gypsies. Other groups have suffered terrible persecution. The Armenians, for instance, suffered their own holocaust at the hands of the Turks during World War I, one generation before the Jews. But, except for the Greeks, what other small nation has left such a mark on world history?

In any case, one Jewish achievement is quite unique: the recreation of a nation out of a multitude of groups who, although they all claimed to be Jews, had become extremely culturally and linguistically diverse and were not even all religious. Jews in the diaspora had little more than the memory of a historical tradition in common—a tenuous link indeed. Each Jewish community in the diaspora had much more objectively in common with Gentiles in their respective countries than with each other. As at least half of world Jewry is not religious, Judaism for many is but a set of symbols rather than a living daily reality. Zionism, the ideology that provided the rationale for the recreation of the state of Israel, did not unite all Jewry either, for it was largely an Eastern-European, Ashkenazic movement that involved the more assimilated Western European Jews only peripherally and the Sephardic-Oriental Jews hardly at all. Theodor Herzl, the father of Zionism, was a Germanized Hungarian, a European intellectual and indeed very much of a germanophile, who made only token attempts to involve Oriental Jews in the Zionist movement (Elon, 1975).

How did the "Israeli miracle" come about? The Israeli nation was recreated by achieving two of the essential conditions of nationhood:

1. the establishment of a territorial basis through the foundation of the independent state of Israel in what had been the British Mandate of Palestine and
2. the adoption of a common language, Hebrew, which, in this case had to be virtually resurrected from its moribund status as a ritual language.

That feat too—the successful revival in less than a century of a virtually dead language—is unique in world history. Others have tried (e.g. the Irish who attempted to revive Gaelic) but failed. Before independence, only a couple of hundred thousand people spoke Hebrew, mostly as a second language; 30 years later, Hebrew was used by over three million, at least half of whom spoke it as their mother tongue. The feat of resurrecting Hebrew as a modern language is analogous to, say, trying to create a Catholic state with Latin as the official language to be adopted by Poles, Austrians, Irish, Spaniards, French, and so on.

What kind of a state is Israel? There are two polar views as to the nature of the Israeli state. One is the official Zionist ideology of the state; the other is the radical Arab ideology. Both have a considerable measure of validity; both are one-sided. Perhaps the most coherent composite view, and the one closest to reality, is given in Smooha's (1978) masterly analysis. Let me briefly state the two opposite views, starting with the official Israeli position.

The justification for the state of Israel (and for the Jewish sectarian nature of the state) is that Jews have a long-standing historical claim to Palestine, that they have had a continuous presence in the region and that they have no other place to call their own where they can feel safe. The Holocaust is always invoked as tragic evidence for the need of a Jewish state where Jews are in majority and can control their own destiny. (Unfortunately, the Holocaust argument fails to impress the Arabs, at whose expense the state of Israel was established, since they had nothing to do with Hitler's Germany. To Arabs, the Holocaust was strictly a European, Christian affair, of which they are made to pay the reparations.)

Zionist ideology calls for an in-gathering of the exiles into the land of Israel to recreate a Jewish state. Therefore, every Jew has an automatic right of admission, and Judaism is the official, established religion of the state (which, however, also recognizes and entrenches special rights to the minority religions of Islam, Christianity and Druzism). Every Jewish immigrant is subjected to strong ideological pressures to make a total commitment to the Zionist state, to learn Hebrew as quickly as possible and to become absorbed into the mainstream of the national Jewish culture. Intensive courses in assimilation are made available (on a voluntary basis) to the immigrants, in which they are subjected to a mixture of Zionist indoctrination and a total immersion in the Hebrew language. Hebrew is the main official language, but Arabic and English are also given some official recognition as secondary languages.

Military service is universal for both Jewish men and women (except for Orthodox women who can be exempted) and is considered a sacred duty to the State. Although long ruled by the Labor Party with a strongly socialist, egalitarian (for Jews), secular, welfare-state ideology, the Israeli State also protects the special rights of the Orthodox minority (about 30% of the Jewish population) who are much more conservative on a number of issues (such as the status of women and the religious nature of the state). Official policy is thus an uneasy compromise within the Jewish population.

Arabs residing within the boundaries of pre-1967 Israel number about 450,000 and make up 13% of the total population of 3.5 million. They are about 76% Muslim, 15% Christian and 9% Druze (Smooha, 1978, p. 280). They have the right to vote, and they elect a few members of the Knesset (Parliament), but they are clearly second-class citizens with restricted rights. All restrictions on the rights of Arabs are justified on grounds of the continuous state of war between Israel and its Arab neighbors—and the imperatives of survival.

The antithesis to this picture of Israel, as a refuge for a persecuted minority and an egalitarian Promised Land for all Jews everywhere, is the Arab ideology of Israel as an aggressive, expansionist, militaristic, sectarian, racist state—a belated extension of European colonialism on Asian soil supported by the capitalist countries, primarily the United States. The evidence for the view of Israel as a case of settler colonialism and an example of what, in the South African context, I have called a "Herrenvolk democracy" [(van den Berghe, 1965) meaning a democracy limited to the ruling ethnic or racial group] is considerable.

Palestine, a piece of the Ottoman Empire dismembered after the Turkish defeat in World War I, became a British Mandate. It was Britain that, in the Balfour Declaration of 1917, first gave official "great power" recognition to Zionist aspirations. At the outset of Zionist colonization, the Jewish population of Palestine was about 24,000 out of a total population of about 500,000 (Smooha, 1978, p. 65). When the British Mandate began in 1918, another 65,000 Jewish immigrants had raised the total to about 100,000, perhaps 15% of the total, if one takes natural increases of the Arab population into account. During the Mandate, Britain allowed (sometimes reluctantly, to be sure, because Britain was caught between the irreconcilable demands of Jews and Arabs) considerable Jewish immigration. Hitler refugees from Germany in the 1930s more than doubled the Jewish population from 175,000 to 400,000, raising it to 30% of the total population of Palestine.

In 1939, Britain began to try restriction of Jewish immigration, but, after World War II, hundreds of thousands of Jewish survivors of the Nazi concentration camps clamored for admission to Palestine. The British found themselves caught in the middle of an escalating civil war between Jews and Arabs, so they withdrew in 1948. The United Nations 1947 partition plan never had a chance to be implemented. Israel proclaimed its independence, May 14, 1948, and was immediately recognized by most Western countries and the Soviet Union. It was jointly attacked by all its Arab neighbors, and a protracted War of Independence (1948–1949) followed, during which hundreds of thousands of Arabs fled from Israel and Jews from the Arab countries (principally from Morocco, Yemen and Iraq) fled to Israel. Over the years, some 630,000 Jews immigrated from Arab countries, and close to a million Palestinian Arabs became refugees in neighboring Arab countries.

It is thus a matter of historical record that the Zionist movement is almost entirely European in origin and inspiration; that about 90% of the 447,000

Jews who immigrated to Israel until independence came from Europe (Smooha, 1978, p. 281), and thus that Israel does historically represent the last wave of European overseas colonization; that Jewish immigration to Palestine was on the whole supported by both governmental and private (mostly Jewish) agencies in the main capitalist and colonial countries, principally Britain and later the United States; and that the State of Israel since its creation has been under the protective umbrella of the Western capitalist countries, again principally the United States but also Britain and France (who were Israel's allies in the 1956 war against Egypt). Israel is thus seen by the Arabs as a client state of the United States and a foreign European enclave on Asian soil. A frequent historical parallel is that of the Christian Crusader states of the 12th and 13th centuries, a parallel bitterly resented by the Israelis but dear to the Arabs because, of course, the Crusaders were in the end expelled after two centuries of precarious rule in Palestine. (The parallel is very imperfect because the Crusaders came without women and never numbered more than about 5000.)

The catalog of Arab grievances against Israel is a long one. Arabs who have left Palestine, often in fear of their lives during the war, have not been allowed to return to their homes. Except for the Druzes and the Bedouins, who are considered loyal to Israel and who may volunteer for armed service, Arabs are excluded from military service. Arab land rights are continually encroached upon by Jewish settlements, and whole Arab communities have been displaced by force. Arabs are subject to continuous and often humiliating vexations and surveillance. They are given "special rights" as separate religious communities of Christians or Muslims. This means that, while Islamic or Christian law is recognized by the State of Israel, Arabs are also treated as communities apart from Jews, are administered through separate quasicolonial agencies, go to segregated Arabic-medium schools and so on. Whereas every Jew anywhere in the world has an automatic right of admission to Israel and a claim to Israeli citizenship, Arabs born and raised in Palestine who fled during one of the wars are not permitted to return. Arabs residing in the pre-1967 areas of Israel, and who have stayed since the foundation of the state, have Israeli citizenship and the right to vote, but their legal rights are frequently infringed upon by arbitrary actions of the government. For example, entire communities have been illegally expelled from their villages for reasons of "security," despite a Supreme Court ruling in their favor. In fairness to Israel, however, it must be stated that Israel inherited its conception of a religious state with separate juridical status to each religious community from the British Mandate, which, in turn, merely extended the Ottoman *millet* system. Thus, the basic structure of the Israeli state is, ironically, a Muslim-inspired theocracy which it shares with its enemies.

The overall picture is quite clear. The State of Israel is benevolent, democratic, egalitarian and assimilationist for the 87% of the population of 3.5 million who are Jews. It is none of these for the 13% of the population (of pre-1967 Israel) who are Arabs, nor, of course, for the Arab population of

1.2 million in the territories conquered in the 1967 war who are completely excluded from the Israeli body politic and treated as a conquered people. For the Arabs, the Israeli regime has indeed most of the features of a colonial state, although it must be said that, by colonial standards, Israel's rule has been relatively mild and benign. It is quite possible for an apolitical Arab in Israel to prosper and to avoid unpleasantness, and it is not true that Israel is a *racist* state in the sense that South Africa is, for instance. Another crucial difference with classical colonialism is that the Jews, even though they now make extensive use of Arab labor, have generally sought to dispense with Arab labor rather than to exploit it.

The conflict between Arab and Jew is fundamentally irreconcilable so long as one community (the Jews in this case) insist that Israel must be a *Jewish* state. Irreconcilable interests necessarily lead to policies that differentiate sharply among ethnies and deepen antagonism. Deep antagonism is, in turn, advanced as a rationalization for ethnic discrimination. Given the present nature of Israel as a Jewish State, this vicious circle is inescapable.

So far, I have presented matters primarily in Arab–Jewish terms, but the situation is made far more complex by a profound double cleavage within the Jewish population. I have already alluded to the cleavage between the 30% of the Jews who are Orthodox, insisting that Israel must be a sectarian state, and the 70% whose religious views and practices are tolerant and lax, and who advocate secularism (although clearly *Jewish* secularism).

The other cleavage is the ethnic one between the Ashkenazim (literally "Germans")—a term used to refer to most European Jews who, in Eastern Europe, spoke Yiddish, a German dialect, or other European languages—and the so-called Orientals (or Sephardim) who came mostly from Arab countries and who are strongly Arabized in language and culture. There are also some Sephardic groups who speak Ladino (a dialect of Spanish), Turkish, Bulgarian or other languages, but they are small and are generally considered subgroups of the Orientals, though they are often socioeconomically close to the Ashkenazim.

This ethnic cleavage between Ashkenazim and Orientals has been meticulously documented in Smooha's (1978) recent study, wherein he sharply questions both the ideology and the practice of assimilation as propounded by the Ashkenazic group and extolled by the Ashkenazic intellectual establishment (Eisenstadt, 1954, 1967). Jews from the Arab countries, even though they are often more strongly anti-Arab than the Ashkenazim, are, in fact, culturally and linguistically Arab and are still only partially assimilated in the Israeli mainstream, as defined by the largely Ashkenazic ruling class.

Orientals make up 55% of the Jews in Israel, a proportion that is steadily rising as their birth rate is much higher than that of the Ashkenazim (Smooha, 1978, p. 280). Yet, they are in an unfavorable position vis-à-vis the Ashkenazim. Their linguistic acculturation to Hebrew has been as successful as that of the Ashkenazim. (In fact, as Hebrew is fairly closely related to Arabic, Orientals often find it easier to learn than native speakers of Indo-European languages.) But Orientals came from much poorer, less industrialized countries and, consequently, started out with fewer "modern" skills, less education, less capital and a "traditional" style of life, making adjustment to a brash frontier society like Israel difficult. For instance, the Oriental family structure tends to be strongly patriarchal, with semisecluded women and a high birth rate. These conditions make for very cohesive kinship networks but render urban adjustment difficult because they contribute to residential overcrowding and lower per capita income.

Smooha (1978) documents in great detail the sizeable and persistant inequalities between Orientals and Ashkenazim. Oriental *family* income has risen over the years from about two-thirds to four-fifths of Ashkenazi family income, but the greater size of the Oriental family reduces the Oriental *per capita* income to roughly half (52% in 1958–1960, 48% in 1968–1969) of the Ashkenazi per capita figure (Smooha, 1978, pp. 154, 282, 286). In fact, in per capita income, the gap has actually increased because of a declining Ashkenazi birth rate. This difference must be seen, however, in the context of a rapidly increasing standard of living in the 1950s and 1960s for *both* groups, but Ashkenazim improved their condition faster than Orientals.

Occupational differences also favored Ashkenazim. For example, 13% of the Ashkenazim and only 2% of Orientals were in professional and technical jobs in 1975; 58% of Ashkenazim were in clerical occupations compared to 33% of the Orientals (Smooha, 1978, p. 157). Smooha concludes that the occupational gap, too, has not substantially decreased since independence. Educational differentials are considerable—but decreasing. Ashkenazim have an average of three more years of education in median number of years of schooling completed, but the gap has been reduced by six months between 1961 and 1975 (Smooha, 1978, p. 159). Incidentally, the difference in mean IQ scores for Ashkenazim and Orientals is almost identical to that between whites and blacks in the United States: 15 IQ points (Smooha, 1978, p. 162).

In the distribution of power, too, Oriental underrepresentation is glaring. In 1973, for example, Orientals with 55% of the Jewish population made up only 11% of the Cabinet, 17% of the Knesset (Parliament), 8% of the members of the executive of the Jewish Agency, 25% of the members of the Central Committee of Histadrut (trade union federation), 3% of top-ranking civil servants, none of the 21 officers of general rank in the armed forces and none of the 19 mayors of the largest cities (Smooha, 1978, p. 309). In several of these and other fields, these figures, though low, represented increases over the 1950s and 1960s, thereby indicating a concern by the Ashkenazic power structure to co-opt some Orientals. This is particularly true in the trade union movement (Histadrut) linked with the Labor Party.

The overall picture of Oriental–Ashkenazic differences is that they are considerable and persistent, despite some narrowing of the gap in some respects. Such success as has been achieved in reducing ethnic group disparities has been due largely to efforts in spreading mass education and to co-optation of Orientals in some key positions through an Israeli version of informal "affirmative action." Nevertheless, the gap remains approximately as wide as between white and black Americans on many socioeconomic, occupational and educational indices, and in performance on standardized IQ tests. This is true in both countries despite an official ideology opposing discrimination and actively promoting equality of opportunity.

In addition to being much poorer and less educated, on the average, than the Ashkenazim and having a culture that makes them resemble the despised Arabs, the Orientals are also phenotypically much more like the Arabs than like the Ashkenazim. Although it would be an overstatement to say that there is a racial distinction made between Ashkenazim and Orientals, it is no overstatement to characterize Israeli society as clearly stratified into three main ethnic groups: the Ashkenazim on top, Oriental Jews in the middle and Arabs at the bottom. The Orientals are clearly an "intermediate" group, sharing many of the objective cultural and phenotypic attributes of the Arabs but belonging to the privileged Jewish group. Although the official ideology of Israel is, of course, to assimilate the Orientals, the assimilation is far from complete, as shown by endogamy rates. There is virtually no intermarriage between Arab and Jew, and a strong stigma attaches to such marriages. In fact, these marriages are legally impossible, except through conversion of one of the spouses, since Israeli law, following the old Ottoman *millet* system, forces everyone, whether religious or not, to marry according to the religious rites of his or her ascribed religious community; thus, by law, every religious community—Jewish, Muslim, Christian and Druze—is totally endogamous.

Between Ashkenazim and Orientals, it would be considered bad taste to express prejudice against intermarriage openly; nevertheless, rates of intermarriage are well below the expected rate. However, they are on the increase, clearly indicating a trend toward a gradual merging of the two groups. Intermarriage rose from 11.8% of all Jewish marriages, in 1955, to 19.1% in 1974 (Smooha, 1978, p. 129). Given near parity of the two groups, the expected percentage, if marriage among Jews were random, would be about 50%. (By means of comparison, the rate of Ashkenazim–Oriental intermarriage in Israel is well below the percentage of Jews who marry Gentiles in the United States.)

The whole issue of assimilation raises the question: Assimilation to what? The Ashkenazim, who are greatly overrepresented in all the leading institutions of Israeli society (academia, the officer corps of the armed forces, the Kibbutz movement, the professions and the top political leadership), have imposed their culture, their values and their view of the world and of their society on the Orientals. To the Ashkenazim, it was axiomatic that Israel was to be built along a predominantly European model, except for the use of Hebrew as the official language. Not only was it the only culture with which they were familiar; they actively rejected as abhorrent the obvious alternative, namely, an Arabized, Oriental Jewish culture. Everything Arabic was the antimodel—the things that Israel was desperately striving to avoid.

This blatant Eurocentrism of the Ashkenazim inevitably became translated into a kind of condencending paternalism vis-à-vis Orientals. They

were regarded as backward and in need of "uplifting" to Ashkenazi standards. Naturally, Oriental intellectuals resented this paternalism, but, at the
same time, they found it difficult to challenge it, much less to suggest the
Arabization of Israel. Yet, increasingly, Oriental intellectuals realize that
Arabization is perhaps best for Israel's survival. Not only are two-thirds of
the population of pre-1967 Israel basically Arabic in language and culture
(i.e. Orientals and Arabs combined), but differential birth rates are certain
to make the Ashkenazim a diminishing minority. Furthermore, in the ma-
cropolitics of the region, a culturally European Israel is even more out of
tune with the area than an Arabized Israel would be. By blending culturally
into the Near-Eastern landscape, Israel might eventually become less of a
sore thumb to its neighbors.

These ideas are anathema to many Ashkenazim, because they represent
the very antithesis of their vision of what Israel should be. If Israel is to
become Arabized, they argue, then it has no reason to survive, forgetting
that the most dazzling florescence of Medieval Jewish culture took place in
Muslim Spain and was crushed and destroyed by European Christians. Israel
is thus not only on the edge of a political conflict between Arab and Jew.
It is in the forefront of a cultural clash between Europe and the Arab world.
The real question is not so much how successful was the Israeli policy of
assimilation? Rather, the lasting historical question will be: Who is assimilating whom? The tide of history seems clearly against the Ashkenazim.
Again, the Jews, to survive, will have to assimilate to their unwilling hosts!
Given a climate of reciprocal cultural and political tolerance, they can make
a dazzling contribution, not only to their own society, but to Arab and,
indeed, to world culture, as they have repeatedly done in the past. If, however, they behave as European colonials, their long-range outlook is no
brighter than that of white South Africans, the other last sizeable European
population enclave in a hostile continent.

SUGGESTED READINGS

The study of ethnic assimilation has for long been almost co-extensive with the study
of ethnic relations in the United States, as is evident from American textbooks on the
subject (Barron, 1957; P. I. Rose, 1974; Shibutani and Kwan, 1965; Simpson and
Yinger, 1972). The works of Handlin (1951, 1957) are classics on the subject. Recently,
the trend has been to emphasize continuing pluralism (Glazer and Moynihan, 1970;
Hraba, 1979; Newman, 1973). On Israel, the contrasting approaches of Eisenstadt
(1954, 1967) and Smooha (1978) are instructive.

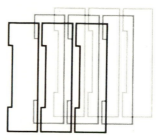

THE FORMATION,
PERSISTENCE
AND DEMISE
OF ETHNICITY

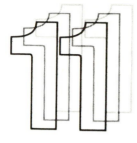

ETHNICITY AND
OTHER BASES OF SOCIALITY

The fundamental argument of this book has been that ethnicity is a special basis of sociality, irreducible to any other, through often empirically overlapping with other principles of sociality. I have argued that ethnicity is an extension of kinship and that the sentiments associated with it are of the same nature as those encountered between kin, albeit typically weaker and more diluted. I have gone one step further to link ethnicity with the sociobiology of kin selection, a step that is bound to elicit passionate rejection and disagreement.

ETHNICITY AS KIN SELECTION

To restate the argument briefly, there is abundant evidence that natural selection favored nepotistic organisms, because, by favoring kin, organisms are contributing to their own inclusive fitness. Genes predisposing for nepotism will spread in an animal population, because their carriers thereby enhance not only their own direct reproduction but also that of related organisms which share certain proportions of their genes with the nepotist. Indeed, nepotism seems to be an important—perhaps the most important—basis of animal sociality. The most social and tightly integrated animal societies, the eusocial insects, are made up entirely of a reproductive couple and specialized, nonreproductive siblings.

It is admittedly a big leap to go from ants, bees and termites to humans, but the hypothesis of kin selection in the furtherance of inclusive fitness has received much corroboration from vertebrates, including mammals, and, as anthropologists have long known, *all* human societies are organized on the basis of kinship. Elsewhere, I have shown that even the most specific and diverse forms of human kinship organization conform remarkably well to expectations derived from sociobiological theory (van den Berghe, 1979a).

The leap is thus not nearly as great or as implausible as most social scientists assume.

The next step in my analysis was an extension of the principles of nepotism from the nuclear and extended family to that group of intermarrying (and thus interrelated) families that for most of human evolution (and still for many people today) makes up the basic solidary social group, variously called sib, deme, tribe or whatever. This constituted the elemental ethny—until a few thousand years ago, a group of a few score to a few hundred people. This was the fundamental peace-keeping group of people who saw each other as related.

Over time, ethnies grew to thousands and even millions of people, and, as they grew, their underlying kinship basis became, of course, correspondingly diluted. Nevertheless, underlying ethnicity, wherever it is found, is some notion of shared ancestry, real or at least *credibly putative*. In the absence of such a belief—however vague and generalized—the basis of sociality is *not* ethnicity but something else.

From the *basis* of ethnicity as an extension of kinship (most likely with genetically selected nepotism), we turned to the *markers* of ethnicity, i.e. to the outward signs used by people to determine whether others share the same ethny or not. The more reliably, quickly and easily a marker is likely to establish or discount common ethnicity, the more likely that marker is to be used. Ethnic markers are usually cultural (especially linguistic), as we have seen, because under most historical situations until recently, cultural markers best differentiated even close neighbors who typically looked very much alike.

RACE AS A SPECIAL MARKER OF ETHNICITY

"Race" as a primary marker of common descent is relatively uncommon and recent, because it does the job of discriminating accurately only after much rapid long-distance migration has taken place and then typically only for a few generations before interbreeding blurs again phenotypical distinctions. I must, once more, reassert that I attribute no *intrinsic* significance to phenotypes in determining group boundaries and, hence, no validity to any classification of our species into rigid subspecies. Nor am I arguing that we have an instinctive propensity to stick to people who look like us. Rather, to the extent that we do so, we are "race conscious" only as a test of common ancestry. The genetic propensity is to favor kin, not to favor those who look alike. This is clearly shown by the ease with which parental feelings take precedence over racial feeling in cases of racial intermixture.

We have *not* been genetically selected to use phenotype as an ethnic marker, because, until quite recently, such a test would have been an extremely inaccurate one. Racism is thus a cultural invention, a simple one to be sure, that is readily invented when the circumstances of long-distance migration across a wide phenotypic gradient make "race" a good test of kinship; there is no evidence that racism is in-born, but there is considerable evidence that ethnocentrism is.

Racism is thus a special case of ethnic sentiment, using a phenotype as an ethnic marker. Because, however, the markers themselves are largely immutable, ascribed at birth and genetically inherited, societies that use primarily phenotypes as ethnic markers are characterized by more rigid and invidious intergroup relations than societies using cultural markers. In practice, many societies, particularly the complex large-scale societies that developed out of European colonial expansion since the late 15th century have adopted a mixture of cultural and phenotypic markers of ethnicity. Nevertheless the analytic distinction between ethnicity and race is useful for the reasons just mentioned.

CLASS AND CLASS CONFLICT

Ethnicity (and race, as a special case thereof) are thus extensions of the principle of kinship. The basis of ethnic solidarity is nepotism. The two other principal ways in which human societies are organized are reciprocity and coercion. Two unrelated individuals can enhance each other's fitness by cooperating in a mutually beneficial manner. Commonality of *interest* is therefore another fundamental basis of sociality in human collectivities. Broadly, we call human groups, organized for the pursuit of common interests, *classes*. Or, to utilize the useful Marxian distinction, a group of people who simply share common interests constitute a "class *in* itself," while a group consciously organized for the pursuit of these common interests is a "class *for* itself."

The third basis of human sociality, coercion, is, in fact, intraspecific parasitism. It arises when one group of people uses force or the threat of force to enhance the fitness of its members at the expense of another group. Different classes, as I have just defined them, can (and often are) linked to each other in such an unequal relationship of parasite and "host," thus making for class conflict in the classical Marxian sense.

It can readily be seen that my analysis is generally compatible with Marxian class analysis. One fundamental limitation of Marxian class analysis, however, is its reification of class as an entity superseding individual actors. It is this reification of class that leads many socialist utopians to expect that, once class distinctions have been abolished in a society, then class conflicts will disappear and general altruism will prevail. The first part of the prediction is true enough, but the second is a non sequitur. Eliminate exploitative relations between classes in a society, and you eliminate that particular basis of group conflict. But if the entire society becomes classless, then the basis of class solidarity, namely individual interest, disappears. Selfish interests are even more likely to emerge than in a situation of class conflict where overlap in individual interests can lead to solidary class action. Classes organize, not in the abstract, but against other classes with antagonistic interests; eliminate class differences, and you destroy the very basis of class solidarity.

Class solidarity, then, is nothing more than the overlap in the selfish individual interests of the members of a class. Workers, for instance, can only be expected to join a trade union if, by so doing, they individually benefit (or hope to benefit). That is, the benefit/cost ratio of unionization must be realistically predicted to be greater than one for successful unionization to take place. A reductionist model of class conflict and solarity in terms of individuals maximizing self interests is thus perfectly adequate to understand "collective" behavior. Conversely, the reification of class adds nothing to the model, and the gratuitous assumption of altruistic behavior in classless societies is empirically falsified. That is why Marxism has been so relatively successful in accounting for class conflicts (where it implicitly adopted the individual reductionist model of classical economics) and such an abysmal failure in predicting, much less changing, behavior in the utopian societies it attempted to create. Socialism has always foundered on the rock of individual selfishness. We are an organism biologically selected to maximize our individual inclusive fitness.

ETHNICITY VERSUS CLASS

The two principal modes of collective organization in complex societies are ethnicity and class. The former is based on some notion of common kinship; the latter on common interest. The analytical distinction between these two types of social formation is crucial; both are, in principle, equally important, and neither is reducible to the other. They are fundamentally different in nature, and trying to redefine one as a special manifestation of the other impoverishes our understanding of plural societies (Leo Kuper, 1974; Leo Kuper and M. G. Smith, 1969).

Ethnicity tends to be the more permanent and the more basic of the two. Since it is based on common descent, changes in ethnic consciousness and boundaries, while they can and do occur, are contained within the limits of people's perceptions of biological relatedness. Thus, for example, ethnic boundaries can extend in scope by lumping together related groups that hitherto saw each other as different; conversely ethnic solidarity can break down into smaller components. Also, the salience of ethnic sentiments and the extent to which they can be mobilized for political purposes can fluctuate greatly in short periods of time.

All these changes, however, take place within a preexisting framework of ties of descent and marriage establishing a newwork of kin selection and sense of "we-ness" between people. Since descent, in the nature of the case, also creates the possibility of cleavage between collateral branches at each generation, the principle of fission and fusion (as called by British structural anthropologists in analyzing segmentary lineage systems) also operates in the definition of ethnic boundaries. This is why the latter often appear to fluctuate widely and capriciously. A closer examination shows, however, that these changes, while indeed responsive to environmental conditions and politically manipulable within limits, are not random, taking place within a preexisting structure with predictable lines of cleavage.

It will be objected that the sense of common descent in ethnicity is often a fiction, which is true enough. But for such a fiction to be effective, it has to be credible, and this cannot be achieved instantaneouly, arbitrarily and at random. It takes time before an alien group becomes assimilated into an ethny, and, as the assimilation process is accompanied by intermarriage, generations of interbreeding to indeed transform the fiction into reality again. Two previously unrelated groups can fuse into one breeding population after a couple of generations of intermarriage.

It will also be objected that, for modern ethnies of millions of people, whatever biological relationship they may have is extremely tenuous at best, and this is quite true. Indeed, feelings of ethnic solidarity are more easily maintained in small, closely related groups than in large ethnies running into tens or even hundreds of millions of people. Nevertheless, even in very large ethnies, the basis of the solidarity remains the same, however diluted it may be. Ethnocentrism appeals to sentiments that have evolved in much smaller groups, and hence the appeal is often of reduced effectiveness, but the appeal strikes a responsive chord to the extent that the larger group is, in fact, a credible descent group. This typically can happen only after several generations of common history.

A commonly noted feature of ethnicity is its "irrationality." Appeals to ethnic sentiments need no justification other than common "blood." They are couched in terms of "our people" versus "them." The ethnic demagogue does not have to argue from logic or to mobilize interests. He merely has to activate preexisting sentiments of common descent. The most effective way to elicit this elemental ethnic solidarity is to create the illusion (or exploit the reality) of a threat by an outside group. Race riots, for instance, flare up by the mere spread of a rumor that one of "them" killed, hurt or simply offended one of "us."

The 1979–1980 seizure of hostages by Iranian militants at the American Embassy in Teheran is a classical example of the mobilization of ethnic sentiments. It elicited a groundswell of ethnic patriotism in the United States, as well as a wave of irrational retaliatory actions against totally innocent Iranians in the United States. Only a court injunction stopped, for example, the Immigration Service from discriminately deporting Iranians from the United States. It is also interesting how ineffective the Iranian militants' actions have been in trying to capitalize on the main line of cleavage in the United States. They released black American hostages in an attempt to exacerbate racial divisions, but they were unsuccessful. The detention of the American hostages was seen by Americans not as the actions of a small group of militants and not as an ideological struggle of Third World peoples against capitalism, but as an affront of Iranians against Americans.

Clearly then, ethnicity is more primordial than class. Blood runs thicker than money. This, however, is not to say that ethnicity is always more important or more salient than class. Nor is it necessarily the case that ethnicity can always be mobilized more easily than class for political action. Class solidarity, unlike ethnic solidarity, is dependent on a commonality of interests, which must be convincingly demonstrated before class solidarity can become effectively mobilized. Even then, it is vulnerable to the countervailing selfish interests of individual members of the class. A successful class organizer must persuade his target audience that they have a selfish interest in organizing for this common interest.

Class is therefore an alliance of convenience, based on selfish opportunism. It is vulnerable to changes in circumstances and can quickly disintegrate, because a class is not a preexisting solidary community, but class formation is not constrained by preexisting groups. Class groups can be formed out of coalitions of disparate groups sharing only a common interest in taking collective action. A classical example is the spectacular success of Jarvis' Initiative 13 in California in 1978. It was not difficult to convince California property owners that it was in their interest to vote themselves a substantial reduction in real estate taxes. The appeal was strictly rational, and it did not require any mobilization of ethnic or any other affiliation. Some minority ethnic groups attempted to organize against the initiative, because they tended to belong to the class that did not own property and whose social services would be negatively affected by the initiative, but they failed to organize an effective countermovement on a class basis, and they resoundingly lost the fight.

THE RELATIONSHIP BETWEEN CLASS AND ETHNICITY

Repeatedly in the case studies we examined in this book, we saw that class and ethnicity, although they are clearly distinct principles of social organization, interpenetrate in complex and varying ways. Indeed, the interplay of class and ethnicity is probably the most difficult problem facing the analysis of complex societies. Empirically, a complete range of situations is found, from a Swiss-type situation where the correlation between class and ethnicity is close to zero, to a Peruvian-type case where the correlation is close to one. In between are situations like those of Québec or Northern Ireland where there is some relationship between ethnic and class status—but far from a perfect one. The intermediate situations are in fact the most common, and the ones where class and ethnic conflicts are most intricately intertwined. A priori, it is impossible and unwise to declare that one factor is more important than the other. The relative salience of class and ethnicity varies from case to case, and from time to time.

A few generalizations, however, seem to emerge from this bewildering diversity of situations:

1. Class and ethnicity seem to be *antithetical* principles of social organization. As one waxes, the other wanes in relative salience. Basically, if the cleavages are primarily ethnic, then the class divisions within the ethnies are correspondingly muted. Typically then, each ethny in the common polity is led by its elite. Each ethnic elite represents and acts on behalf of its respective ethny. The country may be ruled by a coalition of such ethnic elites, with each elite competing with the other for an ethnic distribution of resources under their supervision. Alternatively, if there is a clear ethnic hierarchy, the subordinate elite acts as a representative of its group and an intermediary between the subordinate group and the dominant elite. Some-

times the subordinate elite turns nationalist and revolutionary, challenging the dominant elite, but even then it is acting on behalf of and, presumably, in the interest of its ethnic constituency, on whose support it relies. In all the variants of situations of great ethnic salience, the class distinctions within ethnies are secondary to the ethnic cleavages, and class organization is difficult.

In the opposite case, where class conflicts take precedence over ethnic cleavages, the definition of problems in terms of class interest militates against ethnic solidarity. Such situations are less common than ethnic-salient situations, which seems to indicate that, if ethnic cleavages are marked, they tend to take precedence over class cleavages.

The Andes of Peru are a case in point (van den Berghe and Primov, 1977). There is a clear ethnic distinction between the Spanish-speaking dominant *mestizos* and the Quechua- or Aymara-speaking Indians who are almost all peasants. As there is a near identity of class and ethnic status (i.e. nearly all Indians are peasants), it is a moot question whether Indian peasants are oppressed *qua* peasants or *qua* Indians. The answer is that both factors are at work, although, at the national level, class relations tend to take precedence over ethnic relations. Indians can, however, redefine their class position by leaving the land and ceasing to be peasants. In time, they learn Spanish, become acculturated to local mestizo culture and assimilate into the mestizo group in one or two generations. This class mobility open to Indians automatically deprives Indians of potential leaders, since class mobility is almost inevitably accompanied by a change of ethnic identity. Thus, the class dynamics of the situation strongly militate against an ethnic definition of conflicts.

2. Where ethnic cleavages are complicated by class differences between ethnies, ethnic conflicts tend to be much more virulent. This is so because the issues then often shift from the right of each ethny to autonomy, self-determination and cultural identity, to more radical demands for ethnic equalization of resources and, hence, for an alteration of the class system. Interestingly, the outcome is often not radical, for generally it simply leads to the *embourgeoisement* of the formerly subordinate ethnic elite and a duplication of the dominant group's class structure in the subordinate group. Indeed, we are witnessing this process among American blacks. But the demands for ethnic (or racial) equalization often take very strident forms and elicit much conflict. Here again, we see that the ethnic definition of the problem of inequality deflects from a class solution, even though the subordinate ethnic leadership often adopts radical-sounding rhetoric. Nevertheless, class differences are not irrelevent, for they aggravate ethnic conflicts.

3. Both classes and ethnies vary greatly in their degree of openness and rigidity, with complex mutual repercussions on each other. Broadly, where class groups are rigid and where class mobility is difficult, classes tend to acquire properties of ethnies. Conversely, where ethnic boundaries are fluid and permeable, ethnies tend to acquire the properties of classes.

Examples of rigid classes are "estates" (*Stände* in German), semihereditary

occupational strata characteristic of pre-19th century Europe, in which social classes became much more than simply interest groups. Privileges of
rank, status, wealth and occupational skills were passed on hereditarily at
all levels of society: the nobleman passed on his title and lands to his sons;
the merchant willed his wealth likewise; the craftsman apprenticed his sons
and nephews, and so on. Therefore, each social class came, over time, to
acquire many of the attributes of an ethny, with its own distinct subculture,
style of dress, dialect, institutions and so on.

An even more extreme case of status rigidity is caste, as we have seen in
Chapter 8. Both castes and estates are thus "mixed" types of groups, sharing
some of the properties of classes (notably functional interdependence in the
system of production and complementarity in the division of labor) and
some of ethnies (including, most importantly, a strong tendency to be endogamous). The existence of such mixed types does not invalidate, of course,
the analytical distinction between class and ethny. It merely shows that the
tendency for the two to be in an antithetical relationship is not absolute.
Rigid classes tend to become like ethnies.

The reverse is also true. If ethnies are stratified but if the dominant group
does not resist acculturation and assimilation of members of subordinate
ethnic groups, then it can be expected that members of the subordinate
ethnies will seek assimilation into the dominant one as a means of upward
class mobility. We have seen examples of it in the assimilation of European
immigrants in the United States, the Gallicization of the Flemings in Belgium, the Anglicization of Franco-Canadians outside of Québec and the
Mestizoization of Andean Indians in Peru. To the extent that this process
of ethnic assimilation of the upwardly mobile has taken place over several
generations, those members of the subordinate ethnic groups who have not
assimilated find themselves in an *increasingly* subordinate and marginal
position in both the class and the ethnic structure.

The Andean Indian case is an extreme one: nearly all Indians are peasants,
and nearly all peasants are Indians. The conquered ethny had become first
decapitated of much of its ruling class by the Spanish conquest and then
systematically deprived by interbreeding, acculturation and assimilation
over 20-odd generations of its more enterprising, successful and upwardly
mobile elements. It is little wonder then, that those who today still remain
Indian constitute, in fact, the bottom class of a highly stratified society by
almost any objective correlate of class status one chooses to adopt: illiteracy,
infant mortality, morbidity, life expectancy, per capita income or whatever.

Some scholars have termed such groups "eth-classes" (Gordon, 1964) or
"ethnic classes" [e.g. Rex and Tomlinson (1979) in their study of colored
immigrants in Britain]. Others, stressing the tendency for ethnically or racially differentiated groups in industrial societies to occupy specialized
niches in the division of labor, have spoken of a cultural division of labor
(Hechter, 1971, 1975, 1976, 1978). Others yet have explored the important
consequences of the existence of a "split labor market" by ethnicity or race
on intergroup relations (Bonacich, 1972). All these studies point to the
complicated relationship between class and ethnicity and the analytical

irreducibility of one to the other, much as some would like to try to be class reductionists (e.g. Rex and Tomlinson, 1979). Indeed, Max Weber's classical distinction between a class and a status group (*Stand*) was based on the same distinctions we have drawn here, except that he did not clearly distinguish the ethny from the status group (Weber, 1968). Instead, he tended to identify the two.

CLASS AND ETHNIC MOBILITY

If we dichotomize the degree to which people move in and out of class and/or ethnic groups into "high" and "low," we can schematize the relationship between the two types of mobility as in Schema I. The schema yields four logical combinations, which we have labeled A, B, C and D, but only three of which are found in practice. Cell B is empty for reasons that, by now, are fairly obvious. Given the inertia to remain in one's ethny unless there are powerful incentives to change, it follows that, in a system which offers little opportunity to improve one's *class* position, such incentives to change one's ethnicity are lacking. Even attempts at forced acculturation and assimilation are relatively unsuccessful if ethnic change is not supported by a system of positive rewards (such as access to better jobs, positions of power, high-status spouses and so on).

Type A societies—those characterized by low mobility in terms of both class and ethnic status—tend to be rigidly and highly stratified by both class and ethnicity. That is, they tend to be societies with a high degree of cultural division of labor in which ethnies occupy specialized niches in the economic system. Since class position and ethnicity tend to be closely associated, there is a trend toward occupational roles being hereditary or

SCHEMA I A classification of societies by their class and ethnic mobility.

Class mobility	Ethnic Mobility	
	Low	High
Low	Type A India Ottoman Empire Medieval Spain Tuzi Kingdom of Rwanda	Type B No clear cases
High	Type C Nigeria Belgium Switzerland	Type D Peru Guatemala Mexico

semihereditary. If, say, Jews in the Ottoman Empire tended to be jewelers and money-lenders because Muslims were religiously excluded from these occupations, and if Jews had few other occupational outlets, then, obviously, these specialized occupations would become semihereditary in Jewish families.

By contrast, Type D societies, which have relatively high rates of both class and ethnic mobility, show much more dynamism. Yet, as in Type A societies, the ethnic groups are sharply stratified and specialized, and class status correlates highly with ethnic membership. Type D societies are thus dynamic cases of the ethnic division of labor, in which upward class mobility and change of occupation is possible, but only at the cost of leaving the subordinate ethnies and becoming absorbed into the dominant group. The clearest examples of such societies are in those Latin American countries where the peasantry is heavily Indian and where Indians are nearly all peasants. Indians thus constitute the bottom of a class system dominated by the group (variously called *mestizos, ladinos* or "whites") that, over the centuries, adopted the Spanish language and culture and, at the time of political independence from Spain in the 1810s, assumed power and became the "mainstream" of the new "national" societies.

In Type D societies, the possibility to leave the land and enter nonpeasant occupations is relatively attractive, since the rewards for doing so are often substantial; but this can only be done by migration, generally to urban areas that are mestizo-dominated, and by leaving the cultural and social matrix of the local Indian peasant communities. Eventually this double process of social and geographical mobility leads to a change of ethnicity as well. Even in countries like Guatemala where ethnic boundaries are supposedly rigid and castelike (Tumin, 1952), an analysis of changes in ethnic composition between population censuses clearly shows a continuous process of ladinoization of the Indian population (van den Berghe, 1968).

The classic form of Type D societies is that of a multiplicity of fragmented, atomized, localized but internally unstratified peasant groups that are ethnically distinct from the culturally dominant group. The latter, often a majority of the total population, is much more *culturally* homogeneous but is itself highly internally stratified by social class. Indian peasants are thus a fragmented "ethnic class" at the bottom of a double hierarchy of class and ethnicity. They are dominated, both culturally and in politicoeconomic terms, by a class-stratified "national" mestizo society, the upper class of which rules the society (and traditionally owned much of the land cultivated by the Indian peasants).

Another interesting feature of Type D societies is their brand of paternalism in which extensive networks of patron–client relationships cut across both ethnic and class lines. In Latin America, this takes the form of *compadrazgo*, a ritual tie uniting the biological and godparents of a child and the child himself (*ahijado*) in a life-long set of mutual obligations. One generally seeks a class equal or a superior (but almost never a social inferior) to become a godparent of one's child. Thus, most Indians seek out powerful mestizos to become godparents (*padrino, madrina*) of their children, thereby consolidating a close but unequal relationship across both an ethnic and a class line.

Such ties almost invariably existed, for example, between *hacendados* and their Indian serfs. This paternalism obviously had the effect of perpetuating a quasifeudal relationship and undermining both class and ethnic solidarity among the Indian peasantry. The only tangible way of improving one's lot was to seek the protection and favor of one member of the oppressor class by maintaining a special, personal, privileged relationship with him. Class and ethnic domination reinforced one another as both class and ethnic solidarity was undercut by these particularistic ties of *compadrazgo* across class and ethnic lines.

Type C societies—those characterized by a high degree of class mobility but considerable ethnic stability—are markedly different from both Types A and D. This combination of ethnic stability and class mobility implies that one can change class status without altering one's ethnicity, and, therefore, that each ethny is internally stratified into social classes. To the extent that each ethny has its own class system, the ethnies themselves are less clearly stratified in relation to each other. Indeed, in some cases, the ethnic groups are in substantially the same class position, and one finds a nearly total absence of a cultural division of labor. Switzerland and contemporary Belgium are cases in point.

Sometimes, there are ethnic inequalities as well as class inequalities in Type C societies, but the overlap between the two is only partial. Nigeria is an example. Southern Nigerians, who are largely Christians, are, for a number of reasons traceable to the colonial period, greatly overrepresented in the upper echelons of the "modern" sector, have a much higher literacy rate, have far greater percentages of people with Western-style education and a knowledge of English and so on—compared to Northern Nigerians, who are mostly Muslims. Yet, despite these regional differences in levels of development and "modernization," one cannot rank-order Nigerian ethnic groups in a consensual hierarchy of status. Each ethny feels superior to the others, and each has its internal class distinctions and its elite that represents it in "national" politics.

Since, in Type C societies, social class mobility is possible without changing one's ethny, and since the ethnies themselves are often not clearly stratified, the incentives to assimilate are minimal. There is no point in severing one's ethnic ties, unless this is the main (or, indeed, the only) way of improving one's position. These conditions do not prevail in Type C societies, and this absence of incentives to assimilate largely accounts for the persistence of ethnic differences in these countries. It also accounts for the relative absence in Type C societies of patron–client ties *across* ethnic lines. Indeed, there is a striking contrast between Type C and Type D societies in the operation of networks of patronage and clientelism. In Type C societies, patron–client ties are typically *intraethnic*. The elite distribute favors and resources to ethnic clients, thereby reinforcing ethnic and familistic ties and heightening the salience of ethnicity, at the expense of class, in the political game.

An overwhelming difference between African countries (most of which tend to be of the C Type) and Latin American countries (mostly D Type) is in the relative salience of class and ethnicity. In Africa, class conflicts tend to be muted, while ethnic conflicts are seldom far below the surface. Conversely, in Latin America, ethnic conflicts are almost completely defused through the mechanisms I have just discussed, and class conflicts, especially within the culturally dominant mestizo group, are paramount. This again points to the antithetical nature of class and ethnicity as modes of social organization. Generally, but not necessarily, a stress in one factor is accompanied by a deemphasis in the other. At least, this seems to be the case in terms of consciousness and solidarity. As principles of *domination*, class and ethnicity often reinforce each other, as we have seen in the Latin American societies of Type D.

CONCLUSIONS

Naturally, these societal types are but crude constructs to put some order into an extremely complex reality and attempt some generalizations on the interplay of class and ethnicity. At this level of analysis, we have used general and abstract concepts describing processes at the collective level. This is convenient as a short-hand device to describe a multiplicity of individual actions and decisions. In the last analysis, however, it is people who modify their behavior in accordance with their individual interests. Therefore, processes of ethnic change and persistence must be understood in terms of a model of individual benefit-maximizing behavior. To this model, we now turn in the last chapter.

SUGGESTED READINGS

The relationship between ethnicity and class has occupied a central place in the literature, from the classics by Warner (1941), Myrdal (1944) and Cox (1948), to more recent works by Bonacich (1972), Hechter (1975), Leo Kuper (1965, 1974), Rex and Tomlinson (1979), M. G. Smith (1965a) and W. J. Wilson (1973, 1978). Wilson's latest book (1978) on the declining significance of race and the increasing importance of class for American blacks has been especially controversial.

THE DYNAMICS OF ETHNICITY

Ethnic sentiments, as I suggested, have evolved as an extension of nepotism, the ethny being conceived as an extended kin group sharing common biological descent. Yet, clearly, ethnicity is not a given nor a constant. It waxes and wanes in response to environmental conditions. Groups coalesce and split, form political coalitions and play the ethnic game in a wide variety of ways. Some groups assimilate and lose their identity; others remain separate even under seemingly adverse conditions. Can one make any sense of all this diversity? If ethnicity is primordial and rooted in the biology of nepotism, how can it be so varied and rapidly changing in its manifestations?

There is, of course, no contradiction between a trait having a genetic basis and its being highly modifiable under a range of environmental conditions. A phenotype is always the product of interaction between genotype and environment. Behavioral lability is especially to be expected in an intelligent, self-conscious organism like *Homo sapiens*, which can manipulate situations to its own, conscious ends. Most aspects of human behavior are several steps removed from their genetic underpinnings, and the observable behavior is almost always mediated by a multiplicity of environmental conditions. Ethnicity is no exception. Unless our biological–ecological model can account for variations in expressions of ethnic behavior as well as regularities, it is seriously limited. In this last chapter, I cannot hope to do more than suggest the elements of an answer, along the lines already hinted at previously, especially in Chapter 10.

Sociality is always problematic for any organism. Organisms of the same species are always direct competitors for each other, since they have adapted to the same set of environmental conditions and make substantially the same demands on their habitat. Therefore, mere aggregation exacerbates competition; unless compensated for by countervailing advantages, animals will seek to disperse. Any form of sociality, i.e. of cooperative behavior, between animals must, then, be shown to be fitness-enhancing. Unless animals can increase their fitness by cooperating, there is no reason for them to stick together—and every reason to disperse. This is as true for humans as for other organisms. At least, there is no reason to presume otherwise.

Like nearly all other higher primates (with the exception of the relatively solitary orang-utan), man is a highly social animal, because his survival depends on a minimum support group of at least 20 or 30 individuals, under the conditions of hunting-and-gathering under which he evolved. It is this basic cooperating, interbreeding support group of related individuals that constitutes the template for the ethny. The ethny is thus the primordial social group, the extended kin group, selected through millions of years to maximize the individual inclusive fitness of its members through the operation of nepotism.

So long as our whole species consisted of such microethnies of hunters and gatherers, problems of ethnic change were relatively straightforward. Small, nomadic groups competed and occasionally fought with each other, but their technology made the conquest of other groups unprofitable and their extermination unlikely. Population fluctuated, of course, with the vagaries of the environment, so some ethnies became extinct while others grew in size. But demographic success was limited by resources and technology. Bands split and merged, as can be seen among contemporary hunters and gatherers such as the San of the Kalahari (Lee and De Vore, 1976). Few of these ethnies were completely self-contained populations. Individuals and small family groups migrated between bands and brought fresh blood into the gene pool. At any given time, however, the band formed a fairly well defined group of people, linked by kinship and marriage.

Boundaries and boundary-maintenance between human bands of hunters and gatherers were, in short, not much different from what they are in other species of gregarious primates and social carnivores such as hyenas and African hunting dogs, though, of course, the specific mechanisms (aggression, scent-marking, acceptance rituals and so on) used to maintain, patrol and defend boundaries are species-specific.

STRATIFICATION AND ETHNIC CHANGE

With the development of agriculture, "the plot thickened," for now ethnies became much larger, much more powerfully organized and increasingly capable of either conquering or exterminating each other. Ethnic relations now had an increasing potential for being unequal, one group parasitizing another. This was also the stage at which slavery made its appearance. As we have seen in Chapter 6, slavery is one of the surest ways in which individuals transfer ethnic affiliation and is thus a key institution in understanding ethnic relations. The slave's incentives to acculturate and to become assimilated into the society of the master are, of course, great. This calculus of individual gain explains the prevalence of acculturation and assimilation in slave regimes. This is especially true for female slaves who have the option to breed with their masters (indeed, who often do *not* have the option *not* to breed) and thus to enter their masters' networks of kin selection through their children.

When ethnic groups conquer each other *as groups* (as distinguished from the individual capture of slaves), acculturation and assimilation are less likely than under slavery because the conquered groups typically retain a territorial basis where they can maintain solidary ties. The outcome of conquest situations varies widely. Sometimes it is the conquerors who become assimilated by the conquered; this often happens where the conquerors are a small nomadic minority who dominate settled agriculturalists by the force of arms and who then engage in extensive polygamy with conquered women. Examples are the Mongols in China, the Fulani in the Hausa states of Northern Nigeria and the Tuzi in the Central African kingdoms of Rwanda and Burundi.

More often, it is the conqueror who assimilates the conquered. This can happen even when the conqueror is a small minority (as the Spaniards were in Mexico and Peru, for instance), provided that numerical disadvantage is made up by a superior technology that confers signal advantages to the conquered who assimilate. Literacy, firearms and more efficient uses of energy introduced by the Spaniards in the Americas, for example, gave Indians obvious incentives to learn Spanish ways, including the Spanish language—the key to literacy and access to power.

Where the conqueror is sedentary and the conquered peoples are thinly settled nomads, the outcome is nearly always the ethnic extinction or near-extinction of the nomads. This is less true of pastoralists (who have access to greater and more marketable resources, can sustain larger population densities and are often well organized for warfare) than of hunters and gatherers or incipient horticulturalists. Basically, however, small, stateless ethnies, with the triple disadvantage of small numbers, primitive technology and decentralized political organization, have little chance of ethnic survival in their encounters with conquerors. Either they are physically wiped out by disease or genocide, or their social organization is shattered by conquest and individuals loose their ethnic identity, drifting on the margin of the conquering society.

Their fate is all the more tragic because they have few skills or goods valuable to the conqueror, and therefore are not worth the bother to exploit. Since, however, their primitive technology requires vast expanses of territory to sustain their traditional mode of existence, they are "in the way" of the conquerors, occupying land that can be more intensively exploited with more complex technology. Therefore, the natives get displaced; often this is not followed by assimilation because they have so little of value to offer their conquerors. The fate of Amazonian and many North American Indians, Australian aborigines and the San and Xhoi-Xhoi peoples of Southern Africa are examples of the tragic fate of such groups. Alcoholism, frequently introduced by the conqueror, is often a symptom of this displacement, followed by aimless wandering on the margin of the dominant society. The sociopathology of such groups after conquest is remarkably similar despite great cultural differences between them.

Ethnic hierarchy between conqueror and conquered creates a complex dynamic of ethnic change. The outcome is best understood as the product of a multiplicity of individual strategies of fitness maximization, or, if one rejects the biological viewpoint presented here, as the result of individual cost/benefit decisions. On the one hand, membership in one's own group offers one access to resources and social advantages not readily relinquished. To the extent that the conquered group remains territorially intact (i.e. is not displaced or scattered), is socially cohesive and is allowed cultural and linguistic autonomy, the benefits of staying in an even low-status group continue to be considerable—assimilation a less desirable option. (Besides, assimilation may be resisted by the conqueror and thus not be an option at all.)

Conversely, where the conquered group is spatially scattered with no access to its resources and subjected to socially disruptive policies, membership in it has few benefits; assimilation to the dominant group becomes correspondingly attractive. Inertia tends to favor the retention of ethnic identity, but if the dominant group exerts strong pressures toward acculturation and assimilation or, at least, provides material incentives to assimilate, this inertia can be and often is overcome.

ETHNIC CHANGE: AN INDIVIDUAL CHOICE MODEL

Any close look at the processes of ethnic change (Aguirre Beltrán, 1957, 1967; Barth, 1969; Monica Hunter, 1936; Philip Mayer, 1961), clearly shows that the individual choice model presented here is the appropriate one. These processes take place not at an abstract collective level, but as the result of individuals making more or less conscious decisions dictated by their perceptions of their self-interest. Examples are legion. Many Africans during colonialism deliberately converted to Christianity because it gave them access to literacy and a type of schooling that opened avenues of upward mobility and a regular salary. In the Belgian Congo, for instance, many young men cynically entered seminaries without the slightest intention of becoming priests, but simply because seminaries offered the best available education.

In numerous situations, individuals are found consciously to manipulate ethnic boundaries to their advantage. The way they dress, talk and behave shifts abruptly and predictably depending on the context. Many people literally "commute" culturally between ethnies, presenting an assimilated front in one situation, but being "traditional" in another (Colby and van den Berghe, 1969; Philip Mayer, 1961).

Sometimes this strategy is subtle and requires the precise opposite of assimilation. If the dominant group rewards "traditional" behavior, this calls for "playing the native." One of my Peruvian informants, for instance, generally dressed in Western clothes in his village, but whenever he was coming to the mestizo-dominated city of Cuzco (usually to deal with some government official, lawyer or other high-status mestizo) he always dressed in full, traditional, homespun clothing (van den Berghe and Primov, 1977). In part, this was his way of dressing up: his everyday work clothes were cheap, machine-made cottons, while his homespun clothes were his best ones, reserved for festive and ceremonial occasions. However, when I asked him why he always dressed as an Indian when he came to town, he responded by saying that he got more respectful attention in government offices that way. He was thus deliberately playing "noble savage" to a reformist mestizo government that extolled the merits of Indian culture.

Numerous other examples of the manipulation of ethnic identity for gain have been generated by the policy of "affirmative action" in the United States. There too, when the dominant group rewarded ethnic divergence, the latter was immediately forthcoming. All kinds of people suddenly rediscovered American Indian roots, or capitalized on their Spanish surname or started "playing the nigger" by affecting a lower-class ghetto accent. For example, Hansen (1979) documented in detail this process of playing up and manipulating ethnicity among American Indians in Seattle.

A different context in which ethnicity is consciously manipulated for individual gain is in the fierce competition for access to positions of power and hence to the public purse with its vast potential for graft, corruption and embezzlement, which is evident in many "new nations" of the Third World. In the African context, Andreski (1968) has aptly called the new multiethnic ruling class of these countries "kleptocracies," and African authors, like the Nigerian novelist Chinua Achebe (1959, 1966), have described in vivid detail how ethnic patronage and nepotism are not only rampant but the expected and ethical mode of operation within a traditional network of patron–client ties.

In my study of a Nigerian university, ethnic politics was also a highly conscious game played by individuals for personal gain (van den Berghe, 1973a). Networks of ethnic patronage controlled by key academic and administrative personnel competed with each other over the spoils of the university's resources and perquisites. Every appointment unleashed a fierce competitive struggle between ethnic constituencies, in which the object of the game was to manipulate and pervert to one's advantage the ostensibly universalistic rules and procedures by which the university was supposedly run.

To make my point, I have deliberately chosen especially blatant examples of conscious manipulation of ethnicity for personal gain. This is not to say that ethnic politics are always a thoroughly conscious and cynical game, or that people do not often have deep ethnic attachments that they take seriously. Indeed, I have repeatedly emphasized the depth of primordial ethnic attachments, suggesting a biological basis for its nonrationality. Rather, the model of individual, fitness-maximizing choice is closely analogous, not to say homologous, to that of classical microeconomics. Economists know that buyers and sellers do not always act rationally and do not always possess the necessary information to make the right decisions. Their model predicts outcomes based on the assumption that actors will behave, consciously or not, *as if* they were maximizing benefits and minimizing costs. No other competing model yields a better description of actual behavior.

There is no incompatibility between, on the one hand, blind adherence to one's ethnic group, right or wrong, and, on the other hand, the calculating manipulation of ethnicity and the weighting of ethnicity against other types of sociality, for individual gain. Indeed, nepotism itself is a fitness-maximizing game, albeit often an unconscious one. There are circumstances under which the benefits to be derived from nepotism are superseded by other forms of sociality. Because humans have a considerable capacity for making conscious cost/benefit calculations, ethnicity can be rationally manipulated or indeed superseded by other considerations.

The crucial issue, therefore, is not so much rationality or consciousness, which are merely mechanisms by which humans speedily adapt to rapidly changing environments. Rather, the fundamental postulate of the model is that organisms, consciously or not, tend to behave in individually "selfish" ways, i.e. in fitness-maximizing ways. For humans, ethnicity is not the only relevant consideration. Therefore, ethnicity can only be understood in relation to other social formations, and individual choices (again, more or less conscious and rational) are the outcome of these competing pressures.

This model of ethnicity has the great advantage of resolving the apparent contradiction, evident in much of the literature on the subject, between the "primordialist" and the "instrumentalist" views. Ethnicity is *both* deeply ingrained because it is rooted in the biology of nepotism *and* subject to rapid fluctuations in response to environmental changes. For example, a common phenomenon is the merging of hitherto distinct but related microethnies into larger entities. This typically takes place with an upward shift in the scale of the polity. When a bigger state suddenly comes into existence, the relevance of strictly localized affiliations becomes gradually overshadowed by larger-scale politics. Small, local groups, suddenly thrown into contact with more distant and unrelated peoples, discover their similarities and coalesce into larger groups. In turn, this formation of larger ethnies gives people more weight in playing ethnic politics at the higher level.

This process, which social scientists have sometimes called "supertribalization" in Africa (van den Berghe, 1971a), has happened repeatedly in colonial situations—for example among the Luhya of Kenya and the Ibo and Yoruba of Nigeria. Often, a seemingly trivial exogenous event, like the translation of the Bible by a foreign mission society, is the catalyst that brings about ethnic coalescence. The one local dialect chosen by the mission then becomes the standardized written tongue of an entire region, and a new superethny gradually gains a higher level of ethnic consciousness. The process is only understandable, however, within the context of competition of collectivities and ultimately individuals for scarce resources.

ETHNICITY AND CLASS AGAIN

As we saw in Chapter 11, much ethnic change, and in particular the problem of the demise or persistence of ethnicity, must be understood in terms of the interplay between class and ethnicity. These two alternative and competing principles of sociality make different claims on individuals, and have different "pay-offs" in dissimilar sets of circumstances. In complex, stratified, and multiethnic societies, rates of assimilation are largely explainable by the relative balance of costs and benefits of affiliating on a class versus an ethnic basis, or of affiliating to one ethny or another if that option exists.

Generally, people resist assimilation, unless the benefits are overwhelming. One's ethnic affiliation is not lightly shed. The deep emotional attachment to one's ethny is the outcome of a multiplicity of previous beneficial associations with one's kinfolk, in-laws and other intimates. These relationships are not easily replaced. They are not only intimate and based on a trust born out of long-standing experience; they are also diffuse—that is, they extend over the whole range of one's life and activities. Ethnic ties, in short, constitute an all-encompassing matrix of intimate, affective relationships, conferring the multiple benefits of both kin selection and reciprocity. An ethny is a social womb, largely coterminous with one's closest, longest-lasting and most functionally significant ties.

By contrast, class ties are segmental. They affect only specific aspects of our life, although admittedly the essential one of our material sustenance. Furthermore, class ties, being openly utilitarian, do not commit one emotionally as do ethnic ties. Business partners or professional colleagues may occasionally become intimate friends or in-laws, but they are not normally expected to become intimates. One can resign from a trade union or a professional association in a way in which one cannot resign from a family, an ethny or a caste. In the first case, life goes on largely unchanged; in the latter, one "starts a new life."

The importance of ethnic ties can become especially crucial in the impersonal, anomic environment of a large city, where an ethnic group can be the main and only mediating institution (outside the nuclear family) between the isolated individual and a cold, hostile urban jungle. There is thus nothing paradoxical or problematic about the survival of ethnic collectivities in an urban environment. Assimilation is not a simple function of urbanization, "modernization," "Westernization" or any of these glib concepts that were so popular in the social sciences of the 1950s and 1960s.

Rather, the tendency to assimilate is the product of a set of countervailing costs and benefits for individuals behaving in certain ways. Indeed assimilation is itself a gross label that often provides a poor description of what individuals do. Typically, people do not consciously decide to assimilate or to resist assimilation. They simply take a multitude of small daily decisions to behave in certain ways in certain situations and differently in others, according to their perceptions of what is most appropriate in each case. "Appropriate" means in most cases doing what is profitable, what is agreeable to others on whom one depends, what is likely to produce the desired ends. In short, "appropriate" means "benefit-maximizing."

The language-learning behavior of young children is interesting in this respect. It has been the distressing experience of millions of immigrant parents that, as soon as their children enter school in the host country, the children begin to resist speaking their mother tongue—even at home. Children, of course, quickly discover that their home language is a restricted medium that is not useable in most situations outside the home. When they discover that their parents are bilingual, they conclude—rightly for their purposes—that the home language is completely redundant. They thus start using the language of the host country even at home, unless expressly forbidden or punished for doing so.

If, in addition to the greater use of the host country language, that language is more prestigeful, then the process of linguistic acculturation is further accelerated. Indeed, this is generally the case in many frontier-type societies with massive immigration. Mastery of the new language entails success in school, at work and in "the world." Mastery in the home language brings few rewards by comparison: the smiling approval of a grandmother is but slender counterweight to the powerful forces of assimilation. The home language may even be stigmatized or ridiculed in the larger society, creating a sense of inferiority and self-hatred in the immigrant child, who often compensates through hyperconformity with dominant norms. Ethnic and dialect jokes, for instance, can be powerful stimulants for acculturation and assimilation.

However, if the home language of the child is more prestigeful than the native language of the larger society, parents experience little difficulty in maintaining its use. Then their children become either fluently bilingual (e.g. the mestizos of Andean Peru) or monolingual in the minority home language, as in most colonial situations. This shows that children must be motivated to learn and use a language, and that their linguistic behavior is readily predictable from the structure of rewards and punishments activated by speaking one language as distinct from another.

Seldom do people learn a language as a consequence of a deliberate decision to assimilate. Assimilation is merely the long-range outcome of a long series of minute day-to-day decisions to do certain things and shun others. There is no overall mechanistic tendency to assimilate or not to assimilate. Indeed, there is not even always a necessity to do one or the other. Stable bilingualism or biculturalism, though it requires some effort and entails some strains, can be a viable option too. For instance, there are many areas like Germany, Switzerland, the Basque part of Spain, the Peruvian Andes and others, where most inhabitants are fluent in either two languages or two dialects of the same language (a local one and a "high" one of wider use). People shift back and forth between the two, a phenomenon known among sociolinguists as "diglossia"; but they do not do so at random. They clearly differentiate the situations where they speak one as distinguished from the other. Which is used is situationally determined according to complex and subtle, but clearly nonrandom criteria, which are predictable because they are benefit-maximizing to the language user. This process of manipulating language use for personal gain is at least partly conscious, as shown by the fact that people can often produce a reasonable rationale when asked why they speak one language as opposed to another: ease of communication, formality or informality of relationship, the marking of social distance, establishing a claim to superior status and so on.

With other aspects of culture, as with language, people modify their behavior more or less consciously in response to pressures and counterpressures. Religion, for instance, might be thought to be relatively resistant to pressures to assimilate, since it is based presumably on deeply ingrained convictions. There are, of course, plenty of cases of groups that obdurately refuse to change their religion and, indeed, make religion the core of their ethnic identity and the principal rallying ground for resisting pressures to assimilate. But there are also numerous instances of opportunistic conversion. The general tendency is for people to convert from low-status to high-status religions, as the spectacular progress of both Islam and Christianity in Africa clearly shows. Religious conversion is frequently used as an avenue of upward mobility.

People, then, tend not to assimilate, unless there are advantages to doing so. The more general set of conditions making for assimilation (and acculturation) is one where ethnic groups are clearly hierarchized *and* overlap territorially. The more sharply differentiated the "cultural division of labor" (Hechter, 1976, 1978), the more social class mobility is necessarily linked with a change of ethnic identity. An extreme example would be the Peruvian Andean situation: to become anything but a peasant, an Indian must leave his village and migrate to an urban settlement; but, to survive in town, he gradually learns Spanish, adopts mestizo ways, and ceases to be Indian. Success (usually small-scale entrepreneurial success in a small shop, or wage-employment as a servant, day laborer or small employee) is synonymous with "deindianization."

Overlapping ethnic territories both reduce ethnic cohesiveness and promote relations across ethnic lines. This is especially true in an urban setting where population density is high, and where interaction is both frequent and impersonal. Under such conditions, mere convenience favors the use of the dominant language as the *lingua franca*, thus heightening the incentives to assimilate. This explains why cities are ideal melting pots. Stable multilingualism seldom survives long in a city. Generally, one language achieves ascendancy—at least as a *lingua franca* in the public domain. Once a language achieves that status, its higher prestige and utility further contribute to its spread.

The progress of French in the traditionally Flemish city of Brussels is a case in point. English was in the process of supplanting French in Montréal until the passage of legislation (Laws 22 and 101) aimed at reversing the trend, making Montréal monolingual in French. Bilingualism is simply not a workable alternative in either case. The sheer cost of having to establish which language is most appropriate in fleeting encounters with strangers is too high. A convention to use primarily one language in public is too convenient not to be adopted, and once adopted, the other languages are gradually displaced. African cities are undergoing the same process. Thus, Swahili has become the *lingua franca* of multilingual Nairobi and Dar-es-Salaam, gradually displacing even the formerly dominant English, not to mention the other African languages. In Dakar, Wolof is doing the same to French, Serer and other languages.

The same model of acculturation and assimilation as the product of a multiplicity of selfishly motivated individual decisions also helps to explain what aspects of culture change fastest and most slowly. For example, it has long been noted that technology "diffuses" quickly and easily, presumably because of the obvious advantages which it confers, but also, it has been argued, because it can be easily divorced from other "deeper" aspects of culture. Yet, we have seen how language and religion, presumably "deep" aspects of culture learned in infancy, can also change quickly if the incentives to do so are strong enough.

Cookery, however, is notoriously resistant to acculturation. Often the last aspect of their culture that immigrant groups retain, long after they have lost use of their language, is distinctive cooking and foods. It can be argued that taste for foods is deeply ingrained, being acquired early in life. But there is much more to food than taste. As a food-sharing animal, humans ritualize food consumption to the extent that some scholars claim to be able to reconstruct a culture and its relationship to the natural world from table manners (Lévi-Strauss, 1979). There is no question, however, that cuisine can be retained as an ethnic marker long after other aspects of culture have been cast off. Why is there so little pressure to assimilate culinarily? Precisely because food-sharing is primarily a *family* ritual, reinforcing ties of nepotism and thus, by extension, a good marker of ethnicity.

It should be noted here that the retention of ethnic cuisine is largely a *ceremonial* retention that does not interfere with the enjoyment of other foods, including the enjoyment of other groups' ethnic foods—or some commercialized version thereof. Italian-Americans probably do not patronize fast-food chains and Chinese restaurants any less than other Americans, but family reunions feature *pasta* and *chianti*. Interestingly, the Yankee ritual meal par excellence, Thanksgiving Dinner, has become the ritual meal of the American superethny. All the immigrant groups symbolize their new ethnicity by feasting on foods originally alien to *all* of them!

It may seem frivolous to conclude a book about ethnicity on a culinary note, but much of what social scientists have long treated as frivolous is in fact essential to our nature. The old adage that we are what we eat is only a partial truth. It stresses the environmental side of our existence. We are also unique combinations of DNA molecules programmed to behave beneficently toward those in whom we recognize ourselves. Ethnicity, I suggested, represents a wide circle of recognition of kinship. As a food-sharing animal that ritualizes communal eating among kin, eating together and eating the same things are our very human way of becoming more like one another. They are also our uniquely human way of blending, quite literally, nature and nurture.

That, of course, is precisely what I tried to do in this book. The propensity to favor kin and fellow ethnics is deeply rooted in our genes, but our genetic programs are highly flexible, and our specific behaviors are adaptive responses to a wide set of environmental circumstances. Ethnicity is *both* primordial and situational. Any alternative view of it is, I firmly believe, one-sided.

SUGGESTED READINGS

Among the more ambitious analytical attempts to deal with the topic of this chapter have been the works of Blalock (1967), Blalock and Wilken (1979), Blau (1979), Francis (1976) and Schermerhorn (1970).

BIBLIOGRAPHY

Achebe, Chinua
  1959   *Things Fall Apart.* New York: McDowell.
  1966   *A Man of the People.* New York: Day.

Adam, Heribert
  1971   *Modernizing Racial Domination.* Berkeley: University of Califor-
          nia Press.
  1979   Three perspectives on the future of South Africa, *International
          Journal of Comparative Sociology* 20 (1–2): 122–136.

Adam, Heribert, and Hermann Giliomee
  1979   *Ethnic Power Mobilized.* New Haven: Yale University Press.

Adorno, T. W., et al.
  1950   *The Authoritarian Personality.* New York: Harper.

Aguirre Beltrán, Gonzalo
  1946   *La Población Negra de México, 1519–1810.* México: Ediciones
          Fuente Cultural.
  1957   *El Processo de Aculturación.* México: Universidad Nacional
          Autónoma de México.
  1967   *Regiones de Refugio.* México: Instituto Indigenista Interamericano.
  1979   *Regions of Refuge.* Washington DC: Society for Applied Anthro-
          pology, Monograph 12.

Allport, Gordon W.
  1954   *The Nature of Prejudice.* Cambridge, MA: Addison-Wesley.

Altmann, S. A.
  1962   Social behavior of anthropoid primates, in E. L. Bliss (ed.) *Roots
          of Behavior.* New York: Harper and Row, pp. 277–285.

Andreski, Stanislav
  1968   *The African Predicament.* London: Joseph.

Angle, Paul M., ed.
  1958   Treated Equal? The Complete Lincoln–Douglas Debates of 1858.
         Chicago: University of Chicago Press.

Aptheker, Herbert
  1943   American Negro Slave Revolts. New York: International Publish-
         ers.

Bagley, Christopher
  1972   Racialism and pluralism, Race 13 (3): 347–354.

Bainbridge, William
  1978   Satan's Power. Berkeley: University of California Press.

Balandier, Georges
  1963   Sociologie Actuelle de l'Afrique Noire. Paris: Presses Universi-
         taires de France.
  1970   The Sociology of Black Africa. New York: Praeger.

Banton, Michael
  1967   Race Relations. London: Tavistock.
  1973   Racial Minorities. London: Fontana.
  1977   The Idea of Race. London: Tavistock.

Barash, David
  1977   Sociobiology and Behavior. New York: Elsevier.

Barron, Milton, L., ed.
  1957   American Minorities. New York: Knopf.
  1967   Minorities in a Changing World. New York: Knopf.

Barry, Brian
  1975   Political accommodation and consociational democracy, British
         Journal of Political Science 5 (4): 477–505.

Barth, E. A. T., and D. T. Noel
  1972   Conceptual frameworks for the analysis of race relations, Social
         Forces 50 (3): 333–348.

Barth, Fredrik
  1956   Ecologic relationships of ethnic groups in Swat, Northern Pakistan,
         American Anthropologist 58: 1079–1089.
  1959   Political Leadership Among the Swat Pathans. London: London
         School of Economics Monographs on Social Anthropology, No.
         19.

Barth, Fredrik, ed.
  1969   Ethnic Groups and Boundaries. Boston: Little Brown.

Barton, Josef J.
  1975   Peasants and Strangers. Cambridge, MA: Harvard University
         Press.

Bascom, William
  1969   The Yoruba of Southwestern Nigeria. New York: Holt, Rinehart
         and Winston.

Bash, Harry H.
  1979   Sociology, Race and Ethnicity. New York: Gordon and Breach.

Bastide, Roger
    1950   *Sociologie et Psychanalyse*. Paris: Presses Universitaires de France.
    1971   *African Civilisations in the New World*. London: C. Hurst.

Bell, Wendell, and W. E. Freeman, eds.
    1974   *Ethnicity and Nation-Building*. Beverly Hills: Sage Publications.

Bendix, Reinhard, and S. M. Lipset, eds.
    1966   *Class, Status and Power*. New York: The Free Press.

Benedict, Ruth
    1940   *Race, Science and Politics*. New York: Modern Age.

Bennett, John W.
    1976   *The Ecological Transition*. New York: Pergamon Press.

Bennett, John W., ed.
    1973   *The New Ethnicity*. St. Paul, MN: West Publishing Company.

Berndt, Ronald M.
    1962   *Excess and Restraint. Social Control Among a New Guinea Mountain People*. Chicago: The University of Chicago Press.

Berreman, Gerald D.
    1960   Caste in India and the United States, *American Journal of Sociology* 66: 120–127.
    1972   Race, caste and other invidious distinctions in social stratification, *Race* 13 (4): 385–414.

Béteille, André
    1971   Race, caste and ethnic identity, *International Social Science Journal* 23 (4): 519–535.

Béteille, André, ed.
    1969   *Social Inequality*. Baltimore: Penguin.

Bharati, Agehananda
    1972   *The Asians in East Africa*. Chicago: Nelson-Hall.

Binder, Leonard, ed.
    1966   *Politics in Lebanon*. New York: Wiley.

Blalock, Hubert M.
    1967   *Toward a Theory of Minority Group Relations*. New York: Wiley.

Blalock, Hubert M., and Paul H. Wilken
    1979   *Intergroup Processes, A Micro–Macro Perspective*. New York: The Free Press.

Blau, Peter M.
    1979   *Inequality and Heterogeneity*. New York: The Free Press.

Blauner, Robert
    1972   *Racial Oppression in America*. New York: Harper and Row.

Bloch, Marc
    1939–1940   *La Societé Féodale*. Paris: Michel.

Blumer, Herbert
    1965   Industrialization and race relations, in Guy Hunter (ed.), *Industrialization and Race Relations*. New York: Oxford University Press.

Boeke, J. H.
1953   *Economics and Economic Policy of Dual Societies.* New York: Institute of Pacific Relations.

Bonacich, Edna
1972   A theory of ethnic antagonism, the split labor market, *American Sociological Review* 37: 547–559.
1973   A theory of middleman minorities, *American Sociological Review* 38: 583–594.
1979   The political implications of a split labour market analysis of South African race relations, in P. L. van den Berghe (ed.), *The Liberal Dilemma in South Africa.* London: Croom, Helm.

Boulding, Kenneth
1978   *Ecodynamics, A New Theory of Social Evolution.* Beverly Hills: Sage Publications.

Bovill, E. W.
1958   *The Golden Trade of the Moors.* London: Oxford University Press.

Brass, Paul R.
1974   *Language, Religion and Politics in North India.* New York: Cambridge University Press.
1976   Ethnicity and nationality formation, *Ethnicity* 3 (3): 225–241.

Braudel, Fernand
1973   *Capitalism and Material Life, 1400–1800.* New York: Harper and Row.

Brazeau, Jacques, and Edouard Cloutier
1977   Interethnic relations and the language issue in contemporary Canada, in Milton J. Esman (ed.), *Ethnic Conflict in the Western World.* Ithaca, NY: Cornell University Press.

Brewer, Jeffrey D.
1978   Tourism, business and ethnic relations in a Mexican town, in Mario D. Zamora et al. (eds.), *Tourism and Behavior,* Williamsburg, VA: College of William and Mary.

Buchanan, Keith
1953   The northern region of Nigeria, *The Geographical Review* 43 (4): 451–473.

Buck, Peter
1962   *The Coming of the Maori.* Wellington, New Zealand: Whitcombe and Tombs.

Burkey, Richard M.
1978   *Ethnic and Racial Groups.* Menlo Park, CA: Cummings.

Burns, R. M., ed.
1971   *One Country or Two?* Montreal: McGill–Queen's University Press.

Campbell, Ernest, ed.
1972   *Racial Tensions and National Identity.* Nashville: Vanderbilt University Press.

Cash, W. J.
1941   *The Mind of the South.* New York: Vintage Books.

Cavalli-Sforza, L. L., and W. F. Bodmer
1971   The Genetics of Human Populations. San Francisco: Freeman.

Chagnon, Napoleon A.
1974   Studying the Yanomamö. New York: Holt, Rinehart and Winston.
1977   Yanomamö, The Fierce People. New York: Holt, Rinehart and Winston.

Chagnon, Napoleon A., and Paul E. Bugos
1979   Kin selection and conflict: An analysis of a Yanomamö ax fight, in Napoleon A. Chagnon and William Irons (eds.), Evolutionary Biology and Human Social Behavior. North Scituate, MA: Duxbury.

Chagnon, Napoleon A., and William Irons, eds.
1979   Evolutionary Biology and Human Social Behavior. North Scituate, MA: Duxbury Press.

Chance, Michael R. A.
1967   Attention structure as the basis of primate rank orders, Man 2 (4): 503–518.

Chance, Michael R. A., and C. J. Jolly
1970   Social Groups of Monkeys, Apes and Man. New York: Dutton.

Chirot, Daniel
1977   Social Change in the Twentieth Century. New York: Harcourt, Brace, Jovanovich.

Chopard, Théo
1963   Switzerland, Present and Future. Bern: New Helvetic Society.

Cipolla, Carlo M.
1965   Guns, Sails and Empires. New York: Minerva.

Clough, Shepard
1930   A History of the Flemish Movement in Belgium: A Study in Nationalism. New York: Farrar and Rinehart.

Cohen, Abner, ed.
1974   Urban Ethnicity. London: Tavistock.

Cohen, David W., and Jack P. Greene, eds.
1972   Neither Slave nor Free. Baltimore: The Johns Hopkins University Press.

Cohen, Erik
1972   Toward a sociology of international tourism, Social Research 39 (1): 164–182.
1973   Nomads from affluence, International Journal of Comparative Sociology 14 (1–2): 89–103.

Cohen, Ronald
1978   Ethnicity, problems and faces in anthropology, Annual Review of Anthropology 7: 379–403.

Cohen, Ronald, and John Middleton, eds.
1970   From Tribe to Nation in Africa. Scranton, PA: Chandler.

Colby, Benjamin N., and Pierre L. van den Berghe
1969   *Ixil Country*. Berkeley: University of California Press.

Collier, George A.
1975   *Fields of the Tzotzil*. Austin: University of Texas Press.

Comas, Juan
1972   *Razas y Racismo*. México: SepSetentas.

Connor, Walker
1972   Nation-building or nation-destroying? *World Politics* 24 (3): 319–335.
1973   The politics of ethnonationalism, *Journal of International Affairs* 27 (1): 1–21.
1978   A nation is a nation, is a state, is an ethnic group, is a . . . , *Ethnic and Racial Studies* 1 (4): 377–400.

Cox, Oliver C.
1948   *Caste, Class and Race*. Garden City, NY: Doubleday.
1976   *Race Relations, Elements and Social Dynamics*. Detroit: Wayne State University Press.

Craton, Michael
1975   "Jamaican slavery," in Stanley L. Engerman and Eugene D. Genovese (eds.), *Race and Slavery in The Western Hemisphere*. Princeton, NJ: Princeton University Press.

Curtin, Philip D.
1969   *The Atlantic Slave Trade; A Census*. Madison: University of Wisconsin Press.

Dahl, Robert A., ed.
1966   *Political Oppositions in Western Democracies*. New Haven, CT: Yale University Press.
1971   *Polyarchy: Participation and Opposition*. New Haven, CT: Yale University Press.

Daly, Martin, and Margo Wilson
1978   *Sex, Evolution and Behavior*. North Scituate, MA: Duxbury Press.

Davidson, Basil
1961   *The African Slave Trade*. Boston: Little Brown.

Davis, Allison, W., B. B. Gardner and M. R. Gardner
1941   *Deep South*. Chicago: University of Chicago Press.

Davis, David B.
1970   *The Problem of Slavery in Western Culture*. Ithaca, NY: Cornell University Press.

Davis, Kingsley
1942   A conceptual analysis of stratification, *American Sociological Review* 7: 309–321.

Davis, Morris, and J. F. Krauter
1971   *The Other Canadians*. Toronto: Methuen.

Dawkins, Richard
1976   *The Selfish Gene*. London: Oxford University Press.

Degler, Carl N.
　1971　*Neither Black nor White*. New York: Macmillan.

de Heusch, Luc
　1966　*Le Rwanda et la Civilisation Interlacustre*. Bruxelles: Institut de Sociologie, Université Libre de Bruxelles.

De Kiewiet, Cornelis W.
　1941　*A History of South Africa, Social and Economic*. Oxford: Clarendon Press.

Delf, George
　1963　*Asians in East Africa*. London: Oxford University Press.

de Mestral, Aymon
　1970　*Suisse Romande, Suisse Allémanique*. Lausanne: Nouvelle Revue de Lausanne.

de Reuck, Anthony, and Julie Knight, eds.
　1967　*Caste and Race*. Boston: Little Brown.

Despres, Leo A.
　1967　*Cultural Pluralism and Nationalist Politics in British Guiana*. Chicago: Rand McNally.

Despres, Leo A., ed.
　1975　*Ethnicity and Resource Competition in Plural Societies*. The Hague: Mouton.

Des Pres, Terrence
　1976　*The Survivor*. New York: Oxford University Press.

Deutsch, Karl W.
　1966　*Nationalism and Social Communication*. Cambridge, MA: MIT Press.

Deutsch, Karl W., and W. J. Foltz, eds.
　1963　*Nation-Building*. New York: Atherton.

DeVos, George, and Lola Romanucci-Ross, eds.
　1975　*Ethnic Identity, Cultural Continuities and Change*. Palo Alto, CA: Mayfield.

De Vos, George, and Hiroshi Wagatsuma, eds.
　1966　*Japan's Invisible Race*. Berkeley: University of California Press.

d'Hertefelt, Marcel
　1965　The Rwanda of Rwanda, in James L. Gibbs (ed.), *Peoples of Africa*. New York: Holt, Rinehart and Winston.

Dickie-Clark, Hamish F.
　1966　*The Marginal Situation*. London: Routledge and Kegan Paul.

Dollard, John
　1957　*Caste and Class in a Southern Town*. Garden City, NY: Doubleday Anchor.

Dollard, John, et al.
　1939　*Frustration and Aggression*. New Haven, CT: Yale University Press.

Dore, Ronald P.
1958   *City Life in Japan*. Berkeley: University of California Press.

Drake, St. Clair, and Horace R. Cayton
1945   *Black Metropolis*. New York: Harcourt, Brace.

Driedger, Leo, ed.
1978   *The Canadian Ethnic Mosaic*. Toronto: McClelland and Stewart.

Dumont, Louis
1970   *Homo Hierarchicus*. London: Weidenfeld and Nicolson.

Dunbar, Edward E.
1861   History of the rise and decline of commercial slavery in America, *The Mexican Papers* 1 (5): 177–279.

Duncan, J. Otis, and Stanley Lieberson
1959   Ethnic segregation and assimilation, *American Journal of Sociology* 64: 364–374.

Dunn, James A.
1972   Consociational democracy and language conflict; *Comparative Political Studies*, No. 1, pp. 3–39.

du Roy, Albert
1968   *La Guerre des Belges*. Paris: Editions du Seuil.

Eisenstadt, S. N.
1954   *The Absorption of Immigrants*. London: Routledge and Kegan Paul.
1967   *Israeli Society*. London: Weidenfeld and Nicholson.

Eisenstadt, S. N., and S. Rokkan, eds.
1973   *Building States and Nations*. Beverly Hills: Sage.

Elkins, Stanley M.
1968   *Slavery*. Chicago: University of Chicago Press.

Elon, Amos
1975   *Herzl*. New York: Holt, Rinehart and Winston.

Emerson, Rupert
1960   *From Empire to Nation*. Cambridge, MA: Harvard University Press.

Engerman, Stanley L.
1975   Comments on the study of race and slavery, in Stanley L. Engerman and Eugene D. Genovese (eds.), *Race and Slavery in the Western Hemisphere*. Princeton, NJ: Princeton University Press.
1979   The realities of slavery, a review of recent evidence, *International Journal of Comparative Sociology* 23 (1–2): 46–66.

Engerman, Stanley L., and Eugene D. Genovese, eds.
1975   *Race and Slavery in the Western Hemisphere*. Princeton: Princeton University Press.

Enloe, Cynthia H.
1973   *Ethnic Conflict and Political Development*. Boston: Little, Brown.

Esman, Milton J.
1977   *Ethnic Conflict in the Western World*. Ithaca, NY: Cornell University Press.

Evans-Pritchard, E. E.
  1940   *The Nuer*. London: Oxford University Press.

Fanon, Frantz
  1963   *The Wretched of the Earth*. New York: Grove.
  1965   *Studies in a Dying Colonialism*. New York: Monthly Review Press.
  1971   *Peau Noire, Masques Blancs*. Paris: Editions du Seuil.

Feagin, Joe R.
  1978   *Racial and Ethnic Relations*. Englewood Cliffs, NJ: Prentice-Hall.

Firth, Raymond
  1936   *We, the Tikopia*. London: Oxford University Press.
  1959   *Economics of the New Zealand Maori*. Wellington, New Zealand: Government Printer.

Fisher, Alan G. B., and H. J. Fisher
  1971   *Slavery and Muslim Society in Africa*. Garden City, NY: Doubleday.

Fisher, R. A.
  1958   *The Genetical Theory of Natural Selection*. New York: Dover Press. (First published in 1930.)

Fisman, Joshua A., et al.
  1966   *Language Loyalty in the United States*. The Hague: Mouton.

Fishman, Joshua A., C. A. Ferguson and J. Das Gupta, eds.
  1968   *Language Problems of Developing Nations*. New York: Wiley.

Fogel, Robert William, and Stanley L. Engerman
  1974   *Time on the Cross*. Boston: Little Brown.

Foley, John P.
  1900   *The Jeffersonian Cyclopedia*. New York: Funk and Wagnalls.

Foner, Laura, and Eugene D. Genovese, eds.
  1969   *Slavery in the New World*. Englewood Cliffs, NJ: Prentice-Hall.

Fortes, Meyer
  1969   *Kinship and the Social Order*. Chicago: Aldine.

Fox, Robin
  1967   *Kinship and Marriage*. Harmondsworth: Penguin.

Francis, E. K.
  1976   *Interethnic Relations*. New York: Elsevier.

Franklin, John Hope
  1974   *From Slavery to Freedom*. New York: Knopf.

Frazer, James G.
  1890   *The Golden Bough*. London: Macmillan.

Frazier, E. Franklin
  1957   *Race and Culture Contacts in the Modern World*. New York: Knopf.
  1965   *Black Bourgeoisie*. New York: The Free Press.

Freedman, Daniel G.
  1979   *Human Sociobiology*. New York: The Free Press.

Freyre, Gilberto
  1963   *The Mansions and the Shanties*. New York: Knopf.

1964   *The Masters and the Slaves.* New York: Knopf.

Furnivall, J. S.
 1948   *Colonial Policy and Practice.* London: Cambridge University Press.

Geertz, Clifford
 1967a The integrative revolution, in Clifford Geertz (ed.), *Old Societies and New States.* New York: The Free Press.

Geertz, Clifford, ed.
 1967b *Old Societies and New States.* New York: Free Press.

Genovese, Eugene D.
 1965   *The Political Economy of Slavery.* New York: Pantheon.
 1969a *The World the Slaveholders Made.* New York: Pantheon.
 1969b The treatment of slaves in different countries, in Laura Foner and Eugene D. Genovese (eds.), *Slavery in the New World*, Englewood Cliffs, NJ: Prentice-Hall.
 1974   *Roll, Jordan, Roll.* New York: Pantheon.

Genovese, Eugene D., ed.
 1973   *The Slave Economies.* New York: Wiley, 2 volumes.

Ghai, Dharam P.
 1970   An economic survey, in D. P. Ghai and Y. P. Ghai (eds.), *Portrait of a Minority.* Nairobi: Oxford University Press.

Ghai, Dharam P., and Yash P. Ghai, eds.
 1970   *Portrait of a Minority.* Nairobi: Oxford University Press.

Ghurye, G. S.
 1952   *Caste and Class in India.* New York: Philosophical Library.

Gibbs, James L.
 1965   *Peoples of Africa.* New York: Holt, Rinehart and Winston.

Ginzberg, Eli, and A. S. Eichner
 1964   *The Troublesome Presence.* New York: The Free Press.

Gist, Noel P., and A. G. Dworkin, eds.
 1972   *The Blending of Races.* New York: Wiley.

Glazer, Nathan
 1975   *Affirmative Discrimination.* New York: Basic Books.
 1979   Affirmative discrimination: Where is it going? *International Journal of Comparative Sociology* 23 (1–2): 14–30.

Glazer, Nathan, and Daniel P. Moynihan
 1970   *Beyond the Melting Pot.* Cambridge, MA: MIT Press.

Glazer, Nathan, and Daniel P. Moynihan, eds.
 1975   *Ethnicity: Theory and Experience.* Cambridge: Harvard University Press.

Gluckman, Max
 1958   *Analysis of a Social Situation in Modern Zululand.* Manchester: Manchester University Press.

Goffman, Erving
 1963   *Stigma.* Englewood Cliffs, NJ: Prentice-Hall.

Goldin, Claudia Dale
1975   A model to explain the relative decline in urban slavery, in Stanley
       L. Engerman and Eugene D. Genovese (eds.), *Race and Slavery in
       the Western Hemisphere*. Princeton: Princeton University Press.

Gordon, Milton M.
1964   *Assimilation in American Life*. New York: Oxford University
       Press.
1978   *Human Nature, Class and Ethnicity*. New York: Oxford University
       Press.

Gossett, Thomas
1963   *Race: The History of an Idea in America*. Dallas: Southern Meth-
       odist University Press.

Greeley, Andrew M.
1971   *Why Can't They Be Like Us?* New York: Dutton.
1974   *Ethnicity in the United States*. New York: Wiley.
1979   The American Irish, *International Journal of Comparative Soci-
       ology* 20 (1–2): 67–81.

Greene, Penelope
1978   Promiscuity, paternity and culture, *American Ethnologist* 5:151–159.

Gregory, Robert G.
1971   *India and East Africa*. Oxford: Clarendon Press.

Gretler, Armin, and P. E. Mandl
1973   *Values, Trends and Alternatives in Swiss Society*. New York:
       Praeger.

Grüner, Erich
1969   *Die Parteien in der Schweiz*. Bern: Francke.

Gutkind, P. C. W., ed.
1970   *The Passing of Tribal Man in Africa*. Leiden: Brill.

Gutman, Herbert
1976   *The Black Family in Slavery and Freedom, 1750–1925*. New York:
       Pantheon.

Haldane, J. B. S.
1932   *The Causes of Evolution*. New York: Longmans, Green.

Hamilton, Gary
1978   Pariah capitalism: A paradox of power and dependence, *Ethnic
       Groups* 2: 1–15.

Hamilton, W. D.
1964   The genetical evolution of social behaviour, *Journal of Theoretical
       Biology* 7: 1–52.

Handlin, Oscar
1951   *The Uprooted*. Boston: Little Brown.
1957   *Race and Nationality in American Life*. Garden City, NY:Doubleday.

Hannan, Michael, and John Meyer, eds.
1979   *National Development and the World System*. Chicago: University
       of Chicago Press.

Hansen, Karen T.
    1979   American Indians and Work in Seattle. Seattle: University of
            Washington Ph.D. dissertation.

Hartung, John
    1976   On natural selection and the inheritance of wealth, Current An-
            thropology 17 (4): 607–622.

Hawley, Amos H.
    1950   Human Ecology. New York: Ronald.

Hayashida, Cullen Tadao
    1976   Identity, Race and the Blood Ideology of Japan. Seattle: University
            of Washington Ph.D. dissertation.

Hechter, Michael
    1971   Towards a theory of ethnic change, Politics and Society 2 (1):
            21–45.
    1975   Internal Colonialism. London: Routledge and Kegan Paul.
    1976   Ethnicity and industrialization, Ethnicity 3 (3): 214–224.
    1978   Group formation and the cultural division of labor, American Jour-
            nal of Sociology 84 (2): 293–318.

Helm, June, ed.
    1968   Essays on the Problem of Tribe. Seattle: University of Washington
            Press.

Hernandez, C. A., M. J. Haug and N. N. Wagner, eds.
    1976   Chicanos, Social and Psychological Studies. St. Louis: Mosby.

Herskovits, Melville J.
    1938   Acculturation, the Study of Culture Contact. New York:
            J. J. Augustin.
    1958   The Myth of the Negro Past. Boston: Beacon Press.

Hoetinck, H.
    1967   Caribbean Race Relations. London: Oxford University Press.

Hofstadter, Richard
    1959   Social Darwinism in American Thought. New York: Braziller.

Hollingsworth, L. W.
    1960   The Asians of East Africa. London: Macmillan.

Horwitz, Ralph
    1967   The Political Economy of South Africa. New York: Praeger.

Hraba, Joseph
    1979   American Ethnicity. Itasca, IL: Peacock.

Hsu, Francis L. K.
    1963   Clan, Caste and Club. New York: Van Nostrand, Reinhold.
    1971   The Challenge of the American Dream. Belmont, CA: Wadsworth.

Huggett, Frank E.
    1969   Modern Belgium. London: Pall Mall.

Hunt, Chester L., and Lewis Walker
    1974   Ethnic Dynamics. Homewood, IL: Dorsey.

Hunter, Guy
1966 *Southeast Asia: Race, Culture and Nation.* New York: Oxford University Press.

Hunter, Guy, ed.
1965 *Industrialization and Race Relations.* New York: Oxford University Press.

Hunter, Monica
1936 *Reaction to Conquest.* London: Oxford University Press.

Hutton, J. H.
1946 *Caste in India.* Cambridge: Cambridge University Press.

Huyse, Luc
1970 *Passiviteit, Pacificatie en Verzuiling in de Belgische Politiek.* Antwerp: Standaard Wetenschappelijke Uitgeverij.

Isajiw, W. W.
1974 Definitions of ethnicity, *Ethnicity* 1: 111–124.

Jensen, Arthur
1969 How much can we boost IQ and scholastic achievement? *Environment, Heredity and Intelligence.* Cambridge, MA: Harvard Educational Review Reprint Series, No. 2.

Johnstone, F. A.
1976 *Class, Race and Gold.* London: Routledge and Kegan Paul.

Jones, James M.
1972 *Prejudice and Racism.* Reading, MA: Addison-Wesley.

Jordan, Winthrop D.
1969 *White over Black.* Baltimore: Penguin.

Kalbach, Warren E.
1978 Growth and distribution of Canada's ethnic populations, 1871–1971, in Leo Driedger (ed.), *The Canadian Ethnic Mosaic.* Toronto: McClelland and Stewart.

Karash, Mary
1975 From porterage to proprietorship, in Stanley L. Engerman and Eugene D. Genovese (eds.), *Race and Slavery in the Western Hemisphere.* Princeton, NJ: Princeton University Press.

Karve, Irawari
1961 *Hindu Society.* Poona: Deccan College.

Kedourie, Elie
1961 *Nationalism.* New York: Praeger.

Kennedy, R. J. R.
1944 Single or triple melting pot? *American Journal of Sociology* 49: 331–339.

Kephart, William M.
1976 *Extraordinary Groups: The Sociology of Unconventional Lifestyles.* New York: St. Martin's Press.

Keyes, Charles F.
1976   Towards a new formulation of the concept of ethnic group, *Ethnicity* 3 (3): 202–213.

Kinloch, Graham C.
1974   *The Dynamics of Race Relations*. New York: McGraw-Hill.

Kitano, Harry H. L.
1974   *Race Relations*. Englewood Cliffs, NJ: Prentice-Hall.

Klein, Herbert S.
1978   *The Middle Passage*. Princeton, NJ: Princeton University Press.

Klineberg, Otto
1944   *Characteristics of the American Negro*. New York: Harper.

Kluckhohn, Clyde, and Dorothea Leighton
1958   *The Navaho*. Cambridge, MA: Harvard University Press.

Kogon, Eugen
1950   *The Theory and Practice of Hell*. New York: Farrar, Strauss.

Kohn, Hans
1956   *Nationalism and Liberty: The Swiss Example*. London: Allen and Unwin.

Krausz, Ernest
1971   *Ethnic Minorities in Britain*. London: MacGibbon and Kee.

Kroeber, Alfred L.
1948   *Anthropology*. New York: Harcourt, Brace.

Kunstadter, Peter, ed.
1967   *Southeast Asian Tribes, Minorities, and Nations*. Princeton, NJ: Princeton University Press.

Kuper, Hilda
1974a   *The Uniform of Colour*. Johannesburg: Witwatersrand University Press.
1947b   *An African Aristocracy*. London: Oxford University Press.
1960   *Indian People in Natal*. Durban: Natal University Press.
1963   *The Swazi*. New York: Holt, Rinehart and Winston.
1978   *Sobhuza II*. New York: Africana Publishing Company.

Kuper, Leo
1957   *Passive Resistance in South Africa*. New Haven, CT: Yale University Press.
1965   *An African Bourgeoisie*. New Haven, CT: Yale University Press.
1971a   Political change in plural societies, *International Social Science Journal* 23 (4): 594–607.
1971b   Theories of revolution and race relations, *Comparative Studies in Society and History* 13 (1): 87–107.
1973   *Race, Class and Power*. London: Duckworth.
1977   *The Pity of It All*. London: Duckworth.
1981   *Genocide*. Hammondsworth: Penguin (in press).

Kuper, Leo, ed.
1975   *Race, Science and Society*. Paris: UNESCO.

Kuper, Leo, and M. G. Smith, eds.
1969   *Pluralism in Africa*. Berkeley: University of California Press.

Lane, Ann J., ed.
1971   *The Debate over Slavery*. Urbana: University of Illinois Press.

Leach, E. R.
1954   *Political Systems of Highland Burma*. London: Bell.

Leach, E. R., ed.
1962   *Aspects of Caste in South India, Ceylon and North-West Pakistan*.
        Cambridge: Cambridge University Press.

Lee, Richard B., and Irven De Vore, eds.
1968   *Man, the Hunter*. Chicago: Aldine.
1976   *Kalahari Hunters-Gatherers*. Cambridge, MA: Harvard University
        Press.

Lehmbruch, Gerhard
1967   *Proporzdemokratie*. Tuebingen: Mohr.

Lemarchand, René
1970   *Rwanda et Burundi*. New York: Praeger.

Lever, Henry
1978   *South African Society*. Johannesburg: Jonathan Ball.

Levi, Primo
1976   *Survival in Auschwitz*. Collier: New York.

Le Vine, Robert, and Donald T. Campbell
1972   *Ethnocentrism*. New York: Wiley.

Lévi-Strauss, Claude
1952   *The Race Question in Modern Science*. Paris: UNESCO.
1969   *The Elementary Structures of Kinship*. Boston: Beacon Press.
        (Originally published in French in 1949.)
1979   *The Origin of Table Manners*. New York: Harper and Row.

Lewis, Lionel S., R. A. Wanner and D. I. Gregorio
1979   Performance and salary attainment in academia, *The American
        Sociologist* 14: 157–169.

Lieberson, Stanley
1961   A societal theory of race and ethnic relations, *American Socio-
        logical Review* 26: 902–210.
1963   *Ethnic Patterns in American Cities*. New York: The Free Press.

Lijphart, Arend
1968a   *The Politics of Accommodation, Pluralism and Democracy in the
        Netherlands*. Berkeley: University of California Press.
1977a   *Democracy in Plural Societies*. New Haven, CT: Yale University
        Press.
1977b   Political theories and explanation of ethnic conflict in the western
        world, in Milton J. Esman (ed.), *Ethnic Conflict in the Western
        World*. Ithaca, NY: Cornell University Press.

Lijphart, Arend, ed.
1968b   *Politics in Europe*. Englewood Cliffs, NJ: Prentice-Hall.

278

Lind, Andrew W., ed.
1955   *Race Relations in World Perspective*. Honolulu: University of Hawaii Press.

Little, Kenneth
1947   *Negroes in Britain*. London: Kegan Paul.

Litwack, Leon F.
1961   *North of Slavery*. Chicago: University of Chicago Press.

Lorwin, Val R.
1966   Belgium: Religion, class and language in national politics, in Robert A. Dahl (ed.), *Political Oppositions in Western Democracies*. New Haven, CT: Yale University Press.
1971   Segmented pluralism, *Comparative Politics* 3 (2): 141–175.
1972   Linguistic pluralism and political tension in modern Belgium, in Joshua A. Fisman (ed.), *Advances in the Sociology of Language*. The Hague: Mouton, Vol. 2.

Lowenthal, David
1972   *West Indian Societies*. London: Oxford University Press.

Lugard, Frederick
1929   *The Dual Mandate in British Tropical Africa*. Edinburgh: W. Blackwood.

Lyman, Stanford M.
1974   *Chinese Americans*. New York: Random House.

Lynch, Owen
1969   *The Politics of Untouchability*. New York: Columbia University Press.

MacCannell, Dean
1976   *The Tourist*. New York: Schocken.

MacCrone, I. D.
1937   *Race Attitudes in South Africa*. London: Oxford University Press.

McNeill, William H.
1976   *Plagues and Peoples*. New York: Doubleday.

McRae, Kenneth, ed.
1974   *Consociational Democracy*. Toronto: McClelland and Stewart.

McRoberts, Kenneth
1979   Internal Colonialism, The Case of Québec, *Ethnic and Racial Studies* 2 (3): 293–318.

McRoberts, Kenneth, and Dale Posgate
1976   *Québec: Social Change and Political Crisis*. Toronto: McClelland and Stewart.

Magalhães de Gandavo, Pedro
1922   *The Histories of Brazil*. New York: The Cortes Society. (First published in 1575.)

Mangat, J. S.
1969   *History of the Asians in East Africa*. Oxford: Clarendon Press.

Mannix, Daniel P.
1962   *Black Cargoes*. New York: Viking Press.

Mannoni, O.
1964   *Prospero and Caliban*. New York: Praeger.

Maquet, Jacques J.
1957   *Ruanda*. Bruxelles: Elsevier.
1961   *The Premise of Inequality in Ruanda*. London: Oxford University Press.
1970   Rwanda castes, in Arthur Tuden and L. Plotnicov (eds.), *Social Stratification in Africa*. New York: The Free Press.

Marquard, Leo
1957   *South Africa's Colonial Policy*. Johannesburg: South African Institute of Race Relations.
1962   *The Peoples and Policies of South Africa*. London: Oxford University Press.

Marwick, Brian
1940   *The Swazi*. Cambridge: Cambridge University Press.

Mason, Philip
1970   *Race Relations*. London: Oxford University Press.
1971   *Patterns of Dominance*. London: Oxford University Press.
1974   *A Matter of Honour*. New York: Holt, Rinehart and Winston.
1975   *Prospero's Magic*. Westport, CT: Greenwood Press.

Maunier, René
1949   *The Sociology of Colonies*. London: Routledge and Kegan Paul.

Mauss, Marcel
1924   *Les Rois Thaumaturges*. Strasbourg.

Mayer, Kurt B.
1952   *The Population of Switzerland*. New York: Columbia University Press.
1968   The Jura problem, ethnic conflict in Switzerland, *Social Research* 35: 707–741.

Mayer, Philip
1961   *Townsmen or Tribesmen*. Cape Town: Oxford University Press.

Maynard Smith, John
1964   Group selection and kin selection, *Nature* 201 (4924): 1145–1147.

Mayr, Ernst
1963   *Animal Species and Evolution*. Cambridge, MA: Harvard University Press.

Mellafe, Rolando
1975   *Negro Slavery in Latin America*. Berkeley: University of California Press.

Memmi, Albert
1965   *The Colonizer and the Colonized*. New York: Orion.
1968   *Dominated Man*. New York: Orion.

Mindel, Charles H., and R. W. Habenstein, eds.
1976   Ethnic Families in America. New York: Elsevier.

Miner, Horace
1965   The Primitive City of Timbuctoo. Garden City, NY: Doubleday.

Moodie, Dunbar
1975   The Rise of Afrikanerdom. Berkeley: University of California Press.

Mörner, Magnus, ed.
1970   Race and Class in Latin America. New York: Columbia University Press.

Morris, H. S.
1956   Indians in East Africa, British Journal of Sociology 7 (3): 194–211.

Moynihan, Daniel P.
1965   The Negro Family. Washington, DC: U.S. Government Printing Office.

Munger, Edwin S.
1967   Afrikaner and African Nationalism. London: Oxford University Press.

Murray, Vera
1976   Le Parti Québécois. Montréal: HMH.

Myrdal, Gunnar
1944   An American Dilemma. New York: Harper.

Nadel, S. F.
1942   A Black Byzantium. Oxford: Oxford University Press.

Nagata, Judith A., ed.
1975   Pluralism in Malaysia. Leiden: Brill.

Newman, William M.
1973   American Pluralism. New York: Harper and Row.

Nicolaisen, Johannes
1963   Ecology and Culture of the Pastoral Tuareg. Copenhagen: The National Museum.

Nielsen, François
1980   The Flemish movement in Belgium after World War II, American Sociological Review 45: 79–94.

Nordlinger, Eric A.
1972   Conflict Regulation in Divided Societies. Cambridge, MA: Occasional Paper No. 29, Center for International Affairs, Harvard University.

Novak, Michael
1971   The Rise of the Unmeltable Ethnics. New York: Macmillan.

Oliver, Roland, and John D. Fage
1962   A Short History of Africa. Baltimore: Penguin.

Olorunsola, Victor A., ed.
1972   The Politics of Cultural Subnationalism in Africa. Garden City, NY: Doubleday.

Olson, James Stuart
1979   The Ethnic Dimension in American History. New York:
        St. Martin's Press.

Oster, George F., and Edward O. Wilson
1978   Caste and Ecology in the Social Insects. Princeton, NJ: Princeton
        University Press.

Outers, Lucien
1968   Le Divorce Belge. Paris: Editions of Minuit.

Park, Robert E.
1950   Race and Culture. New York: The Free Press.

Parsons, Talcott
1964   The Social System. New York: The Free Press.

Patterson, G. James
1979   A critique of "the new ethnicity," American Anthropologist 81
        (1): 103–105.

Patterson, Orlando
1967   The Sociology of Slavery. Cranbury, NJ: Associated University
        Presses.
1977   Ethnic Chauvinism. Briarcliff Manor, NY: Stein and Day.

Patterson, Sheila
1953   Colour and Culture in South Africa. London: Routledge and Kegan
        Paul.
1957   The Last Trek. London: Routledge and Kegan Paul.
1965   Dark Strangers. Harmondsworth: Penguin.

Peach, Ceri
1980   Which triple melting pot? Ethnic and Racial Studies 3 (1): 1–16.

Peres, Yochanan
1971   Ethnic relations in Israel, American Journal of Sociology 76 (6):
        1021–1047.

Pescatello, Ann M., ed.
1975   The African in Latin America. New York: Knopf.

Petersen, William
1975   On the subnations of Western Europe, in Nathan Glazer and Daniel
        P. Moynihan (eds.), Ethnicity, Theory and Experience. Cambridge,
        MA: Harvard University Press.
1979   Ethnicity in the world today, International Journal of Comparative
        Sociology 20 (1–2): 1–13.

Pettigrew, Thomas F.
1964   A Profile of the Negro American. Princeton, NJ: Van Nostrand.

Pettigrew, Thomas F., ed.
1980   The Sociology of Race Relations. New York: The Free Press.

Pinkney Alphonso
1975   Black Americans. Englewoods Cliffs, NJ: Prentice-Hall.

Pirenne, Henri
1932   Histoire de Belgique. Bruxelles: Henri Lamertin.

Porter, John
   1965   *The Vertical Mosaic.* Toronto: University of Toronto Press.

Rabushka, Alvin
   1974   *A Theory of Racial Harmony.* Columbia, SC: University of South
         Carolina Press.

Rabushka, Alvin, and K. A. Shepsle
   1972   *Politics in Plural Societies.* Columbus, OH: Merrill.

Redfield, Robert
   1956   *Peasant Society and Culture.* Chicago: University of Chicago Press.

Redfield, Robert, and Melville J. Herskovits
   1936   Memorandum on the study of acculturation, *American Anthro-
         pologist* 38: 149–152.

Rex, John
   1970   *Race Relations in Sociological Theory.* New York: Schocken.

Rex, John, and Robert Moore
   1967   *Race, Community and Conflict.* London: Oxford University Press.

Rex, John, and Sally Tomlinson
   1979   *Colonial Immigrants in a British City.* London: Routledge and
         Kegan Paul.

Richmond, Anthony
   1973   *Migration and Race Relations in an English City.* London: Oxford
         University Press.
   1978   Migration, ethnicity and race relations, *Ethnic and Racial Studies*
         1 (1): 1–18.

Ronen, Dov
   1979   *The Quest for Self-Determination.* New Haven, CT: Yale Univer-
         sity Press.

Rose, Arnold M., ed.
   1951   *Race Prejudice and Discrimination.* New York: Knopf.

Rose, Peter I.
   1974   *They and We.* New York: Random House.

Rothman, Jack, ed.
   1976   *Issues in Race and Ethnic Relations.* Itasca, IL: Peacock.

Rowe, John H.
   1946   Inca culture at the time of the Spanish conquest, in Julian Steward
         (ed.), *Handbook of South American Indians,* Vol. 2. Washington:
         Bureau of American Ethnology.

Royal Commission
   1967–1970 *Report of the Royal Commission on Bilingualism and
         Biculturalism.* Ottawa: Queen's Printer, 6 Vols.

Runciman, W. G.
   1972   Race and social stratification, *Race* 13 (4): 497–509.

Russell, Peter, ed.
   1966   *Nationalism in Canada.* Toronto: McGraw-Hill.

Safa, Helen, I., and B. M. Du Toit, eds.
1975　*Migration and Development*. The Hague: Mouton.

Sahlins, Marshall
1976　*The Use and Abuse of Biology*. Ann Arbor: University of Michigan Press.

Said, Abdul, and L. R. Simmons, eds.
1976　*Ethnicity in an International Context*. New Brunswick, NJ: Transaction Books.

Saywell, John
1977　*The Rise of the Parti Québécois, 1967–1976*. Toronto: University of Toronto Press.

Schermerhorn, Richard A.
1970　*Comparative Ethnic Relations*. New York: Random House.
1974　Ethnicity in the perspective of the sociology of knowledge, *Ethnicity* 1 (1): 1–14.
1978　*Ethnic Plurality in India*. Tucson: University of Arizona Press.

Schneider, David M.
1968　*American Kinship*, Englewood Cliffs, NJ: Prentice-Hall.

Schwartz, Barton M.
1967　*Caste in Overseas Indian Communities*. San Francisco: Chandler.

Sellin, H. Thorstein
1976　*Slavery and the Penal System*. New York: Elsevier.

Shahrani, M. Nazif Mohib
1979　*The Kirghiz and Wakhi of Afganistan*. Seattle: University of Washington Press.

Shepher, Joseph
1981　*Incest: The Biosocial View*. Boston: Garland (in press).

Shibutani, Tamotsu, and Kian M. Kwan
1965　*Ethnic Stratification*. New York: Macmillan.

Shils, Edward
1957　Primordial, personal, sacred, and civil ties, *British Journal of Sociology* 8: 130–145.

Simon, Rita James
1978　*Continuity and Change; A Study of Two Ethnic Communities in Israel*. New York: Cambridge University Press.

Simons, H. J. and R. E. Simons
1969　*Class and Colour in South Africa, 1850–1950*. Baltimore: Penguin.

Simpson, George E., and J. Milton Yinger
1972　*Racial and Cultural Minorities*. New York: Harper and Row.

Smiley, Donald V.
1976　*Canada in Question*. Toronto: McGraw-Hill, Ryerson.
1977　French–English relations in Canada and consociational democracy, in Milton J. Esman (ed.), *Ethnic Conflict in the Western World*. Ithaca, NY: Cornell University Press.

Smith, Lilian
  1963   *Killers of the Dream*. New York: Anchor.

Smith, Mary F.
  1954   *Baba of Karo*. London: Faber and Faber.

Smith, Micheal G.
  1960   *Government in Zazzau, 1800–1950*. London: Oxford University Press.
  1965a *The Plural Society in the British West Indies*. Berkeley: University of California Press.
  1965b The Hausa of Northern Nigeria, in James L. Gibbs (ed.), *Peoples of Africa*. New York: Holt, Rinehart and Winston.

Smock, David R., and Audrey C. Smock
  1975   *The Politics of Pluralism*. New York: Elsevier.

Smooha, Sammy
  1975   Pluralism and conflict: A theoretical explanation, *Plural Societies* 6 (3): 69–89.
  1978   *Israel: Pluralism and Conflict*. London: Routledge and Kegan Paul.

Smythe, Hugh H.
  1952   The Eta, a marginal Japanese caste, *American Journal of Sociology* 58: 194–196.

Sowell, Thomas
  1972   *Black Education, Myths and Tragedies*. New York: David McKay.
  1975   *Race and Economics*. New York: David McKay.

Srinivas, M. N.
  1962   *Caste in Modern India*. New York: Asia Publishing House.
  1969   *Social Change in Modern India*. Berkeley: University of California Press.

Stampp, Kenneth M.
  1964   *The Peculiar Institution*. New York: Vintage.

Stein, Howard, F., and Robert F. Hill
  1977   *The Ethnic Imperative*. University Park: Pennsylvania State University Press.

Steinberg, Lucien
  1978   *Jews Against Hitler*. London: Gordon and Cremonesi.

Steinfield, Melvin, ed.
  1970   *Cracks in the Melting Pot*. Beverly Hills: Glencoe Press.

Stember, Charles Herbert
  1976   *Sexual Racism*. New York: Elsevier.

Stenning, Derrick J.
  1959   *Savannah Nomads*. London: Oxford University Press.
  1960   Transhumance, migratory drift, migration: Patterns of pastoral Fulani normadism, in Simon and Phoebe Ottenberg (eds.), *Cultures and Societies of Africa*. New York: Random House.
  1965   The pastoral Fulani of Northern Nigeria, in James L. Gibbs (eds.), *Peoples of Africa*. New York: Holt, Rinehart and Winston.

285

Steward, Julian H.
  1977   *Evolution and Ecology*. Urbana: University of Illinois Press.
Stine, Gerald James
  1977   *Biosocial Genetics*. New York: Macmillan.
Stone, John
  1973   *Colonist or Uitlander?* Oxford: Clarendon Press.
Sutch, Richard
  1975   The breeding of slaves for sale and the westward expansion of
          slavery, 1850–1860, in Stanley L. Engerman and Eugene D. Gen-
          ovese (eds.), *Race and Slavery in the Western Hemisphere*. Prin-
          ceton, NJ: Princeton University Press.
Tabbarah, Riad B.
  1979   Background to the Lebanese conflict, *International Journal of
          Comparative Sociology* 20 (1–2): 101–121.
Takaki, Ronald T.
  1979   *Iron Cages, Race and Culture in 19th Century America*. New York:
          Knopf.
Tandon, Yash
  1970   A political survey, in D. P. Ghai and Y. P. Ghai (eds.), *Portrait of
          a Minority*. Nairobi: Oxford University Press.
Tannenbaum, Frank
  1947   *Slave and Citizen*. New York: Knopf.
Tax, Sol
  1952   *Heritage of Conquest*. Glencoe, IL: The Free Press.
Thompson, Virginia, and Richard Adloff
  1955   *Minority Problems in Southeast Asia*. Stanford: Stanford Univer-
          sity Press.
Tindermans, Leo
  1971   *L'Autonomie Culturelle*. Bruxelles: Van Ruys.
Trivers, Robert L.
  1972   Parental investment and sexual selection, in B. Campbell (ed.),
          Sexual Selection and the Descent of Man. Chicago: Aldine.
Tuden, Arthur, and Leonard Plotnicov, eds.
  1970   *Social Stratification in Africa*. New York: The Free Press.
Tumin, Melvin
  1952   *Caste in a Peasant Society*. Princeton, NJ: Princeton University
          Press.
Tumin, Melvin, ed.
  1969   *Comparative Perspectives on Race Relations*. Boston: Little,
          Brown.
Tumin, Melvin M., and Walter Plotch, eds.
  1977   *Pluralism in a Democratic Society*. New York: Praeger.
Turnbull, Colin
  1961   *The Forest People*. New York: Simon and Schuster.

1965   *Wayward Servants.* London: Eyre and Spottiswoode.

Turner, Jonathan, and Edna Bonacich
1978   "Toward a Composite Theory of Middleman Minorities" (Mimeographed Paper).

Urquhart, M. C. and K. A. H. Buckley
1965   *Historical Statistics of Canada.* Cambridge: Cambridge University Press.

Vallières, Pierre
1969   *Nègres Blancs d'Amérigue.* Paris: Maspero.

van den Berghe, Pierre L.
1965   *South Africa: A Study in Conflict.* Middletown, CT: Wesleyan University Press.
1967   *Race and Racism: A Comparative Perspective.* New York: Wiley.
1968   Ethnic membership and culture change in Guatemala, *Social Forces* 46: 514–522.
1970   *Race and Ethnicity: Essays in Comparative Sociology.* New York: Basic Books.
1971a   Ethnicity, the African experience, *International Social Science Journal* 23 (4): 507–518.
1971b   The benign quota, panacea or Pandora's box? *The American Sociologist* 6 (3): 40–43.
1972a   Neo-racism in America, *Transition* 41: 15–18.
1972b   Academic apartheid, *Worldview* (October), pp. 25–29.
1973a   *Power and Privilege at an African University.* London: Routledge and Kegan Paul.
1973b   "Pluralism," in John J. Honigmann (ed.), *Handbook of Social and Cultural Anthropology.* Chicago: Rand McNally.
1974   Bringing beasts back in, *American Sociological Review* 39 (6): 777–788.
1975a   Asian Africans before and after independence, *Kroniek van Afrika* 6: 197–205.
1975b   *Race and Ethnicity in Africa.* Nairobi: East African Publishing House.
1978a   *Race and Racism: A Comparative Perspective.* New York: Wiley, 2nd edition.
1978b   *Man in Society: A Biosocial View.* New York: Elsevier.
1978c   Bridging the paradigms, *Society* 15 (6): 42–49.
1978d   Race and ethnicity, a sociobiological perspective, *Ethnic and Racial Studies* 1 (4): 401–411.
1979a   *Human Family Systems: An Evolutionary View.* New York: Elsevier.
1979b   *The Liberal Dilemma in South Africa.* London: Croom, Helm.
1979c   Nigeria and Peru, two contrasting cases in ethnic pluralism, *International Journal of Comparative Sociology* 20 (1–2): 162–174.

van den Berghe, Pierre L., and David Barash
1977   Inclusive fitness and human family structure, *American Anthropologist* 79 (4): 809–823.

van den Berghe, Pierre L., and George P. Primov
1977 *Inequality in the Peruvian Andes, Class and Ethnicity in Cuzco*. Columbia, MO: University of Missouri Press.

Vander Zanden, James W.
1963 *American Minority Relations*. New York: Ronald Press.

Vaughan, James H.
1970 Caste systems in the western Sudan, in Arthur Tuden and L. Plotnicov (eds.), *Social Stratification in Africa*. New York: The Free Press.

Vayda, A. P.
1960 *Maori Warfare*. Wellington, New Zealand: Polynesian Society Moari Monographs, No. 2.

Wade, Richard C.
1964 *Slavery in the Cities: The South 1820–1860*. New York: Oxford University Press.

Wagley, Charles, ed.
1952 *Race and Class in Rural Brazil*. Paris: UNESCO.

Walker, Eric A.
1957 *A History of Southern Africa*. London: Longmans.

Wallerstein, Immanuel
1974 *The Modern World System*. New York: Academic Press.

Wallerstein, Immanuel, ed.
1966 *Social Change, The Colonial Situation*. New York: Wiley.

Ward, David
1971 *Cities and Immigrants*. New York: Oxford University Press.

Warner, W. Lloyd
1941 "Introduction" to Allison W. Davis, B. B. Gardner and M. R. Gardner, *Deep South*. Chicago: University of Chicago Press.

Weber, Max
1958 *The Protestant Ethic and the Spirit of Capitalism*. New York: Scribner.

1968 *Economy and Society*. New York: Bedminster. (First published in 1922.)

Weilenmann, Hermann
1951 *Pax Helvetica*. Zürich: Eugen Rentsch.

White, Lynn
1962 *Medieval Technology and Social Change*. London: Oxford University Press.

Whitten, Norman E., and J. F. Szwed, eds.
1970 *Afro-American Anthropology*. New York: The Free Press.

Willemsen, A. W.
1969 *Het Vlaams-nationalisme*. Utrecht: Ambo.

288

Williams, Robin M.
  1964   *Strangers Next Door*. Englewood Cliffs, NJ: Prentice-Hall.
  1975   Race and ethnic relations, in Alex Inkeles et al. (eds.), *Annual Review of Sociology* 1 (Palo Alto, CA: Annual Reviews).
  1977   *Mutual Accommodation*. Minneapolis: University of Minnesota Press.

Wilson, Edward O.
  1971   *The Insect Societies*. Cambridge MA: Harvard University Press.
  1975   *Sociobiology: The New Synthesis*. Cambridge, MA: Harvard University Press.
  1978   *Human Nature*. Cambridge, MA: Harvard University Press.

Wilson, Monica Hunter
  1936   *Reaction to Conquest*. London: Oxford University Press.

Wilson, William J.
  1973   *Power, Racism, and Privilege*. New York: Macmillan.
  1978   *The Declining Significance of Race*. Chicago: University of Chicago Press.

Wirth, Louis
  1956   *The Ghetto*. Chicago: University of Chicago Press.

Wolpe, Harold
  1970   Industrialism and race in South Africa, in S. Zubaida (ed.), *Race and Racialism*. London: Tavistock.

Woodward, C. Vann
  1955   *The Strange Career of Jim Crow*. New York: Oxford University Press.

Wynne-Edwards, V. C.
  1962   *Animal Dispersion in Relation to Social Behavior*. Edinburgh: Oliver and Boyd.

Young, Crawford
  1976   *The Politics of Cultural Pluralism*. Madison: University of Wisconsin Press.

Zamora, Mario D., et al, eds.
  1978   *Tourism and Behavior*. Williamsburg, VA: College of William and Mary, Studies in Third World Societies, No. 5.

Zolberg, Aristide R.
  1974   The making of Flemings and Walloons, Belgium, 1830–1914, *Journal of Interdisciplinary History* 5: 179–235.
  1975   Transformation of linguistic ideologies, the Belgian case, in Jean-Guy Savard and Richard Vigneault (eds.), *Multilingual Political Systems*. Québec: Presses de l'Université Laval.
  1977   Splitting the difference, in Milton J. Esman (ed.), *Ethnic Conflict in the Western World*. Ithaca, NY: Cornell University Press.

Zubaida, Sami
  1978   Theories of nationalism, in G. Littlejohn et al. (eds.), *Power and the State*. New York: St. Martin's Press.

Zubaida, Sami, ed.
  1970   *Race and Racialism*. London: Tavistock.

NAME INDEX

SUBJECT INDEX

Weak money, 139, 147, 153
West Africa, 90, 94, 96, 104, 113, 114,
    117, 119, 121–126, 137, 162, 178
Western hemisphere, 81, 86, 89, 90, 93,
    97, 111, 115–117, 124–130, 158, 184
West Indies, see Caribbean
Westernization, 256
White ethnics (U.S.), 227
White Highlands (Kenya), 148, 149
Wolof, 260
World system theory, 40–41
World War I, 199, 205
World War II, 2, 57, 114, 148, 149, 170,
    177, 179, 199, 200, 204, 207–208, 224,
    225, 226

X
Xhoisan, 48, 91, 167, 253
Xhosa, 167

Y
Yanomamö, 42–43, 56, 57
Yemen, 231
Yiddish, 233
Yoruba, 16, 56, 62, 256
Ypres, 198
Yugoslavia, 63, 81, 191

Z
Zaïre, 17, 42, 47–53, 82, 173, 213
ZANU, 189
ZAPU, 189
Zanzibar, 33, 147
Zazzau, 122
Zimbabwe, 173, 174, 189
Zionism, 229, 231
Zoroastrianism, 162
Zuilen, 201
Zulu, 62, 87, 167
Zürich, 194, 197